Progress in Tourism, Recreation and Hospitality Management

Volume 6

Belhaven Series

Progress in Tourism, Recreation and Hospitality Management

Published in association with the Department of Management Studies for Tourism and Hotel Industries, University of Surrey, UK.

Progress in Tourism, Recreation and Hospitality Management

Volume 6

Edited by
C.P. Cooper and A. Lockwood

JOHN WILEY & SONS
Chichester • New York • Brisbane • Toronto • Singapore

British Library Cataloguing in Publication Data
A catalogue record for this book is available from the British Library

ISBN 0-471-94859-4

Typeset in 10/11pt Times by Florencetype Ltd, Stoodleigh, Devon
Printed and bound in Great Britain by Biddles Ltd, Guildford and King's Lynn.

Contents

List of contributors   vii
Editorial preface   xvi

Alternative tourism themes

1   Ecotourism: a ruse by any other name   3
    B. Wheeller

2   Issues in ecotourism   12
    C. Wild

3   Alternative tourism: the real tourism alternative?   22
    M. Romeril

4   Issues in sustainability and the national parks of Kenya and
    Cameroon   30
    D.C. Gilbert, J. Penda and M. Friel

5   The emergence of ethics in tourism and hospitality   46
    M. Wheeler

6   Gender and tourism   57
    J. Norris and G. Wall

Tourism in the Pacific Rim

7   Environmental challenges and influences on tourism:
    the case of Thailand's tourism industry   81
    K.S. Chon and A. Singh

8   A critique of tourism planning in the Pacific   92
    S.J. Craig-Smith and M. Fagence

9   Theme parks in Japan   111
    T.S. Mervyn Jones

10   The regulation of the Hong Kong travel trade   126
    P.L. Atkins

Food and beverage management

11   Yield management: the case for food and beverage
    operations   139
    J. van Westering

12   The menu as a marketing tool   149
    A. Cattet and C. Smith

13   Factors affecting future menu compilation   164
    M.A. O'Neill, M.A. McKenna and F. Fitz

14 Food trends in Europe   175
    G. Valterio

15 Food management: developing a national policy   178
    J. Thomson

16 Culinary heritage in the face of tourism   189
    P. Reynolds

Contemporary themes

17 Dynamic innovation in the tourism industry   197
    A.-M. Hjalager

18 Career theory and tourism: the development of a basic
    analytical framework   225
    M. Riley and A. Ladkin

19 Predicting business failure   238
    S. Lewis

20 Geographic information systems in tourism marketing   250
    S. Sussmann and T. Rashad

21 Comprehensive human resource planning: an essential
    key to sustainable tourism in island settings   259
    M.V. Conlin and T. Baum

Tourism statistics

22 Forecasts of international tourism   273
    J. Latham

23 The European hotel industry   283
    A. Pizam and T. Knowles

List of contributors

Peter Atkins
Department of Hotel and Tourism Management
Hong Kong Polytechnic
Hung Hom
Kowloon
Hong Kong

Peter Atkins was course leader for the BA (Hons) Tourism Management course at Hong Kong Polytechnic. His research was in the area of human resources, especially the integration of modern educative techniques in industrial training programmes. He was completing his PhD when he died in 1993.

Dr Tom Baum
School of Accounting, Business and Economics
The University of Buckingham
Hunter Street
Buckingham MK18 1EG
UK

Tom Baum is Professor of International Hotel and Tourism Management and Deputy Dean of School at the University of Buckingham. His research and consultancy interests are in the areas of national tourism policy development and implementation; and manpower/human resource planning for tourism at national and regional levels.

Anne Cattet
56 Chemin de Sanzy
69600 Oullins
France

Anne Cattet was a researcher at the University of Surrey. She is currently lecturing in English.

Michael Conlin
Centre for Tourism Research and Innovation
Bermuda College
PO Box DV356
Devonshire DVBX
Bermuda

Michael Conlin is Dean of the Faculty of Hotel and Business Administration and Director of the Centre for Tourism Research and Innovation at Bermuda College, Bermuda. His current research interests are in the area of human resource planning, with specific reference to small island environments.

Dr Kye S. Chon
Department of Tourism and Convention Administration
University of Nevada Las Vegas
Box 456023
4505 Maryland Parkway
Las Vegas
Nevada 89154-4870
USA

Kye-Sung Chon is Associate Professor of Tourism and Management at the University of Nevada, Las Vegas. He edits the *Journal of Travel and Tourism Marketing* and has research interests which include tourism in developing countries, consumer behaviour in hospitality and tourism industries, and the strategic management of tourism organisations.

Dr Stephen J. Craig-Smith
Department of Business Studies
Gatton College
Lawes
Queensland 4343
Australia

Stephen Craig-Smith is Head of Department of Business Studies at Gatton College, University of Queensland, and Director of the Centre for Hospitality and Tourism Management. His research interests focus on coastal zone management and tourism planning.

Dr Michael Fagence
Department of Geographical Sciences
University of Queensland
Brisbane
Queensland 4072
Australia

Michael Fagence is Senior Lecturer in Geography at the University of Queensland. His principal research interests lie in tourism planning, regional policy and rural development.

Dr Frank Fitz
Department of Hotel and Catering Management
University of Ulster
Newtonabbey
Co. Antrim BT37 0QB
UK

Frank Fitz is a lecturer at the University of Ulster. He is researching foodway analysis in relation to diet, nutrition and healthy eating.

Mr Martin Friel
School of Hotel and Catering Management
Oxford Brookes University
Gypsy Lane
Oxford OX3 0BP
UK

Martin Friel is Lecturer in Hospitality Marketing at Oxford Brookes University. His main research interest is in the study of rural communities and the sociocultural impacts of tourism.

Dr David Gilbert
Department of Management Studies
University of Surrey
Guildford GU2 5XH
UK

David Gilbert is Lecturer in Marketing and course tutor for the University of Surrey's MSc in Tourism Marketing. His research interests relate to the application of marketing to the study of tourism in the form of consumer behaviour and management issues.

Anne-Mette Hjalager
Science Park
Gustav Wiedsvej 10
8000 Aarhus C
Denmark

Anne-Mette Hjalager is an independent consultant and researcher in tourism. She undertakes investigations for local and national authorities and for the European Union.

T.S. Mervyn Jones
Faculty of Transport
Swansea Institute of Higher Education
Mount Pleasant
Swansea SA1 6ED
UK

Mervyn Jones is Director of research and postgraduate course development in the Faculty of Transport at the Swansea Institute. His research interests lie in the transport implications of the growth of leisure and land-use planning in developing countries.

Tim Knowles
Department of Management Studies
University of Surrey
Guildford GU2 5XH
UK

Tim Knowles is Lecturer in Hotel and Catering Management at the University of Surrey. His research interests focus on the European hotel industry with particular emphasis on the impact of European Union legislation. He is the author of a recent text in hospitality management and has extensive experience of the British hospitality industry.

Adele Ladkin
Department of Management Studies
University of Surrey
Guildford GU2 5XH
UK

Adele Ladkin is a graduate student at the University of Surrey. Her research relates to career planning and development with particular reference to hotel managers.

Professor John Latham
Business Division
Southampton Institute of Higher Education
East Park Terrace
Southampton SO9 4WW
UK

John Latham is Professor of Business Analysis at Southampton Institute. He is a mathematician, with a special interest in research methodology and the analysis of tourism demand.

Susan Lewis
Department of Management Studies
University of Surrey
Guildford GU2 5XH
UK

Susan Lewis is Lecturer in Financial Management at the University of Surrey. Her research interests are in the field of financial management in the hospitality and tourism industries.

Dr Martin A. O'Neill
Department of Hotel and Catering Management
Magee College
University of Ulster
Londonderry BT48 7JL
UK

Martin A. O'Neill is a lecturer at the University of Ulster. His research interests are in the area of strategic and operational practice in tourism.

Margaret A. McKenna
Department of Hotel and Catering Management
University of Ulster

Newtonabbey
Co. Antrim BT37 0QB
UK

Margaret McKenna is a senior lecturer at the University of Ulster. Her research includes strategic management and gender issues.

Joanne Norris
Department of Sociology
University of Guelph
Toronto NIG 2W1
Canada

Joanne Norris is a graduate student in the Department of Sociology, University of Guelph. Her research is concerned with aspects of gender and tourism in Bali.

Joan Penda
Department of Management Studies
University of Surrey
Guildford GU2 5XH
UK

Joan Penda is a researcher whose roots and interests lie in the study of problems of tourism impact on the people and environment of Africa.

Dr Abraham Pizam
Department of Hospitality Management
University of Central Florida
PO Box 161400
Orlando
Florida 32816
USA

Abraham Pizam is Professor of Tourism and Hospitality Management in the Department of Hospitality Management at the University of Central Florida, where he has previously served as the chair of the department and the Director of the Dick Pope Sr Institute for Tourism Studies. Professor Pizam is the author of numerous scientific publications in the field of tourism/hospitality.

T. Rashad
School of Travel Industry Management
University of Hawaii at Manoa
George Hall 2560 Campus Road Honolulu
Hawaii 96812
USA

Tamer Rashad has recently completed an MSc on Geographic Information Systems in Tourism Marketing at the University of Surrey.

He is currently at the University of Hawaii administering TRINET. His research interests include applications of interactive multimedia to tourism marketing.

Dr Paul Reynolds
Faculty of Business
Northern Territory University
PO Box 40146
Casuarina
Northern Territory 0811
Australia

Paul Reynolds is Associate Professor at the Northern Territory University, Darwin. He is currently engaged in research in ecoauditing in service industries, and strategies for aboriginal involvement in tourism projects in Australia.

Dr Michael Romeril
Conservation Officer
Planning Department
States of Jersey
St Helier
Jersey
Channel Islands

Michael Romeril is the conservation officer for Jersey, Channel Islands. For a number of years he has advised UNEP and the WTO on tourism/ environment issues. He is Vice President and former Chairman of the Institution of Environmental Sciences.

Dr Michael Riley
Department of Management Studies
University of Surrey
Guildford GU2 5XH
UK

Michael Riley is Lecturer in Management Studies at the University of Surrey. He specializes in human resource management and is course tutor for the department's MSc in International Hotel Management. His research interests lie in labour markets, management development and group behaviour.

Amrik Singh
Department of Tourism and Convention Administration
University of Nevada Las Vegas
Box 456023
4505 Maryland Parkway
Las Vegas
Nevada 89154-4870
USA

Amrik Singh is currently pursuing his graduate studies at the University of Nevada, Las Vegas. His research interests include strategic management and marketing of hospitality and tourism businesses.

Christopher Smith
Department of Management Studies
University of Surrey
Guildford GU2 5XH
UK

Christopher Smith is Lecturer in Food and Beverage Management. His research interests include the marketing, technology and effectiveness of food and beverage operations; the use of computers in food and beverage management; and the educational needs of managers in the hotel and catering industry.

Silvia Sussmann
Department of Management Studies
University of Surrey
Guildford GU2 5XH
UK

Silvia Sussmann is Lecturer in Management Computing. Her current research interests include intelligent user interfaces; the application of advanced software tools in hospitality research education; and the impact of technology on the promotion and marketing of tourism products.

Dr James Thomson
Department of Management Studies
University of Surrey
Guildford GU2 5XH
UK

Jim Thomson is Reader in Food Management at the University of Surrey. He has been an active researcher for many years, with projects on school meal services, geriatric feeding, army feeding and prison feeding. He has produced many publications, particularly in the field of additives and contaminants in food.

Gilbert Valterio
Foundation Nestlé Pro Gastronomia
Rue de la Madeleine 39
CH-1800 Vevey
Switzerland

Gilbert Valterio is the Chairman of the Nestlé Pro Gastronomia Foundation. The Foundation, formed in 1991 to mark the company's 125th anniversary, works to assist hospitality educators to improve their knowledge and teaching skills through a wide variety of seminars, colloquia, research projects, awards and grants.

Professor Geoffrey Wall
Department of Geography
Faculty of Environmental Studies
Isiah Bowman Building
University of Waterloo
Ontario N2L 3G1
Canada

Geoffrey Wall is Associate Dean, Graduate Studies and Research Faculty of Environmental Studies at the University of Waterloo. He has long-standing and varied interests in tourism and is currently involved in the formulation of a sustainable development strategy for Bali.

Jetske van Westering
Department of Management Studies
University of Surrey
Guildford GU2 5XH
UK

Jetske van Westering is a Lecturer at the University of Surrey. Her research focuses on the application of yield management in the hospitality industry, as well as issues of profitability in food and beverage management.

Carolyn Wild
24 Kempster Avenue
Ottawa K2B 8B2
Canada

Carolyn Wild is a tourism and management consultant with research interests in ecotourism and adventure travel. Her experience in tourism and transportation extends from the Arctic to the Outback of Australia.

Marion Wheeler
Research Officer
The Sports Council
2 Tavistock Place
London WC1H 9RA
UK

Marion Wheeler has worked as an independent consultant involved in projects ranging from competitive tendering to sponsorship and event management. She is currently working in the Sports Council Research Unit.

Dr Brian Wheeller
Centre for Urban and Regional Studies
University of Birmingham
Edgbaston
Birmingham B15 2TT
UK

Brian Wheeller is Lecturer in Tourism at the University of Birmingham, where he is course director for the Tourism Policy and Management MSc programme. His research interests include developing a critique of eco/ego/sustainable tourism.

Editorial preface

Progress in Tourism, Recreation and Hospitality Management was launched in 1989 as a collaborative venture between the University of Surrey and Belhaven Press. Belhaven Press has now been taken over by John Wiley & Sons and *Progress* is continuing under this new publisher. The aims of *Progress*, however, remain the same. It is designed to provide an authoritative, annual and international review of research and major issues of concern in the fields of tourism, recreation and hospitality. *Progress* aims to provide leadership in research and has become an established annual volume for researchers, students and staff in academic institutions as well as a source book for practitioners. *Progress* thus fills a gap in the literature: a gap which has arisen owing to the rapid advance of the fields and the difficulties for researchers in consolidating material.

Since the first volume of *Progress* tourism as a subject area has made considerable advances. The academic community is growing, publishing output and conference activity is expanding and new journals and texts are appearing. This increased activity reinforces the need for a publication which attempts to synthesise and consolidate the subject area: a subject area which is not only advancing but also, as Pearce (1993) suggests, is in a constant state of flux with boundaries that are continually expanding, merging and dissolving as new schools of thought emerge. Jafari (1990) groups these schools of thought in tourism into four major categories, each with its own distinctive position or platform:

* the *advocacy* platform, where the benefits of tourism are stressed;
* the *cautionary* platform, which emerged as the problems of tourism became evident;
* the *adaptancy* platform, suggesting that while the cautionary platform has merit, it is possible to reduce the impact of tourism through new strategies and planning; and
* the *knowledge-based* platform, which is a more recent development and takes a scientific approach to the accretion of a body of knowledge of tourism.

Progress clearly is part of this latter platform, and hopes to contribute to the maturity and acceptance of the tourism subject area by providing high-quality research reviews. This is particularly important given that some commentators have termed tourism the 'science of the artificial', expanding and developing through the materials, methodologies and advances in other disciplines (Simon 1969).

The hospitality field, too, has evolved. In the late 1960s and early 1970s, courses in hotel management and catering were dominated by the presence of food and beverage operations; in industry, operations were dominated by the presence of the chef. The books that were produced at these times centred around food production and service, food and beverage control and, to a lesser extent, food and beverage management. The production of Graham Campbell Smith's *Marketing of the Meal Experience* (1967) seemed to herald a new wave of concern for food and beverage management, moving from the purely operational to the strategic. With this head start, one might expect that research into food and beverage would have become well established and new texts at a higher level would have emerged. This is not the case. Despite the publicity and star status awarded to a handful of top chefs, academic interest in the area has not kept pace with the progress made in other fields. Indeed, in Volume 4 of this series Riley and Smith (1992) seemed to be fighting a rearguard action to defend food and beverage operations in hotels against the hotel developers who would prefer to ignore them.

There is some evidence that the tide has turned. Two new UK texts aimed at higher-level study in this field will be published in 1994. The CHME Operations Management Research group has plans for a number of research projects in this area. The Inflight Caterers Association is developing new materials for its specialist high-level courses.

Volumes 4 and 5 of *Progress* saw a restructuring to provide themed groupings of research reviews and also the introduction of an annual commentary on tourism statistics. In Volume 6 we continue this trend by providing groupings of papers around three themes as well as five papers which focus on contemporary issues in the subject areas. The statistical section has been expanded to provide reviews and forecasts of tourism and hospitality statistics.

The tourism themes in this issue of *Progress* belong to the adaptancy and knowledge-based platforms. A range of papers exploring the adaptancy platform are presented as 'alternative tourism themes'. Wheeller comments generally on the papers in this section and provides a searing critique of ecotourism while Romeril provides a balancing view of alternative tourism approaches. More specifically, Wild provides a stimulating review of ecotourism, supported by Gilbert *et al.*'s paper on sustainable tourism initiatives in the national parks of Africa. Wheeler outlines ethical issues in tourism, a theme still in its infancy, and Wall and Norris review another nascent tourism theme, that of gender roles.

Turning to the knowledge-based platform, the second theme reviews tourism in the Pacific Rim. As this is one of the world's fastest-growing tourism regions, there are many issues needing research. Fagence and Craig-Smith review the problems of tourism planning in the Pacific, while Atkins, in a significant case study, draws on another public sector role by considering the regulation of travel agents in Hong Kong. Chon and Singh consider the environmental influences upon tourism development in Thailand and Jones provides an authoritative review of theme park developments in Japan.

The hospitality theme for this issue centres around the area of food and beverage management and shows the wide range of possible avenues that further research and scholarship might take. Jetske van Westering argues that using the yield management techniques that have proved successful for airlines and hotels could also have a positive impact on food and beverage operations. Cattet and Smith report on research conducted in France into the perceived role of the menu as a marketing tool, as well as providing a review of the scope of the literature in this area. O'Neill *et al.* take the menu one stage further and look at the variety of environmental influences that will have a role in shaping menus in the future.

Taking a wider perspective still, Gilbert Valterio looks at some of the current preoccupations with food trends in Europe and how these can help and hinder menu development. Broadening the scope to society as a whole, Jim Thomson provides guidance on how a flexible food and nutritional management policy can be developed to cope with needs at a national scale. Finally, Paul Reynolds discusses the issue of the disappearance of identifiable national food cultures in the face of international tourists' perceived need for a 'safer' version of the local cuisine.

There is sufficient material here to indicate the breadth of interests that can be found in the food and beverage management area and the vast potential for future research. It is to be hoped that more academics will 'dip their toes' into the ocean of possibilities before the tide goes out again.

Chris Cooper and Andrew Lockwood
University of Surrey
March 1994

References

Campbell Smith, G., 1967, *Marketing of the meal experience*, University of Surrey Press, Guildford.

Jafari, J., 1990, 'Research and scholarship. The basis of tourism education', *Journal of Tourism Studies*, 1(1): 33–41.

Pearce, P.L., 1993, 'Defining tourism study as a specialism: a justification and implications', *Teorus International*, 1(1): 25–32.

Riley, M. and Davies, E., 1992, 'Development and innovation: the case for food and beverage in hotels', *Progress in Tourism, Recreation and Hospitality Management*, 4: 201–8.

Simon, H.A., 1969, *The sciences of the artificial*, MIT Press, Cambridge, Mass.

Alternative tourism themes

1 Ecotourism: a ruse by any other name

B. Wheeller

In a fascinatingly revealing article, Kaiser (1987) argued that those of us who have witnessed the evolution of ecological awareness in Europe over the last twenty years now acknowledge that American Indians, more than any other group of people, are seen and presented as models of an exemplary ecological attitude. They are regarded as the patron saints of a close relationship between man and the natural environment. One of the reasons for this seems to be

> the widespread dissemination of a text that is regarded as a manifesto of ecological feeling and thinking – a speech, sometimes referred to as a letter, by Chief Seattle. While American Indians are seen by some to be ecological by birth, Chief Seattle is hailed as the prophet of ecological sentiment that is said to be lacking in Western industrialised nations (Kaiser 1987).

It would appear, however, that Chief Seattle's reputation as a great ecologist is, to say the least, somewhat exaggerated. So, too, I am convinced, is the enormous confidence now being lavished on ecotourism – surely tourism's biggest 'con-trick' yet. (Given what has happened in tourism over the years, this certainly is some accolade.) The plaudits being showered on eco/sustainable tourism emanate from sources that are either distressingly naive or disturbingly devious. In my opinion those naive but sincere advocates, speaking and acting with integrity, command respect even if their beliefs are misplaced. They enthusiastically gulp from the poisoned chalice of ecotourism. However, the majority, and overwhelming influential, players in the ecotourism game have a far more cunning, calculating 'bent'.

Though Seattle did give a speech in 1854, it was apparently bereft of ecological sentiment. According to Kaiser, the Seattle speech that captured the imagination of millions of latent environmentalists was not, in fact, written or delivered by Seattle in 1854 but was prepared, in 1970, as a film script for an environmental documentary, *Home*. The script was written by Perry, a lecturer at the University of Texas. Having read Seattle's original speech, Perry decided to prepare a new version. Using, by way of introduction, only very brief portions of the original speech, Perry then wrote his own ecological text. However, 'the actual film failed to give credit to Perry for his part in the script but gave credit to Seattle for what in fact he had never said or written' (Kaiser 1987). When shown nation-wide, the film had a significant impact. Viewers wrote in for transcripts and these were sent out without making it clear that it was Perry's work, not Seattle's.

Some of the arguments lucidly and evocatively developed by Kaiser were reiterated in a later article with the (hardly original) title 'White man speaks with forked tongue'. This pointed out that the 'environmental oratory of Chief Seattle of the Dwamish Indian tribe – anticipating the green movement by more than a century – has achieved in two decades the status of a kind of ecological Gettysburgh address' (Lichfield 1992). It, too, argued that the Chief's best-known and best-loved sayings are bogus.

Some regard the authenticity of the speech as being, in a sense, irrelevant. If Seattle did not actually deliver the words, then, the argument goes, he should have done: 'if it wasn't written it should have been' (Lindholm 1975). As long as somebody did, and the message gets through and ecological awareness is growing then the *minutia* of source can be ignored. Lichfield's example of the American best-selling children's book, *Brother Eagle, Sister Sky: a message from Chief Seattle* (Jeffreys 1992), is testimony to this. Here debate about authenticity has not deflected from the (assumed) positive effect of bringing the green message to a young audience.

However, there is now a danger that this same reasoning will be used to justify the commercial tourism sector's use of ecotourism and the accompanying evocative, persuasive use of environmental images. While I can see the logic in this – that the industry might well be raising current environmental awareness – on the whole, this justification does not seem acceptable. This is simply because this procedure is, through massaging demand, simultaneously part of the process that is damaging the environment. The tourism industry is primarily concerned with it own interests – which essentially remain profit – and, despite protestation to the contrary, these are chiefly regarded as short-term. New destinations (often ecological havens) are continually being opened up and the spatial spread of tourism to vulnerable areas encouraged. The argument that, for its own survival, the industry must maintain the quality of its product is dubious and the supposed symbiosis between tourism and the environment is, I believe, on the whole, a fabrication (see Wheeller 1991; 1992; 1993a, b).

According to Lichfield (1992), the saga of Chief Seattle is not a literary fraud. 'It is a classic canard, the product of an error of attribution 20 years ago which has achieved near mythical status through the eagerness of environmentalists to embrace a romantic vision'. The distortion of ecotourism by the tourism industry – the deliberate, conscious marketing manipulation – cannot, I feel, be seen in such a generous light. No romantic vision this, rather it is a flagrant case of the *big sell* (Wheeller 1994). Such orchestration is not, of course, restricted to tourism. However, ecotourism's apparent concern, and claims for preserving the product (interpreted loosely as the *environment*), clearly make it particularly prone to, vulnerable to, and (in the case of Savognin) ripe for such marketing ploys.

While most companies and destinations involved in the marketing exploitation of the environment have carefully selected an array of suitable, acceptable *natural* images and well-chosen *soft* text in all their advertising material, Savognin, in Switzerland, has taken the opposite tack and (though still a variation on a theme) deliberately set out to shock. In its very own 'back to basics' campaign, in order to emphasise its ecofriendly credentials, they resort to a photograph of a cowpat, with the accompanying message, 'We want to make it clear that our holiday resort has remained a true real village' (Gmur 1993). The ensuing furore and the spin-off attention it has received (witness a mention here) have, to many, deemed the campaign a success.

By design, this is not, of course, typical of the tourism ecoadvert genre. Much more common are the mushrooming examples such as the 'Natural Habitat' strategy for Bermuda (*The Times* 1994) and the 'Heritage, wild-life and vegetation are zealously preserved' approach of the television advertisement for Turkey (shown on Channel Four on 15 January 1994). Doubts raised by this genre are symptomatic of wider ethical issues that riddle tourism in general and ecotourism in particular.

In the sphere of ecotourism much imminent debate is likely to revolve around the effectiveness, or otherwise, of the glut of codes of ethics held in such high esteem by many advocates of ecotourism principles. These codes of good practice and behaviour are continually being championed as proof of progress (see, for example, Krippendorf 1992). Wheeler (Chapter 5, this volume) cites them as evidence of an organisation appreci-ating that ethical considerations are part of business decision-making. Wild, too (Chapter 2, this volume), briefly mentions codes of ethics. However, without the means to enforce guidelines, surely they are only literally paying lip-service to the problem? To be honest, it seems a little absurd to argue, as Wheeler seems to suggest, that to be truly effective we need further guidelines to enforce guidelines. Is *guidelines* not merely a euphemism for prevarication and procrastination, a substitute for effective action?

The same anxieties of image, prestige and status that bedevil ecotourism are, I believe, endemic to the notion of sustainable tourism in general. There is the ubiquitous desire to be politically correct in rhetoric if not in deed. Bramwell and Lane, editors of the new *Journal of Sustainable Tourism* are aware, but nevertheless appear rather cavalier and somewhat dismissive, of the danger: 'Waldstein (1991) noted that all politicians (and all large corporations) now claim to be passing pro-environment policies. He warns of the "limousine environmentalism" increasingly common in the USA where lip-service masks a lack of positive actions' (Bramwell and Lane 1993). I say 'somewhat dismissive' because, despite acknowledging this fundamental problem – 'It is easy to discuss sustain-ability. Implementation is the problem ...' (Bramwell and Lane 1993) – the overall impression is that they are extremely optimistic that these flaws in sustainable tourism can be rectified.

A similar vein runs through urban tourism. Just as *ego*tourism is a more appropriate nomenclature for ecotourism, so *urbane tourism* is surely a more appropriate terminology for urban tourism. High-profile, elegant, suave and sophisticated in their grandeur (for example, opera houses, theatres, galleries, convention centres), many urban tourism projects are designed to meet the dual purpose of image enhancement and target market satisfaction (not too far a cry from current ecotourism destination marketing). Many of the projects are only urban in the sense of physically being in the city. Roughly (though perhaps not the best word to use here) from the same stable as the egotraveller, their clientele is (or at best likes to be regarded as) educated, suburban and urbane – certainly not ignorant, high-rise inner-city or sub-urbane. Urbane angst? The traveller–tourist split?

When the urbane culture vultures migrate from their city haunts do they become egotravellers? In some respects the ecotourists are selecting, picking out and devouring what they consider to be the best bits of culture. Some say the relationship is symbiotic, others regard it as more parasitical, while a few regard it as purely predatory. Actually to imply that ego-travellers are vultures is incorrect, as vultures live off carrion. It is the impact of ecotravellers on existing societies, not dead carcasses, that is so contentious.

We all *know* that tourism is the world's fastest-growing industry, the world's largest employer, etc. We all know that it is big business. We are now being told, as if it is some sort of great revelation (and saviour), that ecotourism is the fastest-growing sub-sector of the international tourism industry. 'It has a growth rate three times that of tourism overall' (Mackay 1994). If we are (foolishly) to believe that small is automatically beautiful and ecofriendly in sustainable terms, then looking at the recent UK experience, the proliferation of small tour operators would seem to auger well. Under the banner 'Specialist tours thriving', Elliot (1994) writes that 'New figures show that the number of small tour operators has actually increased, not dropped, over the last three years'.

Leaving aside how ecotourism is precisely measured and isolated from tourism *overall*, these revelations should surely be of no surprise to anyone remotely interested in, and who has followed the development of, the rampant growth of global tourism and of the global tourism industry. Tourism is big business. For reasons that are patently obvious, so too is ecotourism (see Wheeller, 1991; 1992; 1993a, b). According to Mackay (1994): 'Recent American research found that this sector [ecotourism] of the market represents potential sales of between $2 billion and $10 billion'. I particularly like this statement, as it is so vague as to almost have a ring of truth about it. Wild (Chapter 2, this volume) also provides some interesting statistics of ecotourism growth. Adventure tourism, regarded by some as the antithesis of ecofriendly behaviour, is now gaining 'respectability' behind a nature-friendly mask. Ecotourism and adventure tourism/travel seem to be becoming inseparable: 'tour operators are preparing for a year when eco-tourism takes centre stage and culminates in the World Congress on Adventure Travel and Eco-tourism in Tasmania' (Mackay 1994). The congress meets at West Point Hotel and Casino, Hobart. Let us hope that this venue is in itself considerably more ecofriendly than the Tropical Hotel, Manaus, Amazonia, where the 1993 conference was held (see Wheeller 1994).

We are familiar with the use of derogatory terminology deriding mass tourism – herds, flocks, hordes, invasion, etc. – and with its counterpart, the soft, ego-boosting linguistic licence that warmly envelopes ecotourism. Unintentionally however, the title of Mackay's article 'The eco-tourists take over', might be a watershed. Inadvertently it perhaps bears (bares?) a portent – that the mantle of invader should perhaps be passed on to the ecotourist. Maybe future headlines will read 'Ecotourists are on the march' or 'An array of ecotourists about to embark'. Such military imagery brings to mind Butler's brilliant paper 'Alternative tourism: pious hope or Trojan horse?' (Butler 1990). His warnings appear to have gone unheeded. Tourism, often in the guise of ecotourism, has invaded previously impregnable areas. The ecotourists are now well and truly out from the confines of the horse's belly and are up and running – with predictable results. Recent warnings to local councils over 'starry-eyed, simplistic sustainability' (Ridley 1994) will no doubt also be ignored in the rush for a politically correct, immediate sustainability fix.

As government bodies, the tourism industry and the 'concerned' pseudo-traveller search for an 'acceptable' type of tourism, the apparent gift horse of ecotourism seems ideal. Certainly, it is not one that is being looked in the mouth. Unable, or unwilling, to resist, to them ecotourism might well be a boon. 'Transparent' might be more appropriate, for though ecotourism suits these parties' short-term objectives, the true consequences of ecotourism are being ignored. Although so much depends on the interpretation of 'acceptable', it is a case of Troy, Troy, Troy again.

The seemingly immutable conundrum of numbers, of the craving for status/prestige and the concomitant dilemma of access or excess, continues to be the bane of tourism, tourism impact and tourism policy. To an extent, the mixed emotions generated by the recent ascents of Everest serve as both testament and litmus paper to this. Boardman described Everest as the 'amphitheatre of the ego' (Shackley 1993). The craving for adventure and achievement expressed through the desire to conquer Everest has led to increased pressure, with obvious results. According to Beaumont (1993):

> The last four decades have not been kind to poor old Everest. The gentlemen climbers who courted her so vigorously – but respectfully – for the three decades before the first ascent on 29 May 1953 have given way to suitors who have dealt more rudely with her reputation.

Another commentator contends that 'Climbers are becoming increasingly competitive as the number of "firsts" is reduced and often exhibit a single minded determination to get to the summit whatever the cost, whether to the environment or to accompanying people' (Shackley 1993). Ironically, Bonnington has pointed out that the image of Everest as a giant litter dump has had some positive financial implications. 'Expeditions are now seeking sponsorship on "clean-and-climb" tickets utilizing the environment as a fund raising gimmick' (Shackley 1993).

No less than 38 mountaineers reached the summit of the peak on the same day – 12 May 1993. The predictable reaction from commentators is that the experience has been diluted, debased by becoming 'popular'. The degree to which the cachet of Everest has apparently been eroded can be measured by the following UK football report: 'The top of the First Division is beginning to resemble Everest, so many teams have visited the summit this season' (Bradfield 1994). Nevertheless, this 'deterioration' of the experience, of the product, has not (apparently) diminished the actual demand for 'adventurers' to go there. According to experts, there seems to be urgent need for codes of practice to be implemented, restriction of permits and a new fee structure to be adopted in order to ameliorate the problem (see Shackley 1993).

Now here is where I have another problem with eco/sustainable tourism. When we are looking at sustainability just what exactly is it we are (hoping) to sustain? Are we sustaining the status quo and fossilising the situation, or are we really aiming for that nebulous h(e)aven – sustainable growth? We are repeatedly being told that the 'product' must be upgraded or at least maintained in quality, otherwise as 'the visitor experience' deteriorates so it will lose its market. Simultaneously we are also being informed that increasing pressure is continuously deteriorating the product. It seems that as the quality of the product falls, demand nevertheless remains buoyant, albeit from a different market. That this new market is somehow deemed inferior seems to be at the heart of this 'quality' debate. But surely, is this not simply what works such as Veblen (1970), Turner and Ash (1975) and Pearce (1983) have been telling us for years?

Veblen's conspicuous consumption is at the hub of the ego/eco/sustainable debate:

> ... this expression, this desire to travel, to go on holiday, to go abroad is here to stay. I reckon one of the basic reasons stem[s] from jealousy. It is here where we show our true colours – or rather colour, green. It is this intrinsic green trait, rather than an environmentally-based one, that will continue to have the most powerful influence on consumer holiday choice. Conspicuous consumption, window to the west, keeping up with the Joneses etc., the green-eyed serpent uncoils as are we continually trying to better ourselves holiday wise (Wheeller 1993b).

For the ensuing chapters in this section the editors have selected a range of contributions on ecotourism. Gilbert and Penda provide a brief background to the concepts of sustainability before adopting a case-study approach. Wild, too, looks at some of the issues raised by Gilbert and Penda, while also probing wider, related issues of concern. Her arguments are backed up by a splendid bibliography. Wheeller, in her contribution, explores some of these ethical aspect of tourism. She raises the question of 'ethical dissonance' – the conflict between what managers believe and what they actually practice. She also refers to Hall's (1989) point that money, ego, information and ignorance often prevent people acting ethically. (So does this account for the hypocrisy of sustainable ecotourism?) Education is seen by many as the way forward for nurturing a 'better' tourism. Dream on. While Wheeler's article casts a brighter glow on this, my intuitive view is that 'ethics' still plays very little part in tourism training (which encompasses the majority of tourism courses) and is only present, in varying degrees, in tourism education.

Norris and Wall contribute a thoughtful, stimulating assessment of gender issues in tourism. With an informative contextual setting which relates gender to development and leisure issues, they explore a range of current gender issues in tourism. If, they argue, gender issues are not an integral part of tourism impact investigations, then such studies are incomplete. If we are seriously discussing notions of cultural sustainability, then surely gender issues have to be fully explored? They also point out, correctly, that:

> A drawback of much of the literature is that many generalisations have been made concerning tourism and its effects, without a clear specification of the type and stage of tourism, and overlooking the importance of regional specificity and the dynamics of culture.

However, while this statement refers to impacts the same, of course, is true of the 'solutions' in the form of eco/sustainable tourism. Their comments reinforce the obvious disparity between what *should be* and what actually *is* while side-stepping how the dilemma can be effectively resolved.

Romeril, however, in his highly commendable, balanced chapter, clearly has considerably more faith and provides not only salient positive points but also an excellent review and bibliography for those wishing to take this debate further. He does, however, recognise the need for a quantum change of attitude among the main protagonists in the economic growth/ sustainability/tourism and lifestyle debate. Furthermore, he sees success only if tourism can modify its obsession with expansionist growth (some tall order this). When Romeril does confront reality he points out that Brazil and Agenda 21 mean little, if anything, and terms such as 'sustain-ability' mean all things to all people. He makes the excellent point of the danger of being caught in the quagmire of jargon and debate – 'surely it is the philosophy and not the semantics that is important'. Unfortunately the philosophy is in itself also somewhat flexible – again all things to all people.

Wheeler, in her chapter on ethics, also discusses, though hardly con-fronts, the same stumbling block of 'what is' rather than the ideal of 'what should be'. She talks in terms of an ethical approach 'that applies the theoretical concepts to business realities'. I am still at a loss to see how this will be achieved – though Weiler's example of Australian nature-based tour operators, quoted in Wild (Chapter 2, this volume), does offer hope. Similarly Gilbert and Penda believe that 'Responsible tourism is an easier option to implement than alternative tourism'. We will see.

These authors do not share, and are not saddled with, my despondency as regards ecotourism issues. They write from a more positive stance.

While I cannot wholly support their ideas, the best I can manage is to hope that I am wrong and they are right in their considered optimism.

The parameters of what precisely ecotourism is have never been clear. They are becoming increasingly blurred as it becomes basically little more than a marketing vehicle, a green light for development. Ecotourism is just another form of tourism – a ruse by any other name. These surely are the realities of ecotourism – 'an altruistic, even noble, concept hijacked for commercial and material purposes' (Wheeller 1994). Currently on board a band-wagon, many proponents of ego/eco/sustainable tourism will soon discover – if they do not already know it – that they have been taken for a ride by a stampeding white elephant.

References

Beaumont, P., 1993, 'Queue at the top of the world', *Observer*, 16 May: 49–50.

Bradfield, S., 1994, 'Football League round-up', *Observer*, 23 January.

Bramwell, B. and Lane, B., 1993, 'Sustainable tourism: an evolving global approach', *Journal of Sustainable Tourism*, 1: 1–5.

Butler, R., 1990, 'Alternative tourism: pious hope or Trojan horse?', *Journal of Travel Research*, 28(3): 40–45.

Elliott, H., 1994, 'Specialist tours thriving', *The Times*, March: 12.

Gmur, F., 1993, 'Darf ein Kurort mit Kuh-Sch . . . werben?', *Reise-Journal, Bild am Sonntag*, 19 December: 34.

Hall, S., 1989, 'Ethics in hospitality', *Lodging*, September: 59–61.

Jeffreys, H., 1992, *Brother Eagle, Sister Sky: a message from Chief Seattle*, Hamish Hamilton, London.

Kaiser, R., 1987, *Chief Seattle's speech(es): American origins and European reception; recovering the world*, Swann and Krapal (eds), California University Press, Berkeley: 497–535.

Krippendorf, J., 1992, *Tourism and the environment. Conference proceedings*, English Tourist Board, London.

Lichfield, J., 1992, 'White man speaks with forked tongue', *Independent on Sunday*, 26 May: 26.

Lindholm, J., 1975, as quoted in Kaiser (1987). *Outdoor America*, December.

Mackay, A., 1994, 'Eco-tourists take over', *The Times*, 17 February: 20.

Pearce, P., 1983, *The social psychology of tourist behaviour*, Pergamon, Oxford.

Ridley, T., 1994, 'Councils warned over starry-eyed sustainability', *Local Transport Today*, 3 February: 1.

Shackley, M., 1993, 'No room at the top', *Tourism Management*, December: 483–5.

The Times, 1994, 'Natural habitat', Bermuda, *Times Magazine*, 5 March.

Turner, L. and Ash, J., 1975, *The Golden Hordes*, Constable, London.

Veblen, T., 1970, *Theory of the leisure class*, George Allen and Unwin, London.

Waldstein, F., 1991, 'Environmental policy and politics', in P. Davies and F. Waldstein (eds), *Political Issues in America*, Manchester University Press. Manchester.

Wheeller, B., 1991, 'Tourism's troubled times: responsible tourism is not the answer', *Tourism Management* 12(1): 91–6.

Wheeller, B., 1992, 'Alternative tourism – a deceptive ploy', in C.P. Cooper and A. Lockwood (eds), *Progress in tourism, recreation and hospitality management*, Vol.4, Belhaven, London: 140–45.

Wheeller, B., 1993a, 'Sustaining the ego', *Journal of Sustainable Tourism*, 1(2): 121–9.

Wheeller, B., 1993b, 'Willing victims of the ego-trap', *Focus*, no. 9: 14.

Wheeller, B., 1994, 'Carry On Up The Jungle', *Tourism Management*, June.

2 Issues in ecotourism
C. Wild

Introduction

The concept of ecotourism came into vogue in the late 1980s. Initially, the term was not widely used, many authors referring instead to nature travel, ecological or green tourism (Laarman and Durst 1987; Jones 1987). In 1989, ecotourism was advanced as a means to promote and finance conservation and economic development (Ziffer 1989). This took a major leap into the international spotlight in 1990 with the publication of *Ecotourism: the potentials and pitfalls* by the World Wildlife Fund (Boo 1990). Since then the term 'ecotourism' has rushed into popular usage, often in advance of serious study.

Much discussion on ecotourism has centred on natural resource conservation, led by wildlife and conservation activists and park protection agencies. Early concerns about tourism's impact on natural areas date back over 20 years as recent overviews of major works and issues in tourism, the environment and ecology have shown (Romeril 1989; Farrell and Runyan 1991). More recently, concern for conservation has seen ecotourism promoted as a means of sustainable development in natural areas, combining conservation with economic development (Whelan 1991). Ecotourism has also been linked to a positive environmental ethic and tourist education (Butler 1992) and is rapidly gaining a cultural tourism dimension and a concern for local communities. Many of these aspects were addressed by Budowski (1976) who foresaw ecotourism, proposing that a symbiotic relationship between tourism and conservation could offer a country physical, cultural, ethical and economic advantages.

Arguments about the definition of ecotourism have been a preoccupation at the growing number of international ecotourism conferences. The first widely quoted definition, thanks in part to its use by Boo, came from Ceballos-Lascurain (1987), who is credited with first coining the word. Ecotourism has now gone beyond the 'travel to ... natural areas' of his definition to travel that includes a positive benefit to conservation. This is reflected in Boo's (1992) recent refinement that 'ecotourism is nature travel that advances conservation and sustainable development efforts'. Incorporating the sustainable development element in a local context, the Ecotourism Society uses the following definition in a 1991 publicity brochure: 'Ecotourism is responsible travel to natural areas that conserves the environment and sustains the well-being of local people.'

The major issues in ecotourism centre around nature conservation and economic development and the role which governments, non-governmental organizations, host communities, the tourism industry and tourists themselves play in accomplishing these joint goals.

Major issues in ecotourism

Nature conservation

Tourism as a means to benefit the natural environment is a major theme of ecotourism. Benefits may include protection, conservation and even rehabilitation of natural resources. Ecotourism can act as an instrument for conservation by increasing the awareness of the value of nature, creating political pressure to conserve natural resources and by providing socioeconomic incentives to maintain wildlife populations and habitat through job creation, influx of foreign currency and capital investment (Filion *et al.* 1992).

Issues of tourism impact, tourist carrying capacity and tourist limitation must be addressed to manage tourism effectively in sensitive ecosystems and protected areas. Conservationists suggest that effective tourism management can actually enhance the quality of the natural resources that attract tourists in the first place, resulting in a 'positive feedback loop' (McNeely and Thorsell 1988). This is a shift from the often impractical aim of protecting sensitive ecosystems from any tourist or human use. One approach suggests the establishment of ecopreserves funded in part by fees from ecotourism. These would take into account the needs of the habitat and the species it supports as well as the human and economic needs of society (Ashton 1991).

Efforts are being made to integrate ecotourism into protected area management. Diagnostic and planning guidelines have been developed to assist in planning the development and management of ecotourism in protected areas (Boo 1992). Sound ecotourism development can result in an increase in funds for conservation and raise tourists' awareness of the pressures faced by natural areas. Awareness must extend to local communities which may stand to gain or loose from ecotourism or increased protection of natural areas they have traditionally used. Conservationists are now being forced to recognize the role of local communities in conservation (Young 1992).

Economic development

The issues associated with economic development through ecotourism are complex. Consideration must be given to the amount of private and public sector investment, foreign exchange benefits, employment impact and economic leakage. Healy (1988) examined nature tourism and economic multipliers to determine the benefit to local economies. Generally, smaller and less developed areas showed greater economic leakage as many goods and services had to be brought in from the outside. Nature tourism which encourages local employment and small business development promotes higher multipliers and greater local economic development. It can also be a viable alternative, as demonstrated on the island of Dominica, where disadvantages of terrain, isolation and climate preclude conventional mass tourism development (Weaver 1991). The challenge is to create economic benefits for local communities to give them the incentive to conserve their natural resources (McNeely 1988).

The existence or establishment of parks can provide a base for local economic development through ecotourism, but this is not necessarily the case. The loss of access to natural resources in protected areas can result in the stagnation of local economies if economic alternatives to resource extraction are not provided (Place 1991). Local communities may know little of the economic value of parks or may even have their livelihoods threatened when protected wildlife stray from park boundaries damaging crops and villages. Compensation may be required and the sharing of park revenues with local communities has been promoted as a means to gain local support for protected areas and wildlife (Leakey 1991). Local communities want to ensure they receive fair economic benefit for their support of conservation (Webley 1991).

A recent examination of the economics of protected areas emphasised the need to place monetary values on the maintenance of biological diversity and other conservation benefits (Dixon and Sherman 1990). The study suggests that the benefits of protected areas are often under-estimated. This type of economic analysis has also been applied to ecotourism to determine who pays, who benefits and how local benefits can be maximised (Sherman and Dixon 1991). Evaluation of both ecological and economic benefits is considered particularly important if policy-makers are to choose between ecotourism and other resource-based development options (Lindberg 1991).

Role of non-governmental organisations and governments

Non-governmental organisations (NGOs) such as the World Wildlife Fund, Conservation International and many other non-governmental groups have been the agents of much of the study and research conducted in ecotourism, as the reports of Boo and Ziffer attest. Policy and planning, public awareness, training and education, community development and technical assistance are just some of the areas related to ecotourism in which NGOs have been involved (International Resource Group 1992). Through their work, NGOs, particularly those involved in resource and wildlife conservation, have had a strong influence on governments and their conservation and tourism policies.

Governments are now beginning to see the benefits of ecotourism, not only for nature conservation but also for the economic development of rural and remote areas. For example, ecotourism has become a centrepiece for Amazonian development and conservation policy in Brazil (Kermath

1991). In Belize, a major shift in the country's economic priorities thrust tourism from relative obscurity to 'the industry spearheading the "Green" movement', demonstrating how quickly policies can change when the benefits of ecotourism are realised (Vega 1992). Other countries are following suit; however, critics question the balance between the economic and ecological motives of these policies and their effectiveness in natural resource conservation. Costa Rica, which has been a leader in ecotourism development, has had to strike a balance between ecotourism and more traditional tourism. Faced with the often conflicting interests of govern-ments, communities and conservationists, tourism development in Costa Rica is matter of trade-offs and constraints in a tug between preservation and profit (Hill 1990).

Governments have important roles to play in ecotourism development at the national, regional and local levels. They must deal with issues of regulation, zoning, financing, infrastructure development, education and training, and the marketing and promotion of ecotourism, among others. Coordination with the private sector and non-governmental organisations is required to establish shared responsibilities. Relationships with tourism operators and local communities need to be built. Trans-border agreements may be needed in multinational tourism developments such as La Ruta Maya, which links five nations (Garret 1989). Clearly, planning for ecotourism is no easy task and governments have been groping for ways in which to develop it. Some government experience shows how computer-based mapping of natural resources can support both tourism planning and resource management (Gale 1991). Dowling (1991) proposes an ecotourism planning model that emphasises the role of people as part of the ecosystem in a regional sustainable development framework.

Governments market ecotourism through their national tourism associa-tions which have long been recognised as playing an important role in preserving the environment (Filani 1975). These tourism authorities need to cooperate with the private sector to enhance the promotion of nature tourism and provide accurate and prompt information to tourists' literature requests (Durst and Ingram 1988). They can also play a positive role in educating the tourism industry to gain support for their govern-ments' conservation goals. Canada, for example, has developed a code of ethics and guidelines for sustainable tourism which the national tourism industry association has adopted (Tourism Industry Association of Canada 1992). A code of ecotourism ethics for Canada has also been proposed (Scace *et al.* 1992).

Host communities

In its applied form, ecotourism often involves travel to small rural or remote towns and villages in undeveloped areas and scenic natural settings. Much of the recent growth in ecotourism has occurred in developing countries particularly in rainforest and tropical zones where local inhabitants may have had little contact with tourists. Local communities and cultures, historical and archaeological aspects of areas visited may be integrated into the travel experience. In many instances, communities may not actively seek ecotourism, but have it thrust upon them or may even be overlooked in tourism development plans.

Tourist contact with host communities can affect local cultures and lifestyles, causing cultural and economic degradation. A community-based approach to ecotourism development and decision-making respects traditional lifestyles and community values. Strong supporters of indigenous community ecotourism development projects maintain that the community should have total control of the project and the right to say 'no' to everything related to it (Aussie-Stone 1992). Others have demonstrated that ecotourism revenues can be used as the economic incentive for socially acceptable, locally managed tourism which promotes indigenous resource conservation in a supply-managed model of ecotourism development (Lillywhite 1992). A community-controlled approach calls for resourceful marketing to match demand with supply and poses the question to what extent communities may be willing to adjust to marketplace demands.

Communities rarely have total control over development. Most ecotourism projects have an outside force or agency, such as governments, developers or NGOs, trying either to develop tourism or to conserve nature or both. Local involvement is stressed, because local cooperation is wanted or needed. A formalised local participation plan is seen as the most effective way to lessen the negative impact of ecotourism on local populations and emphasise the positive aspects (Drake 1991). Whether the approach is formalised local participation or not, current thinking suggests that local communities have considerable potential to do good or harm to ecotourism attractions (International Resources Group 1992) and that ecotourism serves as a conservation tool only when local people become an integral part of the process (Young 1992).

The tourism industry

Recent studies in North America have reported the growth of the eco-tourism market and the increase in the number of ecotourism operators (Ingram and Durst 1989; Rymer 1992; Yee 1992). The exact size of the industry and the amount of growth are difficult to determine. Ziffer (1989) suggests that nature travel represents about 10 per cent of personal and leisure travel for Americans and Europeans. She estimated that about 4 million US citizens spend roughly $12 billion per year travelling overseas for nature travel. Filion (1992), in a broader definition, estimated that at least 157 million international tourists travelled to enjoy and appreciate nature in 1988 resulting in contributions to national income of $155 billion.

The rate of growth in nature tourists was estimated by Ziffer (1989) at 20 per cent per year, based on the growth experienced by tour operators. A sampling of US-based ecotourism operators found a 13 per cent per annum increase in the number of tours operated and a 20 per cent increase in direct revenues over the period 1985–9 (Rymer 1992). This type of growth is estimated by many other countries and is expected to continue. In Australia, for example, it has been predicted that environmental tourism will grow well into the twenty-first century (Moore and Carter 1991).

Entrepreneurs are rapidly developing new ecotours and ecotourism destinations to take advantage of the industry growth. Not all are necessarily conservation-minded. Some operators are associated with environmental groups or make contributions to conservation from tour proceeds. Others provide very little economic benefit to the areas they visit, prompting the question whether it is ecotourism or 'eco-sell' (Wight 1993). But some ecotourism developers and operators are taking the problem of development and conservation seriously. Hacket (1991) shows one company's plans for 'solving the ecotourism dilemma' in the design and development of an environmentally sensitive resort. Restoration of habitat has also been demonstrated in an ecotourism resort development (Selengut and Simon 1991) and a study of Australian nature-based tour operators concluded that they weren't 'faking it' with respect to being environmentally friendly (Weiler 1992).

Tour operators whose very existence depends on conserving wilderness are banding together to develop proactively codes of conduct to protect the ecosystems in which they operate (Falconer 1991). Codes of ethics and conduct are being rapidly developed and adopted by many ecotourism operators, not just for themselves but for the tourists that travel with them (Yee 1992; Blangey and Epler Wood 1993). Tour guides are key in implementing these codes, and many operators have trained ecologists, naturalists or other experts on their staff who play an important role in tourist education and nature interpretation.

There is some documentation of operators' experience with market development and marketing ecotourism (Ryel and Grasse 1991). Ingram and Durst (1989) concluded that image and marketing problems are the greatest challenge facing both tour operators and host countries. A failed project in Panama demonstrates the need for effective marketing and appropriate tourism infrastructure to support ecotourism development (Chapin 1990). Marketing is often direct to the tourist, but the number of speciality travel agents is increasing as more operators use retail outlets. Also, non-specialised agents are beginning to offer ecotours and mainstream tour suppliers are becoming involved in ecotourism (Wild, 1992).

Tourists

Ecotourists range from special interest groups, such as birdwatchers, photographers and scientists, to tourists with a general interest in visiting natural areas and different cultures. The trend towards more meaningful travel, to discover new landscapes and be enriched by direct contact with indigenous populations and their culture, has been recognised for some time (Moulin 1980), but exactly who today's ecotourists are and what their motivations are for choosing an ecotour is just starting to be addressed. A study of Canadian ecotourists showed they are well educated, have incomes well above average and a strong desire to learn about the natural, cultural and historical aspects of their destinations (Eagles 1992; Eagles *et al.* 1992).

More tourists are becoming aware of ecotourism through newspapers, travel magazines and television. Rymer (1992) confirms the growth in the US ecotourism market both in terms of number of ecotourists and in the dollars they spend. He also notes a striking increase in the percentage of tourists concerned about the environmental impact of their tours. Guides such as *The good tourist* (Wood and House, 1991) are appearing to help tourists select companies that have shown a genuine awareness of their role in protecting the environment. The Ecotourism Society is proposing to ask ecotourists to provide feedback on their experiences and to rate their tours as a means of monitoring ecotourism services (Epler Wood 1992).

Summary and conclusions

Integrating all the issues in ecotourism is a difficult task. It requires a multidisciplinary approach and an understanding of the goals of all the stakeholders involved. Government planners, private developers, tour operators and local communities are working together in a coalition of disciplines and interests to make ecotourism work, but many questions have yet to be answered. Who gains, who pays? Does the environment really benefit? Who controls it, who monitors its impact? There is obviously a need for more research and a thought-provoking list of concerns which may be addressed by research is given by Valentine (1992).

Many articles on ecotourism conclude on an upbeat or a hopeful note. Budowski (1976) predicted that a tourist industry based on natural assets of the environment could expect a brilliant future, and tourism and nature were seen as natural partners by McNeely and Thorsell (1988). Ziffer (1989) held out hope for effective ecotourism policies and programmes and Boo (1992) thinks people are poised to believe in ecotourism. Is this optimistic view justified? Certainly sceptics and critics exist, and they can point to examples of things gone wrong; of ecotourism being used as a buzzword or even a marketing gimmick; of ecosystems damaged and communities threatened. But ecotourism projects founded on the notion of sustainable development do exist and are succeeding, and enough positive action seems to be building momentum to permit ecotourism to keep taking strides forward. More wildlands will be lost, but others which are threatened will be saved and in this ecotourism will play a role, and is in fact making a difference. Ecotourism may be viewed as the leading edge of a change in tourism – the conscience of the greater tourism industry, leading the way for more environmentally sound tourism development in general.

References

Ashton, R.E., 1991, 'The financing of conservation – the concept of self supporting eco-preserves', in J.A. Kusler (compiler), *Ecotourism and resource conservation: a collection of papers* (2 vols), Ecotourism and Resource Conservation Project, Omni Press, Madison.

Aussie-Stone, M., 1992, 'Planning a culture hotel for an indigenous community', in *1992 World Congress on Adventure Travel and Ecotourism*, Adventure Travel Society, Englewood, Colorado.

Blangey, S. and Epler Wood, M., 1993, 'Developing and implementing ecotourism guidelines for wild lands and neighboring communities', in K. Lindberg and D. Hawkins (eds), *Ecotourism: a guide for planners and managers*, The Ecotourism Society, Alexandria, Virginia.

Boo, E., 1990, *Ecotourism: the potentials and pitfalls* (2 vols), World Wildlife Fund, Washington, DC.

Boo, E., 1992, *The ecotourism boom: planning for development and management*, WHN Technical Paper Series, Paper #2, World Wildlife Fund, Washington, DC.

Budowski, G., 1976, 'Tourism and environmental conservation: conflict, coexistence or symbiosis?', *Environmental Conservation*, 3(1): 27–31.

Butler, J.R., 1992, 'Ecotourism: its changing face and evolving philosophy', paper presented at the IVth World Congress on National Parks and Protected Areas, Caracas, Venezuela.

Ceballos-Lascurain, H., 1987, 'Estudio de prefactibilidad socioeconómica del turismo ecológico y anteproyecto arquitectónico y urbanístico del Centro de Turismo Ecológico de Sian Ka'an, Quintana Roo', study carried out for SEDUE, Mexico.

Chapin, M., 1990, 'The silent jungle: ecotourism among the Kuna Indians of Panama', in 'Breaking out of the tourist trap, part one', *Cultural Survival Quarterly*, 14(1): 42–5

Dixon, J.A. and Sherman, P.B., 1990, *Economics of protected areas – a new look at benefits and costs*, Island Press, Washington, DC.

Dowling, R.K., 1991, 'An ecotourism planning model', in B. Weiler (ed.), *Ecotourism: incorporating the global classroom*, Bureau of Tourism Research, Canberra, Australia.

Drake, S., 1991, 'Development of a local participation plan for ecotourism projects', in J.A. Kusler (compiler), *Ecotourism and resource conservation: a collection of papers* (2 vols), Ecotourism and Resource Conservation Project, Omni Press, Madison.

Durst, P.B. and Ingram, C.D., 1988, 'Nature-oriented tourism promotion by developing countries', *Tourism Management*, 9(1):39–43.

Eagles, P.F.J., 1992, 'The travel motivations of Canadian ecotourists', *Journal of Travel Research*, 21(2):3–7.

Eagles, P.F.J., Ballantine, J.L. and Fennell, D.A., 1992, 'Marketing to the ecotourist: case studies from Kenya and Costa Rica', paper presented to the IVth World Congress on National Parks and Protected Areas, Caracas, Venezuela.

Epler Wood, M., 1992, 'Defining criteria for a consumer evaluation program: the Ecotourism Society's national survey of outbound tour operators', in *1992 World Congress on Adventure Travel and Ecotourism*, Adventure Travel Society, Englewood, Colorado.

Falconer, B., 1991, 'Tourism and sustainability: the dream realized', in L.J. Reid (ed.), *Tourism – Environment – Sustainable Development: An Agenda for Research*, Travel and Tourism Research Association, Brock University, Canada.

Farrel, B.H., and Runyan, D., 1991, 'Ecology and tourism', *Annals of Tourism Research*, 18(1): 26–40.

Filani, M.O., 1975, The role of national tourism associations in the preserving of the environment in Africa', *Journal of Travel Research*, 13(4): 7–12.

Filion, F.L., Foley, J.P. and Jacquemot, A.J., 1992, 'The economics of global eco-tourism', Paper presented to the IVth World Congress on National Parks and Protected Areas, Caracas, Venezuela.

Gale S., 1991, Assessing Tourism Opportunities, Economic and Inventories, in *1991 World Congress on Adventure Travel and Ecotourism*, Adventure Travel Society, Englewood, Colorado.

Garret, W.E., 1989, 'La Ruta Maya', *National Geographic Magazine*, October: 424–79.

Hackett, M., 1991, 'Solving the ecotourism dilemma', in B. Weiler (ed.), *Ecotourism: incorporating the global classroom*, Bureau of Tourism Research, Canberra, Australia.

Healy, R.G., 1988, *Economic considerations in nature-oriented tourism: the case of tropical forest tourism*, Forestry Private Enterprise Initiative (FPEI) Working Paper no. 39, Raleigh, North Carolina.

Hill, C., 1990, 'The paradox of tourism in Costa Rica', in 'Breaking out of the tourist trap, part one', *Cultural Survival Quarterly*, 14(1): 14–19.

Ingram, C.D. and Durst, P.B., 1989, 'Nature-oriented tour operators: travel to developing countries', *Journal of Travel Research*, 28(2): 11–15.

International Resources Group, Ltd., 1992, *Ecotourism: a viable alternative for sustainable management of natural resources in Africa*, US Agency for International Development, Washington, DC.

Jones, A., 1987, 'Green tourism', *Tourism Management*, 8(4): 354–6.

Kermath, B.M., 1991, 'Nature conservation and ecotourism in Brazilian Amazonia', in J.A. Kusler (compiler), *Ecotourism and resource conservation: a collection of papers* (2 vols), Ecotourism and Resource Conservation Project, Omni Press, Madison.

Laarman, J.G. and Durst, P.B., 1987, 'Nature travel in the Tropics', *Journal of Forestry*, 85(5): 43–6.

Leakey, R., 1991, 'Kenya's parks system and eco-tourism', in *1991 World Congress on Adventure Travel and Ecotourism*, Adventure Travel Society, Englewood, Colorado.

Lillywhite M., 1992, 'Reactive or proactive: Botswana low impact eco-tourism development plan', in *1992 World Congress on Adventure Travel and Ecotourism*, Adventure Travel Society, Englewood, Colorado.

Lindberg, K., 1991, *Policies for maximizing nature tourism's ecological and environmental benefits*, World Resources Institute, Washington, DC.

McNeely, J.A., 1988, *Economics and biological diversity: developing and using economic incentives to conserve biological resources*, International Union for Conservation of Nature and Natural Resources (IUCN), McGregor and Werner, Inc., Washington, DC.

McNeely, J.A. and Thorsell, J.W., 1988, 'Jungles, mountains, and islands: how tourism can help conserve the natural heritage', in L. D'Amore and J. Jafari (eds), *Tourism: A vital force for peace*, First Global Conference, Montreal, Canada.

Moore, S.R. and Carter, B., 1991, 'Ecotourism in the 21st Century', in B. Weiler (ed.), *Ecotourism: incorporating the global classroom*, Bureau of Tourism Research, Canberra, Australia.

Moulin, C.L., 1980, 'Plan for ecological and cultural tourism involving participation of local populations and associations', in D. E. Hawkins, E.L. Shafer and

J.M. Rovelstad (eds), *Tourism planning and development issues*, George Washington University, Washington, DC.

Place, S.E., 1991, 'Nature tourism and rural development in Tortuguero', *Annals of Tourism Research*, 18(2): 186–201.

Romeril, M., 1989, 'Tourism: the environmental dimension', in C.P. Copper (ed.), *Progress in tourism, recreation and hospitality management*, Vol. 1, Belhaven Press, London.

Ryel, R. and Grasse, T., 1991, 'Marketing ecotourism: attracting the elusive eco-tourist', in T. Whelan (ed.), *Nature tourism: managing for the environment*, Island Press, Washington, DC.

Rymer, T.M., 1992, 'Growth of U.S. ecotourism and its future in the 1990s', *FIU Hospitality Review* 10(1): 1–10.

Scace, R.C., Grifone, E. and Usher, R., 1992, *Ecotourism in Canada*, Canadian Environmental Advisory Council, Environment Canada, Hull, Quebec.

Selengut, S. and Simon, R., 1991, 'Maho Bay: a model for environmentally-sensitive and economically-successful development: ecological restoration as a component of resort development and restoration', in J.A. Kusler (compiler), *Ecotourism and resource conservation: a collection of papers* (2 vols), Ecotourism and Resource Conservation Project, Omni Press, Madison.

Sherman, P.B. and Dixon, J.A., 1991, 'The economics of nature tourism: determining if it pays', in T. Whelan (ed.), *Nature Tourism: Managing for the Environment*, Island Press, Washington, DC.

Tourism Industry Association of Canada, 1992, *Code of ethics and guidelines for sustainable tourism*, Tourism Industry Association of Canada, Ottawa.

Valentine, P.S., 1992, 'Review, nature-based tourism', in B. Weiler and C.M. Hall (eds), *Special interest tourism*, Belhaven Press, London.

Vega, M., 1992, 'The ecotourism trend', *Belize Currents*, no. 13: 35–7.

Weaver, D.B. 1991, 'Alternative to mass tourism in Dominica', *Annals of Tourism Research*, 18(3): 414–32.

Webley, J., 1991, 'The effect of eco-tourism on African cultures and lifestyles', in *1991 World Congress on Adventure Travel and Ecotourism*, Adventure Travel Society, Englewood, Colorado, USA.

Weiler, B., 1992, 'Nature-based tour operators: are they environmentally friendly or are they faking it?', paper presented at the First World Congress on Tourism and the Environment, Belize.

Whelan, T., 1991, 'Ecotourism and its role in sustainable development', in T. Whelan (ed.), *Nature tourism: managing for the environment*, Island Press, Washington, DC.

Wight, P., 1993, 'Ecotourism: ethics or eco-sell?', *Journal of Travel Research*, 31(3): 3–9.

Wild, C., 1992, 'The business of packaging adventure travel and ecotours', in *1992 World Congress on Adventure Travel and Ecotourism*, Adventure Travel Society, Englewood, Colorado.

Wood, K., and House, S., 1991, *The good tourist*, Mandarin Paperbacks, London.

Yee, J.G. 1992, 'Ecotourism market survey: a survey of North American eco-tourism operators', The Intelligence Center, Pacific Asia Travel Association, San Francisco.

Young, M. 1992. 'Towards a meaningful ecotourism definition' (preliminary paper), World Wildlife Fund, Sydney.

Ziffer, K.A., 1989, *Ecotourism: the uneasy alliance*. Conservation International and Ernst & Young, Washington, DC.

3 Alternative tourism: the real tourism alternative?

M. Romeril

There was a distinct sense of *déjà vu* at a major tourism and environment international conference held in London as recently as the summer of 1992. Introducing his paper, one of the main speakers told delegates that 'the conference comes at a very timely moment' (Porritt 1992). Virtually the same claim was being made over 20 years ago at the Europa Nostra conference on the same theme (Europa Nostra and European Travel Commission 1973) and the sentiment has been echoed at countless other conferences and workshops on the same subject. One is tempted to ask if there has really been much progress along the path of environmental enlightment in the context of tourism.

It is now a quarter of a century since the first study of tourism and conservation at the International Union for the Conservation of Nature and Natural Resources (IUCN) Tenth Technical Meeting on Ecology, Tourism and Recreation (IUCN 1967). It is ironic, therefore, that, at a time when so many so-called green tourism initiatives are being launched and lauded, there is an increasing groundswell of opinion that questions what can really be accomplished in the way of environmentally sensitive and sympathetic tourism development.

Looking at the historical perspective, the attitudinal changes concerning tourism's impact(s) on the environment are well documented. In the context of the postwar years, which were a time of recovery and growth, an early view was that tourism had few impacts on the natural environment (Zierer 1952). However, the mass tourism which characterised the 1960s began to awaken many to the negative aspects of an industry which still appealed to many as the perfect answer to economic ills. The United Nations Conference on the Human Environment at Stockholm in 1972 distilled the essence of so many substantive environmental arguments prevalent at that time. It argued the necessity for a way forward which integrated the conservation of natural resources within broader economic and social strategies.

In such a context of increasing environmental concern it was impossible to ignore the role of tourism in environmental issues and vice versa. Comprehensive reviews of the environmental impacts of tourism appeared regularly during the next decade or so, and have been well documented (see, for example, Romeril 1989). This raised profile triggered many attempts to find a mutually beneficial, pragmatic relationship between tourism and the environment which would reflect the ideals espoused at the UN Stockholm conference. Budowski's (1976) seminal paper, while reminding us that tourism and the environment could exist in a state of either coexistence or conflict, argued strongly also that symbiosis could be achieved and was the ideal relationship. Support for that ideal was endorsed by subsequent authors (Gunn 1978; Romeril 1985).

The concept has evolved and become modified over the years to reflect changing attitudes on both sides of the argument, and particularly taking account of the expanding breadth of environmentalism and the greater acceptance of the validity of the environmental case. Again the literature is well documented. Thus the earlier ideas of Travis (1982) and Murphy (1983; 1985) were reflected in the comprehensive review of Farrell and McLellan (1987). The call was for the environment to embrace social and physical dimensions as well as the ecological perspective. Such a holistic and integrative approach, which has been advocated by so many, continues to be the subject of fine-tuning. Dowling (1992a) provides the latest refinement. He argues that environmentally compatible tourism development can be achieved through sustainable development but that it will only be attained through appropriate tourism planning.

Sustainable development has been a concept central to nearly all recent major global environmental initiatives. It was advocated by the World Commission on Environment and Development (WCED 1987) in a report generally referred to as the Brundtland Report, and was the core theme of the Earth Summit at Rio de Janeiro in 1992. In many ways the concept varies little from the principles enunciated at Stockholm in 1972, but its clear focus is on long-term economic growth (through the sustainable use of environmental resources). *Inter alia*, this approach should ensure the maintenance of environmental integrity.

With so much apparent progress in global environmental understanding and commitment, and the fact that tourism's clear links with the environment have been recognised for so long, one might be forgiven for thinking that the problems associated with the industry's impact on its primary resource are, or could soon be, a thing of the past. However, such optimism may not be well founded. Of the three options espoused by Budowski (1976), truly symbiotic relationships exist in far too few cases, conflict is not too difficult to find and, even with examples of coexistence, the motives and actuality are often viewed with suspicion by many environmentalists and other unbiased observers. Perhaps the emerging situation could best be described as 'coexistence, often with a strong environmental sympathy'.

The view that progress in resolving tourism/environment issues is perhaps far less tangible than perceived has gained ground as a significant number of authors have questioned the reality of so-called alternative tourism approaches. Butler (1990; 1991) argued that, too often, over-simplistic and naive views of the complex nature of tourism, and also of the environment, led to misleading claims and hopes for alternative tourism. Other authors express their doubts in a more cynical manner. Wickers (1992), for example, claims that while the industry is desperately trying to appear ecologically responsible, much of the noise is marketing babble. Wheeller (1991; 1992a), one suspects with a degree of hyperbole, implies that tourism's very complexity and heterogeneity render it unmanageable. He claims that there is, as yet, no answer to tourism's global impact problems.

The 'impossible to achieve' claim is nothing new to the environmentalist. However, there are few, if any, environmental causes that cannot be overcome if the commitment is there, and if those involved are willing to accept the costs entailed in achieving a positive result in the long term. The present climate surely could not serve as a better reminder to world leaders that definitive action is necessary to build on the valuable contribution to the environmental debate generated by Brundtland. Despite some political cynicism, much was realistically achieved at Rio de Janeiro, with the adoption of Agenda 21 which sets out a programme for world action on sustainable development in the twenty-first century.

There remains concern, however, that a preoccupation with the actual word 'sustainable' will blind us to the underlying, but absolutely necessary, requirements for mankind to achieve these global initiatives. There is a dire need to appreciate the reality which will demand a quantum change of attitude among so many decision-makers, and other 'actors' involved in the industry. The Brundtland Report itself intimates that the integration of economic and ecological considerations into development planning will require nothing less than a 'renaissance' in economic decision-making. The attitude to 'economic growth' illustrates the point, particularly as even Brundtland is considered to remain too fixed on the ethic of expansionism (Ekins 1989). Ekins calls for a redefinition of economic growth – one should reclaim for it its original economic meaning of an improvement in human welfare, rather than an increase in production and consumption. The parameters of choice become clearer when they are between different, and largely undefined, forms of industrial expansion. Given the interactive nature of tourism, it seems an activity particularly well suited to further this goal, but only if it can moderate its obsession with expansionist growth.

The global environmental initiatives address also the fundamental problems of meeting the basic needs of humanity – food, clothing, shelter and jobs. There is a call for the community of nations to evolve a new, more equitable, international economic structure that begins to narrow the gap between developing and developed countries. Again tourism would seem to have a special relevance because of its direct and indirect catalytic role in respect of this objective.

So where do all these noble, and seemingly essential, environmental goals leave us in the real world of tourism development? Is it really true to claim, as Wheeller (1992b) does, that such global declarations, conventions and agreements are synonymous with the tourism initiatives that avoid, 'by the subtle use of sidestepping rhetoric, the unpalatable situation of having to come to terms with the real and, as yet, insoluble dilemma of tourism'?

Sadly, I have to empathise with Wheeller's hyperbole in some respects. Working 'at the coalface', one is faced with the reality of the local decision-making process. To the man wanting to develop his 'modest' beach concession at a sensitive location, Brundtland and Agenda 21 mean little, if anything, and even terms such as 'sustainable', if acknowledged, can be used in a manner which means all things to all people. How often, for example, do we underestimate the power of decision-making dignitaries in the local political scene, who choose to ignore national and regional policies if it suits?

One may wonder why appreciation and understanding of the wider issues are so vital at this (minor) level of activity. The World Conservation Strategy (IUCN 1980) pointed up the enormous potential for good of every individual environmental achievement no matter how small, since their sum would represent a major impact. Therefore, conversely, it must be equally true that the sum of the many negative impacts, no matter how small each one may be in itself, can have a huge detrimental effect.

There is certainly a major difficulty in translating ideal(s) into action (Pigram 1980). However, despite this rather gloomy prognosis, the situation is not without hope. Two apparent stumbling blocks require special attention. There is a need to avoid becoming enslaved in a world of jargon and/or rigid definitions, and there should be a more pragmatic acceptance of the fact that mass tourism will not just 'go away' and it will always need to cater for the desire for a wide spectrum of holiday experiences. There is no single type of tourist and therefore no single standard response to solve all tourism's problems.

The preoccupation with definitions is well demonstrated with the term 'carrying capacity'. The concept of a threshold level of tourism beyond which detrimental environmental impacts will occur promises planners the ideal of a magic formula to solve all problems. The reality is very different and that magic formula remains as elusive as ever. It is true that in particular well-defined environments the concept can be made to work, but all too often the search for an empirical methodology is wasteful of time and energy. What is important is for the philosophy behind the concept automatically to condition the decision-maker to think environmentally. As Wall (1982) pointed out, if the concept encourages tourism planners and managers to give greater consideration to environmental matters, to the qualities of the experiences available to both hosts and guests, and to specify their goals and objectives, then it will have served a useful purpose. One has to hope that a similar semantic preoccupation with the exact definition of sustainability, valuable as the concept is, does not prejudice progress in addressing the issue.

In similar vein, the semantic merry-go-round, or the nonsense nomenclature game as Wheeller (1992b) calls it, does little to hasten progress. So often it seems to offer little more than an academic exercise for those somewhat removed from the action. Alternative tourism, rural tourism, green tourism, ecotourism etc. – what does it matter if the definition is not strictly appropriate if the activity is environmentally sensitive and sound? Surely it is the philosophy, and not the semantics, that is important.

Coming to terms with the fact of mass tourism is also not without semantic overtones as authors wrestle with the exact description of a 'visitor', a 'tourist' and a 'traveller'. Yet again, the answer calls for a degree of pragmatism. Tourism is the world's largest industry. The movement of large numbers of people in pursuit of leisure is unlikely to cease or diminish significantly, but it should not be impossible to cater for mass tourism in an environmentally benign manner. For example, although the Mediterranean costas can never again be natural unspoilt coastlines, they can be improved. The challenge should be to rehabilitate the present ugly urban sprawl and create environments, in their sociocultural as well as their architectural and design context, of the highest standard. At new destinations likely to cater for high numbers of tourists, the challenge should be to create an infrastructure of such quality that the features could become worthy, in time, of conservation in their own right!

Can mass tourism be managed? The honeypot concept is now somewhat dated in leisure planning and yet it is not without merit applied to mass tourism. While perhaps not viewed that way by their originators, theme parks act as valuable honeypots providing leisure opportunities for millions who might otherwise have generated pressures in other more sensitive areas. The Disneyland centres are probably the most famous of theme parks. Despite the criticisms of such theme parks for their artificiality, there is no doubt that they provide the kind of tourism that millions of people want and do so at a fraction of the environmental and cultural costs of today's charter flights and resort hotels around the world (Von Droste *et al.* 1992).

It has been argued that catering for the masses in such a way is a *ghettoisation* (Wheeller 1992a) of tourism which does not accord with the notion of the sensitive traveller being at one with the indigenous population. One can accept this to some extent, but the solving of all environmental problems requires an element of compromise. There is no example of tourism that is devoid of environmental impact and in this instance the social disbenefits are surely offset by other significant and worthwhile environmental gains to an extent which justifies the whole.

The regulation of tourism through pricing mechanisms or other means is another way of controlling large numbers of tourists, though some see this as creating up-market elitism. Such a pejorative interpretation is unfortunate. Restriction, to a lesser or greater extent, will become the norm in our environmentally enlightened future and we will accept the wisdom of the decisions in the light of the overall benefits for society. We already do. Controls already exist at the Great Barrier Reef in Australia and at the Mesa Verde National Park in America, to name but two examples.

While accepting that mass tourism can be successfully managed, it would be wrong to ignore potential trends, which we can only begin to grasp at this moment in time, which could see a diminution of, or at least no further increase in, the phenomenon. At a basic level, the old chestnut of seasonality remains a major influence affecting mass tourism. However, the edges of the high season and the low season are gradually becoming blurred. Advanced technology, especially in the field of computers, changing work patterns, and other demographic trends should all lead to a reduced seasonal flux which may be more significant than initially envisaged. In these 'ozone-affected' days when the incidence of skin cancer is increasing, alarmingly so in some cases, will people still desire, almost like lemmings, the sun, sea and sand holidays which are deemed to be the root cause of the disease?

Moves within the industry are encouraging as it addresses issues raised by the introduction of ecolabelling and environmental audit. The British Standard, BS 7750, for environmental management, provides a valuable yardstick by which to assess the environmental performance of those firms and organisations promoting tourism destinations. Thomsons has already made positive moves in that direction and others will surely follow the example of such a tourism giant. In a more futuristic vein, who can predict the role of 'virtual reality' technology in meeting the hedonistic aspirations of the future tourist? Perhaps local theme parks offering the opportunity, through virtual reality, to travel the world without leaving the home neighbourhood could become the order of the day.

Such radical change may seem somewhat far off or unreal. However, this may not be so given the acceptance that the 'quantum leap' forward or the 'renaissance' already mentioned in the context of economic thinking will be equally necessary in other dimensions of life. Major shifts in human behaviour and far-reaching changes in values and life styles are a *sine qua non* for an environmentally sustainable future. While it may be difficult to conceive, the mass tourist of tomorrow may be a very different 'animal' to that of today, even assuming he or she continues to exist.

The mass market still remains confined to certain areas, notably coastal regions, and does not even exist for about 80 per cent of the year. Therefore, a preoccupation with mass tourism should not prejudice the challenge of ensuring that it is not 'more of the same' in lightly developed or undeveloped destinations. Vast areas of the world, many of high environmental value, are likely to be seen as potential tourist destinations. Well-proven planning approaches integrating tourism and environment interests in a mutually compatible and beneficial manner do exist and clearly show that such areas can be successfully developed if the commitment to environmental objectives is sincere. Dowling (1992b) lists many examples ranging from small scale to large, which generate nature conservation, cultural, heritage, social and spatial benefits.

Many such planning approaches have a tourism or environmental bias or specific context. For that reason, Dowling (1992b) has argued the case for an environmentally compatible tourism (ECT) planning framework as a regional sustainable development framework. The major thrust of his framework is not towards the determination of land-use sustainability or capability, carrying capacity, threshold analysis or pattern analysis. It evaluates and determines environmentally compatible tourism through the identification of 'significant areas', 'critical areas' and 'compatible activities'. Reflecting Murphy's (1985) approach, the role of people as part of the ecosystem is especially emphasised. Its particular merit is the further drawing together of the disparate strands of tourism and environment planning. Tourism and the environment are seen as a unified whole with the community dimension, often ignored or undervalued, given due weighting.

The ECT planning framework has been successfully tested in the Gascoyne region of Western Australia (Dowling 1992b). What it and other planning frameworks prove is that it is feasible to integrate environmental protection and enhancement with the realisation of tourism potential. The ultimate goal is to ensure the wise use of resources, meeting *needs* rather than *demands*, and this is the essence of sustainability.

Sustainability can be achieved through a number of mechanisms, and there is no reason why the myriad forms of tourism, whatever their label, cannot be accommodated within its philosophy. There should be less concern about the definition of, and distinction between, different forms of alternative tourism and more concern that the tourism of the future is alternative from that of the exploitive industry of times past. The tourism industry is not without its fair share of the greed of humankind, and it will take some time yet before all its many lesser actors become endowed with the altruism of the global clarion calls for environmental awareness. Nevertheless, it is at that level that (correct) action is required most of all. A combination of jargon, semantics and rhetoric can all too readily provide a smokescreen for the local politician who wants to promise much yet produce little. However, the tide of change to environmental awareness and action is certainly gathering strength and momentum across the whole spectrum of economic and social activity, and it is not unreasonable to expect, and see, within an acceptable time-scale, far more tangible evidence of the successful linking of tourism with sustainable development.

References

Budowski, G., 1976, 'Tourism and environmental conservation: conflict, coexistence or symbiosis?', *Environmental Conservation*, 3(1): 27–31.

Butler, R.W., 1990, 'Alternative tourism: pious hope or Trojan horse?', *Journal of Travel Research*, 28(3): 40–45.

Butler, R.W., 1991, 'Tourism, environment, and sustainable development', *Environmental Conservation*, 18(3): 201–9.

Dowling, R.K., 1992a, 'Tourism and environmental integration: the journey from idealism to realism', in C.P. Cooper and A. Lockwood (eds), *Progress in tourism, recreation and hospitality management*, Vol. 4, Belhaven, London: 33–46.

Dowling, R.K., 1992b, 'An environmentally based approach to tourism planning', PhD Thesis, Murdoch University, Perth, Western Australia.

Farrell, B.H. and McLellan, R.W., 1987, 'Tourism and physical environment research', *Annals of Tourism Research*, 14(1): 1–16.

Ekins, P., 1989, 'Beyond growth: the real priorities of sustainable development', *Environmental Conservation*, 16(1): 5–6.

Europa Nostra and European Travel Commission, 1973, *Tourism and conservation – working together*, ETC, Dublin.

Gunn, C.A., 1978, 'Needed: an international alliance for tourism-recreation-conservation', *Travel Research Journal*, 2: 3–9.

IUCN, 1967, *Ecology, Tourism and Recreation*, Proceedings of the Tenth Technical Meeting, IUCN, Morges, Switzerland.

IUCN, 1980, *World Conservation Strategy*, IUCN, Gland, Switzerland.

Murphy, P.E., 1983, 'Tourism as a community industry: an ecological model of tourism development', *Tourism Management*, 4(3): 180–193

Murphy, P.E., 1985, *Tourism – a community approach*, Methuen, New York.

Pigram, J.J., 1980, 'Environmental implications of tourism development', *Annals of Tourism Research*, 7(4): 554–83.

Porritt, J., 1992, 'Challenges and choices for the 90s', in *Proceedings of Tourism and Environment Conference*, English Tourist Board, London.

Romeril, M.G., 1985, 'Tourism and the environment – towards a symbiotic relationship', *International Journal of Environmental Studies*, 25(4): 215–18.

Romeril, M.G., 1989, 'Tourism: the environmental dimension', in C.P. Cooper (ed.), *Progress in tourism, recreation and hospitality management*, Vol. 1, Belhaven, London: 103–13.

Travis, A.S., 1982, 'Managing the environment and cultural impacts of tourism and leisure development', *Tourism Management*, 3(4): 256–62.

Von Droste, B., Silk, D. and Rossler, M., 1992, 'Tourism, world heritage and sustainable development', *UNEP Industry and Environment*, 15(3–4): 6–9.

Wall, G., 1982, 'Cycles and capacity – incipient theory or conceptual contradiction', *Tourism Management*, 3(3): 188–92.

WCED, 1987, *Our Common Future*, Report of the World Commission on Environment and Development (the Brundtland Commission), Oxford University Press, Oxford.

Wheeller, B., 1991, 'Tourism's troubled times: responsible tourism is not the answer', *Tourism Management*, 12(1): 91–6.

Wheeller, B., 1992a, 'Is progressive tourism appropriate?', *Tourism Management*, 13(1): 104–5.

Wheeller, B., 1992b, 'Alternative tourism – a deceptive ploy', in C.P. Cooper and A. Lockwood (eds), *Progress in tourism, recreation and hospitality management*, Vol. 4, Belhaven, London: 140–45.

Wickers, D., 1992, 'Whither green', *Sunday Times*, 5 January.

Zierer, C.M., 1952, 'Tourism and recreation in the West', *Geographical Review*, 42: 462–81.

4 Issues in sustainability and the national parks of Kenya and Cameroon

D.C. Gilbert, J. Penda and M. Friel

Introduction

The concept of providing sustainable forms of tourism has become more prominent in the 1990s as a response to the recognition of the environmental problems caused by unorganised tourism and poor planning. This concept is extremely important for countries such as those in Africa where the tourism potential is in danger of being over exploited. Solutions to the adverse affects of tourism are not easy as, according to Lane (1992), the tourism industry cannot afford a decline in numbers. Therefore the industry has to tackle vigorously current problems of demand as well as make allowances for potential future difficulties.

This chapter provides a brief background to the concepts of sustainable tourism and then places them in the context of planning in the Kenyan and Cameroon national parks. Such an approach may lead to the refining of some of the issues related to the current lack of consensus over what are taken to be appropriate forms of tourism.

Different forms of sustainable tourism

The growing awareness of the problems of mass tourism has led observers and researchers on tourism and the environment to attack the past methods and directions of tourism development and to recommend their replacement with alternative forms of tourism. Due to conflicts between mass tourism and the environment, managers, researchers, academicians, planners, tour operators, international bodies – such as the United Nations Environmental Program (UNEP) and the World Tourism Organisation (WTO) – are all working toward the development of new forms of tourism that will diminish impacts on the environment as well as maintain the national and local benefits of tourism. The problem with the current approach is that while some favour small-scale approaches, others see this as no solution to the inherent problems of tourism-related enterprises.

McKercher (1993) has identified the underlying structures or 'fundamental truths' related to tourism development which lead to adverse impact. These relate to the *negative social, environmental and economic impacts* which different tourism authors have tried to address (Mathieson and Wall 1985; Krippendorf 1987; Lea 1988; Millman 1989; Buckley and Pannell 1990; Butler 1990; Boo 1991; Saremba and Gill 1991; Sinclair 1992) by arguing for one or more of the different sustainability approaches:

1. As an industry, tourism consumes resources, creates waste and has specific infrastructure needs. This is seen to have an impact on the social fabric of the host community and, due to infrastructure require-ments, to have wider implications than for just the local tourist area.
2. It has the ability to over-consume resources and put different areas under stress.
3. Conflicts will occur between host communities and tourists as certain resources become scarce or where there are incompatible needs.
4. Tourism is predominantly led by the private sector where decisions are based upon profit motives and where tour companies will not consider investing in socially necessary environmental programmes such as sewage plants.
5. Tourism is a multifaceted industry and activity and its fragmented nature makes it difficult to provide effective controls.
6. Tourists are motivated to indulge in excesses and are therefore consumers not anthropologists.
7. Tourism is an imported market of consumers who consume at the generation point and as such can over-concentrate on one small area.

Green, alternative and sustainable tourism

The problems identified which reflect the concern over social, environ-mental as well as economic impacts have been worrying various tourism writers since the early 1970s. The anxiety generated has led to a diverse range of terms and solutions. Terms appended to tourism such as 'appropriate', 'alternative', 'controlled', 'eco', 'green', 'nature', 'soft', 'responsible' and 'sustainable' reflect an often simplistic approach to creating what authors believe to be a more benign form of tourism or even one with positive benefits. The question posed is whether any of the approaches can provide a solution to a diverse range of problems found in different tourism situations.

To comprehend the vast number of approaches dealing with concern over tourism policies it is necessary briefly to discuss the main typologies of green, alternative and sustainable tourism which seem to subsume some of the other terms previously mentioned. This is not an easy task as there is considerable overlap and confusion between the terms.

Green tourism
Green tourism has often been used as a basis for creating a balanced approach to planning. A working definition of green tourism is given by Bramwell (1990) thus: 'Tourism which enhances the distinctive character of local cultures ... works through host community control, provides

quality employment for local people and keeps economic benefits within the local economy'.

Green tourism is often associated with approaches which concentrate on various interactions in the local environment. Additionally there is the notion of variable degrees of personal contact between visitors and locals (see, for example, Butler 1990; Green 1990; Gordon 1991) also includes the notion of interacting with wildlife which for national parks is an important consideration. Behind these characteristics is the belief in the ability of green tourism to alleviate the problems of mass tourism. It is often argued that a green strategy has to be accomplished slowly step by step. This is argued to be a careful way to manage the environment as development is by cautious steps, compared to mass tourism which has been considered more aggressive and inconsiderate because of the organiser's motive being solely for profit. Slow development is recommended in order to make it easier for the host to absorb change. In addition, those who stress the need for green tourism often stress the need for a locally based set of decisions.

However green tourism is also used as a label by industry in respect of the need to provide traveller codes which places the stress on information such as how to conserve energy, rather than on some of the more basic problems of tourism impact. While tour companies continue to price near to break-even point and suffer the problems of a highly volatile price-sensitive market-place, it is not surprising they are unwilling to implement far-reaching sustainable tourism measures. There is also very little chance that the economic benefits of tourism will remain in the local economy rather than be repatriated to foreign countries. This contradicts Bramwell's earlier definition where, for green tourism, economic benefit should be retained by the local community.

The current response of the industry is due to changing consumer values towards *greenness* (Elkington and Hailes 1992), and tour operators have tried to soften their image by stressing their commitment to creating more 'green tourism'. However, Wheeller (1991), Long (1991) and Wickers (1992) have accused the marketing people of promoting tourist destinations without considering the harm that the tourist movements will cause to the environment. Wheeller (1992b) quotes Wickers' (1992) observation that:

> Much of the noise is marketing babble – another front on which to fight the competition and many companies are simply slapping the green label on any destination where nature is more rampant than concrete. What will happen to that nature as a result of their promotion of it is not a question they care to address.

While authors are keen to stress the benefits of green tourism there are still no figures or research to indicate the level of demand associated with green tourism products. This is not to say that no progress has been made as there is a move to classify the segments. Following authors such as Porritt and Winner (1988) who have looked at the different 'shades of green' of different consumers and Krippendorf (1984) who identified the *critical consumer tourists*, the English Tourist Board (1992) devised a four-category profile of tourism consumers:

- the *inactive*, who have no real interest in the environment;
- the *mainstream*, those who make some green purchases but are not keen;
- the *second wave*, new green consumers who adopt green consumption;
- the *leading edge*, dark greens with full knowledge of green initiatives.

However, although we are told that the 'second wave' is expanding and the 'inactive' declining, we still have little knowledge of the green tourism consumer.

Alternative tourism
Alternative tourism (AT) is often another synonym for green tourism. It is treated by Jarviluoma (1992) as small-scale tourism developed by local people and based upon concern for the local environment and carrying capacity. Some definitions of AT have been propounded which stress social factors, such as that of the Ecumenical Coalition of Third World Tourism (ECTWT) 'a process which promotes a just form of travel between members of different communities. It seeks to achieve mutual understanding, solidarity and equality amongst participants' (Holder 1984). Tourism of this nature requires some responsibility on the part of both tourists and intermediaries (tour operators, travel agents) to travel without causing habitual damage to the environment or social relationships. Alternative tourism is also treated as having developed as a reaction to our being part of growing mass consumerism and the modern industrial world by Cazes (1989). The seeking out of experiences that are more natural is echoed by Smith and Eadington (1992), who defined alternative tourism as 'forms of tourism that are consistent with natural, social and community values and which allow both hosts and guests to enjoy positive and worthwhile interaction and shared experience'.

As with green tourism, there are a number of arguments as to the efficacy of the application of alternative tourism to tourism locations. Butler (1990) treats alternative tourism as an elitist activity for wealthy and highly educated groups, and as a form of tourism which only spreads problems to new unspoilt areas. This argument could as easily be levelled at various 'green tourism' developments.

The question is therefore one of whether *realism* should prevail in terms of acceptance that there will always be conflicts of cost and benefit related to all forms of tourism, or whether *idealism* should dominate, whereby coexistence of tourists' needs and small-scale development is one means of dealing with the conflicts.

Sustainable tourism
Out of the interest in protecting tourist destinations emerged the interest in different forms of sustainable tourism (Smith 1981; Richter and Richter 1985; Krippendorf 1987; Pearce 1992; Sinclair 1992). Since the discussion on sustainable development began in the 1980s, other writers

have followed with definitions such as that of Davidson *et al.* (1992):

> Sustainable development is an alliance of three essential elements: people, their environment and the future. Implicit is the idea of people-centred development which brings social and economic advances but also safeguards the environment and its resources so that options are not closed for the future.

Pearce (1992) argues that alternative tourism policies tend to be formulated as a result of the concentration on particular aspects of mass tourism without necessarily possessing an underlying coherent philosophy *per se*. Although new alternatives to the problems caused by mass tourism are being developed, environmental and other forms of impact are still identified as a negative by-product. As Wheeller (1992a) warns, alternative forms of tourism should not be seen as an answer to the negative impacts of tourism. This is because any form of tourism alternative is to be treated with caution and scepticism, scrutinised and analysed from a realistic point of view. Meanwhile, according to Cohen (1989), the managers, marketing personnel and others involved in planning and selling tourism products should concentrate on eliminating the worst situations of dehumanization and exploitation in tourism rather than resort to arguing about alternative development. Although alternative tourism may be accepted as a set of principles to solve the problems of mass tourism and environmental problems, its success has to rely on changes in management philosophy; the acceptance of appropriate planning; and a willingness to accept objectives which make revenue a lower priority than sustainability.

De Kadt (1992) argues that the analytical tools of assessing conventional tourism should be modified to enable AT to be successful. This would involve an examination of situations through the use of cost-benefit and cost-effectiveness analysis in order to provide guidance on investment choices. De Kadt also appeals to government agencies to assess the costs and benefits of development projects especially on the environment. In addition, he argues there should be a redefinition of the gross national product (GNP), so that ecological implications are included.

Responsible tourism
While a number of arguments exist for AT and green tourism, the authors believe that proponents are often too naive in their expectation that such approaches will immobilize and heal the detrimental impacts of modern tourism. More importantly, we do not believe that economic self-determination will be made available to local communities when the *modus operandi* of tourism to date has been exploitative. The proponents of alternative tourism offer eminently worthwhile arguments, but, given their inherent weakness, we propose the emphasis should be placed on the acceptance of *responsible tourism*.

Responsible tourism is an easier option to implement than other alternative or green forms of tourism. This is because responsible tourism requires not the overthrow of existing forms of tourism but the reform and modification of current industry practices so as to eliminate the worst abuses. Responsible tourism is something in which everyone in society can partake so that through concern there will evolve an improved set of values which will drive improvements in the way tourism is conducted. If alternative tourism is pursued then it should be based on responsible principles, but not all responsible tourism is necessarily of a scale and type that would deem it to be alternative. Responsible tourism should lead to more awareness of the problems of tourism, more careful development, more concern for the host community and environment and a more enlightened approach by the tourist.

Responsible tourism should feed back in welfare to the community. For example, one of the strategies adopted by the Kenya Wildlife Service towards conservation is to enable the rural people to benefit from wildlife, in which an innovative approach includes the payment of monetary compensation to local residents (Economist Intelligence Unit 1991). As attitudes change, planning at the local community level will be led by a culture which requires the cooperation of local government officials, local citizens, professional and business people so that all can participate in decision-making that will benefit the welfare of the environment and community. Therefore responsible tourism also identifies those specific characteristics which were highlighted in the discussion about green tourism. The purpose is directed towards the travellers so that they are educated to be aware of the fragile nature of their environment. It is also more responsive to the needs of the local people and involves them in decision-making. Our definition of 'responsible tourism' is as follows. It charges tourists to be aware of the impact of their actions, the local society to take responsibility to enforce its own will and for all concerned to take a responsible attitude to protecting the resource base of the area so that overall welfare is enhanced. We treat responsible tourism as a sensitising force which softens the impact of tourism through the concern of individual tourism stakeholders. The stakeholders are everyone from the tourist to the community and to the operators who will develop compassion regarding aspects of: environmental low-density and high-density tourism; the high import and low import of goods and services into a tourism area; foreign or local ownership issues; the scale of development between resort and community; and the dominance or subservience of the host culture.

Our idea of responsible tourism does not argue for small-scale development or unnecessary protection, but for modes of individual action which recognise the need to feel and be responsible for the development and activity of a touristic area such that appropriate values are held by all those involved.

Responsible development in African national parks

The debate regarding the environment and tourism has its roots in the 1970s when several authors stressed the ability of tourism to provide a conservation role especially in relation to national parks (Myers 1972; Greenwood 1972; Agarwal and Nangia 1974; Gunn 1978). However with the national parks in Africa it is not just the environmental concerns which are important.

The idea of responsible tourism development in Africa is especially linked to the art and craft works which are sold to tourists as souvenirs. Handicrafts, according to de Kadt (1984), are symbols of the past and representatives of what the present generation should understand. The use of local culture is an example of *commoditisation* with varieties such as 'colourful' local costumes and customs, rituals, feasts, folklore and ethnic arts that are produced solely for tourist consumption (Cohen 1988). This concept of commoditisation is treated as an alienating force which changes rather than sustains African culture. Following such arguments, the implementation of sustainable development in developing countries may lead to some problems because of the need for change to occur in order to meet with the demands of the tourists from industrial societies.

Economic problems

The problems of tourism are also economic. Due to the repatriation of profit by foreign companies and because of regional economic necessity, local people are led to sell what the tourist demands. For less developed countries in Africa this is often the basis of being exploited by the developed countries. This situation is often made worse when the majority of local people have no true employment in tourism-related jobs. For example, in Tanzania, in 1989, the Ngorogoro Conservation Area Authority received 92% of its income from tourism fees. Despite these benefits, none of the Masai is employed in hotels.

Regardless of the social and cultural costs, a Kenyan study by Migot-Adholla *et al.* (1992) concludes that the coastal people are in favour of tourism and would like to see more tourists coming to Kenya. The local people appear to be in accord with the official tourism policy which is in favour of fast tourism growth in Kenya. Yet the opinions of the local people are often based on obtaining short-term benefits for employment and income. However, from the same study, 40 per cent of all respondents 'were not sure which Kenyans actually benefit from tourism'.

Economic impact

Pressure on the environmental infrastructure is unabated as visitors to national parks in Africa have been steadily increasing. One possible reason for the expansion is the growing popularity of adventure holidays and the availability of cheap charter prices. Kenya's marketing strategy enhances value for money by combining beach holidays on the coast with wildlife safaris (Rajotte 1987; Gamble 1989).

Although in many parts of Africa the soil may not be very fertile, it can be used for wildlife and plant conservation. However, due to the upsurge in the search for 'first hand communion with nature', referred to by Almagor (1985) as the 'vision quest', this has produced increasing demand for Kenyan safaris which in turn culminates in environmental impact. However, the wildlife managers face a paradoxical situation by which tourism needs to be developed in order to raise revenue to maintain conservation in the national parks. This can be self-defeating because as demand levels rise there is a ceiling capacity or saturation level for any given park or region, and if acceptable carrying levels are exceeded the costs of tourism begin to outweigh the benefits.

There are six national parks in Cameroon: five are of the savannah type; and one the Korup National Park in Cameroon, is a rainforest which was formed into a national park as recently as 1988. One reason for conserving some of these rainforests is the scarcity of some of the trees. Romeril (1989) and Boo (1991) examined the benefits of conservation and preservation of tourism resources. The benefit of conservation to tourism development is that tourism-related revenue is often channelled back into conservation efforts where tangible related benefits are evident such as ranger services. Positive benefits can also accrue through the improvement of attractions such as landscape or restored ancient monuments and buildings. This is highlighted by Kundaeli (1983), who writes of the efforts made to protect the coastal and marine environments populated by tourists on the East African coast.

The Korup National Park was created by the Republic of Cameroon in conjunction with the World Wide Fund for Nature. The future of the Korup was protected through the formulation of a detailed master plan aimed at conserving its biodiversity. This has been followed up with attempts to implement the objectives of conservation by negotiating with the local people living around the park. The Korup National Park could be taken to be a model for African countries who are designating national parks from areas of rainforest. However, tourism development has not been fully realized in the Korup National Park. The largest proportion of tourists who visit are scientists. In a recent issue of the *New Scientist* magazine, Duncan Thomas a British botanist described a visit to the Korup National Park (Miller 1993). He was working on a project for the National Cancer Institute in an attempt to discover a plant with medicinal properties capable of preventing HIV (the virus which causes AIDS). This further highlights the importance of conservation so that important plants of this rainforest can be preserved for future generations. The estimated number of tourist arrivals to the Korup National Park was 500 in 1989, and will be 1000 annually before the year 2000. The park's plan has also incorporated tourism development, with a review of the physical, sociocultural and economic impacts of the national park to its community, construction of accommodation and the provision of transport to cater for the needs of tourists.

Unlike the designation of national parks in the UK and USA for public recreation and allowing freedom of access because they are public property, the Korup National Park is strictly a conservation area with rigid sustainable development principles, which means that the local community is deprived of the use of the park. Some individuals may question the benefit of such national parks if hardship is caused to the community due to displacement and exclusion policies. To reinforce the plan, meetings are arranged with the local community living in the created buffer zones of the park to discuss issues of conservation, so that ecological damage is minimised. There is awareness of the needs of the park's communities, and to balance the deficit of loss of habitat access the local authorities have attempted to cater for the welfare of the local community by developing local skills.

The application of zoning

Zoning is a useful technique to sustain the national park's resources. Zoning classifies park areas for certain kinds of use or non-use and defines spatial limits of future use allocations. It provides a good framework for land management that balances the park's twin mandate of preservation and visitor access. This sets aside some areas for primary preservation purposes and others for recreation and visitor facilities (Murphy 1985). According to Brown (1982), core zones can be used to protect wilderness areas and help with tourism flows, the rotation of usage patterns and the creation of high-usage *honeypot* points. Sheikh (1990) has proposed zoning with fixed viewing points in Kenya's national parks and strict regulation for the tourists' minibuses as ways to curb the disturbance to the wildlife.

In Africa the adoption of zoning has social as well as environmental impacts. In Kenya in the Masai Mara and Tsavo National Parks local inhabitants are deprived of traditional rights of pastoralism. Zoning in Africa is not straightforward as it often affects the lifestyle of the original community while acting as a useful means of protection. While many human activities are permitted others are ruled out as it is the sustainability of the park which is the basis of permitted activity. This will also apply to Cameroon when the government reformulates its policy on human settlement in the buffer zone.

Whatever zoning occurs there is always a need for some form of tourism facilities. The planning of facilities such as access roads and accommodation in the Korup National Park is the responsibility of the local tourism managers. The existing lodges impose constraints on capacity but in order to be profitable they must have a certain number of beds and achieve a minimum level of bed occupancy. The resulting heavy tourist congregations around a few focal points could lead to localised capacity excesses long before overall capacity is reached. Also poor road and lodge placement in the early stages of tourist development could be to the detriment of a park's formation. This point is widely overlooked by park managers who, too often, start planning only when tourist problems arise. Whatever is contained in a park's tourist-use policy, early planning, including zoning and distribution of lodges, roads and other facilities, must be planned as if for capacity, even though that point may be decades away.

Zoning is often used as a means to protect the environment. However, Gilbert (1993) believes zoning, if not properly planned, can cause many secondary problems. First, the designation of a specific partial development zone may form the basis of an excuse for an increase in infrastructure in the zoned area. It is argued that this may lead, over time, to a change in the character of the area with different human-made developments replacing the original reason for visits to the area. Within a period of time this leads to pockets of development where natural areas are replaced with human-made ones.

Second, the establishment of protected zones may deny a resident community the ability to develop its own local economy. If a zone protects the naturalness of an area, it may attract tourists, yet there is no income in the area and the visitors' expenditure only benefits an adjacent developed zone. Therefore, Gilbert questions whether financial compensation should be given to those protected attractive areas which support, by synergy, other communities in development areas which are able to benefit more freely from tourism arrivals.

Third, policies which encourage small-scale development are often treated as an optimal solution to rural harmonization strategies. While this has positive benefits, it is argued that the smallness of scale often restricts an individual's revenue-generating ability, or viability, due to the creation of higher overheads.

Finally, zoning is often artificial due to the disregard of different geographical boundaries which do not take into account wider issues. The example given is where there could be a disregard of animal migration patterns or regional drainage systems.

The national parks in Kenya are used as a potential tourist attraction to promote wildlife safaris. The Kenyan wildlife resources are distributed over 40 locations in the national parks and national reserves. These parks and reserves occupy a land area of 15 797 square miles (40 914 km^2, 7 per cent of Kenya's land surface area). The wildlife attraction of Kenya is an important asset and has generated a considerable amount of revenue to the Kenyan economy. Mass tourism has been encountered in the Kenyan national parks, especially the popular ones (Amboseli, Masai Mara and Tsavo), whereby the physical problems of congestion, over-crowding, loss of vegetation and poaching are prevalent. These are the savannah parks where animals are grouped together and are therefore more accessible for tourists to make contact and view them. Meanwhile, the contrary position holds for the Cameroon national parks, especially the Korup National Park. Korup has hardly experienced tourism because it was created as recently as 1988, whereas some of the Kenyan national parks are more than 30 years older. It is interesting that sustainability is therefore not so much a tourist as a local community issue. The reason given for the plan to limit physical impacts in the Korup National Park, caused by human activities such as poaching, hunting, fishing and farming, is that it is the only tropical rainforest national park in Africa and there are diverse species of plants and animals spread throughout the park.

Earnings from wildlife viewing and safaris provide up to 25 per cent of Kenya's total foreign exchange income. However, the situation of the wildlife has recently received international concern due to game cropping for meat, game farming, scientific study and heritage concerns. All these activities are now increasing, with a resultant need for wildlife conservation measures (Dieke 1991). As part of the tourist industry's realisation of the need for support, Kenya's Masai Mara receives from tour operators such as Abercrombie and Kent and Africa Bound a donation to its anti-poaching fund of £5 for each visitor.

Social impact

While large numbers of tourists visit Kenya's parks, tourism is still in the early stages of development in Cameroon. The Waza National Park in northern Cameroon is wholly a savannah park with diverse fauna and flora similar to the Kenyan national parks. Meanwhile, the Korup National Park has not yet encountered serious traffic and congestion problems, and the strategy aims towards sustainable tourism development. This was reflected in the life-span of the national parks plan of 30 years. Maintaining conservation policies of land use for tourists and the local community implies the social costs of land ownership problems, resettlement and prohibition of activities. However, the denial of community rights for local people may not be contingent with conservation in the widest sense.

Not all policies are negative as far as the community is concerned. In the Korup National Park, the managers have employed tour guides or park rangers from the local community in order to enable them to partici-pate in guarding the forest. In so doing, they receive payments which increase their income so that they can buy alternative sources of protein rather than hunt animals in Korup. Park rangers assume and take the role of interpreters of the national park. Their role is not easy because, accord-ing to Almagor (1985), a guide's role can be very challenging if the tourists do not belong to the institutionalized category and, instead, seek to explore the area by themselves.

The tourism development of a national park normally involves the government in designating the park on a local community's common ground. This has caused problems in the Kenyan and Cameroonian national parks such as: land disputes, deprivation of land ownership rights for pastoralism, resettlement and tension between the host and the tourists. In Kenya, land acquisition by the government for national parks has caused deprived pastoral rights and led to designation of the local community living around the area as 'squatters'. The national parks in Kenya occupy around 7 per cent of Kenya's territory, yet the ecosystem requirement for their wildlife communities extends across areas between two and ten times the size of the protected territories. The Tsavo National Park is the epitome of conflicts between the absolute purposes of wildlife protection, on the one hand, and the often legitimate needs of human communities, on the other hand. Before the park was formed, the tribes living in the region earned a living from subsistence poaching of elephants. After their rights to own and poach the elephants were curtailed, the people faced a cutback in their living standards. This developed into ecological and social imbalances in the Tsavo National Park, with curtailment of the rights of local people to continue pastoral farming again decreasing their standard of living.

Another cost incurred by the local community is experienced by the Taita people who live in an enclave protruding into Tsavo National Park. They suffer from the deprivations caused by elephants. The tension which exists for the Taita people and the Kenyan authorities is not helped when many living as much as 100 kilometres from the Tsavo National Park are deemed to be squatting on their former farms. Also, in Lake Nakuru National Park, peasant cultivators are banned from using pesticidal chemicals and nitrogenous fertilizers on their farms and in the rivers. The objective of this regulation is to maintain the ecological stability in the park.

This situation facing the local people in the national park environment in Kenya may not be dissimilar to that of the resettled people in the Korup National Park in Cameroon. The designation of this park has put into effect a ban on hunting, fishing and farming in the core zone. Cameroonian law does not permit any human settlement in the park, so attempts have been made to make the law flexible in order that human beings can undertake their normal activities in a buffer zone but on a sustainable basis. The reason given for this ban on human activities in the national park is to achieve conservation so that future generations can utilise the existing resources unimpaired.

Given the changes taking place, a benefit from developing the Korup National Park (and possibly tourism development) is the promotion of local skills. This benefit is also prevalent in the Kenyan national parks. Local skills are developed such as canoe building, furniture making, house construction, woven bags, dresses, 'asaris', animal crafts, ropes, nets and distillates. These activities are meant to replace lost incomes from curtailed hunting, fishing and farming. The specific initiatives in the development of local skills are pursued at the Rural Artisan Centres in Mundemba (the Korup National Park headquarters) and in Nguti which are equipped with basic tools to train students so that they can not only create craftwork but also build houses and furniture. Thus, by educating local people to produce craftwork products, they can be sold to tourists when they arrive at the park.

What is an appropriate form of development?

How do we agree as to what should be the balance between the alternatives? Myers (1975) used the social-cost-benefit approach to analyse the economic impacts of tourism development in the Kenyan national parks.

He stated that social-cost-benefit analysis is useful in planning and that it 'provides a national framework for ... choice, using national objectives and values. It also provides an order of magnitude, evaluates welfare parameters and assists those who formulate policy'.

The social-cost-benefit approach can be illustrated using the Masai Mara National Park and the effects on its inhabitants. Myers (1975) stated that the Masai people are unaware of the amount of land excised from the tribal reserves and the consequences for their wide-ranging pastoralism practices. The national park's development has increased income generation, employment and the livelihood of the local community. However, the Masai suffer opportunity costs by virtue of the protected areas' existence. For example, they bear a direct loss through seasonal wanderings of wildlife on their crops, yet receive very little funding from the safari organisers in Nairobi and Mombasa. One positive development is that the Taita and Masai people have been encouraged to harbour wildlife on their land so that some direct returns from indigenous accommodation and lodges can be gained from tourists (Bachmann 1988). Furthermore, in some areas, the smallholder in agriculture develops livestock production, while others grow grain (Curry and Morvaridi 1992). Therefore responsible tourism can be developed in Kenya in order to sustain the wildlife, the environment and provide more social welfare for the area.

To reduce impacts on the Korup National Park numerous alternative natural attractions have been discovered by Korup Link Tours. This is a tour retail company newly established to develop tourism in the Ndian Division in Cameroon where the Korup National Park is located. These attractions are meant to serve as 'honeypots' for visitors to the Korup National Park so as to alleviate the problems expected with the future growth in tourism traffic. The honeypot attractions are an alternative to the national park with existing features similar to the core zone of the national park. It is hoped that this development will divert tourists from the more sensitive areas of the national park, hence limiting the negative effects of concentrated levels of tourism on the national park environment.

Opinion is divided on the type of tourism development that should be implemented in some of the national parks in Cameroon and Kenya. Ideally, an overall responsible tourism approach favouring appropriate development which maximised the welfare of the community, the environment and the visitor is wanted. As part of this, it is important to decide on the balanced development and attraction of low- and high-impact recreational activities (Buckley and Pannell 1990). The low-impact group are viewed as seeking contemplative and naturalist pursuits, while the high-impact group are judged to require sporting and social activities, the use of cars and forms of activity which damage the ecosystem.

Conclusion

Kenya has gained major economic benefits from tourism development because the authorities promoted green tourism based upon the country's wildlife resources. But this occurred without consideration of the long-term impacts of those activities. Meanwhile, Cameroon has recently recognised that tourism can be an alternative means of income to the agriculture industry of cocoa, coffee, bananas and rubber. It is satisfying to see that Cameroon has a cautious attitude to tourism development, especially in its careful planning over the long term. The Korup National Park is a clear example that sustainable development can be enforced in a national park. However, this has been gained from an institutionalised framework of control where the indigenous population has been relocated or restricted within certain zoned areas. The promotion of ecological visits, for the area, will generate the much needed foreign exchange and protect the existing parks in Cameroon, yet the social cost is the exclusion and restriction of local community access. Kenya does not offer an alternative model, as it requires improvement in sustainable tourism development of its national parks and wildlife safaris, which, due to increased demand, are suffering unacceptable levels of impact.

References

Agarwal, R.K. and Nangia, S., 1974, *Economic and employment potential of archaeological monuments in India*, Asia Publishing House, New Delhi.

Almagor, U., 1985, 'A tourist's vision quest in an African game reserve', *Annals of Tourism Research*, 12(5): 31–47.

Bachmann, P., 1988, *Tourism in Kenya: a basic need for whom?*, Peter Lang, Berne.

Bramwell, B., 1990, 'Green tourism in the countryside', *Tourism Management*, 11(2): 41–2.

Brown, C., 1982, 'Resource planning for recreation and tourism', in *Essays in national resource planning*. CURS, University of Birmingham.

Boo, E., 1991, *Ecotourism: the potentials and pitfalls*, Vol. 1, World Wildlife Fund, Washington, DC.

Buckley, R. and Pannell, J., 1990, 'Environmental impacts of tourism and recreation in the national parks and conservation reserves', *Journal of Tourism Studies*, 1(1): 24.

Butler, R.V., 1990, 'Alternative tourism: pious hope or Trojan horse?', *Journal of Travel Research*, 28(3): 40–45.

Cazes, G., 1989, 'Alternative tourism: reflections on an ambiguous concept', in T.V. Singh, L. Thenus and F. Go (eds), *Towards appropriate tourism: the case of developing countries*, Lang Publications, New York: 117–26.

Cohen, E., 1988, 'Authenticity and commoditization in tourism', *Annals of Tourism Research*, 15(3): 371–86.

Cohen, E., 1989, 'Alternative tourism – a critique'. In T.V. Singh, L. Theuns and F. Go (eds), *Towards appropriate tourism: the case of developing countries*. Lang Publications, New York: 127–42.

Curry, S. and Morvaridi, B., 1992, 'Sustainable tourism. Illustrations from Kenya, Nepal and Jamaica', in C.P. Cooper and A. Lockwood (eds), *Progress in tourism, recreation and hospitality management*, Vol. 4, Belhaven Press, London: 131–9.

Davidson, J., Myers, D. and Chakraborty, M., 1992, *No time to waste: poverty and the global environment*, Oxfam, Oxford.

De Kadt, E., 1984, *Tourism: passport to development?*, Oxford University Press, Oxford.

De Kadt, E., 1992, 'Making the alternative sustainable: lessons from development for tourism', in V.L. Smith and W.R. Eadington (eds), *Tourism alternatives: potentials and problems in the development of tourism*, University of Pennsylvannia Press, Philadelphia: 47–75.

Dieke, P.U.C., 1991, 'Policies for tourism development in Kenya', *Annals of Tourism Research*, 18(2): 269–94.

Economist Intelligence Unit, 1991, 'Managing tourism and the environment: a Kenyan case study', *Travel and Tourism Analyst*, 2: 78–87.

Elkington, J. and Hailes, J., 1992, *Holidays that don't cost the earth*, Gollancz, London.

English Tourist Board, 1992, *The green light – a guide to sustainable tourism*, ETB, London.

Gamble, W.P., 1989, *Tourism and development in Africa: case studies in the developing world*, Murray, London.

Gilbert, D.C., 1993, 'Issues in appropriate rural tourism development for southern Ireland', *Leisure Studies*, 12(2): 137–46.

Gordon, C., 1991, 'Sustaining versus sustainable: landscapes for tourism', *UK Ceed Bulletin*, no. 31: 14–15.

Green, S., 1990, 'The future of green tourism', *Insights*, D5–8, Tourism Marketing Intelligence Service, English Tourist Board, London.

Greenwood, D., 1972, 'Tourism as an agent of change: a Spanish Basque case study', *Ethnology*, 11: 80–91.

Gunn, C.A., 1978. 'Needed: an international alliance for tourism-recreation-conservation', *Travel Research Journal*, 2: 3–9.

Holder, J.S., 1988, 'Pattern and impact of tourism on the environment of the Caribbean', *Tourism Management*, 9(2): 119–27.

Jarviluoma, J., 1992, 'Alternative tourism and the evolution of the tourist areas', *Tourism Management*, 13(1): 118–20.

Krippendorf, J., 1987, *The holiday makers: understanding the impact of leisure and travel*, Heinemann, London.

Kundaeli, J.N., 1983, 'Making conservation and development compatible', *Ambio*, 12(6): 326–31.

Lane, B., 1992, 'Marketing green tourism: is there a market for sustainable tourism products and will these ventures be profitable?', *Leisure Opportunities*, January: 34–5.

Lea, J., 1988, *Tourism and development in the Third World*, Routledge, London.

Long, V., 1991, 'Nature tourism: environmental stress or environmental salvation?', paper presented at the Third World Leisure and Recreation Association International Congress, Sydney, July.

Mathieson, A. and Wall, G., 1985, *Tourism: economic, physical and social impacts*, Longman, London.

McKercher, B., 1993, 'Understanding tourism's social and environmental impacts, *Journal of Sustainable Tourism*, 1(1): 6–14.

Migot-Adholla, S., Mbinddyo, J. and Mkangi Katana, G.C., 1992, *A study of tourism in Kenya with emphasis on the attitudes of residents of the Kenyan coast*, IDS consultancy report no. 7, University of Nairobi.

Miller, S., 1993, 'High hopes hanging on a useless vine', *New Scientist*, January 16: 12–13.

Millman, R., 1989, 'Pleasure seeking "v" the greening of world tourism', *Tourism Management*, 10(1): 275–8.

Murphy, P., 1985, *Tourism: a community approach*, Methuen, New York.

Myers, N., 1972, 'National parks in savannah Africa', *Science*, 178: 1255–63.

Myers, N., 1975, 'The tourist as an agent for development and wildlife conservation: the case of Kenya', *International Journal of Social Economics*, 2: 26–41.

Pearce, D.G., 1992, 'Alternative tourism: concepts, classifications and questions', in V. Smith and W. Eadington (eds), *Tourism alternatives: potentials and problems in the development of tourism*, University of Pennsylvania Press, Philadelphia: 15–30.

Porritt, J. and Winner, D., 1988, *The coming of the Greens*, Fontana, London.

Rajotte, F., 1987, 'Safari and beach resort tourism, the costs to Kenya', in S.G. Britton and W.G. Clarke (eds), *Ambiguous alternatives: tourism in small developing countries*, University of South Pacific, Suva, Fiji.

Richter, L.K. and Richter, W.L., 1985, 'Policy choices in South Asian tourism development', *Annals of Tourism Research*, 12(2): 201–17.

Romeril, M., 1989, 'Tourism – the environmental dimension', in C.P. Cooper (ed.), *Progress in tourism, recreation and hospitality management*, Vol. 1, Belhaven Press, London: 103–13.

Saremba, J. and Gill, A., 1991, 'Value conflicts in mountain park settings', *Annals of Tourism Research*, 18(3): 455–72.

Sheikh, Z., 1990, 'Development of tourism in Kenya: problems and possibilities', unpublished MSc dissertation, University of Surrey.

Sinclair, M., 1992, 'Tourism, economic development and the environment: problems and policies', in C. Cooper and A. Lockwood (eds), *Progress in tourism, recreation and hospitality management*, Vol. 4, Belhaven Press, London: 75–81.

Smith, V.L., 1981, 'Controlled versus uncontrolled tourism in Bhutan and Nepal', *Royal Anthropological Institute Newsletter* (RAIN), 46: 4–6.

Smith, V.L., and Eadington, W.R. (eds) 1992, *Tourism alternatives: potentials and problems in the development of tourism*, University of Pennsylvannia Press, Philadelphia.

Wheeller, B., 1991, 'Tourism's troubled times: responsible tourism is not the answer', *Tourism Management*, 12(1): 91–6.

Wheeller, B., 1992a, 'Is progressive tourism appropriate?, *Tourism Management*, 13(1): 104–5.

Wheeller, B., 1992b, 'Alternative tourism: a deceptive ploy', in C.P. Cooper and A. Lockwood (eds), *Progress in tourism, recreation and hospitality management*, Vol. 4, Belhaven Press, London: 140–45.

Wickers, D., 1992, 'Whither green', *Sunday Times*, 5 January.

5 The emergence of ethics in tourism and hospitality
M. Wheeler

Introduction

Ethics is concerned with human behaviour and is a phenomenon of choice. It is integral to decision-making as with each decision situation come options, choices and differing consequences. Ethics in tourism involves issues such as ecological impacts, truth in menu, destination marketing, employment conditions and codes of conduct. This chapter considers the ways in which ethics has already been linked to tourism, identifies a number of critical issues with ethical components in the industry and argues that ethics does have an important role to play in tourism.

Definition of ethics

Definitions of ethics revolve around phrases such as 'right' and 'wrong', 'good' and 'evil' (Beauchamp and Bowie 1983), and 'just' and 'unjust' (Runes 1964). Hegarty (1990) believes most people agree that there is a fundamental difference between right and wrong. Frequently this determination is made intuitively rather than by a process of formal reasoning. It implies blameworthiness in the event of a wrong and wrongdoer and reward for the gooddoer. In the business environment it is important that this process is externalised, leading to social responsibility of decisions.

Whitney (1990) states that underlying critical issues in business is the element of human behaviour; the 'rightness' or 'wrongness' of what people do as well as the impact of their deeds. Because the rightness and wrongness of behaviour are involved these critical issues are also ethical issues.

However, in order to understand the concept fully, the importance of ethics within the individual and/or organisation must be located. In order to do this, Carroll (1989) advocates the use of the *stakeholder* concept. The stakeholder concept acknowledges there is a need to recognise a view of society from which relationships between the individual, the community and the organisation can be established.

Primary stakeholders are seen as those who have a formal, official or contractual relationship with the organisation; all others are classified as *secondary* stakeholders. Once the relationship is established, the legitimacy of the stakes of the stakeholder is identified. From this the organisation or individual is able to decide what strategies and actions should be taken and

contain corporate *social responsibility*. Social responsibility can be d
as including:

- *Economic* responsibilities: an orientation to produce and sell ᵤ
  and services that society wants, and to sell them at a fair price – a price
  that society feels represents the value of goods and services and
  provides an adequate profit for the business, allowing growth.
- *Legal* responsibilities: to comply with laws under which the business is
  expected to operate.
- *Ethical* responsibilities: those areas in which society expects certain
  performance but which it has not been able or willing to articulate in
  the form of laws.
- *Discretionary* responsibilities: activities which are purely voluntary,
  guided by the business's desire to engage in social activities that are not
  mandated or any of the above (adapted from Carroll 1989, p. 30).

Thus, the central issue with ethics is characterising a behaviour in the
context of a relationship as right or wrong, and this involves social
responsibility in decision-making. Ethics can also be said to arise when
there is confusion or lack of clarity about the appropriate behaviour of an
individual in a given situation. Following on from this, in order for ethics
to contribute to a greater understanding of the tourism industry, the
approach must be one that applies the theoretical concept to business
realities. So far there have been a number of studies that have contributed
to the growing body of knowledge on the subject. They can be divided into
those that consider ethics and decision-making, tourism and hospitality
education and others that have concentrated on specific issues.

Ethical decision-making in tourism and hospitality

Most of the research in this area has concentrated on the hotel industry
in the USA and the documenting of responses to ethical statements.
Whitney (1989) surveyed both students in Michigan and managers in
Washington State. Based on the assumption that a higher level of ethical
development is gained through maturity, he found disturbingly that in
neither group was the individual orientation influential in ethical decision-
making. Therefore, the industry's norms overcame personal beliefs and
values as a base for decision-making.

This theme was followed by research which concentrated on hotel
managers and produced an ethical orientation profile of those surveyed
(Whitney 1990). In this study, respondents were asked to indicate the
extent of their agreement with statements such as 'A company's code of
ethics is more a public relations document than an operations policy' and
'Profit is the sole factor which should influence company and management
decisions'. He found that ethical decisions which draw upon traditional
values may be made more easily than those which violate traditions but are
more common in the business arena. In the latter instance managers will
experience *ethical dissonance*, conflict between the stronger ideological

aspect (what they believe) and the operational aspect (what they practice) of their ethical philosophy.

Schmidgall (1991) examined ethics in the American hospitality industry by means of a survey of hotel managers' reactions to ten hypothetical scenarios, and the results suggested that the industry is often divided as to what is considered ethical and what is not. For example, 55 per cent said it is OK to hire one of their workers to do 'yard work' at their home, but nearly 40 per cent disagreed saying it did place undue pressure on the worker. Responding to another question, 65 per cent of managers said it would be unethical to accept a free case of wine from a supplier, but 25 per cent disagreed, suggesting the gift would not affect the hotel's future purchases.

These studies can be used to illustrate the fact that perhaps hospitality courses are not addressing ethical issues that stimulate individual development, resulting in both hotel managers and students similarly limited in ethical understanding. Whitney (1990) also suggested that hard business realities do not foster philosophical development and the pressure of economic competition causes law and industry norms to supplant personal convictions as the basis for ethical decision-making.

Hall (1989) explained how to 'draw your [ethical] line' in hospitality; by using a sense of ethics to bridge the gap between quality and excellence. Thus, in order to be an ethical decision-maker, the individual must recognise that service excellence requires not only quality but also a sense of morality, and an understanding of the limitations that prevent the reaching of that ideal. The author also made the point that money, ego, information and ignorance are often barriers for many people to act ethically.

Wheeler (1991; 1993) moved away from hoteliers and concentrated on the critical issues and ethical components that a tourism marketeer encounters while working in the local government context. By means of the stakeholder concept the extent to which each group of stakeholders had influence on the marketeer's final decision became apparent. The stakeholders in the local government tourism marketeers' environment are illustrated in Figure 5.1. Those that wielded the most influence, the primary stakeholders in the decision-making process, were found to be the departmental heads, the councillors, the clients/community and professional bodies. The critical issues were a case of coercion and control, compromising personal integrity, responsibility to the local environment and professionalism. Thus, the marketeer's decision situation revolved around balancing the individual ethic (individuals' beliefs and values), the professional ethic (those dictated by the marketing profession) and the organisational ethic (local government).

Ethics in tourism and hospitality education

A number of studies linking the tourism industry to ethics have concentrated on the extent to which ethics is included in undergraduate

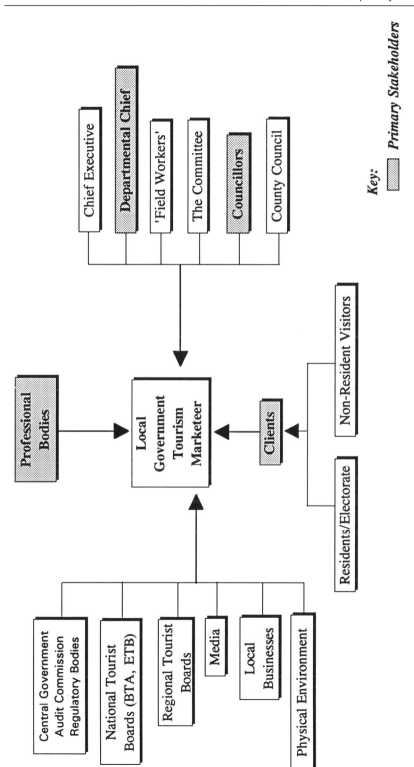

Figure 5.1 *Stakeholders in the local government tourism marketeer*

Source: Wheeler 1991, p. 77.

courses, methods of teaching and the demands placed upon the hospitality educators.

Enghagen (1991a) studied the extent to which ethics is included in the curriculum of hotel, catering and tourism management undergraduate courses in the USA and concluded that it is part of most undergraduate programmes. However, the tendency is for ethics to take the form of an elective rather than a compulsory module, and the author believes that this may result in the students' not seeing ethics as an important issue. Reasons stated as to why ethics was not included were that the curriculum is too full, which implies that the subject is not considered important enough to re-evaluate courses, and a lack of interested and qualified professionals.

The challenge of teaching ethics has two dimensions: to impart a body of knowledge relative to ethical analysis; and to focus on motivating students to act ethically. O'Halloran (1991) stated that at the undergraduate level the teaching of professional ethics, morality and values could take the form of credit classes, outside-class work experience, the integration of these concepts into traditional course work and 'faculty demonstration'. Enghagen (1991b) thought the most appropriate method would be to use ethical theory and analysis, and case studies relevant to tourism and hospitality. The specific approach to teaching ethics for a particular course would take into account such considerations as the nature of the course, the portion devoted to ethical issues, and the background and teaching style of the individual teacher.

Case studies are advocated as the ideal teaching material as they are considered an excellent source of hypothetical moral dilemmas. However, these case studies must be relevant to be effective, in the sense that they contain the service element and concentrate on middle management level issues as this is where the majority of students careers will be located. Perhaps these case studies could be linked to those issues students perceive to be critical in the industry. Enghagen and Hott (1992) found them to be solid waste disposal, conditions of employment, a variety of employment discrimination issues and AIDS in food service. Lieux and Winquist's (1991) idea was to improve both the students' grasp of ethics and writing skills by setting papers on ethical subjects. Students were evaluated on professional behaviour which included criteria such as appropriate documentation, truthfulness, honesty considerations and issues about confidentially.

To monitor and measure the success of ethics in courses, Enghagen (1991b) advocated the use of objectives which have been developed to maintain consistency with what is currently known about human moral development.

Hegarty (1990) discussed the teaching of morality and business ethics to hospitality and tourism students. He concluded that the essential effect of ethics in education is of practical use in clarifying concepts and in helping individuals to make their own decisions on the moral practical questions.

Kwansa and Farrar (1992) worked from the educator's standpoint and devised a conceptual framework on which to base a hospitality educator's code of ethics. Due to their multiple roles as teachers, researchers, administrators and servers of the public good, hospitality educators face ethical dilemmas as they must allocate their time and loyalties among seemingly competing goals. The authors suggested that ethics and professionalism are inextricably linked, and that the development of a code of ethics would provide guidelines and general principles of behaviour in hospitality education and research.

There have also been a number of other studies which have concentrated on specific subjects not already mentioned.

Wheeler (1992) debated the issues of the European Union, the marketing of tourism, the authenticity of the tourist experience, ecological impacts and whether 'green' tourism was an ethical response by the industry. The author concluded that the EU is forcing the industry to become more responsible to the consumer, but that at the same time there is a need to become more responsible to the environment if natural resources are going to remain attractive and the experience authentic. Tourism development has a responsibility to ensure that conditions in which the host community lives do not deteriorate as a result of the development. Thus, thought must be given by the organisations within the industry and also the consumers of the tourist product to the long-term implications of their actions.

Satchell (1987) examined the ethics of headhunting and looked at what would then have been the booming demand for managerial staff, and the fact that executive recruitment agencies faced increasing pressure while trying to improve the headhunter's image.

So far ethics has been mainly related to the tourism industry in terms of hospitality students and hotel managers. The findings indicate that ethical decision-making does not necessarily develop over time, that industry norms prevail, that the teaching of ethics is not necessarily compulsory but can be achieved through the case-study approach. There are, however, many other areas which have yet to be researched. These include marketing practices, managing in an ethical environment, relations with customer and employees, the effect of EU regulations and the study of other groups such as tourist attraction managers, tour operators and airlines. The function ethics has in relation to tourism and hospitality can be clearly identified as twofold. First, ethics is important as a decision-making tool by allowing the individual to recognise that decisions have ethical content. This recognition then acts as a base to develop a more consistent socially responsible approach to decision making. Second, to develop and enhance the profession.

Critical issues and ethical components in tourism

This section outlines a number of ethical challenges apparent in the industry and deserving greater consideration. Four are critical issues in tourism management, and four in hospitality. These issues raise a number of questions focusing on how the individual or organisation should act.

- *Destination marketing.* A holiday brochure's purpose is to create awareness of a tourist location, but it should also be consistent with reality. Has the promotion of bedspaces replaced the promotion of place and experience? There is now the problem of achieving a quality of tourist experience while sustaining both physical and social environments.
- *Authenticity of experience.* At what point do heritage attractions become a calcification of the past? Is the picture one of the past as seen in the way we would like to see it, and not the way it was?
- *Ecological developmental impacts.* Negative effects range from path decay, litter pollution and congestion to the destruction of wildlife and coastline through accommodation development. At what point should development not be undertaken? Who decides? There needs to be a balance between profit, attracting tourists, the priorities of those managing the tourist zone, the priorities of the local community and the collective attitude towards the environment.
- *Green tourism.* Is it the ethical response to tourism development? Is it really helping the tourist industry to become more responsible? Can it be a marketing ploy? Can it be applied in relation to the rate of growth of tourism? Is it really a micro-solution to a macro-problem, given that tourism is growing globally?
- *Truth in menu.* If a menu's primary purpose is to sell food and beverages, should the management not feel justified in representing the quality of the product in a manner to achieve that purpose? Or do consumers have a right to a full and accurate disclosure regarding menu items?
- *Hotel sales and marketing.* With reference to overbooking – it guards against 'no shows' but is it a lie to 'guarantee' a non-existent room for a guest? What guidelines should dictate marketing policies in a competitive environment? Should the organisation accept gifts from suppliers?
- *Alcohol liability.* Selling alcohol gains profit but does it justify unlimited service of drinks to a guest? Who is responsible when a guest drinks too much?
- *Employment.* What efficiencies can a hotel manager ethically employ to keep labour costs down? How can employees protect themselves from exploitation in terms of working hours, pay, benefits, harassment, dress requirements, discrimination and lack of interest in installing and maintaining proper safety and security systems? Is the raiding of competitors' staff justifiable? (Adapted from Whitney 1990.)

These critical issues are by no means an exhaustive list but serve to illustrate the diversity of situations that contain ethical implications. These issues have been talking points in the industry for some time but have not yet been addressed from the appropriate standpoint – the ethical. As can be seen, ethical issues in the tourism industry arise on several levels in the business environment, the individual, the organisational, industry and international and societal levels. The next stage is to see how an ethical standpoint can be applied to working practice.

Guidelines to ethical decision-making

The visible result of an organisation understanding that ethical considerations are involved in business decision-making is the publication and
enforcement of a code of conduct or ethics. This can be used as guidance
to behaviour in specific circumstances. The existence of a code of conduct
is believed to encourage ethical behaviour in the members of a profession.
Research has shown that 'the existence and enforcement of codes of
ethics are associated with higher levels of ethical behaviour' (Ferrell and
Skinner 1988, p. 107).

Coe and Coe (1976) identified governance through a code of ethics as
a key criterion that distinguishes professions from other occupations.
There are other benefits associated with developing a code of conduct:
for example, it enhances the profession's reputation and deepens public
trust; encourages professional socialisation by strengthening professional
identity; serves as a support system; acts as a deterrent to unethical
behaviour through the threat of sanctions; and also provides a basis for
adjudicating disputes internally and externally to the profession.

It is essential that tourism and hospitality professionals are committed
to the idea of a code as being more than a public relations stunt. To be
truly effective, a code of ethics must also contain guidelines for enforcement. Moore (1970) suggests that without the means to enforce adherence
a code of ethics has limited meaning.

Frankel (1989) outlined three types of code. The *aspirational* code is a
statement of ideals to which a professional should strive. The *educational*
code makes a conscious effort to demonstrate how it can be helpful in
dealing with ethical problems associated with the profession. The *regulatory* code sets forth a detailed set of rules to govern professional conduct
and to serve as a basis for adjudicating grievances. A code must be viewed
as a commitment to preserving and perpetuating the group's professional
ideas by justifying its existence and values to society.

Blanchard and Peale (1988) devised a quick 'ethics check' to be used
when analysing an ethical problem or decision in the business context:

1. Is it legal? Will I be violating either civil law or company policy?
2. Is it balanced? Is it fair to all concerned in the short term as well as
   the long term? Does it promote win-win relationships?
3. How will it make me feel about myself? Will it make me proud?
   Would I feel good if my decision were published in the newspaper?
   Would I feel good if my family knew about it?

This test should be applied to the short, medium and long term; if any of
the answers are negative, then the proposed action is not ethical. This test
situation is seen as constituting an evaluation process that results in
improved judgement and ethics over time.

Industry-damaging situations involving ethics have been highlighted
most recently with the admission of a 'dirty tricks' campaign waged by
British Airways against Virgin Atlantic. Until now the industry in the UK
has responded by developing associations such as the Association of

British Travel Agents (ABTA) and the Association of Independent Tour Operators (AITO). Membership of these associations means adherence to working practices and protection for the consumer, but no mention is made of the environment on which the industry is ultimately dependent. It therefore becomes necessary to develop a code of ethics for the tourism profession to monitor working practices and maintain the industry's reputation, integrity and long-term feasibility.

Codes of conduct are not just for those working in the industry but also applicable to those taking part in the tourist experience. High Places, a small independent operator, published in their 1994 brochure the Himalayan Tourist Code and a Guest Code of Conduct (Figures 5.2 and 5.3).

- Limit deforestation – make no open fires and discourage others from doing so on your behalf. Where water is heated by scarce firewood, use as little as possible. When possible choose accommodation that uses kerosene or fuel efficient wood.
- Remove litter, burn or bury paper and carry out all non-degradabie litter. Graffiti are permanent examples of environmental pollution.
- Keep local water clean and avoid using pollutants such as detergents in streams and springs. If no toilet facilities are available, make sure you are at least 30 metres away from water sources, and bury or cover wastes.
- Plants should be left to flourish in their natural environment – taking cuttings, seeds and roots is illegal in many parts of the Himalaya.
- Help your guides and porters to follow conservation rules.

(Published by Tourism Concern, Frobel College, London in *High Places 1994* travel brochure, p. 13.)

As a guest, respect local traditions, protect local cultures, maintain local pride.

- When taking photographs respect privacy – ask permission and use restraint.
- Respect holy places – preserve what you have come to see, never touch or remove religious objects.
- Giving to children encourages begging – a donation to a project, health centre or school is a more constructive way to help.
- You will be accepted and welcomed if you follow local customs.
- Respect for local etiquette earns you respect – loose, lightweight clothes are preferable to revealing shorts and tight-fitting action wear.
- Observe standard food and bed charges but do not condone overcharging. Remember that the bargains you buy may only be possible because of low income to others.
- Visitors who value local traditions encourage local pride and maintain local cultures; please help local people gain a realistic view of life in Western Countries.

(*High Places 1994* travel brochure, p. 14.)

Figure 5.2 *The Himalayan Tourist Code*   **Figure 5.3** *Guest Code of Conduct*

Conclusion

The recognition that decisions in the tourism industry should be analysed from an ethical standpoint suggests a much clearer and deeper understanding of the options available and impacts of those decisions.

The acceptance of this ethical standpoint involves the development and enforcement of a code of conduct, which guides the individual and the realisation that social responsibility has an increasing part to play in decision-making. Social responsibility is especially important as tourism depends on and affects the environment, heritage and the people that work in the industry. Without consideration and action in relation to these aspects, the tourist industry will not remain attractive to the consumer and profit will not be maintained in the long run.

There is plenty of room for further research. Greater focus could be placed on those that work in the industry who are not hotel managers; a much broader range of issues such as industry working practices and environmental implications are waiting to be tackled.

Finally, although the discussion and teaching of ethics provides no immediate guarantee, it does begin a process whereby those exposed to moral reasoning will be more to able to act in the face of ethical challenges which in turn will promote the longevity of the industry.

References

Beauchamp T. and Bowie, N., 1983, *Ethical theory and business*, Prentice Hall, Englewood Cliffs, NJ.

Blanchard, K. and Peale, N.V., 1988, *The power of ethical management*, William Morrow and Co. Inc., New York.

Carroll, A.B., 1989, *Business and society: ethics and stakeholder management*, South-Western Publishing Co., Cincinnati, Ohio.

Coe, T. and Coe, B., 1976, 'Marketing research: the search for professionalism', in K.L. Bernhardt (ed.), *Marketing: 1776–1976 and beyond*, American Marketing Association, Chicago.

Enghagen, L.K., 1991a, 'Ethics in hospitality/tourism education: a survey', *Hospitality Research Journal*, 14(2): 113–18.

Enghagen, L.K., 1991b, 'Teaching ethics in hospitality and tourism education', *Hospitality Research Journal*, 14(2): 467–74.

Enghagen, L.K. and Hott, D.D., 1992, 'Students' perceptions of ethical issues in the hospitality and tourism industry', *Hospitality Research Journal*, 15(2): 41–50.

Ferrell, O.C. and Skinner, S.J., 1988, 'Ethical behaviour and bureaucratic structure in marketing research organizations', *Journal of Marketing Research*, 25: 103–9.

Frankel, M.S., 1989, 'Professional codes: why, how, and with what impact?', *Journal of Business Ethics*, 8: 109–15.

Hall, S.S.J., 1989, 'Ethics in hospitality: how to draw your line', *Lodging*, September: 59–61.

Hegarty, J.A., 1990, 'Ethics in hospitality education', *International Journal of Hospitality Management*, 9(2): 106–9.

Kwansa, F.A. and Farrar, A.L., 1992, 'A conceptual framework for developing a hospitality educators' code of ethics', *Hospitality Research Journal*, 15(3): 27–39.

Lieux, E.M. and Winquist, S.C., 1991, 'Instructions in writing combined with an introduction to ethics in a professional discipline', *Hospitality and Tourism Educator*, 3(2): 34–5, 53–5.

Moore, W.E., 1970, *The professions: roles and rules*, Russell Sage Foundation, New York.

O'Halloran, R.M., 1991, 'Ethics in hospitality and tourism education: the new managers', *Hospitality and Tourism Educator*, 3(3): 33–7.

Runes, D., 1964, *Dictionary of Philosophy*, Adam and Co. Patterson, Littlefields.

Satchell, A., 1987, 'The ethics of head-hunting', *Hospitality*, June: 14–15, 17.

Schmidgall, R.S., 1991, 'Hotel scruples', *Lodging*, January: 38–40.

Wheeler, M., 1991, 'Tourism marketeers in local government: critical issues and ethical components', unpublished thesis, University of Surrey.

Wheeler, M., 1992, 'Applying ethics to the tourism industry', *Business Ethics – A European Review*, 1(4): 227–35.

Wheeler, M., 1993, 'Tourism marketers in local government', *Annals of Tourism Research*, 20(2).

Whitney, D.L., 1989, 'The ethical orientations of hotel managers and hospitality students: implications for industry, education and youthful careers', *Hospitality Education and Research Journal*, 13(3): 187–92.

Whitney, D.L., 1990, 'Ethics in the hospitality industry: with a focus on hotel managers', *International Journal of Hospitality Management*, 9(1): 59–68.

6 Gender and tourism

J. Norris and G. Wall

Introduction

The purpose of this chapter is to present a synthesis of research on tourism and gender from a feminist perspective. It is argued that feminist scholarship and research on tourism have both been growth areas in the past decade but that few attempts have been made to establish relationships between them. While the potential links are wide-ranging and far-reaching, emphasis is placed in this chapter on development studies which have been a focus of attention in both fields. Unfortunately, it is not possible to provide conclusive answers concerning the nature of connections between gender and tourism. Rather the intent is to create a consciousness that such relationships exist and should be addressed. The challenge is to improve clarity in thinking about the experience of tourism for women – women as tourists and women as workers in the tourism industry.

As in other explorations into the meaning and reasons behind goings-on in society, the perspective which is offered stems from particular assumptions. The first and most explicit is the need to study women and women's points of view. The second is the value of studying women and men, and their relations as they are expressed in tourism. The third is to situate tourism, tourists and tourism development within a feminist framework.

The structure of this chapter is as follows. In the next section it is claimed that few links have been made, hitherto, between tourism research and gender studies. The third section outlines the growth of feminist studies in Western societies; various perspectives which come under the umbrella of feminist studies; the evolution and growth of gender studies in development; and the emerging literature concerning gender and leisure studies. A case will then be made for making a connection between gender and leisure studies when conducting research on tourism, whether a 'developed' or 'developing' society is under consideration. Examples of research which might be conducted under the umbrella of gender and tourism are then presented. It should be kept in mind that the purpose of this chapter is to suggest possibilities for future research, rather than to draw conclusions from research already completed.

Tourism studies

The purpose of this section is to present evidence of the dearth of studies which incorporate gender perspectives on tourism. However, it is much easier to demonstrate the presence of something than its absence, and space does not permit a detailed examination of the burgeoning tourism literature or even that specifically devoted to development. Fortunately, there are now numerous texts available which address these topics and a growing number of review papers assess the status of tourism research from different disciplinary perspectives. For example, a recent issue of *Annals of Tourism Research* was devoted specifically to assessments of the contributions to and status of tourism research of a number of social science disciplines (Graburn and Jafari 1991). A reading of such documents confirms the almost total absence of references to feminist scholarship.

The broader field of leisure studies, of which tourism can be considered a part, has begun to incorporate a feminist perspective; this will be discussed in greater detail later in the chapter. However, it continues to be a distinct strand of research which has not yet been integrated into mainstream leisure research. Thus, the comprehensive review of leisure and recreation research edited by Jackson and Burton (1989), which includes chapters on tourism, contains one chapter on women and leisure (Bella 1989). However, this chapter presents a separate perspective which is not incorporated into other contributions.

Of course, tourism researchers have not totally ignored women in their studies: it is an unusual questionnaire which does not ascertain the sex of respondents! However, the resulting data are seldom analysed and presented in a meaningful way. For example, where differences in participation between women and men are identified, they tend to be noted rather than explained. Such research is seldom undertaken from a feminist perspective and indirectly may promote the status quo in that it usually ignores the different constraints and opportunities to which women and men are exposed.

Tourism, tourists and tourist development have each been explored in various ways, depending upon the disciplinary orientations of the researchers. In much research, elements and approaches from several disciplines have been linked and combined so that it can be argued that tourism is an interdisciplinary subject. Feminist scholarship, too, is interdisciplinary but the link with tourism has yet to be firmly established.

Gender studies

> One wonders if women still exist, if they will always exist, whether or not it is desirable that they should, what place they occupy in this world, what their place should be (de Beauvoir 1971).

Growth of feminist studies

Feminist studies emerged as a result of the lack of representation of women in many aspects of political, economic and social life. Although there is a direct connection between feminist writings and the women's liberation movement, the intent here is only to discuss feminism in its literary expression.

Hess and Ferree (1987) see the study of men and women as passing through three distinct phases since the early 1970s. The first phase emphasised the sex differences between men and women. Maleness and femaleness were viewed as biological properties of individuals with clear implications for social behaviour. Those within this perspective who proposed equality between men and women downplayed biological differences, claiming that they 'are rarely relevant for important behaviours, and that the differences are as likely to be instances of female superiority as male' (Hess and Ferree 1987, p. 14). Actual historical experience, though, has clearly indicated a non-egalitarian view of sex differences to be much more prevalent, keeping those who do promote the possibility of egalitarian biological determinism continually on the defensive.

The second phase was marked by a preoccupation with sex roles whereby the biological determinants of maleness and femaleness were combined with social determinism via upbringing in any proportion of nature and nurture that seemed appropriate. Sex differences were no longer intrinsically important issues, since both large and small differences could be explained by socialisation (Hess and Ferree 1987, p. 14–15). In this phase, then, socialisation practices became the culprit. Childrearing was studied to explore the occurrence of sex-specific socialisation practices. A strong critique of this line of reasoning is that when one stresses the importance of sex role socialisation, especially in the socialisation of young children, one assumes continuity throughout the life course (Hess and Ferree 1987, p. 15). In other words, this approach does not take into account the innumerable life experiences that affect the way we think and act. Also, sex role explanations do not give much credence to adult learning or our ability to have control in our lives.

The third phase is one which has ignited an explosion of feminist studies in diverse research areas. A new perspective with a new conceptual focus has been created: the centrality of gender. Gender is seen as 'a principle organizing social arrangements, behaviour, and even cognition' (Hess and Ferree 1987, p. 16). Gender itself is a socially constructed system which suppresses any natural similarities that may occur between men and women. It is a property of systems, rather than people.

Because gender is relational rather than essential, structural rather than individual, analysing gender requires consideration of changes in systems over time. The alteration in social structures themselves as well as variation in individual relations within these gender systems demand attention to both macro and micro levels of structure and change (Hess and Ferree 1987, p. 17).

This perspective has been employed to examine many aspects of society: gender stratification in economic relations; gender relations in the family; gender and the state; gender and ideology, to name but a few. These explorations have led to further, more refined, approaches which focus on particular aspects of the gender system. The conceptualisation of patriarchy, the function of domestic labour in capitalist society, and distinctions between 'private' and 'public' spheres were three early areas of investigation which provided a more systematic approach to gender studies. As conceptual and analytical depth grew, particular frameworks, or paradigms, became distinguishable.

Streams of thought in feminism

> ... feminism is a philosophical framework that has application to numerous facets of society, yet is reflective of each individual's unique life experiences and values (Henderson *et al.* 1989, p. 47).

This quotation attempts to capture the essence of feminism by stressing the all-encompassing nature of a feminist framework that coexists with personal experience and expression. Although women such as Tong (1989) have provided outlines of various frameworks that discuss this multifaceted subject, it is difficult to make general statements about feminist theory or review it comprehensively as a single body of work.

Approaches to the study of gender span liberal, socialist and Marxist perspectives. Each is attached to particular conceptual and analytical abstractions which are offered to explain the structure of society and relationships between the men and women in it. Bearing this in mind, Stanley and Wise (1982) have identified three widely accepted assumptions about women that are common to all feminist theories: women are oppressed and share a common set of oppressions; the personal is political in that personal experience is affected by the 'system' in everyday life; and a feminist consciousness and an understanding of what it means to be a woman can be developed. These assumptions suggest that, in any discussion of theory, it is essential that women not be simply *added in* to what already exists in a patriarchal world.

The above assumptions can be related to common goals. Henderson *et al.* (1989) recognise the different foci of feminist researchers, but suggest that, despite this, feminism and feminist writings are united in the quest for specific goals: to make visible women's power and status; to redefine existing societal structures and modes of existence; and to enable every woman to have equity, dignity and freedom of choice through power to control her life and body, both within and outside the home.

The next two sections will outline more specifically gender orientations in two particular areas of study: development studies and leisure studies.

Gender Studies in Development

Boserup (1970) provided the first overview of women's role in the development process in a comparative analysis of women in Asia, Africa and Latin America. Her thesis was that women were being ignored in the development of the Third World. Therefore, 'development' was gender-specific – specifically beneficial to men. Her analysis was not critical of the development process itself, for she remained quite firmly within the neoclassical modernisation paradigm and she did not present a clear-cut feminist analysis of women's subordination. Her work did provide, though, a starting point for the next decades of feminist research in development studies.

A school of thought that was established after this pioneering research was the liberal, feminist, Women in Development School (WID), which parallels the liberal modernisation perspective. Their philosophy of development for women lies in the diffusion of values, capital, technology and political institutions from the West (Bandarage 1984, p. 497). They argue that integration of women into the development process will facilitate their participation in the formal (public) economy. The limitations of this perspective stem from a lack of class analysis, combined with the fact that women are already integrated into the development process but their work is invisible

The Marxist perspective differs from the liberal in that it sees the poverty of women and men as a structural feature of capitalism as a social and economic system (Bandarage 1984, p. 500). Marxists agree with liberal WID thinkers that economic modernisation (capitalist development) marginalises Third World women, but they believe that, to understand this inequality, one must look at social class inequality and the unequal and uneven development of capitalism world-wide. Marxists also acknowledge, unlike liberal WID advocates, that not all men benefit from technological innovations, nor are all women similarly affected by technological and other aspects of change (Bandarage 1984, p. 501). Comparing the two approaches to gender in development, the Marxist is superior in that it comes from a materialist perspective and is less prone to generalise about men and women as homogeneous groups. Marxism is deficient, however, because its position on women's oppression, like men's, is based on the abstract forces of capitalism, commercialisation and proletarianisation, thereby ignoring women's oppression by men (Bandarage 1984, p. 505).

The birth of radical feminism challenged this omission by introducing personal relations as political issues. The focus on the domestic sphere of life and personal relationships between men and women opened up for debate areas that had been previously ignored by both liberalism and Marxism (Bandarage 1984, p. 505). Radical feminism, focusing on the 'universality of patriarchy', tends to overlook the interrelations between sexual and other forms of social oppression such as class, race and nationality (Bandarage 1984, p. 506). To try and bridge this gap, a theoretical perspective has been created to synthesise Marxist theory on capitalism and radical feminist theory on patriarchy. This is socialist feminism or the analysis of gender and class in the political economy.

Theories of gender in development have provided a body of literature which illuminates the invisibility of women. Although there are conflicting ideologies within the general paradigm, the growth of this literature confirms the appropriateness of making gender central to development studies. The revolutionary nature of the growth of this field of study is apparent, but its limitations to date are also evident. There is a lack of

systematic research on the consequences of rapid growth and technological change on women and on gender relationships. Heyzer (1987),
focusing specifically on women in South East Asia, identified two main
areas of study which need to be enhanced: the reactions of women to
technological and other kinds of production changes, and the resulting
conflict and contradictions that occur at both macro and micro levels as
a result of these changes. The view of women as agents of change rather
than as merely passive victims of circumstances animates research into
how women themselves interpret and respond to structures of opportunity and constraint. It also forces recognition of the limited alternatives
for action facing women who wish to resist oppression (Hess and Ferree
1987, p. 14).

Gender and leisure

In the 1970s mainstream leisure studies texts, women's experience was not
considered at all; if mention of women was made, it was only in reference
to the family. Talbot (1979) produced the first study that focused on
women's leisure. This served as an impetus for additional research in the
1980s. In 1980, Stanley (cited in Stanley and Wise 1982, pp. 6–7) made a
major contribution concerning the 'meaning of leisure'. She proposed that
women are not to be viewed as 'deviant' from men, but that women are
a heterogeneous group with many different interests (Wimbush and
Talbot 1988, pp. 7–8).

As a result of the relationship between women and leisure being
brought to the forefront, writers in leisure studies attempted to use less
sexist language. Although this may be viewed as a progressive step, the
drawback was that their inclusion of gender produced a series of even
more pluralistic analyses which treated class, age, race and gender as
though they were similar and cumulative factors (Wimbush and Talbot
1988, p. 9). Gender became an additional component which was noted
in participation in sex-typed activities, but little was known about why or
how this related to gender differences and inequalities in society in
general. Results were not interpreted in light of the different personal
and social contexts of women and men (Henderson *et al.* 1989, p. 100).
Therefore, what feminist contributions to the sociology of leisure have
done is to stress the importance of analysing leisure in the context of
individuals' lives as a whole. This holistic approach makes one more
aware of why, for instance, women spend more of their leisure time at
home than men do (Wimbush and Talbot 1988, p. 12).

Conceptual frameworks that are relevant to the study of women and
leisure and the comparative study of men's and women's leisure are being
developed to provide more fruitful analyses of the context and meaning
of leisure. An area within the study of women's leisure that is drawing
attention is constraints on leisure. Women's experience of *time* is a
particular focus. Women are, in general, the facilitators of others' leisure

– husbands, children and parents – rather than the recipients of leisure (Wimbush and Talbot 1988, p. 14). When do women have the time to partake in their own leisure? Do they feel there is time to spare to explore activities solely for their own individual enjoyment? Research studies have shown that women's experiences of time are much more fragmented than those of many men, particularly for women not in any form of paid employment (Wimbush and Talbot 1988, p. 11). A historical analysis of leisure illustrates that women have not had the same opportunities for leisure as men. Some of the constraints include: economic oppression in the workforce; family obligations; and maintaining responsibility for the family as well as being an economic provider. A feminist perspective on leisure provides a means to address and attempt to understand women's experience of leisure, as well as push for social change that will recognize women's leisure needs. Feminism and leisure are inextricably linked by components of choice and freedom (Henderson *et al*. 1989, p. 45).

If one takes leisure and feminism and puts them on a series of continua, there are many similarities. Both are more visible today than at any other time in history, both as movements and as streams of thought. At the core of leisure are the elements of freedom and choice, while at the core of feminism are the elements of freedom and integrity; thus, freedom is central to both concepts (Henderson *et al*. 1989, p. 51). It has been hypothesised that if women are given opportunities to take control of their leisure, they may be able to create social changes in other aspects of their lives (Henderson *et al*. 1989).

No attempt has been made here to define leisure or to categorise and compare the experience of leisure for women and men. Rather, the objectives have been to make explicit the relationship between gender and leisure and to illustrate how a feminist perspective can shed some light on the subject.

The purpose of exploring research in the areas of development and leisure studies in greater depth stems from their relevance to gender and tourism studies. The gender and development literature has contributed greatly to a better understanding of women's work in so-called 'developed' and 'developing' societies (Leacock and Safa 1986). However, technological change and the forces of modernity have been viewed through a limited lens with emphasis mainly on work in agricultural and factory production. The rapid growth of international tourism to developing countries since the 1950s has rarely been broached by gender and development researchers. In the growing gender and leisure material, the beginnings of rigorous conceptual and analytical frameworks are emerging, but most definitions and discussions of what leisure means to women do not include women as tourists. Much of the literature focuses on gendered leisure in everyday life, and how women and men differ in what they like to do in leisure time as it relates to their daily routine. This is a legitimate area for research but it has limitations as a basis for discussion of women as tourists and women workers in the tourism industry.

Tourism, gender and development: why make the connection?

Thus far, it has been argued that neither the general area of tourism studies nor the general area of gender studies provides a coherent, systematic overview of relationships between gender and tourism. Therefore, for purposes of explication, six topics which exhibit gender–tourism relationships are outlined briefly.

The tourists

Typologies have been devised to describe variations among tourists. For example, Cohen 1972 devised a typology of four tourist roles which makes a distinction between more *organized* types of tourist and the more *exploratory*. These types relate to demands for particular kinds of tourist experience and facilities, such as accommodation and modes of travel. Although such typologies provide useful insights into some aspects of tourism, they have not attempted to distinguish between motivations of male and female tourists. In fact, no research has been located which focuses specifically on this particular area. Yet this is a worthy area of study because as women gain more diverse opportunities in the fields of education, sexual relations and employment, new (leisure) lifestyles emerge.

> ... a number of social forces have been instrumental in changing the lives of women ... technology that can potentially free women from housework and unwanted pregnancies; liberalization of divorce and abortion laws; new views on sexual morality and an increasing emphasis on permissiveness and individualism; and the women's movement with egalitarian educational and economic goals (Henderson *et al.* 1989, p. 4).

A historical perspective on tourism reveals that women, just as men, have been concerned travellers. Russell (1988) examined women travellers from as far back as the seventeenth century and found numerous reasons why particular women decided to travel to a distant land:

> to escape from domesticity or the drudgery of a routine job; to recover from a broken love affair; to experience the thrill of danger; to demonstrate that women's name is definitely not frailty; to bring the Bible to China; to study plant life or unknown peoples; to delve into the past; to expiate a private guilt; to honour a dead partner; to glorify their country; to find something interesting to write about – or simply to have fun (Russell 1988, p. 15).

Russell's book is anecdotal, not theoretical. She does not interpret the meaning or significance of the various reasons women had for travelling, nor does she attempt to draw any conclusions concerning women travellers through history. However, she does contribute a detailed, thorough account of the experiences of several women travellers. Somewhat similarly, Kroller (1987) has documented the journeys and experiences of Canadian women travellers in Europe between 1851 and 1900. These are welcome additions to literature on the history of tourism as mention is rarely made of women travellers in the past.

In a study of long-term budget travellers, Riley (1988) attempted to distinguish the motives of young, educated, mainly middle-class travellers. She found that most of them were escaping from the dullness and monotony of their everyday routine, their jobs, from making decisions about careers, and desired to postpone work, marriage and other responsibilities (Riley 1988, p. 317). Riley mentions escaping constraints of marriage and romantic relationships, but not in a gender-specific sense. There is potential to extend her analysis to distinguish whether more women than men, or vice versa, turn to travel as a form of escapism and to determine what it is that they are escaping to and from. She 'surprisingly' reports that a large number of budget travellers, perhaps a quarter, are women, but that is the extent of her analysis by gender. However, she does note in passing that women more than men said that they wanted to travel to establish independence from their families and feel comfortable with doing things alone (Riley 1988, p. 324).

Not only is it necessary to explore the nature of female tourists to recognise and appreciate women's experiences, but the patterns of travel and tourist wants of women are also of direct interest to the tourist industry. Types of accommodation and kinds of attractions can be oriented to gender-specific wants. For example, a number of hotel chains now set aside particular floors solely for female customers. The industry has adapted to the growth of sex tourism in particular regions, usually catering to the sexual needs of male tourists. However, not all gender-oriented tourist activities and services need have negative connotations.

Tourism employment

This section examines the employment of women in the tourist industry. Although there has yet to be a systematic, wide-ranging, study of relationships between gender and tourism, a number of unconnected empirical case studies have been undertaken which incorporate women tourism workers or focus upon women workers in the tourist industry (Armstrong 1978; Samarasuriya 1982; Rupena-Osolnik, 1983–1984; Lever 1987; Miller and Branson 1989; Swain 1989; Levy and Lerch 1991). The number of references indicates that this is an emerging area of study.

Most of these studies concentrate upon the introduction of tourism into rural rather than urban areas. All of them note that, in spite of potential increases in economic standing that women may attain due to employment in tourism, strong cultural barriers, the lack of government initiatives and the lack of organisation among the women workers themselves inhibit women from aspiring to leadership roles both in the political and community senses.

Armstrong's study in highland Scotland found that women were the main workers in the industry (especially in the bed and breakfast sector) and, because of this, they had become involved in local politics to protect their interests (Armstrong 1978, p. 63). Their only avenue to pursue this was through organising voluntary associations. These voluntary organisations were not recognised as legitimate political parties. Therefore, women could only enter politics informally, 'through the back door'. The primary organisation, the Women's Rural Institute (WRI), despite repeated efforts, remained powerless due to many social and economic factors, the main one being that traditional male leadership and male networking systems did not acknowledge the head of the WRI as a legitimate political figure. The result was that women remained in informal politics and, although important locally, had little influence beyond their village.

Swain's (1989) study of the Kuna ethnic group in Panama also focuses on indigenous tourism development and the role opportunities that tourism generates for women and men. Swain details the division of labour in the production of mola artwork of fabric appliqué and the gendered access to political roles. Kuna women produce mola artwork of fabric appliqué and maintain a marketable image of ethnicity; Kuna men produce and maintain the political forum that shapes the group's interactions with outside interests, including tourism (Swain 1981, p. 83).

Despite this strict demarcation of gendered roles, Swain describes the division of labour as reflecting an interdependence of the sexes. She discusses bilateral inheritance among Kuna people which is reinforced by an individual's right to personal earnings (Swain 1989, p. 92). Kuna women have organised cooperatives and working groups to support themselves economically and socially. Swain's optimistic account emphasises the importance of local control in tourism, and she suggests that local employment in indigenous tourism could affect the evolution of Kuna gender roles. Maybe one day mola-making may be considered Kuna work, not women's work (Swain 1989, p. 103).

Levy and Lerch (1991) and Samarasuriya (1982) provide the most detailed studies on women and employment in the tourism industry: the former investigate women workers in Barbados; and the latter examines women workers in a small, coastal village in Sri Lanka. Both studies focus upon the relationships among gender, employment in tourism and status in society. They discuss the limitations and barriers women face in light of the positions they are able to enter in the labour market, potential income attainment, job security, work satisfaction, access to resources, social mobility and socioeconomic class. The studies adopt a 'development' perspective (development for whom?). However, they differ with respect to the type of tourist development under scrutiny. In Barbados, employment in large-scale hotels was the focus; whereas in Sri Lanka, more small-scale, locally controlled (guest house) tourism was under study.

Levy and Lerch offer more information concerning gender relations than Samarasuriya, looking at employment of both men and women, whereas Samarasuriya only considers women's employment. The advantage of Samarasuriya's study is that it provides greater depth by categorising and detailing several occupational relations women have to the tourism industry.

Despite the different type of development in the two case studies, many similar consequences affected women workers in both regions. In both cases, access to tourist employment was more limited for women than men. In the Barbados study, none of the women sampled entered tourism employment in a managerial position. Those who were able to attain supervisory positions were in traditional women's areas, such as house-keeping and reception (Levy and Lerch 1991, p. 78). In the Sri Lankan study, socioeconomic class was the factor most constraining where women could enter the labour market. Only middle-class women ran officially registered guest houses, while the poorest women hawked their wares on the beach or by the roadside. Despite class differences, most of the women, regardless of the nature of their employment, did not profit from their endeavours.

Reproductive roles of women, including childcare and household domestic duties, were emphasised as necessarily being combined with women's work in tourism. In Barbados, women relied on social networks to help with the burden of domestic duties. Thirty-five per cent of all women sampled and 50 per cent of female household heads reported that problems with childcare were their biggest concern (Levy and Lerch 1991, p. 81). Women's employment, income, and job security were all noted as being significantly inferior to those of men, and many women took on additional earning strategies, such as baking and sewing, because their remuneration from tourism was not sufficient to make ends meet. Women in the Sri Lankan study also had the primary responsibility of domestic duties and childcare, with implications for their tourism employment. Samarasuriya describes the situation as it relates to women shopkeepers engaged in petty trading:

> Most of the women in the business continue to do so even with little profit because it does not hinder their tasks as mother and housewife. As the shop is part of the house, or garden, they can still look after children, cook the meals and attend to other household chores (Samarasuriya 1982, p. 45)

In both studies it is evident that there are areas of employment deemed 'women's work'. In hotels in Barbados, most of the women employed worked in housekeeping, reception and other service occupations with the lowest job security (due to a lack of unionised women workers) and income levels. In the Sri Lankan study, it is noted that even the women who did own and manage their own guest house or restaurant (there were only a few) did not gain increased status, due to the low value ascribed to women's work. In short, women's mode of reproduction defines the nature of women's mode of production.

The unstable nature of women's employment in the tourist industry is similarly expressed in Lever's (1987) study of Spanish migrant workers. Much of the seasonal, unskilled employment, with long hours and low pay, is undertaken by rural women who migrate due to lack of stable employment at home. The exploitation of what is deemed women's work is again expressed in a different regional context. In Lloret de Mar, a Costa Brava resort, women are seen as 'cheaper' than men, not in terms of pay, but because they sweep and tidy up at the end of the day and do other little jobs men refuse to do (Lever 1987, p. 453). Women predominate in the more precarious occupations that have no job security and low hourly wages, and their work again is a continuation of household and domestic duties, such as chambermaiding and dishwashing. Women view the work as backbreaking and poorly paid, but they see it as a way to enter a career in tourism. Management is happy because there is no need to offer training for these jobs and thus workers (women) can be easily replaced (Lever 1987, p. 454). The lack of unionised women workers was also noted in this study. Lever commented that women were likely to see unions as potentially useful but were less likely to join because men dominated the more stable jobs and were more likely to stay away from their *pueblo* for the whole year (Lever 1987, p. 563). Lever concludes by viewing tourism migration as bringing temporary improvement for individual migrants but representing no more than a 'half-way house'. She sees migration as 'a way of shelving the problem of long-term development of rural areas' (Lever 1987, p. 470).

The last study which will be mentioned is that of Miller and Branson (1989) on women and tourism in Bali, Indonesia. The historical and cultural perspective which is adopted provides an appropriate context in which to approach and attempt to understand women, men, and economic and social change. They discuss the forces of culture on women in Bali: religious, ideological and political. They postulate that the current processes of economic and political change transform women's roles but warn against the assumption that economic autonomy for women automatically leads to political or religious freedom.

> The changes increasingly domesticate women, threatening their economic autonomy in and beyond markets . . . and redefining familial responsibilities to fit a view of the family in which the man is the 'breadwinner.' Men are increasingly evident in trading activities at both the administrative and commercial levels. The Balinese view of commercial activity of trading as 'female' is being redefined in line with the government's stress on the need for economic initiative and for men to lead in development. Both the nation state and the national economy are viewed, by the government and Western advisors alike, as 'male' (Miller and Branson 1989, p. 111).

This article illustrates that there is little to be gained from examining women's roles in economic production, without also considering their definition according to the dominant religious and political traditions, and their place in the household. Recognition must be accorded to the mutual influence of these ideological and institutional factors to avoid an ahistorical and incomplete analysis of women's experience.

The nature of the tourist industry is such that various types of development can occur (this is discussed in the next section) which determine options for direct employment and also affect potentials for indirect employment. Regional differences, diverse tourist wants and types of tourism all affect women's employment opportunities. Despite these variations in the manifestations of tourism, similar cultural and societal constraints were apparent in all of the studies reviewed. Traditional views concerning what is defined as a 'women's work' limited the avenues women could pursue for employment; domestic and childcare duties were the responsibility of women and either had to be combined with tourist employment or extended to other family members (usually daughters or grandmothers); and lack of organisation among women workers, either through unionisation, access to political power or government initiatives, prevented women from 'getting ahead' in the tourism industry.

Type of tourist development

This topic is closely related to tourist employment in that the type of tourist development largely determines employment opportunities that exist for women and men. The scale of development has implications for gender relations.

A general distinction can be made between *large-scale* and *small-scale* tourism. The former refers to large complexes associated with mass tourism. Such places have the capacity to accommodate a large number of visitors, supply a variety of recreational opportunities and are often largely self-contained. Critics of large-scale development come from both developing and developed countries (Turner and Ash 1975; de Kadt 1979; Holden 1984; English 1986; Singh *et al.* 1989; Weaver 1991). They postulate that the benefits of large-scale development do not trickle down to the local population receiving tourism. In fact, this kind of tourist development may even make many people worse off than before its introduction. Therefore, small-scale or alternative tourist development which is locally and/or nationally controlled, that involves direct employment of the local population, and distributes the benefits of tourism among the local population is viewed by many as the *appropriate* type of tourist development. The distinction between small-scale or alternative tourist development and large-scale or mass tourist development has provoked many commentators and critics to debate the usefulness of such a distinction (Cazes 1989; Cohen 1989; Wheeller 1991). However, a question which has yet to be addressed is where gender fits in this debate.

In the previous section, gendered employment patterns were examined in various tourist settings. It was distinguishable that women in both large-scale (Barbados) and small-scale (Sri Lanka) tourist developments experience constraints which affect the avenues they can pursue in tourist employment. Such research should be extended to compare the experiences of women in both situations. A superficial analysis suggests that women have more opportunity in small-scale tourist developments because of the emphasis on local control; however, as was illustrated in the case of women in rural Scotland, while women were the majority of workers in the tourist industry, that did not give them access to political power.

Tourist development under local control does not necessarily lead to benefits for local women. The majority of political and community leadership in most societies is male so that, whether power is in the hands of locals or foreigners, many of the effects on women may be similar.

Images in tourism

This section will critique marketing and advertising in tourism promotion. It is argued that depictions of 'woman' as 'native' in traditional anthropology are maintained in modern tourism advertising. Such imagery and ideology has relationships to current sex tourism. Tiffany and Adams (1985) critique the depiction of women in accounts of traditional anthropologists and attempt to demystify romanticised images of so-called 'primitive' women.

In their search for the primitive, anthropologists have succeeded in reinforcing this contrast to Western men's lives. Like non-Western peoples, women are the losers in these invidious comparisons. Women, the archetype of what men are not, provide the focus of a political inequality that is general among men. Appearing in various roles as Amazons, virgins and matriarchs, women represent a projection of civilised men's imagination (Tiffany and Adams 1985, p. xi).

The objectification and dichotomisation of women has been prevalent in images of society throughout history. Women are constantly depicted in relation to something else: in relation to men, sexuality, motherhood and domesticity. In other words, women present a problem which is addressed through patriarchal structures or explained by biological determinism. Tiffany and Adams discuss the evolution of the discipline of anthropology and the nature of the 'civilized' male anthropologist versus the 'primitive' local female, and demonstrate that the historical roots of female images as mothers, virgins and whores predominated in early Western thought and continue to be the dominant cultural representations of women today.

It is especially relevant to be aware of this context when discussing images of women in tourism because images of First World women tourists and Third World women hosts to tourism are frequently compared and contrasted. Common themes in tourism brochures are the passive, yet alluring, native woman versus the active, sexually provocative, white woman tourist. In both instances women are being defined sexually, but on different levels. In the first case, there is an objectification of women and the native host woman is portrayed as being submissive and as promising something male tourists can control and dominate. In the second case, the sexy, yet independent, white female tourist is active rather than passive and promises a potential sexual liaison with other male tourists on more equal grounds. This separation between women in the West and women in East also makes an ideological distinction between those women who are 'emancipated' and those women who are not. This theme is further explored in the next section on the growth of prostitution in developing countries.

The ideological constructs of the advertising industry infuse the tourism industry. Advertising is a form of discourse which provides the recipient with a range of cultural elements with which fantasy, meaning and identity can be constructed and created. Without advertising, the tourist product often means little other than household-related services, such as food, accommodation and shelter, which are provided to the traveller away from home (Truong 1990, p. 124) The possibility of sexual liaisons with non-white native women as well as with more promiscuous women tourists is portrayed in the mysterious, alluring, black woman, on the one hand, and the buxom, bikini-clad, white woman, on the other. The presentations imply that there is freedom for the white woman tourist to express her sexual desires (away from potential constraints at home) while the black woman provides sexual pleasure for white male tourists.

Britton (1979, p. 326) calls for a dramatic 'reorientation of image'. He does not specifically discuss the depiction of women in advertising but provides a more general commentary upon the advertising of destinations in the Third World. He critiques the imagery of the paradisiacal, utopic societies that have never existed anywhere and demands a more diverse, realistic depiction of destinations and their peoples. However, he does not discuss gendered representations as a central feature of his analysis, thereby limiting his case for a more humane form of advertising.

Prostitution and tourism

> They were poor girls whom fortune failed in need:
> They sold their charms and threw their youth away.
>   Old age caught them alone and desolate –
> Unmarried, childless, where could they seek help?
>   Alive, they drained the cup of bitter dregs;
> And dead, they eat rice mush in banyan leaves.
>   How sorrowful is women's destiny.
> Who can explain why they are born to grief?
>   (Nguyen Du, quoted in Truong 1990, p. 131)

Prostitution is one topic which has attracted attention in the tourism literature to the role of women. Even so, the women involved in the industry are given inadequate opportunity to express their views. It is insufficient to generalise about the oppression of women without being aware of the various reasons why particular women enter prostitution. There are many instances of forced, violent, exploitative subjugation of Third World women, but if stereotypical assumptions and depictions about Third World women are to be avoided, what they have to say must be heard in their own voices.

Although it is important to understand the meaning of prostitution to the individual women and men who work in the industry, one should be aware of the organisational links between prostitution and the sex-related entertainment industry to distinguish the various forms of prostitution involved. There are organised sex package tours which are an extreme form of the merging of prostitution and tourism. These tours involve tour operators, airlines, hotels and entertainment establishments and require a high degree of coordination among the components of the tourism industry (Truong 1990, p. 127). Sex tours to Thailand, the Philippines and South Korea are frequently advertised, especially through large Japanese and German travel agencies (English 1986, p. 51). One German travel agent advertised that:

> Thailand is a world full of extremes and the possibilities are limitless. Anything goes in this exotic country. Especially when it comes to girls . . . Rosie travel has come up with the answer. For the first time in history, you can book a trip to Thailand with erotic pleasure included in the price (English 1986, p. 51).

There are other forms of prostitution that have less overt linkages to the tourism industry. 'Services' are purchased locally in various locations, such as bars, nightclubs and massage parlours, and then carried out by individual purchase of the means of transport and accommodation, or individual purchase of a package tour (Truong 1990, p. 127). In this situation, there is no formal link between prostitution and tourism, except through the supplying of information on prices, locations, and the forms of sexual services available at the destination.

There is a tension between the morality of selling sex and the potential revenues that such a practice generates. The concurrent existence of established and casual workers in the industry is one outcome of this (Truong 1990, p. 127). The economic potential of prostitution forces governments either to turn a blind eye or to try to regulate the activity. At the same time, the moral issues surrounding prostitution impose limits on the degree of public tolerance. In developing countries especially, there are many vested interests in this practice: many people and organisations, both foreign and domestic, want a piece of the pie. Complete regulation of prostitution is seldom possible because the labour force, female labour in particular, is not well organised.

Female prostitution in developing countries signifies the continuous interplay between the new international division of labour and the manipulation of the sexual division of labour (Mies 1986). The mobilisation of female labour in the entertainment industry has become integral to government policies and business practices. In short, female sexuality has become an economic asset. The Philippines offer one example of government involvement in regulating female sexuality in efforts to bring in foreign exchange. During the 1970s, the Filipino government established what was called the 'hospitality' industry and proceeded to license, train and give regular medical check-ups to 'hospitality girls' working in bars and massage parlours. A specific division of government, the Bureau of Women and Minors, was responsible for this (Holden *et al.* 1986, pp. 61–2). The

Bureau developed a training course as a prerequisite to licensing. Most of the girls come from poor, farming families or destitute families living in urban slum areas. 'Employment agencies' recruit women in the provinces, promising jobs in the city, paying their parents an amount in advance and then forcing the young women into prostitution (Holden *et al.* 1986, pp. 63–64). The number of 'girls' increased from 10 000 in 1976 to approximately 300 000 in 1986, with an estimated 20 000 child prostitutes (girls and boys) between the ages of 9 and 12. (Holden *et al.* 1986, p. 62). The Bureau director refuses to acknowledge these women as prostitutes but prefers to refer to them as 'workers'.

Government involvement, combined with less explicit organisation in the exploitation of female sexuality, creates an ideological depiction of the traditional female role in conjunction with the ideologies of nationalism and development. This presents a contradiction for the female (or male) prostitute because, even though the 'glorification of self-sacrifice for the household and nation justifies the act of prostitution, ... the criminalization of prostitutes makes labour organization impossible' (Truong 1990, p. 128).

Thus far prostitution has been discussed in the form of Third World women servicing First World men. This form has been the most evident in tourist destinations and continues to be, but a form of prostitution which should also be explored is Third World men servicing First World women. To date, no material on this subject has been found which explores the phenomenon from the First World women's point of view. This is a relevant area of research because women tourists are a growing phenomenon, travelling alone, in pairs or in groups. Is there a demand for male sexual services in tourist destinations in the Third World? If so, where and to what extent? How does this relationship fit into the more 'traditional' organisational structure for satisfying male tourists? Much of the literature which addresses the motivations of male tourists seeking the services, company and even long-time companionship of Third World women, explains that women in the West are too 'feminist' or 'emancipated', and that they want a woman who will cater to them and not make any particular demands. The ideological distinction between women who are emancipated and those who are not, and how imagery in tourism advertising feeds off this distinction, was mentioned in the previous section. What, we ask, does the emancipated female tourist want? Does she also seek out sexual services to fulfil desires which she cannot satisfy at home? Is she looking to dominate and control the male gender, but only able to do so in a context in which she is viewed as having high status?

Bowman (1989) explored sexual relationships between Palestinian merchants and female tourists in Jerusalem, but he discussed it only from the perspective of the male merchants. He reported that sexual relations with female tourists were a way of gaining status among fellow merchants. Their failure to gain economically was compensated by their (imagined or real) masculine mastery over foreign women. Bowman (1989, pp. 84–5) acknowledged his difficulty with exploring the motivations of women tourists in relationships with the merchants, thus limiting his account to 'the domain of male tales'.

This article demonstrates the need to understand situations from the perspectives of both genders. While Bowman's account was legitimate and well expressed, the women tourists, who were so central to the situation, had no voice. A similar situation was mentioned previously in reference to female prostitutes in developing countries.

Research on prostitution is appropriate and should be continued, but it is also necessary to research relationships which are less extreme and in which women, especially Third World women, are not commonly viewed as being continually oppressed.

Tourism and the family

In previous sections some aspects of tourism and the family have been mentioned and attention has been drawn to the danger of viewing topics and situations in isolation. In the case of tourism employment, family situations and household status largely determine employment opportunities for women who often combine reproductive and productive duties in order to access the market. In Sri Lanka, this entailed working out of the home or taking children to work, and in Barbados family networks were set up to help with childcare responsibilities.

Tourism has a demonstration effect with implications for the cultural institution of the family in host societies. One among many issues which deserve attention is contact between local and travelling youth. What kinds of relationships develop? Are authentic exchanges of cultural beliefs and values possible? Is there a move away from traditional ways of life on the part of local youth, towards emphasis on consumerism and Western attitudes? Does tourism have dramatic effects on the moral and sexual conduct of a community? What about changes in work ethics? These are very broad questions which demand systematic investigation to see if they apply in particular situations. A drawback of much of the literature is that many generalisations have been made concerning tourism and its effects, without a clear specification of the type and stage of tourism, and overlooking the importance of regional specificity and the dynamics of culture.

Kousis (1989), in her study of tourism and the family in a rural Cretan community, concludes that tourism can cause family change but that it is economic not ideological factors which induce this change. Her data reveal that the influence of family control, the importance of marital arrangements, and the dowry system have not lost the significance they enjoyed before tourism (Kousis 1989, p. 318). What has changed are employment patterns, family size and land-holding and wealth-owning patterns. Again it is noted that females constitute the majority of workers, both women who are self-employed and those who work for an employer. This article also touches on the presence of single female tourists in the Cretan community and how they affect the sexual, moral codes.

The relationships between local males and female tourists involved a delicate and controversial issue. Some of the local men, often called *kamakia* or harpoons (metaphorically implying that the male was the harpoon and the female was the fish), systematically dated foreign women. In the full-scale tourism phase, there were about ten groups (or cliques) of single males between the ages 16 and 30 who regularly dated female tourists (Kousis 1989, p. 329).

Although the sexual, moral codes changed with the introduction of tourism, the effect was restricted to male Cretans. Strict sexual conduct of local females was unchanging, despite the relaxed relationships between local males and foreign women. Thus, the gap in sexual codes for men and women was widened.

Kousis's article raises issues which are rarely considered before tourist development takes place or when tourism policies are being implemented. Systematic exploration of the interaction between factors of change, the local sociocultural context and family relations is often lacking. Gender is central to all of these concerns.

Another neglected area of research concerns gender and family relations while families are on vacation. Women are often caretakers of others' leisure, especially that of husbands and children. Does being in the tourist role modify women's 'fragmented' leisure time? Are women still in charge of the family's leisure satisfaction first, and their own second? Do women organise the family holiday – destination, accommodation, leisure activities – from start to finish? Numerous questions could be explored in this area, many of which would be of interest to those in the industry. Work done in feminist leisure studies, which has explored the nature of female leisure experiences, may provide a useful starting point for such investigations.

Discussion

Six topics have been discussed which exhibit relationships between gender and tourism. A distinct theoretical framework has not been provided, nor have all aspects of such relationships been covered. The topics were selected because of their importance for understanding the gendered processes which are apparent in tourist development but have yet to be addressed as a primary focus in tourism studies. By including women's perspectives, understanding of human behaviour can be broadened and improved. Women need to become a subject of discourse as they experience tourism and should be involved in the formation of ideas about themselves: as tourists, tourism employees and hosts to tourism. Women need to be placed at the centre of thinking, having the right to define and decide what is valid, true and meaningful about their lives (Henderson *et al.* 1989). The practice and investigation of tourism, at both theoretical and empirical levels, should move beyond its androcentric orientation and incorporate female perspectives.

Which way to go?

The need to incorporate gender perspective in tourism studies and to make a commitment to the systematic study of women and tourism has been pointed out. This having been said, where should one begin and how is it to be done? Much can be drawn from previous work in the areas of gender in leisure and development studies, as well as in the general feminist studies literature. Feminist leisure studies have viewed leisure from the angle of the social division of labour and stratification which provide guidelines for an analysis of leisure in terms of the historical specificities of production and reproduction (Truong 1990, p. 97). This perspective on leisure can be extended to apply in the study of tourist behaviours and practices to explore implications for gender. 'Social time' is another conceptual addition that stems from feminist leisure studies. New patterns of leisure (or tourism) may promote more leisure for one part of society at the expense of the remainder. Truong (1990) puts forth particular questions which address this issue. Who has access to leisure and 'free time'? To what extent can 'free time' be considered unproductive? Does 'free time' have a liberating effect? In the context of this chapter, tourism can be substituted for 'free time'. A gender perspective on these questions could be very illuminating concerning the nature of tourism.

The gender in development literature provides analytical constructs with which to examine the international gendered division of labour, and women's experience in changing economic, political, social and technological times. Tourism constitutes the entry of leisure into the international division of labour and creates an interplay between discourse, culture, economy and technology and between the developed and developing countries. It has been shown that women from developing countries are being integrated into the structure of production of the tourist industry, but in particular ways. It follows that the study of tourism must be placed within the relationship between reproduction and production and be analysed in historically specific terms, taking into account social differentials on the basis of class, gender, race and age (Truong 1990, p. 97).

The theoretical and empirical contributions to tourism research studies that have come from many disciplines also have much to contribute to gender and tourism studies. Even though gender has not been a central construct in many analyses, models and theoretical frameworks can be modified and extended to include women's perspectives. They also provide a base against which the lack of gender attention can be assessed. Understanding tourism within a feminist framework goes beyond stereotypical images and accounts, and moves towards understanding the symbolic meanings of tourism for women and the social issues surrounding tourism. If tourism has the ability to promote dramatic social, cultural, economic, geographical and political changes, then gender relations among those in host communities, gender relations among tourists, and relations between the two should be investigated. If gender relations are not an integral part of such investigations, then they will be incomplete.

References

Armstrong, K., 1978, 'Rural scottish women: politics without power', *Ethnos* 43(1–2): 51–72.

Bandarage, A., 1984, 'Women in development: liberalism, Marxism and Marxist-feminism', *Development and Change*, 15(3): 495–515.

Bella, L., 1989, 'Women and leisure: beyond androcentrism', in E.L. Jackson and T.L. Burton (eds), *Understanding leisure and recreation. Mapping the past and charting the future*, Venture Publishing, State College, Pennsylvania: 151–79.

Boserup, E., 1970, *Women's role in economic development*, St Martin's Press, New York.

Bowman, G., 1989, 'Fucking tourists: sexual relations and tourism in Jerusalem's old city', *Critique of Anthropology*, 9(2): 77–93.

Britton, R.A., 1979, 'The image of the Third World tourism marketing', *Annals of Tourism Research*, 6(3): 318–29.

Cazes, G.H., 1989, 'Alternative tourism: reflections on an ambiguous concept', in T.V. Singh, H.L. Thuens and F. Go (eds), *Towards appropriate tourism: the case of developing countries*, P. Lang, Frankfurt-am-Main: 117–26.

Cohen, E., 1972, 'Towards a sociology of international tourism', *Social Research*, 39: 164–182.

Cohen, E., 1989, 'Alternative tourism – a critique', in T.V. Singh, H.L. Thuens and F. Go (eds), *Towards appropriate tourism: the case of developing countries*, P. Lang, Frankfurt-am-Main: 127–42.

De Beauvoir, S., 1971, *The second sex*, Alfred A. Knopf, New York. Edited and translated by H.M. Parshley.

De Kadt, E., 1979, *Tourism: passport to development?*, Oxford University Press, New York.

English, P.E., 1986, *The great escape? An examination of North–South tourism*, The North–South Institute, Ottawa.

Graburn, N.H.H. and Jafari, J. (eds), 1991, 'Tourism social science', *Annals of Tourism Research*, 18(1): 1–169.

Henderson, K.A., Bialeschki, M.D., Shaw, S.M. and Freysinger, V.J., 1989, *A leisure of one's own: a feminist perspective on women's leisure*, Venture Publishing, State College, Pennsylvania.

Hess, B. and Ferree, M.M., 1987, *Analyzing gender: a handbook of social science research*, Sage, London.

Heyzer, N., 1986, *Working women in South-East Asia: development, subordination and emancipation*, Open University Press, Milton Keynes.

Holden, P. (ed.), 1984, *Alternative tourism. Report of the Workshop on Alternative Tourism with a Focus on Asia*, Ecumencial Coalition on Third World Tourism, Chiang Mai, Thailand.

Holden, P., Pfafflin, G.F. and Horlemam, J., 1986, *Third World people and tourism*, Ecumencial Coalition on Third World Tourism and the Third World Tourism Ecumencial European Network, Bangkok.

Jackson, E.L. and Burton, T.L. (eds), 1989, *Understanding leisure and recreation. Mapping the past and charting the future*, Venture Publishing, State College, Pennsylvania.

Kousis, M., 1989, 'Tourism and the family in a rural Cretan community', *Annals of Tourism Research* 16(3): 318–32.

Kroller, E.-M., 1987, *Canadian travellers in Europe 1851–1900*. University of British Columbia Press, Vancouver.

Leacock, E. and Safa, H.I., 1986, *Women's work: development and the division of labour by gender*. Bergin and Garvey Publishers, South Hadley, Massachusetts.

Lever, A., 1987, 'Spanish tourism migrants: the case of Lloret de Mar', *Annals of Tourism Research*, 14(4): 449–70.

Levy, D.E. and Lerch, P.B., 1991, 'Tourism as a factor in development: implications for gender and work in Barbados', *Gender and Society*, 5(1): 67–85.

Mies, M., 1986, *Patriarchy and accumulation on a world scale*. Zed Books, London.

Miller, D.B. and Branson, J., 1989, 'Pollution in paradisc: Hinduism and the subordination of women in Bali', in P. Alexander (ed.), *Creating Indonesian cultures*, Oceania Publications, Sydney: 91–112.

Mohanty, C.T., Russo, A. and Torres, L., 1991, *Third World women and the politics of feminism*, Indiana University Press, Indianapolis.

Riley, P.J., 1988, 'Road culture of international long-term budget travellers', *Annals of Tourism Research*, 15(3): 313–28.

Rupena-Osolnik, M., 1983–4, 'The role of farm women in rural plurictivity: experience in Yugoslavia', *Sociologia Ruralalis*, 23–24: 89–94.

Russell, M., 1988, *The blessings of a good thick skirt: women travellers and their world*, Collins, London.

Samarasuriya, S., 1982, *Who needs tourism? Employment for women in the holiday industry of Sudugama, Sri Lanka*, Research Project Women and Development, Columbo and Leiden.

Singh, T.V., Thuens, H.L. and Go, F.H. (eds), 1989, *Towards appropriate tourism: the case of developing countries*, P. Lang, Frankfurt-am-Main.

Stamp, P., 1990, *Technology, gender and power in Africa*. International Development Research Centre, Ottawa.

Stanley, L. and Wise, S., 1982, *Breaking out: feminist consciousness and feminist research*. Routledge and Kegan Paul, London.

Swain, M.B., 1989, 'Kuna women and ethnic tourism: a way to persist and an avenue to change', in V.L. Smith (ed.), *Hosts and guests: the anthropology of tourism*, University of Pennsylvania Press, Philadelphia: 71–81.

Talbot, M., 1979, *Women and leisure*, Sports Council/Social Sciences Research Council, London.

Tiffany, S.W. and Adams, K.J., 1985, *The wild woman: an inquiry into the anthropology of an idea*, Schenkman Publishing Company, Cambridge, Mass.

Tong, R., 1989, *Feminist thought*, Westview Press, Boulder, Colorado.

Truong, T.-D., 1990, *Sex, money and morality: prostitution and tourism in Southeast Asia*, Zed Press, London.

Turner, L. and Ash, J., 1975, *The Golden Hordes*, Constable, London.

Weaver, D.B., 1991, 'Alternative to mass tourism in Dominica', *Annals of Tourism Research*, 18(3): 414–32.

Wheeller, B., 1991, 'Tourism's troubled times: responsible tourism is not the answer', *Tourism Management*, 12(2): 91–6.

Wimbush, E. and Talbot, M., 1988. *Relative freedoms: women and leisure*, Open University Press, Milton Keynes.

Tourism in the Pacific Rim

7 Environmental challenges and influences on tourism: the case of Thailand's tourism industry

K.S. Chon and A. Singh

Introduction

Thailand, a nation of more than 55 million people, is one of the developing world's most dynamic economies. A favourable economic climate in the 1980s propelled the Thai economy into achieving one of the highest growth rates in the world, with an average annual gross domestic product (GDP) growth of 10 percent from 1986 to 1990 (Asia Year Book 1992).

The contribution of tourism to the Thai economy cannot be underestimated. Tourism plays an ever increasing and crucial role in the growth and development of Thailand's economy as the country shifts from an agricultural base to a more industrialised and service-based economy. Tourism is Thailand's largest source of foreign exchange earnings, with receipts accounting for about 5 per cent the country's GDP (Friedland 1992). A rapid growth of tourism in conjunction with a strong international demand has yielded high economic returns, stimulated the nation's economy, created jobs, encouraged investments, and raised the standard of living. Through strong marketing efforts by both the public and private sector, the number of international visitors increased from 1.86 million in 1980 to 5.3 million in 1991 (see Table 7.1), an average annual growth rate of 11 per cent (Tourism Authority of Thailand 1991). Likewise, tourism receipts jumped by over 29 per cent annually from $1.2 billion in 1985 to $4.3 billion in 1990 (Economist Intelligence Unit 1991).

However, Thailand's tourism industry faces new challenges in the 1990s. While the government pushed both tourism growth and export industry growth to improve the economy, it did so at the expense of the long-term health of tourism. As the economy grew, pollution and traffic worsened and were not addressed. The AIDS problem and political unrest which are somewhat related to each other, also added to the problem. At the same time, as the government was promoting tourism, it was not addressing the issues that would eventually lead to the challenges the tourism industry faces in the 1990s.

In this chapter we will review tourism developmental and promotional trends in the Thai tourism industry. A review of Thailand's tourism environment will set the stage for a discussion of the problems that arose as a result of the tourism boom, and their impact on the Thai tourism industry. In addition, we will evaluate marketing strategies employed by

Table 7.1 *International tourism arrivals, Thailand, 1976–91*

Year	Arrivals (thousands)	% Change
1976	1098	–
1977	1220	11.11
1978	1453	19.10
1979	1591	9.50
1980	1858	16.78
1981	2015	8.45
1982	2218	10.07
1983	2191	−1.22
1984	2346	7.07
1985	2438	3.92
1986	2818	15.59
1987	3482	23.56
1988	4230	21.48
1989	4809	13.69
1990	5299	10.19
1991	5100	−3.76

Source: Tourism Authority of Thailand (1991)

the Thai government and the tourism industry to revive this ailing industry. Finally, we will discuss the future outlook of Thailand's tourism industry.

Tourism development in Thailand

Tourism development and promotion in Thailand attracted the attention of the Thai government beginning in 1979 when tourism was included in the fourth National Economic and Social Development Plan (1972–81) (Tourism Authority of Thailand 1991). The plan was aimed at strengthening the Thai economy in the areas of international trade, investment, and tourism to boost foreign exchange earnings and to create and expand employment opportunities.

The success of the policy was evident when tourism became the fastest-growing and most important sector of the Thai economy. From 1980 to 1987, international tourist arrivals to Thailand increased at an average of 10.5 per cent annually. Tourist arrivals expanded from under 2 million in 1980 to 3.5 million in 1987 before rising to 5.3 million in 1990 (Tourism Authority of Thailand 1991). The number of arrivals peaked in 1990 to 5.3 million before declining by 3.75 per cent to 5.1 million in 1991 (Owens 1992).

Along with the increase in arrivals, tourism income increased more than three and a half times from $1.2 billion in 1985 to $4.3 billion in 1990 (Tourism Authority of Thailand 1991). The success of tourism promotion in Thailand from 1987 to 1988 rests largely on the high level of cooperation between the Thai public and private sectors. To celebrate the auspicious sixtieth birthday of King Rama IX, his status as the longest reigning monarch of the Chakri dynasty was commemorated by declaring the year 1987 as 'Visit Thailand Year'. As part of the celebrations, festivals, fairs, processions and cultural displays were organised throughout the country. A diversity of tourist experiences in national parks and historical sites were provided, while the scope of activities was expanded to promote the cultural heritage, history, folk arts and crafts, and natural environment of Thailand. Special tour packages were also introduced, combining several Thai destinations such as Bangkok plus Chiang Mai, Pattaya and Phuket. International marketing efforts, through a strong presence at trade shows in the main tourist markets of Europe, North America, Asia and Australia, were equally instrumental in promoting Thai tourism. The marketing campaign continued with the promotion of the 'Thailand Arts and Crafts Year' in 1988–9. The marketing efforts were fruitful, as evidenced by the increase of visitor arrivals during the years.

Asia and Pacific markets represented about 60 per cent of all arrivals in 1990 with 3.3 million tourists, an increase of 12 per cent over the previous year. The region's overall travel growth remained at an impressive level of 10–15 per cent annually. Taiwan and South Korea recorded the largest growth rates largely due to the lifting of overseas travel restrictions in these two countries. Visitor arrivals from Australia, Hong Kong and Singapore continued to grow during the period. European visitors increased by 11 per cent over 1989 (Table 7.2), and this increase coincides with a relative decline of European arrivals in Mediterranean destinations (Economist Intelligence Unit 1991).

Tourist expenditure patterns also exhibited a change, as tourists spent more time and money on shopping. In 1986, international tourists spent almost 44 per cent of their budget on lodging/food and 27 per cent on shopping. By 1990, shopping expenditure accounted for 39 per cent, while spending on accommodation and food decreased to 38 per cent (Table 7.3). Inexpensive arts and crafts are some of the most popular shopping items for international visitors.

Increased marketing efforts to Asian visitors, who typically stayed only half as long as Europe and North American visitors, resulted in an increase in the length of stay from 6 nights in 1987 to 7.6 nights in 1989 (Tourism Authority of Thailand 1991). In terms of the purpose of visits, business travel surged ahead of leisure travel due to an increase of international trade and convention businesses in the country. In 1990, business travellers increased by 27.8 per cent, while leisure travellers showed an increase of only 8.5 per cent. Convention attendees account for approximately 70 per cent of business travellers from Asian/Pacific countries (Economist Intelligence Unit 1991).

The rapid growth and success of the Thai tourism industry can be attributed to a number of factors. The prosperity and high economic growth rate of Asian countries was a major factor in encouraging regional travel. Asian economic growth recorded the world's largest average annual expansion at 5.5 per cent. As a result, Asian tourists from newly industrialised countries (South Korea, Taiwan, Hong Kong and Singapore) travelled in greater numbers. At the same time, tourists from West Germany and Japan, Thailand's major markets for many years, recorded increases in

Table 7.2 *Arrivals in Thailand ('000s) by origins, 1986–90*

	1986	1987	1988	1989	1990
U.S.A	196.4	235.8	257.6	340.0	367.8
Canada	36.7	44.2	56.2	61.6	69.0
N. America	233.1	280.0	313.8	401.6	436.8
% change		+20.1%	+12.1%	+28.0%	+8.8%
Germany	119.4	148.4	190.3	222.1	243.1
UK	147.2	184.4	279.6	200.3	227.9
France	100.4	131.6	157.3	187.0	197.4
Italy	52.0	65.9	86.4	92.5	108.1
Switzerland	38.1	45.1	60.1	75.3	81.1
Netherlands	34.0	41.5	50.8	54.1	63.5
Sweden	27.5	35.9	48.8	54.1	67.4
Europe	518.6	602.8	873.3	885.4	988.5
% change		+16.2%	+44.9%	+1.3%	+11.6%
Malaysia	652.9	765.2	867.6	736.0	751.6
Japan	259.4	341.9	449.1	555.6	652.3
Taiwan	111.2	194.7	188.7	399.7	503.2
Hong Kong	84.0	132.3	154.4	395.7	382.8
Singapore	194.1	240.0	248.5	290.4	335.7
Australia	94.7	110.7	138.4	218.9	252.2
South Korea	30.6	37.1	65.4	111.6	147.7
India	119.5	117.6	127.5	120.0	128.2
Asia/Pacific	1546.4	1939.5	2239.6	2827.9	3153.7
% change		+25.4%	+15.5%	+26.3%	+11.5%

Source: Tourism Authority of Thailand (1991)

arrivals as their countries continued to lead in world economic performance. A rising trend in long-haul travel in Europe and North America, spurred by larger and more fuel efficient jet aircraft which facilitate non-stop travel, increased Thailand's role as a popular commercial aviation hub. Thailand also occupies an advantageous geographical location because it is a convenient stopover or transit point between Europe, Australia and the Far East. Accordingly, new air links were established with other airlines that created new markets in Canada, Finland, Spain and Switzerland (ESCAP 1991).

In line with the expansion of the tourism sector, there was a corresponding boom in the lodging industry. Average occupancy rates in Thailand increased from about 60 per cent in 1986 to 87 per cent in 1990. At the same time, average room rates more than tripled from about $30 in 1986 to $114 in 1990 (Table 7.4), but posed no threat to demand due to a shortage of rooms. Thus, the Thai government introduced policies that promoted hotel construction through special incentives in order to encourage investment in the lodging industry.

Table 7.3 *Visitor expenditures in Thailand, 1986–90 (per cent)*

	1986	1990
Accommodation	26.6	23.1
Shopping	27.4	39.0
Food and drink	16.9	15.1
Entertainment	10.0	7.6
Local transport and tours	15.6	13.3
Others	3.4	1.9
Total	100.0	100.0

Source: Tourism Authority of Thailand (1991)

Table 7.4 *Thailand hotel industry statistics, 1986–90*

	1986	1987	1988	1989	1990
Number of rooms (thousands)	117	124	136	148	169
Average room rates (in US $)	$30.00	$62.10	$84.84	$101.26	$114.57
Average occupancy (%)	60.8	82.6	90.1	87.1	85.9

Source: Tourism Authority of Thailand (1991); World Tourism Organisation

In an effort to lengthen the visitor's stay, tour operators diversified their package tours by combining trips to remote border areas with trips into Indochina. Consequently, the number of repeat visitors returning to Thailand increased from 1.8 million out of 3.5 million total visitors in 1987 to 2.3 million out of 4.8 million in 1989. Overall, about 47 per cent of all tourists to Thailand are repeat visitors (ESCAP 1991). Germany, Switzerland, Australia, Malaysia and Singapore provided the bulk of repeat visitors. Repeat visitors were attracted by the opportunities to travel up-country and experience the diverse attractions of northern and southern cultural and historical sites, jungle treks, beaches and scuba-diving.

New challenges

After four years of extensive tourism growth from 1987 to 1990, the Thai tourism industry started experiencing difficulties that led to lower arrivals and depressed market conditions in 1991 and 1992. The rapid expansion of tourism that brought forth mass tourism resulted in the deterioration and disorderliness of the tourism industry. The Gulf war and world economic recession in the USA and Europe, as well as political unrest, pollution, high prices, competition and hotel room over-supply, disrupted tourism. Fairly expensive airfares and hotel room rates, especially in Bangkok, made European packages to Thailand 20 per cent more expensive than those to alternative destinations such as Singapore (Owens 1992). In addition, the country's tourism industry failed to market itself aggressively after the successful campaigns which occurred from 1987 to 1990. Thailand's woes continued with the crash and pillaging of a Lauda Air 767 jet in late May 1991, which attracted widespread media and public attention in key markets (Economist Intelligence Unit 1991). Together with an ongoing image problem over AIDS, the sex industry and environmental neglect at some destinations, Thailand's positive tourism image began to decline in the minds of visitors, primarily from the negative publicity. Consequently, tourists were avoiding Thailand in favour of Singapore, Malaysia and Indonesia (especially Bali). From 1989 to 1990, visitor arrivals in Indonesia increased from 1.6 million to 2.2 million, while the visitor arrivals in Malaysia increased from 3.9 million to 7.5 million (ASEANTA 1991).

Another major contributing factor for the slow and moderate growth of Thailand's tourism industry is the winding down of Thailand's current economic and investment boom. The effects of the various constraints to be discussed in the next section consequently led to a decline in tourist arrivals in 1991 by about 4 per cent to 5.1 million

Constraints to growth

The Gulf war dealt a severe blow to European and Middle East airlines by forcing the suspension of services to Thailand and rerouting others. Flight cancellations from Europe and Asia reached 20 per cent and 15 per cent, respectively, in the first three months of 1991 alone. As many as 20 per cent of tour operators in Thailand went out of business, and the cancellations cost the tour trade at least $20 million in lost bookings, with European inbound tourism bearing the brunt of the decrease (Economist Intelligence Unit 1991). The impact was heightened with a terrorist warning in Thailand that affected arrivals from the USA, Australia and the UK. The overall impact was a 35 per cent cancellation of visitors from Japan, Europe and North America, and occupancy rates also declined from the shortfall in visitors. For example, the occupancy rate for Bangkok's five luxury hotels (Oriental, Regent, Dusit Thani, Hilton and Sangri-La) in January 1991 dropped to about 60 per cent from 85 per cent in the same period in 1990 (Goldstein 1991).

The emergence of AIDS in Thailand, primarily among the Thai citizens, coincided with the boom in international tourism toward the late 1980s. Thailand found itself facing a 'sexual paradise' image problem connected with AIDS and prostitution. The risk of contracting AIDS discouraged many tourists from visiting Thailand. More than 300 000 Thais are thought to be HIV positive, and this figure is expected to increase rapidly. Facing a downfall in tourist arrivals, the Thai tourism authorities minimised the existence and threat of the disease so that Thailand would not lose its attractiveness as a tourist destination. The tourism industry sensed no threat from AIDS and consequently did not take any restrictive or preventive measures to protect those at risk (Cohen 1988).

The effects of overbuilding will be more strongly felt in Bangkok than in the rest of the country. Lower occupancies and average room rates are the result of the tourism slump and the industry's over-built state. The arrival slump could hardly have come at a worse time. Since 1986, the supply of rooms in Bangkok had increased by about 24 per cent and is expected to double to almost 40 000 rooms by the end of 1992, up from about 20 000 in 1990 (Goldstein 1991). As a result of the excess supply and downfall in tourist arrivals, room rates fell by 25 per cent in Bangkok in 1991 while the decline nation-wide was up to 50 per cent. Bangkok hotel prices rose by 250 per cent between 1987 and 1990. Higher occupancies prompted hotels to break their contracts with tour operators and to turn away leisure guests in favour of full-rate business guests (Carey 1992).

The ravaging of Thailand's environment by rapid industrialisation has contributed to problems of pollution in cities, resorts and beaches. The air in Bangkok is highly polluted, and European tour cancellations are attributed to the high level of pollution in Bangkok and at some resorts such as Pattaya. The 1986 report of the National Environment Board said that coral reefs around some of the country's main islands were being damaged by litter and boats dragging their anchors (Economist Intelligence Unit 1991).

International investors are seeking alternative countries in South East Asia for their investment, citing the inability of successive Thai administrations to correct severe infrastructure defects, especially Bangkok's rapidly deteriorating traffic network. Additionally, tourists are spending more time in the northern city of Chiang Mai or in the resort island of Phuket or Ko Samui in the south to avoid the traffic congestion in Bangkok.

Since the fall of the absolute monarchy in 1932, Thailand has experienced ten successful coups, a number of failed ones, and 14 new constitutions (Branagan 1992). Another bloodless military coup in late February 1991 resulted in the overthrow of the government. Tourists from Japan, Taiwan and Hong Kong who were highly conscious of political instability chose other destinations over Thailand. Coupled with the Gulf war, tourist arrivals from Asia fell by 20 per cent (Economist Intelligence Unit 1991).

The pro-democracy uprising in late May 1992 dealt a major blow to the Thai economy and tourism industry. As a result of the uprising, the National Economic and Social Development Board (NESDB) revised its pre-May projection of GDP growth from 7.9 per cent to 7.6 per cent for 1992 (Pura and Owens 1992). The most immediate effect, however, was on the tourism industry which is likely to incur a potential loss of millions of dollars in tourism revenues. Tourism revenue, which in 1991 brought in $4.48 billion, is expected to fall to $4.2 billion from a previously estimated $5 billion. Tourist arrivals are forecast to be at 5.1 million visitors for 1992 (or no growth over 1991) and down about 4 per cent from 1990 (Carey 1992).

The severest blow has come from cancelled bookings by Japanese tourists who constitute the lion's share of Thailand's tour market. Cancellations by the Japanese tourists, who comprised the second largest group of arrivals after Malaysians at 559 000 in 1991, ran as high as 40 per cent. Airlines were also affected by Singapore Airlines cancelling a number of flights while Thai Airways had to cancel more than 200 scheduled flights during the crisis. Many Thai professionals are even boycotting the airline in protest over military ties (Carey 1992).

In the lodging industry, Bangkok's premier hotels reported occupancies of 20–30 per cent, down from normal occupancy rates of about 60 per cent. Pattaya hotels are less than 30 per cent full, while occupancies for hotels in Chiang Mai and Phuket range between 30 per cent and 35 per cent. Average occupancy for the nation as a whole is expected to be much less than 60 per cent for 1992 (Handley 1992). Consequently, prices and room rates fell rapidly. Despite the crisis, new hotels continue to open, thereby worsening the over-building situation. The 700-room Sol Twin Towers and the 420-room Royal Garden Riverside opened in June 1992, thus adding another 1000 rooms to the supply in Bangkok. In the pipeline are the 1400-room Imperial Queen's Park, and the 477-room Ramada Renaissance Hotel. New hotels such as the luxurious Sukhotai, Grand Hyatt Erawan and Mansion Kempinski are under pressure to discount rooms, by following the lead of other hotels in Bangkok, as a way of surviving the slack season and building market share. For example, the Grand Hyatt Erawan cut its listed room rates by 30 per cent, while the Sukhotai, which had an occupancy of less than 30%, discounted its rooms by 40–50 per cent.

The political unrest was, however, instrumental in arousing the nation and drawing the world's attention to the magnitude of the problems facing Thailand, and the need to take immediate action. The eventual price Thailand will have to pay to restore its image and confidence hinges on an orderly, timely and wholehearted commitment to resolve the current problems and revive the ailing tourism industry through vigorous marketing and promotion.

Marketing strategies

The most important aspect of the tourism revival campaign is the cooperation between the private and public sector, a cooperative effort that has been absent since the highly successful 'Visit Thailand Year' in 1987. The Tourist Authority of Thailand (TAT), the main tourism agency responsible for marketing and promoting Thailand, has embarked on a tourism recovery programme to restore the tourism industry. TAT's first objective, aimed at the high-spending Japanese tourists, is to assure them that Thailand is safe to visit. Advertising and promotion in major tourist markets is also aimed at restoring confidence among tourists that Thailand is a safe and stable country. The second objective addresses the problems of pollution, cheating, touting and tourist hijacks that were becoming rampant and gaining notoriety. Familiarisation trips to Thailand for the foreign press and travel agents were conducted by Thai tourism representatives to encourage travel to Thailand. The TAT also increased its presence in Japan, South Korea and Taiwan by opening three new sales offices in 1992. Airlines, travel agents and hoteliers are restructuring low-cost holiday packages to entice visitors. To avoid sparking off rate wars, hotels are emphasising value by offering free upgrades and complimentary extra room nights.

A major public relations and promotional campaign called 'The World Our Guest' was developed in August 1992 to coincide with the 60th birthday of Queen Sirikit. An estimated 11 000 visitors to Thailand were given free hotel rooms, airline tickets, meals and tours as part of the promotion, which was declared an unqualified success by the TAT. The campaign was intended to kick-start Thailand's declining tourism industry.

Due to the AIDS crisis, the government has attempted to change the tourist image by stressing the cultural, natural attractions and bargain shopping in Thailand rather than sexual attractions. Even the new Prime Minister of Thailand, Chuan Leek-Pai, who was elected in September 1992, has vowed to restore Thailand's image abroad, by taking steps to clean the environment and to address the AIDS issue. His new cabinet of numerous financial advisers will undoubtedly reflect the emphasis on economic development as a top priority (Handley 1992).

The TAT is increasing its cooperation with the national tourism authorities of the Association of South East Asian Nations (ASEAN) to promote multidestination travel. The inauguration of 'Visit ASEAN Year 1992' is an example of cooperative marketing by the tourism agencies of the six member countries of ASEAN (Thailand, Malaysia, Indonesia, Brunei, Philippines and Singapore). Furthermore, the year 1992 was designated as 'Women's Visit Thailand Year' in order to encourage more women to visit Thailand, a country where the ratio of male tourists is higher. The current marketing campaign is expected to increase visitor arrivals, encourage domestic and regional travel, increase tourist expenditure, and promote the various tourist destinations and experiences that the country has to offer. The opening of the national convention centre in Bangkok with a main hall seating capacity of 10 000 (the largest in Asia), is expected to spur hotels to improve servicing of meetings and conferences in order to attract business travellers and market Thailand as a convention site.

The signing of a Cambodian peace treaty in October 1992 was a positive step that provided Thailand the opportunity to market itself as the gateway to Indochina for tourists desiring to visit Vietnam, Cambodia or Laos. Tour operators can combine tour packages that include trips to countries in Indochina, such as Cambodia, to visit the historical and religious Angkor Wat. As Indochina, especially Vietnam, is in the development stage of exploratory visits for overseas investments and tourism, Thailand will benefit significantly by having direct access to Indochina's emerging markets.

Future of Thailand's tourism

In the long term, Thailand's infrastructure bottlenecks, the result of inadequate planning coupled with rapid growth, will ease. A second international airport is planned north-east of Bangkok that will be capable of handling about 20–30 million passengers annually by the year 2010. The airport's completion should relieve the congestion at Bangkok's Don Muang Airport. Bangkok will grow to be the regional hub in Asia for air traffic, but will still face stiff competition from other destinations such as Singapore. Also, an elevated highway is under construction which will expedite the traffic between the existing airport and downtown Bangkok. Further, by 1997, communications are expected to improve when Thailand gets an additional 3 million telephone lines in Bangkok, rural areas, and the country's first telecommunications satellite.

With relatively inexpensive accommodations, first-class hospitality, an increase in international flights, a growing economy and infrastructure improvements, Thailand will be able to maintain tourism growth through the 1990s. One asset that Thailand can be proud of is that Thailand and hospitality service appear to be a perfect match, one in which every employee wants a guest to be happy. Thailand's past experience shows that tourism demands self-discipline, planning and marketing to be successful. Whether or not it will fulfil its promise as Asia's biggest holiday destination will also depend upon the depth of commitment from the tourism industry, and the lessons learned about the results of inadequate planning.

References

ASEANTA, 1991, *ASEANTA Annual Report '91*, ASEAN Tourism Association, Singapore.

Asia Year Book, 1992, *Far Eastern Economic Review*, Review Publishing Co. Ltd, Hong Kong: 209–10.

Branagan, J., 1992, 'Growing up painfully', *Time*, 1 June: 70.

Carey, S., 1992, 'Recent slump could bring needed dose of reality to Thailand's tourist industry', *Asian Wall Street Journal*, 13 July: 2.

Cohen, E., 1988, 'Tourism and AIDS in Thailand', *Annals of Tourism Research*, 15(4): 467–86.

ESCAP, 1991, *Economic Impact of Tourism in Thailand*, Economic and Social Commission for Asia and the Pacific, Bangkok.

Economist Intelligence Unit, 1991, 'Thailand', *International Tourism Report*, 1: 69–87.

Friedland, J., 1992, 'Tourists stay away in droves', *Far Eastern Economic Review*, 4 June: 56–7.

Goldstein, C., 1991, 'Balmy weather ahead', *Far Eastern Economic Review*, 11 April: 42–3.

Handley, P., 1992, 'Limited damage', *Far Eastern Economic Review*, 2 July: 48.

Owens, C., 1992, 'Thai officials encouraged by economy say future hinges on political stability', *Asian Wall Street Journal*, 14 September: 4.

Pura, R. and Owens, C., 1993, 'Economy should weather storm from political strife, analysts say'. *Asian Wall Street Journal*, 22 June: 5.

Tourism Authority of Thailand, 1993, *Annual Report on Tourism in Thailand, 1990*, Bangkok.

World Tourism Organisation, 1992, *Travel and tourism barometer*, World Tourism Organisation, Madrid.

8 A critique of tourism planning in the Pacific

S.J. Craig-Smith and M. Fagence

Introduction

It has been observed that tourism destinations in the South Pacific are thought to offer 'the stuff of which many tourist dreams are made' (Economist Intelligence Unit 1989, p. 71). Even if this is so, there is evidence that despite being part of the Asia-Pacific region which is recording the fastest rate of tourist growth in the world, the South Pacific region seems not to have attracted its due share of the boom in international travel. It is true that the four 'honeypot' destinations of Guam, Saipan, Fiji and Tahiti have little difficulty in at least maintaining their market share; however, other South Pacific destinations are being constrained, for example, by their ability to raise the finance for many infrastructure developments. In addition, various internalised or regional difficulties (some of which are derived from the region's location, its history and its different systems of land ownership and government) and some exogenous decisions in the boardrooms of multinational corporations and international airlines have created obstacles to tourism growth. Recent enthusiasm for pursuing approaches to tourism respecting environmental and cultural sustainability has not made the tourism planning task any easier. The disparate nature of the 21 Pacific island nations and the absence of a region-wide coordinating agency have contributed to ongoing difficulties in tourism planning and strategy formulation.

The study of circumstances in the South Pacific is becoming an identifiable 'growth industry'. In order to draw the various economic, cultural, environmental and strategic strands together, the Economic and Social Commission for Asia and the Pacific (ESCAP) commissioned a study to focus on the crucial planning and strategic issues. That study (Craig-Smith and Fagence 1992) forms the basis of much of this report, which itself forms part of an ongoing study of tourism planning in the region.

The geographical context

In a rapidly shrinking world, the island nations of the South Pacific afford one of the last untapped tourism destinations. Scattered across the vast expanse of the Pacific Ocean are more than 30 000 islands, with the greatest concentration in its south-west quadrant. Within this south-west sector lie 21 island nations displaying tremendous diversity in scenery, wildlife, economy and social composition. It is estimated that 1200 languages – one quarter of all human languages – are found in this region (Pawley and Green 1985). Owing to their geographical isolation relative to the primary geopolitical poles of the world, these islands remained largely undiscovered by Europeans until the early nineteenth century and were some of the last areas of the world to be absorbed into the great maritime empires of Europe (Campbell 1989).

Much of the present-day mystique of the micro-states in this region is due to their relative isolation and small size. Collectively the 21 nations in this region comprise a mere 550 000 square kilometres of land (an area roughly equivalent to France) and some 6 million people (a population smaller than Greater London or Paris), and are scattered across 30 million square kilometres of ocean (an area comparable to that of Africa). Many of the island nations are too small even to feature on a world map.

On physical, ethnic and social grounds the 21 nations can be divided into three geographic regions – Polynesia, Melanesia and Micronesia. French Polynesia, the Cook Islands, Niue, Tonga, American Samoa, Western Samoa, Tokelau, Wallis and Futuna, and Tuvalu all lie within *Polynesia*, occupying a triangular area of ocean from Easter Island in the east to Hawaii in the north and New Zealand in the south west. Fiji, New Caledonia, Vanuatu, the Solomon Islands and Papua New Guinea all lie in *Melanesia*, which occupies an area west of Polynesia between Australia and the Equator. Nauru, Kiribati, the Marshall Islands, the Federated States of Micronesia, Palau, Guam and the Commonwealth of the Northern Marianas all lie in *Micronesia* (meaning 'small islands') and are located to the north of Melanesia north of the equator.

All too frequently people from outside this region have the common perception that the islands are much the same, offering the same basic ingredients of coral reefs, palm-fringed beaches, a slower way of life and friendly natives. While this popular image is partially true, it falls a long way short of the real position, the problem being that the islands are better known for their image than their reality. On physical grounds the islands of the region can be divided into high islands and low islands. Some countries comprise only high islands, some only low islands and some have both. On the whole the high islands are of volcanic origin and have good soils, abundant water and lush vegetation, as typified by Viti Levu in the Fijian island group. On the other hand, the low islands are of coral formation and generally have no topsoil, sand with a high salt content, limited vegetation, no springs or rivers and, where rainfall is low, there is a scarcity of water, as typified by Tongatapu in the Tongan island group (Stanley 1989).

Superimposed on this geographic and ethnic milieu is a veneer of European colonialism. From the eighteenth century onwards France, Germany, the Netherlands, Spain and the United Kingdom (together with the USA and Japan at a later date) all scrambled for territorial influence and control of the sea lanes. Spain and Germany were the first major colonial powers to lose their Pacific toehold and the United Kingdom has gradually relinquished its territorial control, but French and American colonial power is still significant in spite of increasing ethnic resentment (Fagence 1992). While many of the islands are now independent, there is still a strong American and French presence. The 21 nation states considered here comprise almost all the island nation states of the central and south Pacific. The Hawaiian and the Galapagos islands have been deliberately excluded from this analysis.

For reasons which will become apparent in a subsequent section, the 21 nations are showing an increasing interest in developing tourism, partly to reduce their dependence on foreign aid and partly because of a lack of other economic alternatives. As much as it might be desirable for the 21 countries to pool resources and consider joint marketing and promotion, ethnic, cultural and colonial differences have precluded such a move at present. There is no single body working for the interests of all 21 nations. Fiji, Kiribati, Papua New Guinea, the Solomon Islands, Tonga, Tuvalu, Vanuatu and Western Samoa are all 'Africa Caribbean Pacific' (ACP) countries as defined by the European Community and enjoy EC aid through the auspices of the Lomé Convention (Lee 1987). These eight countries, together with American Samoa, the Cook Islands, the Federated States of Micronesia, French Polynesia, the Marshall Islands and Niue, collectively belong to the regional tourism organisation, the Tourism Council of the South Pacific (TCSP). While this organisation has an interest and responsibility for all 14 countries, its level of support for the ACP countries is much higher than for the other six. No one organisation collectively represents all the countries in the region. The United Nations Economic and Social Commission for Asia and the Pacific (UNESCAP) commissioned the authors of this chapter to undertake a major overview of tourism planning in the region, and especially to recommend means by which tourism planning performance in the region could be improved.

A brief literature review

The growth of tourism development and activity in the Pacific region has generated commensurate growth in published commentaries, reports, strategies and so on. In addition to the published output from the various national tourism agencies, some of the important non-governmental organisations in the region – such as the TCSP, South Pacific Forum (SPF), South Pacific Region Environmental Programme (SPREP) – and the many research centres and institutes have contributed to the growth in commentaries on various aspects of tourism. Jenkins (1980) pointed out a number of common denominators in the published sources: the focus on economic impact assessments, on marketing and feasibility studies, and an interpretation of the role of tourism in national economic development. That assessment remains true, although there is an increasing attention to matters of social and environmental concern. Even so, there continues to be a Western or developed nation bias in many of the interpretations and commentaries, and some of the national tourism plans are based on concepts, ideas and organisational structures which have not been 'translated' from conventional tourism planning orthodoxy to fit the special circumstances of the South Pacific region (Fagence and Craig-Smith, in press).

Useful introductions to the general developmental circumstances of the South Pacific include Cole and Parry (1986), Brookfield and Ward (1988), Oliver (1989) and Fairbairn et al. (1991). Whereas these sources are descriptive of contemporary circumstances, Kirste and Herr (1985) have speculated on future circumstances in the region. Among the earliest sources which deal specifically with tourism are Dommen (1972), Finney and Watson (1977) and Varley (1978). More recently, Kissling and Pearce (1990) have assessed the peculiarities of tourism and travel patterns in 'Destination South Pacific'. Dwyer (1986) and others have interpreted the economic impact of tourism on selected island nations, and some commentators (such as Farrell 1985) have discussed the responses of island tourist destinations to the vagaries of international economic fluctuations and changes in airline policy. Farrell considers some of the problems examined in the next section of this paper, and suggests the region should seriously consider opting for specialisation in tourism development. A similar advocacy for formal and complementary tourism planning and development is implicit in McNaught's (1982) examination of the influences of mass tourism and modernisation in Pacific island communities. The commentaries of McNaught and Farrell recognise the reality of international tourism and travel rather more than Kenaston (1980, p. 105) with his assertion that 'the future of tourism in the South Pacific will be exactly what the South Pacific wants it to be'. The TCSP has recognised the need for the region to specialise with its promotion of the concept of the 'South Pacific Village' (Yacoumis 1989).

By far the largest proportion of publications on tourism in the South Pacific has concentrated on economic issues. Important contributions to the interpretation of economic impacts and opportunities have been made by Britton (1980a; 1980b; 1982), Fairbairn (1985; 1988; 1992), Fairbairn and Parry (1986) and Tisdell et al. (1988; 1990), each working independently or with various collaborators. The vulnerability of the economies of the island nations to exogenous events and policies of the developed nations is well recorded. That vulnerability is exacerbated by the tendency in the region 'towards social, spatial and economic polarization (Britton 1980b, p. 8) leading to tourism development enclaves. Britton's studies seem to support the hypothesis that the level of tourism development in a developing country is determined by the degree of importance of that country to metropolitan interests. This form of neocolonialism has been commented upon by Fagence (1992) in his assessment of the legacy of Europe in the Pacific region, extending from the eighteenth century to the present day with the ongoing aid and support of EC grants to selected Pacific nations. In addition to the overview of regional tourism performance, some commentators provide more detailed assessments of selected island nations (Browne and Scott 1984; Britton 1983). Inter-pretations of the scope and nature of development issues, including tourism, facing small island economies are common (see, for example, Crocombe 1989; McKee and Tisdell 1990), while examinations of the performance and prospects of Pacific island economies in the face of changing world economic structures as lessons for the future have been undertaken by international agencies (World Bank 1991; Thirlwall 1992) as the basis for assessing future financial and technical support. Fairbairn has focused sharply on studies of multinational enterprises in the region (Fairbairn and Parry 1986), of island indigenous entrepreneurs (Fairbairn 1988) and most recently on the need for donor aid to assist private sector development (Fairbairn 1992).

Some of the commentaries on economic aspects of island tourism have been set in the context of 'micro-states'. Mellor (1987) has examined the political circumstances of the Pacific island micro-states, and Milne (1992) has commented on the role tourism plays in the national economies of five selected Pacific island nations. The important issues of transport and communication between the micro-states in the region are examined by various commentators in Kissling (1984). The north–south or metropolitan–periphery linkages have been considered by English (1986) and more generally by Hoivik and Heiberg (1980). There are parallels to be drawn for the South Pacific from Wilkinson's (1987; 1989) interpretation of micro-state dependence and the fit of Caribbean experi-ence to the classic development cycle models. Wilkinson's (1989) general examination of tourism strategies for island micro-states includes an extensive literature review. A continuing influence on micro-state tourism in the Pacific region is the legacy of the various colonial powers, some of which exhibit a reluctance to loosen the ties of domination.

There are few communities and island nations in the region which have avoided the examination of the sociologists. Oliver (1989) has provided a benchmark assessment of many of the native cultures before the impact of the waves of colonisation. The sensitivity of indigenous groups to outside influences has been examined by Biddlecomb (1981) in her commentaries on the contrasts between islanders and tourists in their respective values and expectations, while Rajotte (1980) has edited a collection of responses of Pacific islanders to tourism and tourists. The potential of cultural differences and cultural artefacts as a principal attrac-tion for tourism activity has generated a number of independent and commissioned studies. For example, King (1992) has reviewed the poten-tial of cultural tourism in Fiji, and Sofield (1991) has posited a corpus of principles to guide sustainable ethnic tourism. Middleton, for TCSP (1990a), reviewed museums and cultural centres in the South Pacific, and Watling (1987) has provided a commentary on archaeological sites in Fiji, with an interpretation of the cultural heritage potential for conservation (Watling and Francis 1991). The stereotype of indigenous people in the South Pacific is examined in Schmitt's (1990) review of the image of Hawaii portrayed in films. For many island nations the develop-ment of 'cultural' or 'ethnic' tourism provides a complementary focus of attraction. This opportunity – sometimes referred to as 'secondary tourism' – has attracted support from international funding agencies (UNDP 1988).

'In developing countries, limitations inherent in the private sector require government to take an operational role in the tourism industry' (Jenkins and Henry 1982, p. 519). Government involvement is an important aspect of pursuing a rational system of tourism planning. The South Pacific region has a history of inter-nation and inter-island rivalry and hostility, a situation which is scarcely conducive to a coordinated and comprehensive approach to tourism planning in the region. A number of agencies perform complementary roles in economic, environmental and tourism 'planning'; however, coordination and cooperation are sometimes frustrated by the separate and overlapping responsibilities designated to the supernational agencies. The patterns of organisations and their responsibilities have been described by Arase (1988), Yahuda (1988), Elak (1991), Harris (1991) and Woods (1991). Studies of selected Pacific island nations by the Pacific Islands Development Program (PIDP 1990) drew attention to the difficulties of tourism planning and organisation within the case-study nations and across the region, and the matter was highlighted in the report to UNESCAP by Craig-Smith and Fagence (1992). Loose networks of cooperating island nations seem to achieve more when they are bound by funding opportunities and technical assistance; this is the clear message of Lee (1987a; 1987b) in his commentaries on EC support for the region.

It is the various regional and international agencies which have been responsible for promoting serious considerations of planning for sustainable tourism development, and they have achieved this through the conduct of regional seminars, conferences and workshops. In 1980 UNESCO conducted a workshop in Rarotonga (Pearce 1980) to consider the contribution of research to tourism development and planning in the region. Two years later the Asian Productivity Association convened a symposium in Kathmandu to consider the social and economic impact of tourism in the Asia-Pacific region (Hawkins 1982). This symposium considered 'snapshots' of the state of tourism in 12 countries, including Tonga and Fiji. ESCAP (1986) organised a seminar in Suva to consider the development of tourism in Pacific island countries, with a number of regional case studies. An innovative satellite-link conference was conducted across the region in 1982 to explore the various approaches and responses to tourism in the South Pacific (Rajotte 1982) and a special session of the annual PTRC Seminar in London was convened to examine tourism planning in developing countries (PTRC 1986). More recently, in 1991, the TCSP organised a regional conference in Suva to consider tourism and national development planning (TCSP, forthcoming). That conference was followed by a jointly organised seminar (by ESCAP, TCSP and SPREP) which considered the means of promoting sustainable tourism development in Pacific island countries (ESCAP, in press). The Craig-Smith and Fagence review of tourism planning in the region was an integral element of the ESCAP initiative. Other agencies, such as the Pacific Asia Travel Association (PATA), have held conferences in the region to stimulate constructive action in tourism planning and development.

Some of the Pacific island nations have been more committed than others to the production of national tourism strategies. PIDP (1990) was responsible for a series of tourism development assessments in the late 1980s (for the Commonwealth of the Northern Mariana Islands, Cook Islands, the Federated States of Micronesia, French Polynesia, Kiribati, Marshall Islands, Papua New Guinea, Solomon Islands, Tonga and Western Samoa). The international agency UDP was responsible for securing tourism plans for Fiji (UNDP 1973) and Western Samoa (UNDP 1984), while the Fijian government commissioned a master plan from Coopers and Lybrand (1989). In the last few years the TCSP has taken responsibility for the preparation of tourism development plans for a number of TCSP member countries (funded by provisions of the Lomé Convention, with grants from EC: Solomon Islands (TCSP 1990b), Western Samoa (TCSP 1992a) and Tuvalu (TCSP 1992b)). These plans provide a measure of consistency and continuity in plan structure and approach. As a general guide to member countries, the TCSP Planning and Development Division has prepared guidelines for the integration of tourism development with environmental protection (TCSP 1989). This initiative may prove to be more successful than the issue of guidelines for the preparation of tourism sub-regional master plans by ESCAP (1978). A matter of particular concern is the extent to which tourism planning orthodoxy which is appropriate to the circumstances of developed nations is being adopted without due 'translation' in the very different circumstances of the South Pacific (Fagence and Craig-Smith, in press). Perhaps the series of plans being prepared by the TCSP will introduce a standard and structure more appropriate to the needs of the region.

The sources of difficulties

As stated earlier, the popular image of Pacific islands is a long way from reality, and it ignores a multitude of social and economic problems (Connell 1986). Most of the Pacific islands suffer from two sets of problems: one group of problems is common with most other developing world economies, and another group often compounds the first because the islands comprise minute specks of land in a vast expanse of water.

Within a non-consumer subsistence economy it was possible for the islands and their inhabitants to exist in relative ecological harmony. The first inhabitants of the region originated from South East Asia and over countless generations navigated and migrated eastwards across the vast unknown expanse of ocean. As a general rule the further one travels in an easterly direction the more recent the original human habitation: New Guinea and adjacent areas of Melanesia have supported humankind for upwards of 30 000 years, while parts of Micronesia have been inhabited for fewer than 5000 years (Sharp 1963). In eastern Polynesia human habitation has only occurred in the last 2000 years, and no ancient societies ever reached the Galapagos Islands off South America.

Small populations, constant migration, very little contact with the outside world and few consumer demands meant that the region could support the demands placed upon it. Native plants and animals, garden plots and food from the ocean kept the inhabitants of the region at a reasonable standard of subsistence. All this changed once colonising powers entered the area. The islands were viewed as sources of raw materials to be exported from the region in exchange for cash and infrastructure (Ali 1980). Colonialism brought with it an exposure to a consumer society and engendered an expectation by the indigenous inhabitants of consumer rewards. This process is so far advanced today that only by depending very heavily on outside aid and other assistance can many of these countries even attempt to satisfy the expectations of their citizens.

One of the most pressing problems facing the region is population growth: in some countries this is in excess of 3 per cent per annum (Crocombe 1989). Over the entire region the average population density is around 110 per square kilometre, but this disguises local extremes which can exceed 1000 per square kilometre on some of the coral atolls. In parts of Melanesia the population is doubling every 20 years, with 50 per cent of some island populations below 18 years of age. The resources of many island states cannot cope with existing population demands, let alone a 3 per cent annual increase. Population growth is giving rise to population movement. In countries with a relatively large urban base such as Fiji, 50 per cent of whose population is already urbanised, migration is often focused on the towns. In keeping with many developing nations, the urban areas are ill equipped to cope with this rural influx. In all countries, but particularly in the less urbanised regions, migration focuses on nations around the Pacific Rim, in particular Australia, New Zealand, Canada and the United States (Chapman 1985; Connell 1986). American Samoa, the Cook Islands, Niue, Tukelau, and Wallis and Futuna have more of their citizens in other countries than resident within home boundaries. Most of the island nations of the region have sizeable expatriate communities abroad.

Limited resources pose other problems: small areas of usable land for crop production severely limit production output and thus export capabilities. Small nations are particularly vulnerable to cyclones and other associated meteorological phenomena which are capable of wiping out a nation's entire production in a matter of a few days. Furthermore, with such small areas of land involved, economies of scale are rarely achieved. While the oceans abound with resource potential, most of the small island nations have insufficient resources for economic exploitation. Furthermore, the costs of transporting raw materials to metropolitan markets can be prohibitive.

Further problems face the small Pacific island nations. A small infrastructure, few financial resources, and a very small skilled labour force preclude large-scale processing or manufacturing. This situation forces a heavy reliance on the export of raw materials. Two problems flow from this: first, there is very little value added to the exported commodities; and second, the raw materials are extremely vulnerable to world-wide competition and fluctuating demand. There is a structural problem in employment. As people abandon subsistence agriculture in search of paid work the local economy must produce sufficient income to sustain a waged labour force (Fairbairn 1985). Small islands in isolated locations find it difficult to compete in an international economy. On many of the islands only the government can offer paid employment. Eighty-seven per cent of all paid work in Niue is provided by the government, 50 per cent of all jobs in the Cook Islands are for the government, and about 40 per cent of all American Samoan jobs are underwritten by government funds.

Accessibility is another major problem (Kissling 1984). While at the global scale many of the islands enjoy military strategic interest, at the regional scale most of the islands have poor communication access. Most transportation is across the Pacific rather than within it. Long-haul aircraft can connect North America to South East Asia and Australasia with little need to 'stop over' within the region. Hawaii in the north and Fiji in the south act as sub-regional transport nodes but travel between islands is slow, expensive and often unreliable. As most of the countries have unrealistic expectations of running a national airline landing rights are zealously guarded and regional transport is uncoordinated. It is not unusual for journey times to be quicker from one island to another via a Pacific Rim airport than directly between the two islands concerned. As each island nation usually comprises more than one island, even inter-island transport within the same nation is a problem. In the extreme case of Kiribati, the distance between its most easterly and most westerly islands is greater than the distance across continental United States.

Social structure and land tenure are further difficulties (Acquaye *et al.* 1987; Crocombe 1986). In many islands land does not belong to an individual but to a community, with the individual having certain use rights. This complicated method of land holding, together with absentee land-owner rights, makes development very difficult. Furthermore, negotiation procedures vary not just from island to island but from region to region within the one island. At a recent TCSP regional conference held in Fiji in November 1991, one participant frankly admitted that while he was qualified to conduct land negotiations within his part of his native land, customs were so complicated he would not endeavour to conduct negotiations in other parts of his own country. Land ownership and use rights create major development problems.

While this list is in no way meant to be encyclopaedic, it does give an overview of some of the key problems facing the region. Faced with a task of trying to fulfil the material expectations of its citizens, the region has had to rely heavily on overseas aid. So far aid has been reasonably freely available for two reasons: the major donor countries, mostly on the Pacific Rim or in Europe, have been in a financial position to give overseas aid generously; and in the cold war era the islands enjoyed considerable strategic importance, especially for US bases watchful of a communist presence in South East Asia. In the early 1990s, with the decline in the communist threat and economic depression at home, the major donor countries are inclined to be less generous.

The attraction of tourism

With total exports estimated to be worth around US $2.5 billion for the 21 countries and overseas aid valued at $1.2 billion per year in 1988, tourism has been seen by island governments as a means of boosting export potential and reducing dependence on an uncertain aid income (Stanley 1989).

In global terms current tourism use of the region is minuscule. In spite of very imprecise data, it is estimated that approximately 2 million overseas tourists visit the region annually (Craig-Smith and Fagence 1992). This represents approximately 0.5 per cent of world visitation figures. To put this in a world perspective, 2 million is roughly equal to the number of visitors to Australia and compares with 36 million visiting the United States and 55 million tourists visiting Italy annually. There is considerable inequality in visitor levels between the various countries at present. Guam, Saipan, Fiji and French Polynesia – the four honeypots – account for 1.6 million visitors or 80% of the 21-nation total. New Caledonia, American Samoa, Western Samoa, PNG, the Cook Islands, Vanuatu and Tonga collectively receive a further 325 000 regional visitors or 16 per cent, leaving ten countries attracting only 4 per cent of the regional visitation total. Income to the region from tourism is estimated to be in the order of $1.5 billion; this level exceeds aid payments and represents approximately 25 per cent of regional income (including aid payments).

The already significant cash contribution made by tourism to the region has encouraged almost all island governments to climb on to the tourism bandwagon. The activity is particularly appealing because of its perceived glamour, its beneficial impact on the environment and its ability to bring the market to the region. This saves the region taking its exports to the market (Bull 1991).

For the eight ACP countries Bjarnason (1991) estimated that 35 000 full-time equivalent (FTE) jobs were related to tourism, and for all 14 TCSP member countries the number was between 50 000 and 55 000. If these statistics are correct it can be surmised that approximately 13 international tourists create one FTE job. Although this is significantly fewer than the Australian estimate of 20 international tourists needed to create one FTE tourism job, the nature of the Australian economy and Australian wage levels may account for the disparity. On the 13 to 1 ratio it can be estimated that the 2 million annual visitors to the region generate approximately 150 000 jobs or 12 per cent of the region's total employment. There is considerable economic leakage from these island economies, with an estimated income multiplier of approximately 0.8. Nevertheless, tourism contributes significantly to national incomes and employment.

Table 8.1 *Tourist arrivals and percentage (where known) of locals employed in tourism, Pacific islands, 1990*

	Tourist arrivals	Proportion of region's tourism (%)	Local employment in tourism (%)
American Samoa	56 373	2.88	
Comm of N. Marinas (Saipan)	380 056	19.39	37
Cook Islands	33 900	1.74	20
Fed. States of Micronesia	18 060	0.92	2
Fiji	279 000	14.24	
French Polynesia	132 361	6.75	8
Guam	780 404	39.83	
Kiribati	3 300	0.18	
Marshall Islands	3 500	0.18	
Nauru	1 035	0.06	
New Caledonia	85 213	4.35	
Niue	649	0.03	
Palau	15 000	0.78	
Papua New Guinea	40 742	2.08	3
Solomon Islands	9 200	0.46	2
Tokelau	25	0.00	
Tonga	29 011	1.48	7
Tuvala	700	0.03	
Vanuatu	43 009	2.19	
Wallis & Futuna	100	0.00	
Western Samoa	47 600	2.42	6
Total	1 959 238	100	

Although tourism is presently promoted for economic gain, the island governments are aware of certain positive social and cultural impacts. One of the greatest benefits is employment opportunity. Money earned from tourism jobs gives a greater level of economic independence to the workers who may become less tied to traditional forms. For workers with a reasonable education there are opportunities in tourism entrepreneurship. These opportunities provide access to a middle class in a society hitherto dominated by hereditary chiefs. Some of the social benefits of tourism are considered to be improved mobility, greater job opportunities and the ability to purchase consumer goods. In addition, infrastructure development for tourism has the potential to provide improved transport facilities, more retail outlets, a better health service, improved drinking water and sewerage systems.

Tourism planning in the region

The various matters considered in the two previous sections provided some of the background for the study of sustainable tourism development in Pacific island nations commissioned by UNESCAP in 1991, and reported in Craig-Smith and Fagence (1992). In addition to the conventional review of the present situation of and prospects for tourism activity in the South Pacific region, and an analysis of the principal problems and issues, the study focused on the potential for a region-wide tourism planning strategy. It is this particular focus on tourism planning which marks this study out from others.

Very early in the study process it became apparent that tourism planning in the South Pacific region was likely to be impeded by two matters. First, the special circumstances of the region seemed to be ill suited to the application of orthodox tourism planning theory. This matter has been developed further (Fagence and Craig-Smith, in press). Second, as the Economist Intelligence Unit (EIU 1989) report had pointed out, the existence of so many overlapping agencies and interests in the region, especially with each agency pursuing its own agenda, was scarcely conducive to cooperation and coordination. It became apparent that these two matters, singly and in combination, could frustrate the realization of the full potential of the region (EIU 1989, p. 71). The difficulties flowing from these circumstances would be variously influenced and further exacerbated by the influence of indigenous cultures, the legacy of colonialism and the recent imposition of internationalised neocolonialism.

Tourism planning in the South Pacific has not achieved the model of coherence and integration advocated by Travis (1985); the model of an interlocking system of tourism planning extending across the spectrum of levels from local and regional to national and international has no exemplar in this region, although in a few cases there have been attempts to develop lateral if not hierarchical relationships. The most usual case in this region is for considerable diversity in emphasis, scope, content, focus and implementability. There is no lack of official recognition of the potential advantages of coordination, cooperation and coherence which could be achieved by consistency in the strategy production process. For example, in the opening address to a regional conference in Suva (Fiji), it was acknowledged that

> in many ways the future of tourism in the individual countries of the Pacific is bound up with the future of tourism in others ... given the common interest, it must be greatly to our advantage to present a common front to the world (Kamikamica 1991, p. 11).

In support at the same conference, Yacoumis (1991, p. 7) observed that tourism 'requires an integrated institutional and planning framework'. In tourism marketing various initiatives have been pursued since the 1970s, with differing degrees of success. Early initiatives were dogged by national parochialism or changes in the route strategies of the international airlines in the region; more recently, the 'South Pacific Village' strategy, promoted by the TCSP and supported with funds from the EC, seems to have achieved measurable success.

In the case of tourism planning, at both the national and regional levels, the reality of practice has been at variance with the rhetoric. Some examples drawn from across the region will testify to the differences in emphasis, scope, content, organisation and even seriousness of intent.

While some island nations such as Tonga and Fiji have conspicuous and separate tourism policies within the structures of their national development strategies (in some cases supported by special statutory provisions, such as the Tonga Tourism Act 1976), others such as Kiribati and the Marshall Islands have incorporated tourism as integral elements in broadly based economic development plans. In the case of Kiribati, two ministries have responsibility for tourism matters, with coordination being effected through the Tourism Advisory Committee which was established in 1986. For the Federated States of Micronesia the national tourism development policies have been merged into the current National Development Plan (NDP). Another 'model' of tourism policy-making operates in the Commonwealth of the Northern Mariana Islands where the principal administrative body is the Mariana's Visitors Bureau (MVB). This agency is untypical of visitors bureaux in general in that the functions assigned to it include research, promotion, regulation, supervision of tourism enterprises, development of tourism facilities, tourism manpower development and the formulation of the comprehensive tourism development plan.

In his review of the differential performance of TCSP member countries, Bjarnason (1991) reported that there was no mention of tourism in the NDP of Tuvalu (1987–91). The NDP of Kiribati (1987–91) omitted specific reference to tourism in its set of objectives, policies and strategies. In the Solomon Islands, the general NDP (1985–9) omitted specific references to tourism, whereas the plan for the western provinces of that country (1988–92) listed tourism as a matter of policy significance. Some recognition was accorded tourism with a set of tourism-specific objectives in the plan for Western Samoa (1988–90), while Fiji, Papua New Guinea and Tonga have long-standing commitments to tourism development as part of their respective national economic development strategies.

This differential performance and commitment to tourism development and planning in national strategies has been exacerbated by a lack of coherence and consistency in the structure and content of those plans which exist. The 'plans' prepared for some island nations in the 1970s were essentially marketing strategies. By the late 1980s there was an increasing realisation that tourism plans should incorporate responses to the concerns of environmental and social impact, to the matters of land tenure and ownership, and to the challenge that 'even within a tourist region only certain areas are absolutely necessary for tourist development' (Baud-Bovy and Lawson 1977, p. 181). In its studies of ten Pacific island nations, PIDP (1990) proposed a basic structure for national tourism plans. However, the reality of the situation in the different case studies forced departures from the 'model' framework, reflecting what were considered to be the crucial issues. For example, in the Kiribati exercise there was a strong focus on social and economic safeguards, and for the Solomon Islands an emphasis was on rendering tourism development more appropriate to indigenous circumstances; the creation of appropriate planning and implementation processes was important for the Cook Islands and the Federated States of Micronesia.

The TCSP has embarked upon a process of tourism plan creation using a standardised framework (Bjarnason 1991) fine-tuned to the special circumstances of each case. Three plans have been prepared so far: Solomon Islands (TCSP 1990b), Western Samoa (TCSP 1992a) and Tuvalu (TCSP 1992b). These have been funded through the ACP programme of the EC. Further plans in this 'model' would provide the basis of consistency from which progress to regional coordination in the South Pacific would become possible. There is a tendency in the non-TCSP plans for tourism development to appear largely unconstrained, with conspicuous concentrations near international airports, in enclaves in major cites, or in isolated sites in areas of spectacular natural attraction. The basis for such patterns seems to be inclined more towards industry pragmatism than to efficient tourism planning (Gunn 1977). It is this evidence of pragmatism which has generated the response of some Pacific island governments and some non-government organizations (the NGOs such as ESCAP, TCSP and SPREP) to promote workshops and conferences in the region at which the need to pursue ecologically and culturally sustainable tourism development received priority consideration.

The South Pacific region has undoubted tourism attraction; it is also a region in which unconstrained tourism development could seriously damage the environment and the cultural heritage. As so many of the island nations are becoming acutely dependent on foreign aid and the income from international tourism, there is little spare capacity for errors of judgement. The emerging need is for tourism planning, not necessarily at a sophisticated level, for each island nation, and cooperation and coordination across the region.

Conclusion

In the big picture of international tourism, the South Pacific region is not a major destination. With the exception of the four honeypot destinations of Guam, Saipan, Fiji and Tahiti, the regional performance in tourism attraction has been described in a recent report by the Economist Intelligence Unit (1989) as 'lacklustre'. Destinations in the region are particularly sensitive to such matters as boardroom changes of policy by international airlines, by the impacts of cyclone damage, and by political disturbances. In addition, many destinations are hampered by the lack of funds to provide simultaneously for airport development, hotel accommodation and associated infrastructure and services. For some island nations there is a shortage of trained personnel. Other impediments to the optimal development of tourism in the region include degrees of national rivalry, some national indulgence in the expensive symbolic trappings (such as a national airline), customary land-tenure systems which are not fully understood by offshore entrepreneurs, a negligible domestic tourism market, and a low level of local entrepreneurship. These are some of the matters being addressed by the TCSP.

One of the ongoing problems in the region is variable commitment to regional policy cooperation. Evidence from recent regional seminars suggests there is increasing recognition that cooperative action is needed to conserve scarce natural resources, to increase the sustainability levels of local customs and traditions, to maintain international attention, to create the circumstances in which inter-nation transport (especially by air) is viable, and to contribute to mutually beneficial trading linkages. However, segmented national interests intrude, perhaps borne of the suspicion that participants in cooperative tourism strategies may not benefit equally (PIDP 1990). While cooperation in manpower training, research and data collection, promotion, and negotiation with international funding agencies may be possible, an equivalent level of cooperation with tourism master planning seems difficult to achieve at the present stage of development.

This is a region which faces considerable challenges from its own history, its geographical location, its dispersed distribution of attractions, its colonial legacy and the impact of neocolonialism from the international aid agencies, its propensity to create its own political uncertainties, its systems of customary land tenure, its vulnerability to climatic disturbances, and its susceptibility to metropolitan entrepreneurship and decisions well away from the region. These and other factors create a feeling of uncertainty about the future of tourism development in the region. The ambivalence of some island nations contrasts strongly with the avid pursuit of any tourism potential by other nations; the regard for sustainability is uneven across the region. There can be little doubt that any nation which is determined to be involved in tourism planning should prepare and implement a conspicuous tourism development strategy. However, the study team which reported to ESCAP indicated a scepticism about the feasibility of creating a comprehensive and coordinated regional strategy (Craig-Smith and Fagence 1992). Even given the good will and willingness of the island nations to cooperate in the production of such a strategy, a crucial problem area would seem to be the adequacy of current tourism planning orthodoxy to cope with the special circumstances of the region. Whereas many of the challenges listed here and considered throughout this chapter are being examined, there is a tendency for each to be investigated as a discrete matter. If there is to be a coordinated and comprehensive tourism planning strategy for the region, a useful preparatory step would be the coordination of the various research endeavours. Perhaps one or more of the regional umbrella organizations will take up this particular challenge.

References

Acquaye, E. *et al.*, 1987, *Land tenure and rural productivity in the Pacific islands*, University of the South Pacific, Suva.

Ali, A. 1980, *Plantation to politics*, University of the South Pacific, Suva.

Arase, D., 1988, 'Pacific economic co-operation: problems and prospects', *The Pacific Review*, 1(2): 128–144.

Baud-Bovy, M. and Lawson, F., 1977, *Tourism and recreation development*, Architectural Press, London.

Biddlecombe, C., 1981, 'Pacific tourism: contrast in value and expectations', Pacific Conference of Churches, Suva, Fiji.

Bjarnason, J., 1991, 'Tourism and national development planning', paper presented to TCSP Regional Conference on Tourism and National Development Planning in the South Pacific, Suva, Fiji, November.

Britton, S., 1980a, 'The spatial organization of tourism in a neo-colonial economy: a Fiji case study', *Pacific Viewpoint*, 21(2): 144–65

Britton, S., 1980b, 'A conceptual model of tourism in the Third World', in D. Pearce (ed), *Tourism in the South Pacific*, Department of Geography, University of Canterbury, New Zealand on behalf of UNESCO: 1–12.

Britton, S., 1982, 'Political economy of tourism in the Third World', *Annals of Tourism Research*, 9(3): 331–58.

Britton, S., 1983, *Tourism and underdevelopment in Fiji*, Development Studies Centre, Australian National University, Canberra.

Brookfield, M. and Ward, R., 1988, *New directions in the South Pacific*, Academy of Social Sciences, Canberra,

Browne, R. and Scott, D., 1984, *Economic development in seven Pacific islands*, IMF, Washington, DC.

Bull, A., 1991, *The economics of travel and tourism*, Pitman, Melbourne.

Campbell, I., 1989, *A history of the Pacific islands*, University of Canterbury Press, Christchurch, New Zealand.

Chapman, M., 1985, *Mobility and identity in the island Pacific*, University of the South Pacific, Suva.

Cole, R. and Parry, T., 1986, *Selected issues in Pacific island development*, National Centre for Development Studies, Australian National University, Canberra.

Connell, J., 1986, *Migration, employment and development in the South Pacific*, South Pacific Commission, Noumea, New Caledonia.

Coopers and Lybrand, 1989, *Final report, Tourism Master Plan*, prepared for the Government of Fiji, Suva.

Craig-Smith, S. and Fagence, M., 1992, *Sustainable tourism development in Pacific island nations*, report to UNESCAP, University of Queensland, Lawes.

Crocombe, R., 1986, *Land tenure in the Pacific* (revised edition), University of the South Pacific, Suva.

Crocombe, R., 1989a, *The South Pacific* (5th edition), University of the South Pacific, Suva (see Chapter 1).

Crocombe, R., 1989b, 'Some problems facing Pacific island countries', *Pacific Perspective*, 14(1): 1–7.

Dommen, E., 1972, *The tourist industry in the South Pacific*, University of the South Pacific, Suva, Fiji.

Dwyer, L., 1986, 'Tourism in the South Pacific', in R. Cole and T. Parry (eds), *Selected issues in Pacific island development*, National Centre for Development Studies, Australian National University, Canberra: 226–49.

Economist Intelligence Unit, 1989, 'The Pacific Islands', *International Tourism Report*, 4: 70–99.

Elak, A., 1991, 'The challenge of Asian-Pacific economic co-operation', *The Pacific Review*, 4(4): 322–32

English, E., 1986, *The Great Escape?*, North-South Institute, Ottawa.

ESCAP, 1978, 'The formulation of basic concepts and guidelines for the preparation of tourism sub-regional master plans in the ESCAP region', *Transport and
Communications Bulletin* (ESCAP), 52: 33–40

ESCAP, 1986, *Development of tourism in Pacific land countries*, ESCAP, Bangkok.

ESCAP, in press, Papers of Regional Seminar: Promotion of Sustainable
Development in Pacific Island Countries, ESCAP Bangkok.

Fagence, M., 1992, 'The legacy of Europe in the Pacific region', in *Proceedings*,
Tourism in Europe Conference, Durham, England, July 1992, Centre for
Tourism Studies, Newcastle Polytechnic, F1-11.

Fagence, M. and Craig-Smith, S., in press, 'Challenge to orthodoxy: tourism planning in the South Pacific', in *Papers of Tourism Research Conference*, Sydney,
March 1993, Bureau of Tourism Research, Canberra.

Fairbairn, T., 1985, *Island economies: studies from the South Pacific*, University of
the South Pacific, Suva, Fiji.

Fairbairn, T., 1988, *Island entrepreneurs: problems and performances in the South
Pacific*, University of Hawaii Press, Honolulu.

Fairbairn, T., 1992, *Private sector development in the South Pacific*, University of
New South Wales Centre for South Pacific Studies, Sydney.

Fairbairn, T. and Parry, T., 1986, *Multi-national enterprises in the developing South
Pacific region*, PIDP, East-West Centre, University of Hawaii, Honolulu.

Fairbairn, T. *et al.*, 1991, *The Pacific islands: politics, economics and international
relations*, East-West Centre, University of Hawaii, Honolulu.

Farrell, B., 1985, 'South Pacific tourism in the mid-1980s', *Tourism Management*,
6(1): 55–60.

Finney, B. and Watson, K., 1977, *A new kind of sugar: tourism in the Pacific*, East-
West Centre, University of Hawaii, Honolulu.

Gunn, C., 1977, 'Industry Pragmatism v tourism planning', *Leisure Sciences*, 1(1):
85–94.

Harris, S., 1991, 'Varieties of Pacific economic co-operation', *The Pacific Review*,
4(4): 301–11.

Hawkins, D., 1982, *Social and economic impacts of tourism in Asia-Pacific Region*,
Asia Productivity Organisation, Tokyo.

Hoivik, T. and Heiberg, T., 1980, Centre-periphery tourism and self-reliance,
International Social Science Journal, 32(1): 69–98.

Jenkins, C., 1980, 'Tourism policies in developing countries: a critique', *Tourism
Management*, 1(2): 22–9.

Jenkins, C. and Henry, B., 1982, 'Government involvement in tourism in developing countries', *Annals of Tourism Research*, 9(4): 499–521.

Kamikamica, J., 1991, Opening address to TCSP Regional Conference on
Tourism and National Development Planning in the South Pacific, Suva, Fiji,
November.

Kenaston, T., 1980, 'The future of tourism in the South Pacific', in D. Pearce (ed.),
Tourism in the South Pacific, Department of Geography, University of
Canterbury, New Zealand: 105–110.

King, B., 1992, 'Cultural tourism and its potential for Fiji', *Journal of Pacific
Studies*, 16: 74–89.

Kirste, R. and Herr, R., 1985, *The Pacific islands in the year 2000*, Centre for Asia
and Pacific Studies, University of Hawaii, Honolulu.

Kissling, C., 1984, *Transport and communication for Pacific microstates*, University
of the South Pacific, Suva.

Kissling, C. and Pearce, D., 1990, 'Destination South Pacific', in C. Kissling (ed.),
Destination South Pacific, CHET, Aix-en-Provence, France: 1–11.

Lee, G., 1987a, 'Tourism as a factor in development co-operation', *Tourism Management*, 8(1): 2–19.

Lee, G., 1987b, 'Future of national and regional tourism in developing countries', *Tourism Management*, 8(2): 86–8.

McKee, D. and Tisdell, C., 1990, *Developmental issues in small island economies*, Praeger, New York.

McNaught, T., 1982, 'Mass tourism and the dilemma of modernization in Pacific island communities', *Annals of Tourism Research*, 9(3): 359–81.

Mellor, N., 1987, 'The Pacific island microstates', *Journal of International Affairs*, 41(1): 109–34.

Milne, S., 1992, 'Tourism and development in South Pacific microstates', *Annals of Tourism Research*, 19: 191–212.

Oliver, D., 1989, *The native cultures of the Pacific islands*, University of Hawaii Press, Honolulu.

Pawley, A. and Green, R., 1985, 'The Proto-Oceanic language community', in R. Kirk and E. Szathmary (eds), *Out of Asia: peopling the Americas and the Pacific*, Journal of Pacific History monograph, Australian National University, Canberra.

Pearce, D., 1980, *Tourism in the South Pacific*, Department of Geography, University of Canterbury, New Zealand (on behalf of UNESCO).

PIDP, 1990, *Pacific islands tourism case studies: regional summary*, Pacific Islands Development Program, East-West Centre, University of Hawaii, Honolulu.

PTRC, 1986, *Planning for tourism in developing countries*, PTRC, London.

Rajotte, F., 1980, *Pacific tourism as islanders see it*, University of the South Pacific, Suva, Fiji.

Rajotte, F., 1982, *The impact of tourism development in the Pacific* (satellite conference), Trent University, Peterborough, Canada.

Schmitt, R., 1990, *Hawaii in the movies, 1898–1959*, University of Hawaii Press, Honolulu.

Sharp, A., 1963, *Ancient voyages of Polynesia*, Paul, Auckland, New Zealand.

Sofield, T., 1991, 'Suitable ethnic tourism in the South Pacific – some principles', *Journal of Tourism Studies*, 2(1): 56–72.

Stanley, D., 1989, *South Pacific Handbook*, Moon Publications, Chicago.

Thirlwall, A., 1992, *The performance of prospects of the Pacific island economies in the world economy*, Pacific Islands Development Program, East-West Centre, University of Hawaii, Honolulu.

Tisdell, C. *et al.*, 1988, *Economics of tourism: case study and analysis*, University of Newcastle, Newcastle, Australia.

TCSP, 1989, *Guidelines for the integration of tourism development and environmental protection in the South Pacific*, TCSP, Suva, Fiji.

TCSP, 1990a, *Review of museums and cultural centres in the South Pacific* (prepared by V. Middleton), TCSP, Suva, Fiji.

TCSP, 1990b, *Solomon Islands tourism development plan, 1991–2000*, TCSP, Suva, Fiji.

TCSP, 1992a, *Western Samoa tourism development plan, 1992–2001*, TCSP, Suva, Fiji.

TCSP, 1992b, *Tuvalu tourism development plan, 1993–2002*, TCSP, Suva, Fiji.

TCSP, forthcoming, *Papers of Regional Conference on Tourism and National Development Planning in the South Pacific*, November 1991, TCSP, Suva, Fiji.

Travis, A., 1985, *Collected papers on leisure and tourism*, Occ. Paper 12 (new series), CURS, University of Birmingham, Birmingham.

UNDP, 1973, *A tourism development plan for Fiji* (prepared by Belt, Collins and Associates), UNDP/WTO.

UNDP, 1984, *Tourism master plan for Western Samoa, 1984–93*, prepared by UNDP/WTO, Department of Economic Development, Government of Western Samoa.

UNDP, 1988, *Secondary tourism activity development in Fiji – approaches, policies, controls*, UNDP/WTO.

Varley, R., 1978, *Tourism in Fiji: some economic and social problems*, University of Wales Press, Cardiff.

Watling, R., 1987, *Fiji archeological sites: an identification study*, TCSP, Suva, Fiji.

Watling, R. and Francis, J., 1991, 'Cultural heritage conservation' paper presented to Regional Seminar on the promotion of sustainable tourism development in Pacific island countries, Suva, Fiji, November.

Wilkinson, P., 1987, 'Tourism in small island nations: a fragile dependence', *Leisure Studies*, 6: 127–46.

Wilkinson, P., 1989, 'Strategies for tourism in island microstates', *Annals of Tourism Research*, 16: 153–77.

Woods, L., 1991, 'Non-governmental organizations and Pacific co-operation: back to the future?', *The Pacific Review*, 4(4): 312–21.

World Bank, 1991, *Toward higher growth in Pacific island economies: lessons from the 1980s*, World Bank, Washington, DC.

Yacoumis, J., 1989, 'South Pacific tourism promotion', *Tourism Management*, 10(1): 15–28.

Yacoumis, J., 1991, 'Tourism in the South Pacific an overview', paper presented to TCSP Regional Conference on Tourism and National Development Planning in the South Pacific, TCSP, Suva, Fiji.

Yahuda, M., 1988, 'The "Pacific Community": not yet', *The Pacific Review*, 1(2): 119–27.

9 Theme parks in Japan

T.S. Mervyn Jones

Introduction

It is necessary at the outset, before discussing the dramatic growth in theme park type developments (TPTDs) in Japan, to comment upon the unresolved question of what elements – real, perceived or prescribed – constitute a theme park.

The American Marriot Corporation defines a theme park as a 'family entertainment complex orientated towards a particular subject or historical area, combining the continuity of costuming and architecture with entertainment and merchandise to promote a fantasy-provoking atmosphere'. The manager of Britain's Alton Towers states that his theme park is a 'modern leisure park, the basic fairground approach, put into a much better setting, dealt with on a far more sophisticated level, with charm and charisma and not just orientated to one small sector of the market – but to the whole family'. S. Ohoka (Japan Development Bank) argues that 'theme parks are extraordinary spaces created using a uniform design according to a specific theme . . . we are now in an age in which we can enjoy leisure. In such an age theme parks have emerged as high quality recreation grounds which fully meet the leisure desires of children and adults.'

The dilemma with these few definitions is that they are neither comprehensive nor singularly specific. Clearly the taxonomic problem is what to include to be all-embracing, or simply to be immediately comprehensible and general. If the former argument is accepted, the definition should include physical, marketing, managerial, sociological and psychological references, as these could all claim to be legitimate elements, and do contribute to the success or failure of 'theme park' operations, and need to be understood. This chapter therefore, attempts to classify the Japanese theme parks in terms of their major foci under ten general headings/themes coded as follows:

1. Fantasy (various)   F
2. Amusements (including rides ranging from very exciting
to passive)   AR
3. Heritage/historical (including industrial)   H
4. Educational/including science/nature, etc.   Ed
5. Entertainment (live and passive, including parades)   Et
6. Environment/earth (including oceans/animals/plants)   EE
7. Outer space/the universe   Sp/U
8. Commercial (when predominant and planned mainly
as a shopping complex)   Cs

9. Overseas/a foreign country/city/specific region   O
10. Film/theatre/religious   Fl/T/R

Chronological development

The first leisure-orientated TPTD in Japan was opened in 1965 near Nagoya. This is a historical or heritage centre, which consists of a reconstruction of a Meiji village, and features culture, lifestyle, working situations and trades as well as agricultural implements. It also depicts the architecture of that period.

The second major leisure-orientated development was built in 1975. This took the form of a film-set theme and was located in Kyoto – a former major film-making centre in Japan. It is in part historical and educational, but also has a strong entertainment element.

In 1983, three further TPTDs opened, and were quite different in size, themes and organisational structures and included. *Tokyo Disneyland*, sited close to central Tokyo was backed up by considerable experience and well-tested formulae for success in the United States. *Holland Village* was built near Nagasaki. It was well planned and built but was a new venture for the consortium which paid for the development and for the Japanese management who ran the theme park. The third development, known as *Little World*, was again essentially a historical attraction adjoining the established *Meiji Village* near Nagoya.

A further heritage theme was created at the historical location of Nikko in 1986, where early Japanese history is presented, including the Edo period with all its artefacts. These six pre-1988 sites (see Table 9.1) were to highlight the evolutionary first phase of TPTDs in Japan.

Since 1988 there has been a virtual explosion of leisure-orientated TPTDs throughout Japan. These often have promotion and direct financial backing from the local authority in whose area they are located. Between 1988 and mid-1992 there were no less than 21 major developments (Table 9.2 and Figure 9.1).

These sites, however, are generally on a smaller scale in terms of physical size, investment and infrastructure than that of Tokyo Disneyland.

As indicated in Tables 9.1 and 9.2, the stated themes of the TPTDs do vary, in terms of their sponsors (both private and public), their respective sizes and particularly their development costs which range from under £7 million to over £800 million (see Table 9.3).

An evaluation

In attempting to evaluate TPTDs in Japan, there are a number of important variables that may be identified. It must be stressed that these variables are not mutually exclusive but do allow themselves to be placed in discreet groups (Table 9.4).

Table 9.1 *Theme parks in Japan before 1988*

Opening date	Location city/prefecture	Stated name	Stated theme[1]	Classification[2]
March 1965	Inuyama-City/ Aichi	Meiji Museum Village	Meiji era	H/Ed
October 1975	Kyoto-City/ Kyoto	Toei Uzumasa Film village	Film-making	H/Ed
March 1983	Inuyama-City Aichi	Little World	Foreign village	O/Ed
April 1983	Urayasu-City/ Chiba	Tokyo Disneyland	Disney animation fantasy	F/AR/Et
July 1983	Nishisonogi Town/Nagasaki	Nagasaki Holland Village	17th century Holland	O/H/Ed
April 1986	Fujiwara-Town/ Tochigi	Nikko Edo Village	Edo period	H/Ed

Source: Adapted from *Nikkei Business*, 8 July 1991.

Notes:
1. These themes have been directly translated from the Japanese.
2. See text for the explanation of this classification.

In terms of physical/location factors, the 100 per cent owners and operators of Tokyo Disneyland, The Oriental Land Co. Ltd (whose main shareholders are Mitsui Real Estates and Keisei Electric Railways, while minor shareholders include Chiba Prefecture and Urayasu City), are the first to acknowledge that their success is due in large measure to their location so near to central Tokyo. Within only a 50 kilometre semi-circular catchment area, there are over 30 million people; this number is doubled when the catchment area is extended westwards to around three hours' journey time by Shinkanshin to the Osaka/Kyoto conurbation. This exceptional level of accessibility to Tokyo Disneyland from Japan's principal city and its two major regions, which incidentally accounts for over 70 per cent of its annual visitors, is a most critical variable.

Again the management at the highly successful Osaka Tempozan marketplace and aquarium also conclude that their location and subsequent catchment area, with its large population and good accessibility, have been critical to its success. Certain other Japanese TPTDs whose catchment areas and hence their locations are less favourable – for example, Reomo World (Shikoku) and Noboribetsu (Hokkaido) – have been noticeably less fortunate in reaching their projected visitor targets, although these particular theme parks have succeeded in promoting their respective regions.

Turning to the second group – management operations – it is generally accepted that Japanese management is tenacious, efficient, highly trained and market-orientated. Certainly the Japanese TPTDs exemplify the

Table 9.2   *Theme parks in Japan from 1988*

Opening date	Location city/prefecture	Stated name	Stated theme[1]	Classification[2]
April 1988	Mise-Village/ Saga	Donguri[3] Village	Pasture land in Southern France	O/Ed/EE
August 1988	Manno-Town/ Kagawa	Shikoku New Zealand Village	Farm Village in New Zealand	O/Ed/EE
November 1988	Kushikino-City/ Kagoshima	Kushikino Gold Park	Gold	H/Ed
March 1989	Tamano-City/ Okayama	Oji Fancy Land	Fantasy characters	F/Et
June 1989	Matsusaka-City/Mie	Mie Children's Castle	Science for children	F/AR/ED
July 1989	Koromogawa-Village/Iwate	Tohoku New Zealand Village	Pasture in New Zealand	O/Ed/EE
July 1989	Yamagata-City/ Yamagata	Yamadera Fuga Country	History of Mutsu	H/Ed
July 1989	Obihiro–City/ Hokkaido	Gluck Kingdom	German town in the middle ages	H/Ed
January 1990	Ureshino-Town/Saga	Hizen Dream Road	Edo Era	H/Ed
April 1990	Mano-Town/ Niigata	Sado Nishi Mikawa Gold Park	Alluvial gold mining	H/Ed
April 1990	Shuzenji-Town/ Shizuoka	Shuzenji Rainbow Village	Foreign village	O/Ed
April 1990	Kitakyushu-City/Fukuoka	Space World	Space and the Universe	Sp/U
Apri 1990	Saikai-Town/ Nagasaki	Nagasaki Saikai Paradise	Buddhism	R/H/Ed
July 1990	Ashibetsu-City/ Hokkaido	Canadian World	19th century Canada	O/H/Ed
July 1990	Noboribetsu-City/Hokkaido	Noboribetsu Marine Park 'Nikusu'	Nordic town and an aquarium	EE/H/Ed
July 1990	Osaka-City/ Osaka	Osaka Tenpozan Harbour Village	Ocean/Aquarium	C/EE/Ed
July 1990	Takamiya-Town/Hiroshima	Hiroshima New Zealand Village	Farm village in New Zealand	O/Ed
October 1990	Itsukaichi-Town/Tokyo	Tokyo Sesame Place	Television programme *Sesame Street*	AR/F

Table 9.2 (*continued*)

Opening date	Location city/prefecture	Stated name	Stated theme[1]	Classification[2]
December 1990	Tama-City/ Tokyo	Sanrio Pyuro Land	Communication of parents and children	AR/Ed
April 1991	Ayauta-Town/ Kagawa	Reoma World	Green space and water	EE/AR/F
April 1991	Hinode-Town/ Oita	Harmony Land	Character and village specialties	F/EE/Ed

Source: Adapted from *Nikkei Business*, 8 July 1991.

Notes:
1 These themes have been directly translated from the Japanese.
2 See text for the explanation of this classification.
3 Literally means 'Acorn'.

importance of management operations in all its guises: customer service, cleanness of the development, and smooth operations behind the scenes (both of the active and more passive entertainment's). Marketing with strong public relations sections, and the creation of impressionable brand images, particularly in the planning and early stages of the development, have also played a prominent role.

A number of the most successful TPTDs in Japan illustrate clearly the importance of a number of features of this group. Holland Village[1] in Nagasaki (Kyushu), with its obvious disadvantage of location away from the most populous catchment areas of Japan, is a classic case, its popularity and hence profitability being due to its management policies, especially the training and motivation of staff.

The stereotype used by a number of post-1989 Japanese TPTDs has been Tokyo Disneyland, both in terms of general layout, type of attractions and management style. Consequently, visitors tend to be processed through the park, which offers a clean, secure, informed environment. An important lesson that these newer and smaller *clone* type developments are beginning to learn, is that Tokyo Disneyland, with its ten years of operation and profits, is continually adapting with new themes and rides. These innovations, although spectacular and popular, are very expensive – Tokyo Disneyland's Splash Mountain Ride (1991) cost around £100 million. The importance of planning and costing ahead for this adaptability is critical in these particular types of TPTD. Management is therefore a critical ingredient for success.

Political, entrepreneurial and financial factors may literally be considered as the *raison d'être* of TPTDs in Japan. Without business sponsorships and hence the entrepreneurial spirit, a number of theme parks would not have come into existence, for example Reoma World (Shikoku).

Figure 9.1 *Theme parks in Japan*

An important feature of Japan's TPTDs, both before and after the 1988 boom has been the continual and effective involvement of prefectural and, particularly, local government. The influential 1987 Resort Law (passed by the Japanese Diet) effectively encouraged local government to create or renew resort area type developments (including theme parks). The Japan Development Bank was mandated to 'pump-prime', by offering low interest rates to local government for such developments. The result has been strong political support during the conceptual and planning stages as well as financial contributions to projects. There is, however, wide variation in involvements from a shareholding of 3% in the case of Tokyo Disneyland to nearly 30% investment in Space World.

Politicians in Japan have been known to vie with each other to attract a TPTD to their own locality, in the hope that it will create the demand for labour, and therefore will regenerate a declining area, or simply promote an otherwise less commercially successful locality. For example, the virtual gift of reclaimed land in Tokyo bay by China prefecture to Tokyo Disneyland, was considered by both parties to be beneficial.

A selection of the key variables of social and technological changes, in respect to Japan, include: rising disposable incomes (Table 9.5), increasing available free time (in terms of actual hours worked (Figure 9.2); and demographic changes (greater life expectancy, hence an elderly population). Directly relevant are people's present and future expectations of their leisure time, which are related to lifestyles, life stage and the technologies available, especially electronics with its capacity to create simulators of virtual reality. A further important variable within this group is the redeployment of labour. The area around Kita Kyushu, once predominant in steel-making and shipbuilding, now looks to the leisure industry to absorb its labour force, at least in part.

These four groups of factors are present in all the Japanese TPTDs. (They may also be relevant to Europe's present theme parks, but could have even greater significance for future developments, and for those still in the embryonic planning stage.) It is important to note that the post-1988 Japanese boom slowed down considerably in 1993, and a number of proposals, especially by enthusiastic local governments, have been cancelled, or are awaiting a decision (Table 9.6). One example is the high-tech Tsukuba space port proposal (some 75 kilometres from Tokyo) which would have cost over £1.2 billion.

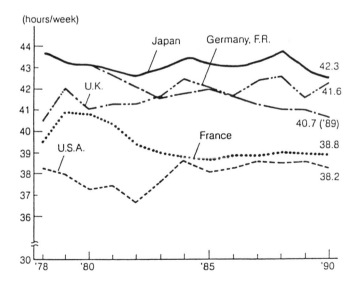

Figure 9.2 *A comparison of actual hours worked in manufacturing industry.* Japan and selected other countries, 1978–90

Source: Bank of Japan, Comparative International Statistics, 1991

Table 9.3 Size, development costs, investing companies and attendance data for a selection of theme parks in Japan

Name	Size/area		Investment cost[1]		Main investing companies	Annual attendance data 1991–2 (million)
	Hectares	Acres	¥ 100 million	£ million		
Tokyo Disneyland	82.6	204.1	2070	863	Mitsui Real Estates, Keisei Train Co., Chiba Pref. Urayasu City, etc.	15.7
Nagasaki Holland Village	10.0	24.7	162	67.6	Nagasaki-Motor Bus Co., Kogyo-Bank, Daishinto	2.0
Nikko Edo Village	44.0	108.7	105	43.8		1.8
Donguri Village	8.5	21.0	19	7.9	Yokoo, Mise-Village	0.5
Shikoku New Zealand Village	13.0	32.1	20	8.3	Saijo Metal	0.4
Kushikino Gold Park	3.0	7.4	16	6.7	Kagoshima, Kushikino-City	0.4
Mie Children's Castle	1.2	3.0	29	12.1	Mie healthy growing children Co.	0.1
Gluck Kingdom	9.2	22.7	40	16.7	Zenrin Jisho Construction, etc.	0.7
Tohoku New Zealand Village	67.0	165.5	27	11.3	Saijo Metal	0.4
Yamadera Fuga Country	3.0	7.4	20	8.3	Sanmangoku, etc.	0.1
Hizen Dream Road	6.5	16.1	34	14.2	Wadaya–Besso	1.0

Space World	33.0	81.51	300	125.0	Shin Nihon Steel, Kita Kyushu City, etc.	2.0
Canadian World	48.0	118.6	45	18.8	Ashibetsu-City, Tokyo Group, etc.	0.4[2]
Noboribetsu Marine Park 'Nikusu'	7.5	13.5	75	31.3	Shimizu Real Estates, Noboribetsu-City, etc.	0.7
Osaka Tenpozan Harbour Village	4.0	9.9	215	89.6	Osaka–City, etc.	3.6[2] (4.2)
Tokyo Sesame Place	2.9	7.2	50	20.8	Tokyo Summer Land, etc.	0.5[2]
Harmony Land	20.8	51.4	115	47.9	Sanrio, Oita-Prefecture, etc.	1.0[2]
Reoma World	69.0	173.4	700	291.7	Japan Golf Co.	5.0[2] (4.0)

Sources: verbal information from Japan Travel Bureau Research Division; *Business Japan*, October 1991; *Nikkei Business* 8 July 1991

Notes
1   The median conversion rate for 1988–91 of 240 Japanese yen = £1 has been used
2   Estimate only
( ) Actual attendance

Table 9.4 *An evaluation of Japanese theme parks: suggested influencing factors*

Group 1 Physical/location	1. 2. 3. 4. 5.	Location Accessibility Catchment area potential Land availability Promotion of regional/city identity
Group 2 Management operations	6. 7. 8. 9.	Management operations: (i) High standards of customer service (ii) High standards of cleanness (iii) High standards of security* (iv) Visitor perception Staff training Marketing including (i) Advertising (ii) Public relations (iii) Creation of a 'brand image' Theme adaptability (hardware and software)
Group 3 Political, entrepreneurial and financial	10. 11. 12. 13.	Political initiatives and investment Business sponsorships Land acquisition costs Substantive infrastructure costs
Group 4 Social and technological changes/trends	14. 15. 16. 17. 18.	Rising disposable incomes Increasing available free time Increased perceptions of leisure opportunities (life style/life stage/new technologies) Demographic changes Restructuring of labour markets (including labour availability)

* It is worth noting that security is virtually taken for granted in Japan but this factor is of much greater significance in the United States and Europe.

The affluent Japanese are now realising the very high costs involved in providing high-tech and sophisticated software and hardware for the types of mass entertainment to be found in mega-developments such as Tokyo Disneyland.

TPTDs are supply-led investments, and according to the Japanese Development Bank (which has partially funded in large measure the post-1988 local government initiatives in the leisure and resort industries) they are beginning to think seriously about a more rational and researched

Table 9.5 *A comparison of per capita incomes and annual real growth rates in some selected countries*

Country		Per capita income (US dollars)	Real annual growth rates, 1986–90 (%)
1.	Switzerland	29 100	+ 2.5
2.	Japan	23 500	+ 4.7
3.	Sweden	21 800	+ 0.9
4.	USA	20 900	+ 2.8
5.	West Germany	19 300	+ 3.1
6.	Australia	17 500	+ 3.4
7.	France	17 000	+ 3.1
8.	United Kingdom	14 700	+ 3.1

Source: Adapted from Comparative International Statistics 1991.
Economic Planning Agency Japan.

approach to the distribution of theme parks in terms of their type, size and location, particularly in respect of the finite domestic market. Research will be needed in respect of the longer-term goals of some of the existing and proposed TPTDs (for example, the expansion plans for Tokyo Disneyland, House Tempos, Nagasaki and the proposed Kobe Magical Journeys theme park). It is worth emphasising that their collective stated objective is to develop strong markets from neighbouring Pacific countries such as Singapore, Taiwan, South Korea and Australia.

The future

The remainder of the 1990s is likely to be the critical period for TPTDs in Japan as it may be in other parts of the developing and developed world: Europe, Australia, Asia (including mainland China) to mention only three continents currently interested in the theme park concept. Unfortunately, systematic research has not been undertaken on a number of critical issues in connection with this growing phenomenon, itself a response to the growth of mass leisure expectations. The empirical research so urgently needed by developers, government organisations, land-use and transport planners, marketing groups, sociologists and the leisure industry in general may be conveniently grouped under three very broad headings: identity; investment; and impacts.

The increasing number of theme parks world-wide highlights how fundamental the *identity* question has and will become. There is so much

Table 9.6 A selection of theme parks in Japan under construction, cancelled in the planning stages, or awaiting a decision, 1992

Stated name	Location	Size/area		Investment cost		Main investing companies	Situation (mid–1992)
		Hectares	Acres	¥100 Million	£ Million		
European Village	Fukushima, Kitashiobara-Town	71	175.4	185	77.1	Itochu Shoji, Asuka Construction, etc.	1988
Tsukuba Space Port	Ibaraki, Tsukuba-City	317	783.0	3000	1250	Mitsubishi Shoji	Cancelled
Narita Japan Village	Chiba, Narita-City	50	123.5	300	125	Narita-City, Nissho Iwai, etc.	Postponed/may cancel
Cosmo World	Kanagawa, Yokohama-City	33	81.5	500	208.3	Cosmo Development (Cosmo Oil)	1995
Izumo Myth Land	Shimane, Izumo-City	190	469.3	1000	416.7	Izumo Resort Development	2000
Tivoli Park Kushikino	Okayama, Okayama-City	16.8	41.5	800	333.3	Okayama-Prefecture, etc.	Postponed/may cancel
Shikoku Festival Village	Kagawa, Nakaminami-Town			12	5	Kotohira Bus	Cancelled
Kyushu Asia Land	Kumamoto, Arao-City	86	212.4	1800	750	Mitsui Bussan, etc.	Postponed/may cancel
Huis Ten Bosch	Nr Nagasaki	120	296.4	1300	541.7*	Kogyo Bank, Nagasaki	Opened March 1992

(House Tempos)						Motor Bus, etc.	
Magical Journeys	Kobe, Hyogo	50	123.5	1500	625.0	Kobe City, etc.	To be opened 1993 or 1994
Nagasaki Vaticano	Nagasaki	6	14.8	1000	416.7	N/A	Decision N/A
Twin Dome City	Fukuoka	20	49.4	2000	833.3	N/A	Decision N/A
Wildlife Park	Wakayama	3	7.4	7	2.9	Wakajama Prefecture, etc.	Postponed/may cancel
21st Century Marine Dream City	Nr Kobe Hyogo	180	444.6	1700	708.3	Hyogo Prefecture, etc.	N/A
Alsace Village	Ito Shizuoka	1.5	3.7	41	17.1	Shizuoka Prefecture	Decision N/A
Fairy Woods	Nagano	119.5	295.2	13.9	5.8	N/A	Decision N/A
Japan Santa Land	Aomori	26	64.2	90	37.5	N/A	Decision N/A

Sources: Adapted from Business Japan, October 1991; and verbal information from Japan Development Park and from Professor S. Komori on behalf of Kobe City government

* First phase only.

variation in theme types, differentiation, scale and size of operation and product specification and presentation and in the marketing strategies adopted. It is therefore important for the leisure industry governments and planners to have some accepted quantitative and/or qualitative bench mark that investors, analysts and policy-makers can refer to when making consequential decisions on TPTDs in their respective countries.

Directly related to the identity question is the need for a better understanding of the *investment* opportunities and drawbacks of this particular growing supply-led tertiary sector. Huge investments have been required for some of the larger-scale TPTDs in Japan: for example, Tokyo Disneyland (£863 million approximately, at 1983 prices, first phase only); Reoma World, partially modelled upon Tokyo Disneyland (£542 million approximately at 1991 prices). Similar sums have been invested in the high-tech Twin Dome City proposal in Fukuoka (£833 million) and in the Marine Dream City proposal near Kobe-City (£708 million). Although planning, land commitment and local and prefectural government involvement have reached an advanced stage in these two latter named developments, they could still be cancelled due to uncertainty, now that it is beginning to be realised how high are the financial risks associated with these larger and high-tech developments.

The inevitable *impacts* of TPTDs need to be fully realised and measured, therefore a few key questions must be addressed concerning physical, social and economic impacts. How many mega theme parks can Europe or any continent accommodate? What are the likely generative effects of such theme parks on the creation of other leisure developments, locally and regionally? What is likely to be the modal split of the visitors? Will theme park type entertainment, especially fantasies (including virtual reality) and rides become the norm for mass entertainment, and if so, for which social groups? Will there be a long-term 'cultural' price to be paid for this form of leisure entertainment? How important in terms of employment (including redeployment) are theme parks likely to become? Will theme parks be able to make an economic contribution to the region in which they are located? What might be suitable measurement indices? It is suggested that the theme park concept is with us for the foreseeable future. Its many manifestations will become increasingly important in terms of land use, traffic generation, mass entertainment (of the reactive type) and service employment. Research on this subject by a number of academic disciplines is therefore both pragmatic and urgent.

Note

1 On 25 March 1992 this particular TPTD was changed from its present form, with the same management opening a similar but much larger TPTD known as *Huis Ten Bosch* (House Tempos) about 24 kilometres away. This particular development has cost £100 million to date.

References

Alder, J. and Martin, B., 1990, 'An experience of captivity', *Newsweek*, July: 50–51.

Anthony, S., 1990, 'Top draw Osaka aquarium', *Australian Business*, May: 94–5.

Brown, J. and Church A., 1987, 'Theme parks in Europe', *Travel and Tourism Analyst*, February: 35–46.

Economic Intelligence Unit, 1990, 'Attendance trends and future developments at Europe's leisure attractions', *Travel and Tourism Analyst*, Report no. 2: 52–75.

Ferguson, A., 1989, 'Maximising the mouse', *Management Today*, September: 56–62.

Lewis, R.K., 1990, 'In the US and beyond, museums enter the age of aquariums', *Museum News*, December: 21–2.

Lowe, J., 1985, 'Science parks in the UK', *Lloyds Bank Review*, 156: 31–42.

Institute for Social and Economic Affairs, 1992, *Japan: an international comparison*, Keizai Koho Centre, Tokyo.

Johnson, S., 1988, 'British theme parks: room for more but no takers', *Leisure Management*, 8(7): 38–44.

Johnson, S., 1990, 'Roller coaster fortunes', *Leisure Management*, 10(3): 41–3.

Jones, T.S.M., 1987, 'Discover urban development', *Public Space*, no. 9, Nihon Kotso Bunka Kyokai, Tokyo: 1–17.

King, D. 1985, 'Will leisure parks be a theme for the future?', *Marketing Week*, November: 38–42.

Learner, C., 1990, 'A theme for the future', *Leisure Management*, 10(10): 51–6.

Martin, B. and Mason, S., 1990, 'What's the attraction?', *Leisure Management*, 10(8): 22–5.

Ministry of Labour, 1992, *Japanese Working Life, Profile*, Institute of Labour, Tokyo.

Moutihno, L., 1988, 'Amusement park visitor behaviour' *Tourism Management*, 9(4): 291–300.

Nemoto, Y., 1990, 'Japanese theme parks come of age', *Funworld*, October: 16–17.

Ohoka, S., 1991a, 'Theme parks provide outlets for leisure-seeking children and adults', *Business Japan*, October: 34–5.

Ohoka, S., 1991b, 'Meeting the potential for waterfront development', *Business Japan*, December: 50–53.

Ohoka, S., 1991c, 'Metropolitan bay development: a renaissance of urban life', *Business Japan*, August: 38–41.

Ohoka, S., 1991d, 'Urban development and regional development in Japan taking a new turn', *Business Japan*, July: 40–43.

Oliver, D., 1989, 'Leisure parks present and future', *Tourism Management*, 9(3): 233–4.

Shurmer-Smith, 1988, 'Eurodisneyland: will it pull Paris east', *Town and Country Planning*, 57(4): 120–21.

Tucker, D., 1991, 'Themes and schemes', *Leisure Management*, 11(2): 22–4.

Tourism Research and Marketing, 1990, *UK Theme Parks. A Market Report*, Tourism Research and Marketing, London.

Acknowledgement

I wish to record the help received from Professors H. Hirooka (Hosei University, Tokyo) and Y. Konishi (Kobe University, Kobe) and S. Ohoka (Japan Development Bank) in the preparation of this chapter.

10 The regulation of the Hong Kong travel trade

P.L. Atkins

Introduction

During 1986–8, Hong Kong suffered a number of travel agency failures and abscondments – among them Peninsular Tours (*South China Morning Press* (*SCMP*), 23 February 1986), Austravel and PC Travel (*SCMP*, 1 February 1987) – leaving many thousands of people with frustrated travel plans, and with losses of HK $30 million. The Travel Agents Reserve Fund, established under the Travel Agency Ordinance of 1985 following a previous bout of complaints and bankruptcies, was unable to acquit the losses. The fund made up of annual fees of HK $2500 from each travel agent and administered by the Department of Economic Services, was exhausted. The governments intention to levy an additional fee of HK $5000 on travel agents to cover the shortfall was met by industry objection and in several cases refusal ('Legco orders travel trade to pay victims', *SCMP*, 16 May 1987). These incidents were widely reported in both the UK and Chinese press, with much commentary about their impact on both Hong Kong consumers and international tourists.

Over the same period the Hong Kong Consumer Council received a large number of complaints about travel agents' failure to provide reasonable or promised service and demanding additional fees and supplementary payments. As a result the Consumer Council lobbied the government for more stringent and enforced protection (*SCMP*, 18 February 1988).

These incidents brought to a head the need for additional regulation in travel agency operations, both from the point of view of the protection of consumers, and to allow for the continued development of this increasingly significant economic activity (*SCMP*, 18 February 1988).

Tourism inbound to Hong Kong is already the third highest earner of foreign exchange, and one of the largest areas of economic activity. World-wide, tourism is considered by some as the largest industry (Richter 1990); and common to all commentators is the view that its future holds continued growth, making it an important topic for government concern.

While most Hong Kong commentators dwell on the aspect of inbound tourism, which in terms of arrivals has grown by 2.68 times since 1979, outbound tourism has grown almost as rapidly, 2.5 times, and is projected to grow at least as much and possibly even outstrip inbound tourism growth (Table 10.1).

Table 10.1 *Tourist arrivals and departures, Hong Kong, 1979–95*

Year	Visitor arrivals (millions)	Departing residents (millions)
1979	2.2	0.8
1980	2.3	0.9
1981	2.5	1.1
1982	2.6	1.1
1983	2.8	1.1
1984	3.1	1.1
1985	3.4	1.2
1986	3.7	1.3
1987	4.5	1.4
1988	5.6	1.6
1989	5.4	1.8
1990	5.9	2.0
1991 *	6.2	2.2
1992 *	6.6	2.5
1993 *	7.0	2.8
1994 *	7.5	3.1
1995 *	8.0	3.5

Sources: Hong Kong Tourist Association, Hong Kong government

* Projected figures

Hong Kong

Hong Kong is widely known as an international tourist destination, an East-meets-West environment, and a major business and commercial centre, as well as, more recently, a growing conference and exhibition centre. Visitor arrivals to Hong Kong have doubled in the decade 1980–1990, an enviable position of marginally faster growth than the Asia–Pacific region, which itself demonstrated higher growth than the rest of the world at 45 per cent.

Hong Kong travel agents also act as intermediaries for international agents and operators. The failure of travel agencies in Hong Kong has implications not only for outbound tourism, but also for arriving and onward bound international tourism.

The predicted demand for outbound tourism from Hong Kong may to a large extent be determined by the lack of any significant domestic tourism potential in Hong Kong.

Although there are a few opportunities for the pursuit of leisure (counting parks, cycle paths and the outlying islands), Hong Kong is small, crowded and its resources so heavily utilised, that domestic tourism does not really exist to any degree. Richter (1989, p. 3) argues that domestic tourism far exceeds the value of international tourism, and goes on to suggest that this is why tourism already stands as the biggest economic activity in the world. The lack of domestic opportunity for tourism in

Hong Kong is a significant factor in the projections for the growth of outbound tourism business.

It can therefore be argued that whatever the style of and approach to the control of travel agents and tour operators, to allow for the progressive and smooth growth of this economic activity, regulation and consumer protection are necessary.

The Hong Kong government's approach to intervention and regulation

The government department responsible for the supervision and regulation of all business enterprise in Hong Kong, including travel agencies, is the Department of Trade. It is widely accepted that Hong Kong is one of the most unregulated free market economies in the world. It has been offered as a model by Western politicians wanting to remove or reduce government involvement in their own national business and trade environment. Yee (1989) suggests that the reasons are cultural, and argues that the common denominator in Chinese success in many diversified areas, is the ability to seize opportunities and respond flexibly to changing conditions.

The Hong Kong government, and individuals within it, appear to believe in the philosophy of non-intervention as the most positive way to encourage economic activity, economic growth and the territory's well-being ('The laid back lawyer hopes for stability', *SCMP*, 16 June 1986). Such is the belief in this philosophy that the Chairman of the Consumer Council, following the collapse of Austravel (*SCMP*, 20 February 1987), is reported as having said: 'Extensive investigative powers cannot be immediately introduced, and any attempt by a Government Instrument to regulate private sector finances would be disastrous'.

This aversion to direct intervention is the foundation for the development of travel agency regulation in Hong Kong, using a self-regulatory model, but without the experience, traditions and established processes of, say, the Association of British Travel Agents (ABTA). The self-regulatory process and mechanisms, while already being significantly effective, will undoubtedly develop and flourish over the ensuing years.

It is important to note that, according to a number of researchers and commentators (Richter 1989, pp. 3, 14; Atkins 1987, pp. 170, 113) the central and overriding government interest and motivation in tourism is maximizing the economic benefits, or, as in this case, encouraging economic activity.

The Hong Kong business environment

Hong Kong is a successful industrial and commercial centre; its success, however, is rarely investigated. Reddin (1990), in one of the few analytical works on the success of Chinese entrepreneurship, concludes that much of the self-evident success is due to three factors: the need for achievement and the ability to take risk; family values; and materialism related to the lack of stability and doubts about the future.

The family is very important in Chinese culture, but family values can be characterised as utilitarian (Reddin 1990, p. 274). Families stick together and demonstrate high levels of loyalty, because that is the most profitable and rewarding thing to do. Reddin sees this as having three distinct features: Confucian ideals, especially concerning the family; materialism; and adaptability (based on the need to accommodate to the environment). These factors tend to determine a seriousness in any business concern; they lead to organisations that are small and family-based; and a great deal of flexibility in business objectives, activity and behaviour (Yee 1989, p. 185). Adaptiveness is the most commonly used explanation of Hong Kong's economic success.

Whereas instability is usually considered a deterrent to business growth, the historical social and political instability in the Chinese culture has encouraged materialism as a hedge against future difficulties, an insurance against future misfortune.

Consumer protection in Hong Kong

Based on the British legal system, but with the addition of Chinese customary law, Hong Kong's legal system is unique. When Hong Kong adopted British law on 5 April 1843, it adopted all the laws in force on that date but did not automatically adopt any that followed. Although the situation changed slightly in 1966 when a Hong Kong Ordinance introduced the possibility of taking account of changes in common law and equity, where locally relevant, Hong Kong law, despite its base, is not the same as British law. Its development since 1843 has been largely independent. The Legislative Council (LEGCO) is the current legislature.

Consumer protection in Hong Kong is less well developed than in the UK, USA and other Western economies. It is covered by the Sale of Goods Ordinance (SOGO). Services were specifically excluded from this legislation, but protection was extended to this area by the Control of Exemption Clauses Ordinance, 1990. Before then, protection was the province exclusively of common law, with recourse available under the law of contract, consumer protection being based in general terms on the *caveat emptor* (let the buyer beware) principle, requiring the consumer to take all precautions for himself or herself.

There have in the past been many fearful stories of tourists being cheated ('Rethink on consumer protection', *Hong Kong Standard* (*HKS*), 23 September 1985; 'New law planned to protect shoppers', *SCMP*, 20 October 1986; 'Time to protect the consumer', *HKS*, 17 August 1988). While regrettable, these incidents are related to the common law position in Hong Kong of *caveat emptor*. The 'cheated' tag is attached by consumers from different cultures who were not suitably well informed or prepared.

Additionally, having returned home, it is very difficult for tourists to do anything about being duped. This situation, of a lack of consumer protection is common in the South East Asia region, reflecting the very recent economic development of the region, and the still developing organisations, institutions and processes that Western economies take for granted.

Hong Kong travel agency operations

Not surprisingly, travel agencies in Hong Kong reflect many of the characteristics of Chinese-owned business in general. They are highly adaptive, entrepreneurial, small in size and family-orientated. One only has to look at the collapsed travel agents, Austravel and PC Travel ('Junior partner throws light on Peninsular', *SCMP*, 26 July 1986), to see the family connections in their financing and operations.

The flexibility of travel agents in Hong Kong is further illustrated by the estimates and analysis of Travel Industry Council (TIC) membership and member operations (Table 10.2), compared say, to ABTA of the UK.

Table 10.2 *Comparison of TIC and ABTA membership figures*

	ABTA No.	(% of all)	TIC No.	(% of all)
Travel agents	2970	91.0	326	30
Tour operators	700	21.5	180	15
Operators/agents	344	9.5	601	55
Total Membership	3260		1070	

Sources: TIC Annual Report, 1991; estimates from the TIC Executive Director. ABTA figures from Howarth Book of Tourism, 1990

Regulation of travel and tourism in Hong Kong

The licensing of travel agents has been a requirement since 1986, when the government passed the first Travel Agents Ordinance, appointed a Registrar of Travel Agents, and imposed some minor requirements on entry into the travel agency business.

Until 1988 there were only three requirements for the issuing of a licence: that the principal was not nor had recently been a bankrupt; that the proposed business had premises and paid-up capital; and that the owners and executives did not have criminal records.

The Travel Agents Ordinance, of 1986 also established the Travel Industry Reserve Fund. This fund, managed by the Department of Trade, sought to provide compensation payments to consumers who suffered from travel agency failures. The reserve fund was funded by an annual payment from travel agents, and in the ensuing two years it was demonstrated that this payment was insufficient to cover the level of failure and abscondments that occurred.

It was only in 1988 that the government examined the travel trade organisations to explore which of them was representative enough to execute the role of the official trade organisation and the activity of regulation and enforcement. The result was the Revised Travel Agents Ordinance of 1989, which incorporated additional requirements for the granting of a licence, including membership of the TIC.

Registrar of Travel Agents

The Registrar of Travel Agents, is charged, by the Travel Agents Ordinance, to license operators in the travel trade. He has the benefit of an Advisory Committee on travel agents, whose chairman and membership are appointed by the Governor. There are a large number of conditions related to the suitability of an applicant, most of which are delegated to the TIC to ensure.

These requirements include, the owner or partners being fit to conduct business, suitable premises, financial suitability (paid-up funds, etc.) and membership of an approved organisation, membership of the TIC, as well as an experience requirement of the manager or staff. In the case of refusal of a licence to an applicant, the Ordinance provides for the right of appeal.

Travel Industry Council of Hong Kong

The TIC is a registered public company, charged under the Travel Agency Ordinance with a number of functions within the travel industry: control of entry to the travel trade; training and upgrading of travel agents; improving consumer protection on travel and tourism products; and collecting and managing the TIC Reserve Fund.

TIC structure and activities

The TIC has a Board of Directors, a Board of Directors of the Reserve Fund and a Board of Directors of the TIC Bonding Fund. There is some overlap of membership between the boards.

The administrative structure of the TIC is based around six departments: Membership; Tours Registration; Accounts; Secretarial; Administration; and Public Relations. Its main activities are based around each of its 15 standing committees, each with a secretariat, and each with its own chairman and committee members. The committee is made up of elected representatives from TIC membership, plus co-opted members from relevant other organisations. There are also some mandatory non-TIC members; for instance, the Reserve Fund has on it two members of the Trade and Industry Branch of the Hong Kong Government.

The TIC employs an executive director and 22 full-time staff, to execute its many functions. Its major requirement is to fulfil its regulatory role and to service, organise and coordinate the 15 standing committees.

Membership
After a dramatic increase in membership during 1988–9, membership has levelled off during the early 1990s, standing at 1070 members in January 1992 (see Table 10.3). Entry and exit from the industry are about equal, and represent a 7 per cent turnover in membership each year.

Association members are the supporting associations, from which TIC draws its membership. Membership of one of the associations, justifies and is a requirement of membership of the TIC. Most of the TIC members (73 per cent) are only members of one association, 18 per cent are members of two, and the rest are members of three or more.

Affiliate members may only trade as travel agents; they may not themselves package and promote their own packages.

Ordinary members have the right both to act as travel agents and to design, organise and execute package tours, so in general terms these are tour operator/travel agency members.

Table 10.3 *TIC membership*

	June 1989	*June 1990*	*June 1991*	*Jan 1992*
Ordinary members	758	781	781	781
Affiliate members	326	298	272	326
Total	1084	1079	1053	1070

Source: TIC annual report, 1991

Codes of practice and regulations
The TIC produces codes of practice for the guidance of its members, which in law have no weight whatsoever, but which are the basis for the actions of the disciplinary and compliance committee.

The TIC codes currently available are the following:

* General Code of Conduct for TIC Members Travel Agents
* Code of Business Practice for Tour Operators
* Business Practice Code of Advertising Practice for Travel Agents
* Recommended Practice for Conditions of Tour Booking.

These codes of practice are proposed by the committees, amended and after consultation with members, and approved by the TIC Board.

Enforcement of regulations
The TIC is responsible for the compliance of the travel trade with the regulations of the Travel Agents Ordinance. After entry to the TIC, and having gained a licence, this compliance is mainly concerned with the 1 per cent levy. The levy is applied to all packages (defined as transport, accommodation and sightseeing, when purchased at one and the same time), their published price, and not to other travel and tourism products.

The TIC enforces payment of the levy not by carrying out investigations itself, but through a security firm which employs people to pose as customers, purchase tourism products, and report any failure to *frank* the receipt. The process of franking is carried out by the agent using a franking machine hired from the TIC for that specific purpose. This independent investigator approach and process is endorsed by the ICAC, and its aim is to ensure impartiality and fairness.

The TIC also collects and processes complaints of any nature about its members, and can enter into a conciliation and eventual arbitration process with the disputing parties.

TIC sources of funds
In addition to the 1 per cent levy on the invoice price of travel and tourism packages paid by the travel agent to the TIC Reserve Fund, the TIC publishes and sells certain documents, and runs training courses from which payments are received.

The TIC Reserve Fund is for the compensation of consumers in the event of a travel agent's failure or abscondment and is not, except for a single annual payment, available for the administration of the TIC itself.

It is interesting to note that the new Legislative Councillor for the Tourism Constituency, was elected on six promises, one of which is to reduce the 1 per cent levy, a promise he is committed to acting on. The TIC is charged by the government with setting standards, ensuring compliance, educating and developing its travel agent members, but is so restricted with regard to resources that it is not easily able to innovate or develop its role. Travel agents have demonstrated extreme sensitivity about the amount of the Reserve Fund levy, as well as its usage ('Travel crises fund paying for expenses', *SCMP*, 2 March 1991). The problem for the TIC is how can it operate effectively, when it has little discretion over its income, and therefore the level of its activities. It takes all of present budget just to maintain the present level of activities; expanding and developing them is not possible without additional funding.

In 1991 the TIC received from the TIC Reserve Fund HK $5,566,758 for administration and expenses. This represents approximately 94 per cent of the TIC's total operating costs. This amount is bid for by the TIC and allocated by the Reserve Fund Board of Directors.

Most of the application of TIC funds is for staffing, given its structure and supporting committee network. The second major expenditure is for premises, once again, not unsurprising in Hong Kong where land and property prices are so high.

Travel Industry Reserve Fund
The reserve fund is growing at the rate of approximately HK $32 million a year, and after just two years' operation is already a source of some antagonism from TIC members who cannot see the need for such a vast reserve fund, nor for the continued 1 per cent levy. This antagonism is reflected in sensitivity to the TIC itself, and the anxiety that it may be using the Reserve Fund to finance its general activities, rather than as a

reserve for travel agency failures or abscondments. In the event of abscondments or failure the consumer is able to claim compensation of 70 per cent of the price paid.

Future potential of and likely developments in the TIC

Perhaps the biggest single issue for the TIC is whether or not its role should be developed or expanded. While its achievements are impressive, there are many areas where it could develop further: for example, consumer protection for a wider range of products; and higher investment in the professional and technical development of its members. Whereas there is pressure from members to reduce the levy, and to reduce the size and activities of the TIC, its failure now or at any time in the future may open the industry to greater government control and regulation, presumably something TIC members would object to strongly.

In order to meet the objectives of further development of its activities, the TIC requires access to more funding. The limited consumer protection, only being for packages and not for the full range of travel and tourism products is a good example, as is the upper limit of 70 per cent compensation. In this context it might be useful for the Reserve Fund to explore ways of supporting and developing the TIC's work, rather than reducing the levy.

The positive achievements of the TIC are many, yet each of its achievements indicates an area of future potential:

* The TIC has produced 7 codes of practice, and has plans for several more.
* It executes some 20 training programmes, and maintains 15 committees focusing on each of its necessary and mandatory roles and strategic aims.
* Its main achievement is its effectiveness in reducing the number of complaints from consumers, and satisfactorily arbitrating and concluding those that occur.
* Reducing the level of failures and abscondments from the industry to nil, and becoming a forum and focus for the disparate and diverse organisations involved in the travel agency sector.
* Ensuring compliance of the travel trade with levy requirements and membership qualifications.

The Chairman and the Executive Director (*TIC Annual Report*, 1991) recognise there is still much to be achieved; however, no amount of wisdom and insight can overcome the lack of available funds.

Conclusion

There is no doubt that the case of travel agency regulation in Hong Kong points up a number of general issues. In particular the tensions between the various players are illuminating. On the one hand, the government sees inbound tourism as important to the economy and therefore justifies regulatory action in the travel agency sector. There are also issues of consumer protection here. On the other hand, the travel agency sector itself has traditionally comprised small family businesses and often has a negative reaction to government regulation. Recent legislation and the tide of opinion in Hong Kong suggest that in the early to mid-1990s the travel agency sector in Hong Kong will move away from regulation. However, this is not an isolated case, as deregulation of the tourism sector is fashionable in many locations around the world.

Postscript

The Travel Agents Amendment Bill of 1992 affects a number of issues discussed in this chapter. First, the levy was reduced to 0.5 per cent in 1992; it will continue to be charged on all packages at their published price. Second, compensation to consumers on the failure or abscondment of their agent will be increased from 70 per cent to 80 per cent. Third, the Travel Industry Central Reserve Fund has been reconstituted as an independent fund. Fourth, a floor limit (minimum reserve) of HK $70 million has been established for the fund, below which the 1 per cent levy would be reinstated. Finally the levy will now be divided between the Travel Industry Reserve Fund (70 per cent) and the Travel Industry Council (30 per cent).

References

Atkins, P.L., 1989, 'National tourism administrations of EEC member states', MSc thesis, University of Surrey.
Reddin, S.G., 1990, *The spirit of Chinese capitalism*, de Gruyter, New York.
Richter, L.K., 1989, *The politics of tourism in Asia*, University of Hawaii Press, Honolulu.
Yee, A.H., 1989, *A people misruled – Hong Kong and the Chinese stepping stone syndrome*, API Press, Hong Kong.

Food and beverage management

11 Yield management: the case for food and beverage operations

J. van Westering

Introduction

Since its inception in the 1950s, progress has been endemic to yield management (YM). Its implementation and mercurial impact on the American airline carrier industry in the 1970s are now somewhat legendary: YM marketing strategies were credited with achieving record profits in an industry in recession. Given this enviable effect in a parallel capacity-constrained service, the hotel industry recognised YM's potential and, in the mid-1980s, moved to adopt YM, its strategies and systems being concentrated on maximising revenue in rooms occupancy; Orkin's (1988) YM formula, itself legendary, dominated 1980s strategies.

Advances in computer technology and accompanying software development in the late 1980s (Hott *et al.* 1989) enabled sophisticated automated approaches to facilitate the application of YM to room occupancy; for investors this rendered YM 'immediate', with users claiming a 5 per cent revenue increase (Gamble 1992). However, investment, not surprisingly, has been restricted to the larger hotel groups, and with a few exceptions has been concentrated in the USA. Similarly, the key research projects have been virtually confined to the USA. Nevertheless, European ventures are increasing (Lee 1990; Akaydin 1993; Falck 1993). The major focus for contemporary advances in YM lies in computer software growth, although research and development are already surpassing these systems.

Progress points to the commercial application of artificial intelligence (AI)/expert systems (Sieburgh 1988; Hott *et al.* 1989; Relihan 1989) for predicting demand and ascertaining market pricing – key YM strategies. The indication is that these systems will increase the immediacy of YM, giving investors the crucial competitive advantages sought. Such possibilities are yet to be realised, with much research and development and commercial investment required, but it could be that they will be the norm by the mid-1990s.

While the full benefits of YM will not be realised without computer-based resources (particularly in forecasting demand) others can be achieved with little such investment. YM development comprises other elements: concurrent progress must be made in staff/guest education, product marketing, and the coordination of corporate policies (Lieberman 1993). Failure to invest in these areas could undermine the whole venture

(Hoyle 1970; Kimes 1989). Additionally the theoretical basis of YM should be carefully re-examined and its parameters widened; for example, the use of the market segment profit analysis (MSPA) approach to YM could ensure the application of YM to all hotel cost centres (Dunn and Brooks 1990; Brotherton and Mooney 1992). YM strategies would then be applied to all the hotel's services; logically YM would then be applied to food and beverage (F&B). YM strategies would be extended and adapted in such a reassessment process.

Yield management: current situation in the hotel industry

Irrespective of such progress, the fact is that the theory is far in advance of the practical application of YM. Regardless of the efficacy of theory, actually implementing innovation is a complex venture. It seems trite to quote Hoyle's (1970) 'innovation is difficult' understatement here; however, there is clear evidence that would-be innovators in the hotel industry are indeed failing to anticipate the difficulties; unless the innovation is based on deliberate and planned change 'yield management might be doomed to failure' (Kimes 1989). YM strategies have now been used in the hotel industry rooms division for some 15 years. Those familiar with the field of innovation will acknowledge that such a time-span is minimal: Rogers (1962; 1971) emphasised the long-term nature of the process (of successful innovation), citing 50 years, while Havelock (1971) reduced the figure to 35. YM in the USA is almost 40 years old; its strategies are well formulated, and its systems under constant scrutiny and development (Schmidgall 1989)

Caution, however, is important; a reminder that virtually all YM users are USA-based is crucial – YM in Europe remains, as yet, almost at the conceptual level, with minimum practical realisation. Only in the USA are significant hotel adoptions and successes regarding revenue maximisation documented. Whereas the use of YM in the airline industry has resulted in increased revenue running into millions of dollars (James 1987), the benefits for rooms division in the hotel industry are seen as, in general, qualitative rather than objectively quantifiable, although increased revenue has been cited extensively. The lack of public data – thus validating revenue increase claims – has prompted scepticism regarding the US enthusiasm for YM; this in itself is cited as one reason for the slow European response and apparent reluctance to invest in and adopt YM (Gamble 1991).

YM's slow progress in Europe is reinforced by the minimal amount of home-based literature and documentation available. Hence Lee's (1990) study of five London hotels using YM strategies (in room occupancy) somewhat disappointingly, yet not surprisingly, revealed that YM strategies had had scant impact on the UK hotel industry. Falck's (1993) work on YM in Finland reflected a similar response.

In Europe YM is considered too expensive (Falck 1993): £250,000 is reputed to have financed the UK Lanesborough Hotel's PMS (Property Management System) from Encore Systems (USA) (Anon 1992); few hotels are in such an advantageous position. Of the current eight publicly incorporated European hotel companies, Gamble (1991) suggests that only three might have the financial resources to implement YM systems. There are an estimated 58 240 establishments providing accommodation in the UK; 47 000 of these are small hotels (less than ten bedrooms) yet it is estimated that only around 3000 have any PMSs with many of these attached to groups (Anon 1992). As technology becomes a more crucial factor in the successful running of a hotel or a hotel group, PMS will be essential; there are already over 40 suppliers in the market. One supplier, HIS, has a major contract with De Vere for YM systems: there are currently approximately 80 UK installations. Clearly YM is gaining some impetus in Europe – but the indications are that to date the larger UK hotel groups have enjoyed sufficient profitability without investing heavily in YM (Gamble 1991). Smaller groups and individual UK hotels, suffering the financial losses incurred by chasing too few customers, might benefit from YM installations, and here simpler, less costly methods of implementation could be effective – prestigious installations not being essential for many properties.

Despite the caution and slow implementation it is clear that YM is having an impact on the industry (Sieburgh, 1988; Kimes 1989; Lee 1990). In the USA, YM has effected major upheavals in hotel organisational health (Schmidgall 1989). The much-needed key strategies and infrastructure are in place; although, to date, these have been related almost solely to room occupancy. YM has been applied in this area to reassess procedures and to maximise revenue. The London Copthorne Tara (Hotel and Caterer), the Hyatt and Hilton chains (Orkin 1988; Schmidgall 1989), and the Royal Sonesta (Sieburgh 1988) all subscribe to such claims while the five London hotels surveyed in Lee's (1990) study 'all professed to enjoy an increase in net profit and average room rate as a direct result of implementing yield management'. Similar service industries – car rentals and theatre ticket sales (Gamble 1992; Lieberman 1993) and pharmaceuticals, health care and manufacturing services (Wolff 1989) for example – clearly encouraged by such claims, have adopted YM; hotel F&B outlets, notorious for low profit margins and revenue losses, might, as a service industry, benefit from a similar approach.

Restaurant profitability has been viewed with increasing alarm during the last two decades. At one time losses in this department were acceptable and even justifiable, the quality of the food operation being used to attract customers to the hotel (Schmidt 1987). However, hotel restaurants can no longer continue as such in an ancillary role, pursuing 'safe mediocrity' (Riley and Davies 1992) without pursuing maximum revenues; long-term global recession problems preclude such luxury, no possible revenue source can be underplayed or overlooked, and all hotel services must contribute to the overall revenue, profitability and viability of the hotel. F&B outlets should equate themselves with rooms division in their determination to maximise revenue. Hotel F&B outlets are key cost centres (Dunn and Brooks 1990) of the hotel; restaurants, conference/banqueting space, and other services, including minor operating departments (MOD: parking and in-house shops, for example) may contribute substantially to a hotel's overall profitability; by concentrating only on the rooms function of a hotel, the YM system could be ignoring revenue opportunities in other parts of the hotel (Kimes 1989).

Yield management: the case for Food and Beverage

YM was initially adopted by the hotel industry because it was seen to have several attributes in common with the airline industry – characteristics which made them both 'ideal candidates for yield-management systems' (Kimes 1989). F&B services appear similar to carrier/rooms division services (all have relatively fixed capacities and all serve segmented, clearly identifiable markets, for example), indicating that benefits might be gained by applying YM to this section of the hotel industry. It is arguable that, since F&B is seen to be failing, some structure to enhance revenue should be imposed upon F&B. YM might provide an answer. Implementation of YM in F&B will not happen overnight; clearly the process needs to be developed over time: however, since YM strategies have now been used in the hotel industry for 15 years, its application to F&B might now be appropriately investigated and implemented. The conditions which enabled YM to be applied to other service industries successfully are clearly relevant. Kimes (1989) postulated six essential conditions which an industry or service should meet for implementation of YM to be effective – the industry must deal with segmented markets; a perishable inventory; advanced sales; fluctuating demand; low marginal sales costs; and high marginal production costs. F&B has all these characteristics – its space/products are often sold in advance; are perishable; deal with segmented markets/different types of customer; show varied demand patterns; and have low marginal sales costs and high marginal production costs – all reinforce the potential for applying YM to F&B. YM was initially applied to failing or industries experiencing problems. Given the financial losses usually associated with F&B outlets, it is surprising that YM has not been used as a tool to assist this section of the industry. YM is directed towards maximising revenue, and yet there appears to be some reluctance to apply it, or indeed alternative organisational systems, to the F&B industry as a whole. Some limited use has been recorded in the banqueting departments of some hotels (Dunn and Brooks 1990).

There is minimal information available on the application of YM to F&B. Previous research in the field of F&B has focused on such issues as: forecasting (for staffing, and food and beverage sales) (Schmidgall 1989); pricing; productivity; working conditions; technological innovations and profitability (this being increasingly linked to leasing F&B space to outside companies!) (Scarpa 1993). Such research has tended to tackle singular concerns rather than taking a holistic view. The two key problems in F&B, low profitability and staffing, are interrelated and overlapping; issues such as fluctuating demand, fixed space, a high payroll percentage, high staff turnover, stressful working conditions, unsociable hours and escalating personnel and training costs can no longer be treated individually – they need confronting together. YM could be directed to address the problems of profitability and staffing simultaneously – in order to attack problems at their source, sometimes principles have to change.

The application of yield management to Food and Beverage

YM is essentially a pricing strategy (Relihan 1989; Dunn and Brooks 1990) which aims to maximise revenue and does so by manipulating demand which in turn effects more profitable staffing patterns. For example, filling a restaurant with lower-paying customers, as a pricing strategy, improves liquidity and ensures full employment of staff. With staffing costs often around 35–40 per cent of turnover, overheads in F&B are the main concern of management. Forced reduction of payroll costs will unavoidably lead to reduced service levels. Hence the emphasis on increasing turnover by many F&B managers, often through special promotions – for example, weeks in which a country or ingredient features in order to attract customers from outside or to increase the custom of the in-house customer. Although these campaigns are often reasonably successful they usually create other costs such as PR and leave a minimally lasting effect. Voucher systems (Beefeater) and Early Bird offers (Harvester) are further examples of such manipulation; the response to these cannot be anticipated or controlled. Demand has to be spread; strategies must be used to change the patterns and widen markets. Current economic experience suggests that markets closer to home should be exploited to ensure restaurant development; gone are the times when the restaurant only served in-house guests.

YM aims to maximise revenue by allocating the right kind of space/ product to the right kind of customer at the right price. For F&B this means that pricing should be used according to fluctuating demand; even if demand cannot be controlled, it can be manipulated. In order to increase turnover, F&B should look for different markets and be willing to exploit its biggest advantage – the almost unlimited hours of the day in which food and drink can be served. Changes in the population's eating behaviour emphasise the relevance of the latter – the more recent 'grazing' (Jones 1993) trend might direct F&B managers to rethink services available.

The application of YM to F&B entails the cyclical process of forecasting occupancy, setting prices accordingly and using the yield statistic. A simple adaptation of Orkin's (1988) formula could be applied. The F&B yield statistic (YS) can be expressed as follows:

$$\text{Yield} = \frac{\text{Actual covers revenue}}{\text{Covers revenue potential}} \times 100\%$$

The actual covers revenue (ACR) is the product of covers sold (CS) and average spend (AS). The covers revenue potential (CRP) is the product of the covers available (CA) multiplied by the potential spend (PS). Thus the YS shows the relationship between the available covers and the potential revenue from these covers, and expresses this as a percentage. This percentage depends, of course, on how the potential amount of covers and average spend are calculated.

Given that we can break down ACR and CRP, we can derive the following yield management formula:

$$\text{Yield} = \frac{CS}{\text{Potential covers}} \times \frac{AS}{PS} \times 100\%$$

In this equation potential covers could be read as the total amount of covers available, or a multiple of this depending on seat turnover. Potential spend could also be set in different ways according to circumstances; in an *à la carte* restaurant this might be, for example, the total price of an expensive three-course meal with aperitif, half a bottle of wine, coffee and digestif.

The YS and the yield management formula are used for several purposes. For reasons of control and comparison, the yield percentage of a restaurant can be calculated for each meal period, as is shown in the example below, or per hour.

In this example the yield percentage of a restaurant is calculated for a dinner period. The restaurant contains 50 seats; its potential spend has been calculated as £40.

Dinner:	Day	Covers sold	Average spend	Yield
	1	30	£33.00	50%

Using the YM formula for day 1 the yield percentage is calculated as follows:

$$\text{Yield} = \frac{30}{50} \times \frac{33.00}{40.00} = 49.5\%$$

This can be repeated for all other days of the week:

2	35	£33.00	58%
3	30	£25.00	38%
4	15	£23.00	17%

and so on.

Based on records and according to influences such as hour of the day, the day of the week, the season and weather, the number of bookings and the number of in house customers, the yield statistic can be fixed to a particular percentage for the purpose of forecasting, as in the following example.

Dinner:	Day	Covers sold	Average spend	Yield
	1	30	£35.38	53%
	2	35	£30.28	53%
	3	40	£26.50	53%
	4	45	£23.55	53%

Potential covers: 50
Potential spend: £40

The YM formula can then be used to set prices or to target customer numbers. In the above restaurant example, the overall yield for the whole of the dinner period is set at 53%. This yield is reached by carefully setting prices in order to attract the forecasted number of customers or by using the projected number of customers to set prices as follows:

$$\text{Yield} = 53 = \frac{\text{covers forecasted} = 35}{50} \times \frac{Z}{40}$$

This calculation will prescribe which average spend should be reached. Based on this average spend, prices could be set. If the forecasted number of customers is higher than 35 as in the above example, the outcome of this calculation will be a lower price; when the number is lower, it will be higher. It is possible that of the forecasted number of customers several bookings might already have been received. Here YM pricing strategies in F&B could adopt different approaches to those applied to rooms division, where those who book well in advance will pay a lower rate than those booking at the last minute. In F&B the opposite could be the case – those booking far in advance are seeking a definite place to have their meal or party, while those seeking a daily meal on the off-chance will be seeking value for money. If the calculation is made first for the full-price paying customers, it can then be calculated how high or low the price for other customers may be set. If this is then repeated for each dinner hour different prices can be offered to customers depending on bookings and time; in this way demand would be really managed.

Once the yield statistic has been determined, the yield of the restaurant can be monitored hourly, daily, weekly or monthly. This information may be used to set up a database; forecasting procedures can then be established and constantly updated. The use of PMS, controlled by an in-house YM consultant, would alert a staff response to changing demand situations. With the aid of this information, strategies and tactical plans could be revised. Feedback would determine the effectiveness of the forecasts, the impact of tactics, and the performance of the workforce in their efforts to raise the restaurant's yields. This presupposes the necessity of sophisticated technology, although for F&B this is not essential as bookings are neither complex nor far in advance. Many hotel PMSs are run on PCs; added functions could be built into such systems.

Once applied, the YM statistic indicates high- and low-demand times. With demand concentrated around certain times in the day (breakfast, lunch and dinner), it should be possible to find new markets to fill the vacant times in between. This could be done by providing a new product or attracting new custom for the old product, and employing another pricing strategy. In order to do this a general change in philosophy and attitude towards pricing is needed.

To allow the market to accustom itself to variable prices, an in between period, where prices alter according to the hour without being linked to bookings, could be used. By allocating lower prices to non-profitable hours and days of the week, new markets could be selected for the same product – for example, OAPs being offered the hours between 11 a.m. and 12.30 p.m. for lower-priced lunches. Usually this market is under-targeted by the hotel industry, although it has already been successfully exploited by restaurant chains.

Another important aspect of the yield statistic is that it links covers (= space) to spend, expressing this as a percentage for easy comparison. The concept of F&B space has always been undervalued, with the number of meals sold and average spend being regarded as the key issues. In drawing attention to the value of this space, Akaydin (1992) proposed that hotel restaurants could be more profitably combined into one large area (single restaurant) which could accommodate different styles of restaurant operation, instead of providing two or three different restaurants in one hotel (an example being the Marriott Hotel, Slough). These could be divided into high- and low-spend areas. Akaydin (1992) recommended the use of partition walls so that each area could be enlarged or reduced according to demand. The associated merits of this idea would be greater efficiency in use of kitchens and staff, with staff training between sections more easily promoted. Additionally, such organisation would require only one restaurant manager.

Yield management: customer response

Consumers seem resigned to the fact that major service industries charge different prices for the same service with, to the consumer, scant reason. For example, airlines are quoted as changing their prices several thousand times a day in response to competitive pressures (Kimes 1989); they, in contrast to hotels, vie with fewer major competitors, and their customers have limited choice – they cannot seek cheaper seats indefinitely, and reservation systems soon indicate prices available. Hotels, however, contend with infinite competition; thus consumer response and attitudes to changing prices are less easy to handle. Basically if hotel customers baulk at changing prices they can patronise the competition. Given that consumers have grown accustomed to purchasing flights, theatre tickets, holidays, etc. at different prices according to demand, it might be assumed that variable prices for the restaurant product will eventually be accepted. It seems likely that customers will concede the logic of paying more for their precise requirements: for example, a personal service securing the seats and time of their choice for the family reunion or facing price increases from weekdays to weekends for the same meal. On weekdays, however, restaurant prices must compete with the supermarket/ready-made meal, takeaway outlets and consumers' lack of time; market trends indicate that only exceptional value will entice more customers during the week. Hoteliers may initially have to invest heavily in client education if YM is to succeed in aiding revenue increase in hotel F&B. Consumers need to be educated to recognise the benefits of YM to themselves.

Conclusion

Hotel F&B departments have long been generating less profit than desired; this has led to the franchising out of F&B space in hotels on a large scale. Another possible answer might be the application of YM. In order to apply YM to F&B it might be that YM has to be *adapted* as well as *adopted*, the idiosyncrasies of the industry being thus met. The size of problems in F&B certainly requires an approach that overhauls traditional values and principles. Whereas other parts of the industry such as single restaurants and restaurant chains have been centres of progress in recent years it is in such a drastic overhaul where the financial power of hotel F&B could be decisive in innovation. This is one of the ways progress in the field might be made.

YM is a recent innovation; evidence indicates that it is a force to be reckoned with; it has already gained ground in the hotel industry at various levels. The benefits being gained in the rooms division side of the hotel industry should be used to benefit F&B. The application of these strategies to F&B seems long overdue. The reticence of hotels to include F&B in mainstream developments is inhibitive; the need for F&B to be placed in the forefront of hotel developments is critical to its growth, profitability and image. If F&B is to move from a secondary position, it, too, must be fully incorporated into a YM programme.

References

Akaydin, S., 1992, 'Yield management in food and beverage operations', unpublished MSc thesis, University of Surrey.

Anon, 1992, *Caterer and Hotelkeeper*, Reed Business Publishing.

Brotherton, B. and Mooney, S., 1992, 'Yield management – progress and prospects', *International Journal of Hospitality Management*, 11(1): 23–32.

Dunn, K.D. and Brooks, D.E., 1990, 'Profit analysis: beyond yield management', *Cornell Hotel and Restaurant Administration Quarterly*, 31(3): 80–90.

Falck, V., 1993, 'Yield management in Finnish hotels', unpublished MSc thesis, University of Surrey.

Gamble, P., 1992, 'Building a yield management system – the flip side', *Hospitality Research Journal*, 14(2): 11–21.

Havelock, R., 1971, 'The utilisation of educational research and development'

Problems of Curriculum Innovation 13 to 15, 13, E283, Open University Press, Milton Keynes: 13–15.

Hott, D.D., Shaw, M. and Nusbaum, E.F., 1989, 'Measuring the effectiveness of an AI/expert yield management system', *Hospitality Education and Research Journal*, 13(3): 343–50.

Hoyle, E., 1970, 'Planned organisational change', *Journal of Curriculum Studies*, 1(2).

James, G.W., 1987, 'Fares must yield to the market' *Airline Business*, January: 16–19.

Jones, M., 1993, 'Restaurants', *Caterer and Hotelkeeper*, 16 September: 33–4.

Kimes, S.E., 1989, 'The basics of yield management', *Cornell Hotel and Restaurant Administration Quarterly*, 30(3): 14–19.

Lee, K.G.Y., 1990, 'A critical evaluation of yield management', Unpublished MSc thesis, University of Surrey.

Lieberman, W., 1993, 'Debunking the myths of yield management', *Cornell Hotel and Restaurant Administration Quarterly*, 34(1); 34–41.

Orkin, E.B., 1988, 'Boosting your bottom line with yield management', *Cornell Hotel and Restaurant Administration Quarterly*, 28(4): 52–6.

Relihan, W.J., 1989, 'The yield management approach to hotel-room pricing', *Cornell Hotel and Restaurant Administration Quarterly*, 30(1) 40–45.

Riley, M. and Davies, E., 1992, 'Development and innovation: the case of food and beverage in hotels' in C.P. Cooper (ed.), *Progress in tourism, recreation, and hospitality management*, Vol. 4, Belhaven Press, London.

Rogers, E.M., 1962, *Diffusion of innovations*, Macmillan, London.

Rogers, E.M., 1971, *Communication of innovations: a cross-cultural approach*, Macmillan, London.

Scarpa, J., 1993, 'F&B can no longer be just an unprofitable guest amenity', *Restaurant Business*, January: 108–16.

Schmidgall, R.S., 1989, 'While forecasts hit targets, GM's still seek better guns', *Lodging*, 15 (3): 101–2, 104–5.

Schmidt, A., 1987, *Food and beverage management in hotels*, CBI, New York.

Sieburgh, J., 1988, 'Yield management at work at Royal Sonesta' *Lodging Hospitality*, 44(11): 235–7.

Wolff, C., 1989, 'Newcomer yield management synthesizes old disciplines', *Hotel and Motel Management*, 204(5): 106.

12 The menu as a marketing tool

A. Cattet and C. Smith

Introduction

In a period of fierce competition, both chain and independent operators need to understand the market in which they operate if they want to remain competitive. They aim to offer each customer a unique 'dining experience' every time, but not all restaurateurs focus their attention on the menu or are aware of its importance. The restaurant's main product is seen to be its food, and the menu is thus the principal means of selling. As customers cannot examine the goods beforehand, they rely on the menu for all communications about the product.

A survey of a selected sample of food-service managers, conducted mainly in France, defined their attitudes towards the use of marketing in the planning and design of menus with a further objective of determining whether they were using the menu as a marketing tool. In a more perfect world, menus would unfailingly sell, satisfy and inspire repeat visits and each item would produce profit for the operator. In reality, however, imperfect menus contribute to restaurant failures, and the process of menu development and marketing becomes critical.

The menu as a recent invention

The habit of introducing a list of dishes only appeared in the middle of the eighteenth century after the introduction of the fork and the plate. At that time, they were not called menus but 'tariffs', taking the form of long lists of dishes lacking any structure, serving only to indicate prices. However, by the nineteenth century, meals had taken on a fixed form and structure, in both France and England. The French had established standard set menus consisting of group servings to be served in six to eight courses. Very quickly, menus ceased to be only a useful and practical tool and became a kind of 'symbol' and a promotional tool for restaurant and hotel.

The impact of French gastronomy

It was only around 1840 that real restaurant menus appeared. Escoffier, Carême, Soyer and other noted French chefs pioneered the lengthy, verbose menus of the Victorian era. It remained to Escoffier and his colleagues to develop the menu alongside their creation of the modern kitchen system. He burned much midnight oil over the composition of his menus and revealed the problems involved in this in the preface to his *Guide Culinaire*. The essence of Escoffier's revision of the menu structure was simplicity.

But even today's shorter menus follow the structure of the classical French menus as far as the succession of courses is concerned. They always start with something light to stimulate the appetite, build up to the main course, and then become lighter towards the end of the meal. Today, international styles influence all kinds of menu as cuisines and methods of cooking become incorporated into current food preparation styles.

The commercial menu

The elaborate, colourful, glossy restaurant menus of today have a history that goes back only to the turn of the twentieth century, when the menu for the day of Parisian restaurants of the 1880s and 1890s was drawn up on a large poster-sized card and placed at the front of the restaurant for everyone to see. French artists of the period, such as Renoir, Gauguin and Toulouse Lautrec, painted *cartes* in exchange for meals and money. Toulouse Lautrec is famous for his caricatures of Parisian women, some of whom were used as models for menus. Over the years, the physical size of the menus grew and grew and between 1890 and 1920 certain restaurants advertised their dishes on a piece of paper which had the format of a small poster. But during the twentieth century, menus were more often used folded in two or four, and became real brochures; more dishes were offered than today. Commercial food-service operations should structure their menu formats around the needs of their customers as well as the limitations of the kitchen.

Conclusion

France was known throughout the world for its classic cuisine which should suggest a perfectly planned menu in the style that we know. An old-time menu served merely to list the available dishes and inform patrons of their prices. Waiters, by gently steering diners to those items whose sale was the most advantageous to the house, performed the primary function of today's menus – selling. But as the restaurant industry grew, especially after the Second World War, the shortage of trained personnel grew increasingly more acute, to the point that the menu has now become one of the restaurateur's most important merchandising tools.

The marketing concept within food-service operations

It is essential that food-service operators identify and address the needs and attitudes of their specific markets as selling will never be successful unless markets have been chosen and understood. The specific needs of the marketing concept in the service sector emphasize the characteristics and service aspects of the food-service product itself. The traditional concept of marketing is narrow as it views marketing skills as applicable only to consumer goods and services for the creation of profit. However, this view has been challenged, particularly by marketers whose skills are being applied to the food-service industry.

The marketing concept

Current definitions of the marketing concept seem to focus on the process by which exchange of mutual satisfiers occurs. The definition of marketing offered by Kotler (1988a), stresses the mutual exchange process which is central to the marketing concept. The Chartered Institute of Marketing (1984) uses a similar definition, but adds the notion of profitability when 'Marketing is the process responsible for identifying, anticipating and satisfying customers requirements profitably'. In other words, the aim of marketing is to satisfy customers while maximising the internal efficiency of a company.

In recent years, however, the marketing concept has received much criticism due to the emphasis on 'profitable' sales volume, because where a want exists and the marketing opportunity appears unprofitable, the marketer generally will not produce the item. Whatever the definition of marketing is, it is more than just a sales plan, more than just a research programme to find out exactly where your sources of business or markets are. Marketing is more an attitude of mind, a way of thinking, which is why it can appear rather difficult to apply to a business and cannot be accomplished overnight. It requires permanent effort to be successful.

According to Buttle (1986, pp. 31–2), it should be clear that selling is not the same as marketing. Selling is just one part of the promotion component of the marketing mix. Selling concentrates on moving what is produced, whereas marketing helps to determine what is produced. Marketing helps to determine what should be offered for consumption. Levitt (1981) mentions that selling is not marketing and that it concerns itself only with the tricks and techniques of getting people to exchange their cash for your product. Levitt adds that selling is not concerned with the values that the exchange is all about and it does not, as marketing invariably does, view the entire business process as consisting of a tightly integrated effort to discover, create, arouse and satisfy consumer needs.

Marketing in the service sector

Levitt (1981) distinguishes between tangibles and intangibles while Christopher et al. (1980) suggest that the distinction is that service products are those which produce a series of benefits which cannot be stored.

However, not all authors agree with the notion that differences exist. Wyckham *et al.* (1975) and Judd (1968) for example, think that services are not different from products.

The characteristics that are commonly cited as making services different are heterogeneity, intangibility, perishability and inseparability. Nevertheless, there has been criticism of this functional approach; Goodfellow (1983) has shown that many so-called services do not exhibit one or more of these characteristics, whereas a number of physical goods do.

This confusion about the nature of services comes from the fact that the area of service marketing is relatively new. In the past, marketing texts and writings confined their attention and most of their examples to consumer goods and the idea that planned marketing can be equally applied to services has taken a long time to be accepted. The discussion of how marketing may be applied to the service sector has been restricted. Lovelock (1977) remarks that all services deliver a number of utilities and that before purchasing consumers will evaluate alternatives against them such as form, location, time, psychic (feelings about service) and value.

In general, the field of service marketing is confined to those exchanges in which the service element is core. Shostack (1977) calls these 'service dominant'. Most definitions of services insist on their intangible aspect. They are impalpable, cannot be smelt, tasted nor easily grasped mentally, which makes choice rather difficult for the customer.

According to Sasser (1978, pp. 8–12, 14–18), the food-service product is made of tangible and intangible elements, some of which are controllable and others uncontrollable by the restaurant manager, leading to an unpredictable outcome. He states that 'consumers perceive risks in selecting services, higher than in selecting products' and that with a product high in experience qualities, such as the restaurant product, the customer can only evaluate after purchase. That is why, food and drink has to be 'packaged' to convey an impression of the level of service and the other elements so that expected customers can translate appearance into confidence about performance. The menu can help in achieving that.

Service organisations will have to put a special focus on the tangible aspect of their organisation to give customers a better perception of what they are offered. In the case of a restaurant, operators will have to put special effort into the menu which represents one of the indicators given to customers to assess the product in advance.

Adaptation of the traditional marketing mix for food-service operations

According to Buttle (1986, pp. 188–91) the infinite variation with which food-service marketers combine their core products (food and beverages to meet the demand of customers suggests that customers seek rather more than the utilitarian satisfaction of a full stomach. These core products are enhanced by being tailored to satisfy the demands of specific sources of custom. Marketing can, through judicious pricing, promotion and distribution of a product, encourage consumers to buy or use more. This is where the marketing mix intervenes which is the convenient means of organizing all the variables controlled by the marketer that influence transactions in the marketplace. It is a 'checklist approach' where marketers attempt to list and organize the variables under their control to influence demand.

It has become customary to consider the marketing mix as the four *P*s: product, price, promotion and place. However, this original marketing mix was primarily invented for situations in which manufacturing organisations were operating and, according to Cowell (1984, pp. 67–76), 'Marketing Practitioners in the service sector find the Marketing Mix may not be inclusive enough for their needs'. For example, people who perform or deliver services are not taken into account in the existing framework. Setting, atmosphere and layout may be important influences in the purchase of some services (especially in the food-service sector). Booms and Bitner (1982) brought together another version of the marketing mix for services, which contains three additional *P* elements (people, physical evidence and process) and, according to Cowell, 'any of these seven elements could influence the success or failure of the overall programme'.

Conclusions

People normally use appearances and external impressions to make judgements about realities. Shostack (1977) argues that consumer decisions concerning an intangible-dominant entity will be based on the tangible clues that surround it. If customers are given some clue as to the quality of a restaurant's food and level of service before entering the place and deciding to dine there, they reduce their risk, as Renaghan (1981) suggests, because their choice is an informed one. Indeed, as more authors recognize, there is a need for operators to resort to marketing strategies for improving their performance and differentiating themselves in the marketplace. Certain tools such as the menu are very important in achieving this. Satisfaction will be dependent on the perceptions that customers have developed about the particular restaurant and the service actually performed.

There are many factors which influence the image that may be formed by a food-service operation. All the elements of the marketing mix such as price, the service itself, advertising and promotional campaigns will contribute to customer and client perceptions as well as physical evidence. The menu is the key factor in any food-service establishment. It reflects the market image of the management and owners, conveying their overall thought and attitude in the quality of its planning and it 'tangibilises' the food-service product. Consumers today are requiring greater sensuality within the meal experience.

Planning an effective menu

The survival of small or large food-service operations will depend on responsiveness to the needs of customers, achieved through a well-planned menu. The restaurant manager will have to manage the 'product' and the image of the restaurant and match them with the expectations of the targeted customers. As part of their marketing strategy, food-service managers' priority should define a clear image and positioning of their restaurants by giving enough tangible and physical clues to customers about the product on offer, the menu being one of the most important. This is why, as in any other art, the drawing up of a menu requires planning and the observance of a few principles if the operator intends to use it as a marketing tool.

Menu goals and objectives

The menu is an expression of the restaurant's objectives. It positions the restaurant in the marketplace and is the articulation of the operation a restaurateur is running. It works as an element of reference. Menu and marketing strategies for restaurants closely parallel Maslow's pyramidal hierarchy of needs. A restaurant can be a place to eat and nothing more, or it can provide a 'dining experience', with food, ambience and service to match. Restaurant classification begins with the simplest operation whose menu is very basic and whose objective is only to satisfy the physiological need for food, but culminates with the luxury restaurant's sophisticated décor, service and elaborate menu which can lead to self satisfaction.

Market assessment

The demographics and preferences of the target market have to be analysed. In the 1990s, social and demographic changes will continue to have a major impact on restaurateurs' menus. Compared with a decade ago, different food products, cooking styles and ingredients are all appearing on menus. Quinton (1991) suggests that restaurants will have a family-orientated atmosphere and a greater provision of children's menus and facilities. Kochak (1991) sees family-oriented restaurants ideally positioned for the future. Changing demography is also creating a large market of 'seniors' to which quality and price are essential.

According to Ganem (1990), consumer demand for attention to nutrition is increasing. More working women will demand lighter and more healthy menu items. Better-educated, well-travelled consumers desire products with less sugar and salt, improved flavour, more natural and varied texture and freshness. Ganem also mentions the individualised way consumers approach dining out which is influenced by social image and the expression of lifestyle. This reinforces the statement 'you are what you eat'.

Quinton also suggests that customers are moving towards diversity and individualised control. They know what they want, when and how they want it. By building a little foresight and flexibility into the menu with subtle changes, a restaurant can give diners what they want about as fast as they know they want it. As marketing studies the changes in existing markets and searches for new ones, operators should regularly try original and fresh menu ideas and promote them. Moreover, intense competition at all levels of the industry is also forcing operators to remain flexible with regard to menus.

Salads are served as entrées or appetisers, and soups can be main dishes. Operators were quick to create dishes that could be presented either as small courses or main courses. Many enlarged the appetiser menu, and some created special menus to meet the market demand of flexible mini-meals for people in a hurry but who want to eat well. Now frequent diners want smaller portions but they want the food to sing with flavour. The *à la carte* menu with an expanded appetiser section becomes smart menu planning. However, restaurateurs have to be cautious when intending to change their menus. A menu for an established restaurant needs to evolve slowly; if a favourite dish suddenly disappears from the menu, guests are not happy.

One of the biggest intangibles in developing a menu for a particular market area and particular clientele is the concept of perceived value which can be viewed by customers in a variety of ways. Value can be seen in the presentation of the menu and the appearance of an item as it is served. Or it may be seen in the method of service or the ambience of the dining room. It is indeed difficult to measure a consumer's perception of value because so much of it is subjective and emotive. Thus, developing a menu that gives customers perceived value is a major challenge.

Assessing the competition

The competition is an important factor to take into consideration when making a menu. Indeed, it is suggested that the menus of the operator's direct competition are a good guide to customer needs and can help determine what the community has a general tendency to eat. It can assist the restaurateur in finding out if there are any predictable demands for the types of product that he intends to offer, but consistent duplications should be avoided. Although there are circumstances, such as family-style steak houses, in which menus may be very similar, customers are looking for variety. Items should not be borrowed from the competition's menu or customers may be disinterested because they are bored with the repetition and the item taken out of context. Product differentiation is required. On the other hand, lack of customer interest can reflect inadequate selling techniques.

The menu as the centre of profit

According to Miller (1983), the menu is the ultimate profit centre of the restaurant. Regardless of the status of the restaurant, or if the profits are declining, the menu must always be the focal point as 'the key to any restaurant's success is whether or not the menu produces more customers and contribution dollars'.

In his model for menu-making, Miller advocates detailed analyses of all menu items to track declining or increasing sales, and prompt action to add or delete items as necessary. According to him, monitoring the sales of individual menu items is critical to the success of an ongoing operation. The restaurant owner/operator must be quick to take advantage of trends, adding those menu items that may increase sales and profit and eliminate those that are not selling well and/or are no longer profitable. There is no need to maintain the listing of any item that is not profitable to the operation unless it increases volume. Menus must also stimulate additional sales of profitable items. Let the menu set the guidelines, then limit it to what your customer wants to purchase, what you prepare and serve well, and what is more profitable. In this way the operation will survive a transitional period and again become the profit-making operation that it once was.

Conclusion

The final objective is to find menu items that will be marketable, popular and profitable. Marketing consists of finding marketable items and presenting them to the customer in an attractive way. Which items depends a great deal on the menu planner's ability to determine needs and to read customer trends. Keeping in tune with new changes in consumer spending habits and the popularity of new items will help. Once the marketable items have been found, the menu planner must develop effective marketing techniques to sell them. How well the customer can see, read and understand the menu item description will affect how well the dish will sell. A well-made menu should lead customers to the items the restaurant most wants to sell, and that can be done through menu design.

The impact of the physical menu

Communication via the menu

The physical menu is the medium by which the restaurateur and his customers communicate. This is one of the most intimate connections he has with them. As such, the menu must be devised so that all lines of communication are wide open and no misunderstanding can occur. The menu writer must 'speak' clearly to the customer and the customer must 'hear' his message and react to it. Communication via the menu can be better understood by examining the classical communication models (see Figure 12.1). Decisions about the cover, the descriptions, the art, the location of the various food items are all very important to the communication process. The menu writer: considers the meaning of

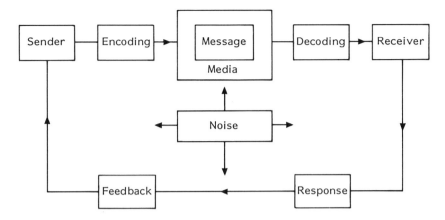

Figure 12.1 *Kotler's modified communication model*
Source: Kotler 1991, p. 568.

the message; expresses meanings in words or symbols; and transmits a message via the printed menu. This allows the customer to: receive the message; translate words and symbols; and understand and accept the meaning.

Visual format

The number of components which make up the visual format are chosen to reflect the image of the food-service operation and to present the items to the customer in a manner constructed for maximum saleability.

The menu cover
The cover makes the all-important first impression. There is no second chance. It is critical that the menu cover creates the desired atmosphere. It should offer the impression of what the restaurant is all about and should begin to presell the rest of the menu. The operator has to remember that the menu cover is a major part of his overall advertising programme and its major function should be to market and identify the restaurant. The menu cover and the menu itself can be anything that suits the restaurant décor and is compatible with the operation. Moreover, certain information should be included on every menu cover such as the restaurant's location, hours and special services.

The layout
The layout is an important part of marketing the menu and should be designed to highlight high-profit items. The principal duty of the menu writer is to direct the customer's attention to those items that the restaurant operation wants to sell. How well the customer can choose items

depends a great deal on how much time is spent on the layout and how well special items are highlighted. Although there is no reliable scientific study of eye focus, it is generally understood by researchers as well as menu writers that the eye focuses on and travels over a menu in a more or less predictable way.

According to some eye-focus studies, the customer's eye crosses the centre part of the menu seven times as he studies the entire menu. Hence, the centre area, being prominent and containing the items that the operator most wants to sell, is critical to his sales strategy and menu planning. The law of primacy and recency explains a customer's typical eye movement across the menu and the most important areas are those in the centre and the right-hand side of the menu.

Typography
Restaurants are often noisy, full of visual distractions and dimly lit. Making a menu readable and legible is doubly difficult. The typeface that is selected for the menu will have a definite effect on the customer. Like layouts, typefaces are used to highlight high-profit items or sections to promote sales. If a line of copy extends too far across the page, customers' eyes will tire before they reach the end. Beautiful menus do not communicate well if they are not legible and readable. Menus that do a good job at both are printed in typefaces that are easy to recognise.

But before the menu designer or planner decides how to use a typeface to market the menu most effectively, management must decide what to sell in the menu. Either the operator wants to sell the entire menu, in which case the menu would be designed in such a way that each item will be presented with the same emphasis; or he just wants to concentrate on high-profit or special items and will then use special typefaces to feature these sections, hoping to draw the customer's attention to them. The menu relies heavily on the printed word to sell the food-service product; the typeface used deserves a lot of consideration because the purpose of a well-thought presentation of menu items is to increase the size of the customer's bill. Moreover, the texture and weight of the paper or stock upon which the menu is printed are its lasting qualities. Operators, then, should be very selective about their menu material because once again it is conveying their restaurant's image.

Colour in the menu
More than any other aspect of the external menu, colour affects the customer psychologically. To select colours for the menu, the menu planner should first establish what the desired impact on the customer is to be. Will colour be used to create a mood or to promote sales? It is no accident that red appears on menus a lot because red is the colour that advances forward in the human field of vision first, something printed in red is impossible to ignore. Physiologically, the body responds to the colour red with a quickened heartbeat and pulse rate and a shot of adrenalin. Primary blue, on the other hand, is said to appease and sedate.

But brighten that blue to the electric colour you often see on menus, and the effect is one of excitement. Colour is one of the more important elements in menu design, and its overall effect on customer purchases should not be ignored.

Illustrations
Beyond choice of colour, the method of menu illustration plays a significant role in displaying information about a restaurant's personality and food. Photography can be an effective selling tool as well. In addition to affecting customer perceptions about food, the use of photography aids sales staff. The pictures help sell the food-service product when words fail. But while photography works well in some cases, it might not be the answer for everyone and some establishments resort to other kinds of illustrations.

An effective logo condenses the character of a restaurant into one symbol. Because so much goes into its development, many restaurants choose to use the logo as the chief design element on their menu. Problems in creating a logo design can be an early warning signal for an under-developed concept. Indeed, if you cannot communicate through an image what the restaurant wants to be, it might mean that you have not thought the concept through enough.

The menu copy
The menu copy is the written description on the menu that is used to sell individual food selections, promote the restaurant, and inform the customer of the services the restaurant has to offer; it is the principal way of marketing the restaurant product. As such, it should be treated as a piece of advertising that can influence customers in their choices of menu items. The copy that describes the menu items is a significant part of the communications goal. Volumes have been written to help restaurateurs do a better job with the copy portion of their menu. According to Scanlon (1985), information on the menus has to add appetite appeal without becoming too wordy.

Conclusion
The physical menu must be consistent in every aspect because consistency also gives an impression of thoroughness and exactness, which goes far when customers sum up their overall impression of a restaurant. The menu's appearance, from the way it is laid out to the paper it is printed on, is a powerful selling message. The placement of menu items, the art, and colour are all critical elements as they should all help the operator in accomplishing his objectives with regard to profit, sales and image. In order to satisfy the needs of the customers the design, colours and format of the printed menu must be considered as well as the contents of the menu. Also part of the physical menu is the choice of the right words to describe the dishes, as it might help increase sales. If customers accept what the operator has done, obviously it means that he has written

a good menu; they will then take action, buy the profitable items you want them to buy, and, most important, return to the restaurant as regular guests.

Marketing theory in practice

A need for market research to decide about the menu contents?

The results of a survey carried out in France of restaurant managers' attitudes towards the menu as a marketing tool showed two distinct kinds of response according to the type of restaurant management. When dealing with the eating habits and the development of new products, most of the independent restaurateurs interviewed recognised that they did not use any market research as they already knew the types of food enjoyed by their local market. They admitted that they put their own experience first, specialised in the food that they did best and enjoyed most and did not really question themselves as to what new tastes were on the market.

They nearly all mentioned the fact that customer feedback helped them to obtain a great deal of information, and that represented for them their own market research. They considered that market research at their level was a waste of time and money. Surprisingly enough, even the most exclusive of the independent restaurateurs did not see any point in carrying out market research and tended to rely on their exclusivity and believe that this was enough to attract a steady stream of customers.

Conversely, all the hotel food and beverage managers interviewed stated that their own research and marketing department carried out frequent market research on changes in consumers' eating habits. It could be said that they felt more concerned about the market and made greater use of marketing techniques in their menus because of management directives from head office. They followed a more comprehensive approach to using the menu as a marketing tool.

The results of this survey showed that the chain-related operators interviewed put effort, time and money into keeping up with general dining trends, enabling them to renew their menus on a frequent basis to keep abreast of the new tastes appearing on the market. Indeed, some hotels presently put a lot of emphasis on healthy food and do include a special calorie-counted menu which adds to their profits. It seems that the only way for a restaurateur to run his restaurant successfully today is with a clear awareness of what his customers and potential customers want, and how they perceive his restaurant.

However, one common element that all the respondents considered important was the use of price as a marketing tool. They all agreed that the concept of value for money is vital and it seems to be one of the primary concerns of the restaurateurs interviewed.

A well-planned and designed menu: part of the marketing strategy of an operation

All of the independent restaurateurs interviewed said that they did not resort to any particular marketing techniques when deciding the placement of menu items. Most of them were even ignorant about the true effectiveness of such techniques. Basically their main requirements were that their menus should be clearly presented, and easy to read and understand. However, it is impressive to note the contrast with the chain-related operators, for example, whose menu's layout is very precise. The construction of their menu has been well researched by the company in such a way as to present the highest-contribution dishes in key areas to increase their sales. Attention to these select areas has been achieved by boxing dishes in groups, and the use of a carefully selected variety of colours to maintain a high degree of interest

The description of menu items seems to be an area of growing importance and research among certain restaurateurs. Indeed, this is a challenge that all the hotel food and beverage managers interviewed found difficult to face. They put a lot of effort and time into it, on the grounds that it was worthwhile. However, they found it even more difficult for their 'light' menus, as they wanted to find words that created a notion of freshness, at the same time as being informative. Moreover, they did not want their customers to feel frustrated because the calories are counted, so the description of the dish becomes the field where the notion of creativity is really important.

The situation is different for independent restaurateurs, especially those belonging to the mid-range category. The impression resulting from the survey is that they did not pay any attention to it. Following the rule 'keep it simple', most of the time they used a limited description as they said that they would rather explain the dish verbally to the customer. Higher up the scale, the restaurateurs interviewed said they did devote quite a lot of time and attention to it, trying to avoid pompous words, as the time of pretentious and flamboyant descriptions is over.

Summary

A very clear difference emerged in the answers given by managers according to the management type of the operation. Most managers of independent restaurants considered the menu as a support that gave an idea of the nature and the policy of their establishment. They felt that its importance was rather limited and tended to rely more on the contact they had with their customers to market what they had to sell. Small or local restaurants could not justify expenditure on market research.

Even the more famous restaurant managers interviewed did not consider the menu as being a market tool and did confess that a lot of 'marketing specialists' come to them offering their help in planning a more effective menu but they refuse, arguing that the menu is not an important tool for them and that being in the Michelin guide is their best marketing tool.

Conclusion

According to the results of this survey, it was surprising to note the gap between the literature and the evidence collected: how little interest managers have in their menu and how they limit its importance and function to a mere list of dishes.

When the restaurant is more established, its reputation comes first and acts as its marketing tool. The impression was also given that most restaurateurs are ignorant of what marketing is and sometimes resorted to it without even knowing. This is different in the case of chain-related establishments as they have marketing departments, which probably explains why they seem to be the only ones within the sample who put any effort into using marketing techniques when planning and designing their menu and effectively using it as a marketing tool. Therefore, a conclusion drawn from the survey is that the attention that managers give to the menu is linked to their attitude towards marketing.

References

Booms, B.H. and Bitner, M.J., 1982, 'Marketing services by managing the environment', *Cornell HRA Quarterly*, May: 35–9.
Buttle, F., 1986, *Hotel and food service marketing: A managerial approach*. Cassell, London.
Chartered Institute of Marketing, 1984, *Code of Practice*, Bourne End, CIM.
Christopher, M., McDonald, M. and Wills, G., 1980, *Introducing marketing*, Pan, London.
Cowell, D., 1984, *The marketing of services*, Heinemann, London.
Ganem, B.C., 1990, *Nutritional menu concepts for the hospitality industry*, Van Nostrand Reinhold, New York.
Goodfellow, J.H., 1983, 'The marketing of goods and services as a multidimensional concept', *Quarterly Review of Marketing*, 8: 19–27.
Judd, R.C., 1968, 'Similarities and differences in product and service retailing', *Journal of Retailing*, 43: 1–9.
Kochak, J., 1991, 'Casual theme', *Restaurant Business*, 20 November: 155–66.
Kotler, P., 1988, *Marketing management* (6th edn), Prentice Hall, Englewood Cliffs, NJ.
Kotler, P., 1991, *Marketing management* (7th edn), Prentice Hall, Englewood Cliffs, NJ.
Levitt, T., 'Marketing intangible products and product intangibles', *Cornell HRA Quarterly*, 22(2), August: 37–44.
Lockwood, A. and Jones, P., 1989, *The management of hotel operations*, Cassell, London.
Lovelock, C.H., 1988, *Services marketing: text, cases and readings*, Prentice Hall, Englewood Cliffs, NJ.
Miller, J., 1983, 'Pricing your menu', *Foodservice Marketing*, 45: 66–67.

Quinton, B., 1991, 'Menus and markets', *Restaurants and Institutions*, 27 March: 12–29.

Renaghan, L.M., 1981, 'A new marketing mix for the hospitality industry', *Cornell HRA Quarterly*, August: 31–5.

Sasser, W.E., Olsen, R.P. and Wyckoff, D.D., 1978, *Management of service operations: texts and cases*, Allyn and Bacon, Boston: 8–12.

Scanlon, N.L., 1985, *Marketing by menu*, Van Norstrand Reinhold, New York.

Shostack, G.L., 1977, 'Breaking free from product marketing', *Journal of European Marketing*, April: 73–80.

Wyckham, R.G., Fitzroy, P.T., and Mandry, S.D., 1975, 'Marketing of Services', *European Journal of Marketing*, 9(1): 59–67.

13 Factors affecting future menu compilation

M.A. O'Neill, M.A. McKenna and F. Fitz

Introduction

Lee (1987) tells us that food service is a volatile industry reliant on nearly unpredictable swings in consumer behaviour. The current economic recession and consumer expectations of quality and wide choice have resulted in the food industry facing unprecedented challenges as competition is increasing for an ever decreasing amount of real disposable income. Schaffer (1984), among others, believes that the essence of any economically based organisation's long-run success is its ability to survive and prosper. In acceptance of this viewpoint it is recognised that there must be a continual awareness of the macro-environment in which the organisation operates. It is only through extensive research, aimed at gaining a detailed understanding of this, that the food production and service industry of today can hope to survive and compete effectively tomorrow. As Higgins and Vincze (1986) state, 'if a business is not growing, not changing, not meeting the current needs of society and preparing to meet its future needs it is declining'. The menu with potential for development and introduction of new food items affords one such means of future growth. Against this background, the proposition of this chapter is that future growth and success within the food service industry lies in the internal manipulation and exploitation of the menu. The development and introduction of new menu items must form the strategy for future growth.

Recognising that a systematic approach to new product development must be followed if an organisation is to remain operationally viable amid the competitive climate of today's business environment, attention here is focused solely on the value of environmental information needs in the pursuit of operational and strategic objectives. In accepting the importance of the menu as a marketing tool, the objective of this chapter is to identify the most important factors which have implications for the development of future menu products.

Menu development and organisation environment

As with all growth strategies there is an element of risk involved, a threat that is accentuated all the more by the fact that in an operational environment where things never remain static there is no way of forecasting accurately for the future. Feltenstein (1986) highlights the risk when he asserts that, 'no matter how carefully orchestrated the process, developing new products is a risky business: there are no guarantees of product success'. In an attempt to reduce both the perceived and actual risk involved in any such growth strategy, he advocates the utilisation of a systematic approach towards new product development, entailing the assembly of a new-product task force, idea generation, screening and development through to actual launch.

A similar viewpoint is advanced by Buttle (1986), who, when referring to new product development, states that

> New products can emerge in many ways, ranging from simple idea germination through to development or as a consequence of market analysis. Successful development, however, should follow a systematic process which entails the following: new product strategy development, idea generation, screening and evaluation, business analysis, development, testing and commercialisation.

Essentially both theorists are espousing the adoption of a more strategic approach aimed at developing and maintaining an optimal balance between the deployment of an organisation's resources and development opportunities in an ever changing environment. Fundamental to this approach is the fact that developmental decisions are based on accurate and continuous observation and assessment of the industry and organisation environment. Success therefore, will depend on an organisation's ability to match environmental conditions with its own capabilities and resources.

As well as a knowledge of the product, market and competition, a prerequisite for success is a detailed awareness of the business and market environment. Taken together, organisation and environment form a larger 'ecosystem' characterised by relatively open exchange and interaction processes. Within this system, the environment provides an ecological 'niche' for the organisation, by supplying it with inputs of necessary resources; and the organisation, to remain viable, achieves satisfactory relationships with its environment by returning to it acceptable outputs. Much therefore depends upon the make-up of this environment, its characteristics and components (Shortt 1987).

In recognising that only some of the elements of the total environment surrounding an organisation affect its activities, it is necessary to divide the environment between general environmental conditions of concern to all organisations and specific environmental influences of significance to one particular organisation only. This part of the environment is likely to be more controllable than the general environment and it includes those factors that are internal or intrinsic to the organisation: system technology; system process; human resources; financial resources; and operational and administrative structure. These are those factors relevant to a specific organisation's system of transforming raw inputs into desirable outputs or menu items. While such factors do have an impact on an organisation's effective capacity and ability to supply that which is demanded, they are largely organisation-specific and unlikely to impinge on any other organisation's ability to supply.

The more general environment presents the difficulties of uncertainty and continual change, which, when unprepared for, can lead to such outcomes as loss of market share or bankruptcy. A change in the more general environment is obviously not organisation-specific, and what might present itself as an opportunity for one organisation may be a source of deep concern to another. The effects are thus likely to be more severe, with implications being felt throughout the entire system and an organisation's competitive environment.

For the purposes of this chapter, attention will be directed to this more general environment and in particular to those environmental factors relating to future menu development: social and cultural aspects; demographic trends; technological change; and competitive considerations. These are illustrated in Figure 13.1.

Environmental factors affecting menu choice

Social and cultural

Under this classification it is proposed to examine issues such as consumer power and quality expectations. In the simplest of terms, all organisational activities must focus around the needs and expectations of consumers, as effective marketers realise successful companies exist only if they have a sufficient number of customers. This centrality of consumers is further highlighted by Ballantyne (1990) in his references to the customer value chain, defined as a series (or linkage) of things producers of goods and services do to produce value for their customers. Hence the food service industry as a whole and individual organisations within, must successfully identify what customers require from particular product or service offerings prior to any considerations of what is valued and consequently produced. Underlying this concept of the customer value chain must be the concept of quality. Today's consumers have become much more quality-conscious in terms of purchasing behaviours. Modern consumers require products and services which not only meet their performance requirements and expectations but actually surpass them. For manufacturers of goods it is a complex task to undertake this successfully, but in the case of producers of services the problem is compounded as account must be taken of the tangible and intangible aspects of the product or service on offer. In order to attempt to fulfil consumer needs and wants, Horovitz and Poon (1991) offer the following recommendations: get the customer's point of view, make the customer the star of the show, respond to all customer complaints, allow the customer to dictate service delivery, and over-respond to the customer. In other words the food service industry must identify its customers, ascertain their wants and needs and supply these with consistent and required quality. In the identification of customers, some of the aspects to be considered are the market

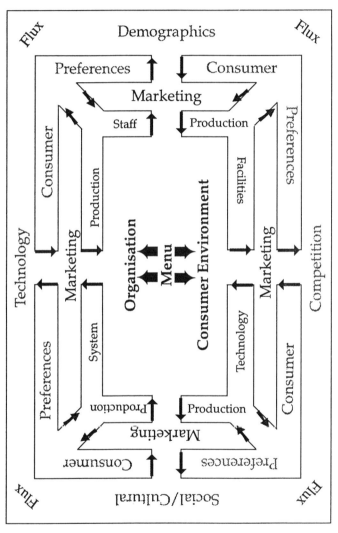

Figure 13.1 *The menu of the future: a strategic environmental analysis model*

Internal Organisational Environment   External Organisational Environment   Finance, Personnel and Marketing encompassed within an Information Feedback Loop

segment(s), for example whether the organisation is catering for the fast food or the family/atmosphere market, and where the products or services are to be consumed, that is, on or off the premises. The second step is to ascertain the requirements of the chosen market segment(s). The Arbor Inc customer window (Cory *et al.* 1987), as illustrated in Figure 13.2, may prove a useful tool as a means of gathering customer data and using the data in the deliverance of a quality product or service. There has been a

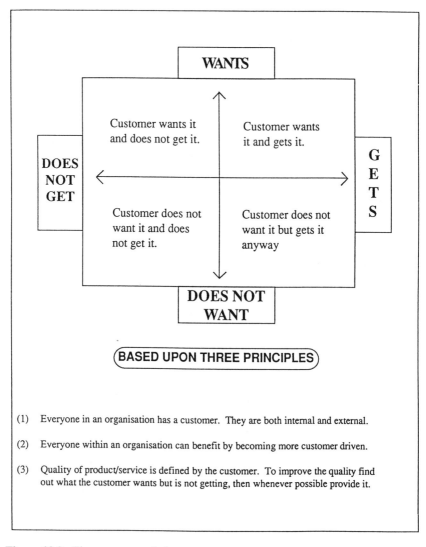

Figure 13.2 *The customer window concept*

Source: Cory *et al.* 1987

recent upsurge in healthy eating, calorie-conscious products, vegetarian-
ism and a move towards eating in as opposed to eating out. Food service
operators must take account of these trends and may find themselves
investing heavily in the implementation of total quality management
aimed at service right-first-time on each and every occasion that opportunity presents. To summarise, with the emphasis now heavily placed on
quality as opposed to quantity, there has been, and no doubt will continue
to be, a great proliferation in the variety of foodstuffs and menu items at
a relatively low cost available to today's consumer.

The healthier eating phenomenon

During the last decade the move towards healthy eating has generated
among many consumers a negative perception of a number of traditional
foods that were hitherto highly valued within our culture. Additional
characteristics of the healthier eating phenomenon include:

• the development of a food-nutrition-health orientation in which nutritional quality is of increased importance in determining food choice;
• changes in traditional food preparation methods;
• increased interest in the effects of production and processing methods
  on food quality;
• increased demand for products subjected to light processing, and
  concerns about the effects of modern farming techniques on the environment, increasing the popularity of 'natural' and 'organic' products.

The increasing interest in health-related food quality attributes among
consumers has become an issue of great importance for food manufacturers, educators, nutritionalists, policy-makers, caterers and marketers
and requires specific responses to meet the new consumer demands. Daly
and Beharrel (1988) have suggested that the new consumer trends and
concerns have originated and developed as a result of pressure from three
main sources. The first and perhaps the major source for change has been
the growing consumer concern over the role of diet in the aetiology of the
so called 'nutritional diseases of affluence' (coronary heart disease, hyper-
tension, diabetes and cancers). The second source of pressure for change
arose from the development and promotion of healthy eating options; and
the final factor can be attributed to the role of public articulators on the
effects of diet and health and the impact of the publication of a range of
influential reports on the role of diet and disease.

Demographic trends

Panyko (1990) believes that by identifying the demographic trends of
tomorrow, marketers can determine what questions they should be asking
today. The food service industry has traditionally been viewed as having
a very stable demand base. Indeed, there has been a commonly held

belief that if the worlds population were to increase, so, too would the demand and consumption of food. Similarly if population growth were to slow down, so, too, would the demand for food. Panyko, however does not subscribe to this and states that demographic factors alone do not sway consumer demand. However, they do provide an insight into likely future demand as well as facilitating the identification of potential growth areas to allow the targeting of particular age segments. Currently there appear to be two key issues in relation to demographic trends: a slowing-down in population growth and consequently an ageing population and an increased incidence of women in the workforce.

The ageing population is not a new idea. It is well recognised that the proportion of older people in the population of most developed countries is increasing, while the fastest growing segment in European countries and in the United States of America is 35–40-year-olds. This maturing of the baby boomers who helped contribute to the fast-food explosion of the 1960s and 1970s, now presents a lucrative sector to the food service industry, with increases in their earning power hopefully reflected in increases in their spending power. These individuals having grown up in the fast-food environment, have made eating out a fundamental part of their lifestyle and are now in a position to influence future generations as heads of households. Similarly, the older generations and their concern for quality of life and timeliness present unique opportunities. In order to capitalise on these, a profile of the over-50s must be drawn up and the products/services on offer positioned accordingly.

The increased incidence of women in the workforce must also be considered. Lawless and Hart (1983) conclude from their research that working women have a positive impact on food service sales. Working women increase the amount of real disposable income in the household and as they become more career-orientated, with resultant less time to spend on household chores and food preparation, there is a corresponding expansion in the use of convenience foods and increased opportunities for eating out.

Technology

The introduction of new technology entails considerable financial, managerial, legal and social changes within the organisation at all stages in the service production and delivery process. Technological changes in relation to food preparation and service include the following: the advent of irradiation; blast freezing; freeze drying; new and reusable packaging; and an increased shift to different methods of cooking, such as broiling, grilling, cook-chill and freezing. Palmer (1983) offers an interesting insight into the future by stating that by the turn of the century food service robots may serve a diverse menu of cooked foods directly to the customer. A number of areas of concern are readily identifiable in relation to the impact of technology on the producer, for example, the loss of the personal aspects of service. According to recent research, corporate hotel users in the

United Kingdom ranked service as a more important factor than location when choosing a hotel, and it is not unreasonable to assume that similar results would emerge in relation to eating-out establishments, dependent, of course, on the meal occasion. However, there are various benefits in terms of reduced preparation times, and resultant cost advantages with the skilful use of modern technology. The question must no longer be whether to employ these techniques, but when.

Competition

In the present era, while the total demand for food and beverages has remained relatively stable over the years, consumers have considerable choice, both in the numbers of places in which to eat and in the types of food available. Figures 13.3 and 13.4 illustrate the outlets competing for consumers' money and the options open to consumers for consuming foods and beverages. Panyko (1990) states

> Meals today can range from home-prepared fresh ingredient foods to refrigerated, frozen or shelf-stable convenience products, and from take-out from a supermarket or fast food establishment to home delivered meals, be they from the local pizzeria or a white-tablecloth restaurant.

Robichaud and Khan (1988) assert that consumers crave change and diversity in their dining experience. With this in mind, a number of prime areas of opportunity for new menu product development and introduction have arisen: breakfast foods; light and nutritious snacks; new taste sensations; complex cook-freeze meals available in the high street store; and an ever increasing and varied amount of take-away foods. Some of these trends include the increased demand for home delivery, with the result that many of the larger restaurant service outlets are now beginning to compete with the smaller operator for the eat-at-home market.

Conclusions

While growth can no longer be guaranteed in the face of a very diverse market environment, today's providers of food and beverage services must face the challenges of increased consumer discretion and other factors. New menu product development and innovative breakthrough offer a means of growth. In order to fulfil this objective, there must be complete understanding of the macro-environment. Past experience has proven that little can be guaranteed in respect of the food industry's future. By carefully researching and analysing those factors that may have a bearing on consumer decision-making, the food service industry might be better placed to placate ever shifting consumer food behaviour within society. The factors discussed are by no means exhaustive, but when viewed in conjunction with other aspects such as government, political,

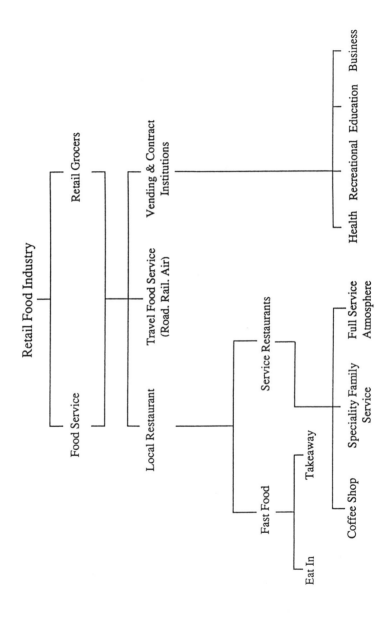

Figure 13.3 *Competition for consumers' spending on food*

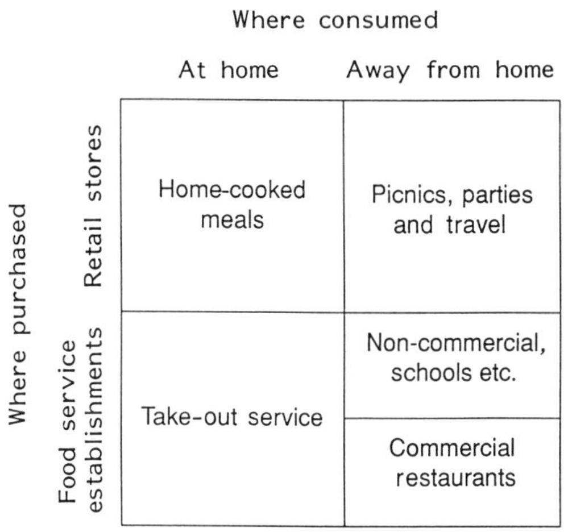

Where consumed

At home   Away from home

Figure 13.4 Options for eating and drinking

Source: Lawless and Hart (1983)

economic and those factors affecting the demand and supply sectors of industry, they do permit a useful insight as to the environment within which the food industry exists to serve today.

References

Armistead, C.G., 1988, 'Customer service and operations management in service business', *The Service Industries Journal*, 9(2): 247–260.

Ballantyne, D., 1990, 'Coming to grips with service intangibles using quality management techniques', Centre for Services Management, Cranfield School of Management.

Buttle, F., 1986, *Hotel and food service marketing: a managerial approach*, Holt, Rinehart and Winston, London.

Cory, M., Kary, B., Orleman, P., Robertshaw, W., Ross, G., Wallace, W. and Wittenbracker, J., 1987, 'The customer window', *Quality Progress*, June, 20: 37–43.

Daly, L. and Beharrel, B., 1988, 'Health, diet and the marketing of food and drink: some theoretical problems', *British Food Journal*, 90: 5–9.

Dittmor, P.R. and Griffin, G., 1993, *The dimensions of the hospitality industry: an introduction*, Van Nostrand Reinholt, New York.

Feltenstein, T., 1986, 'New product development in food service', *Cornell HRA Quarterly*, Nov, 27(3): 62–71.

Higgins, J.M. and Vincze, J.W., 1986, *Strategic management and organisational policy: text and cases* (3rd edn), Dryden Press, London.

Horovitz, J. and Poon, C., 1991, 'Putting service quality into gear', *Quality Progress*, January, 24(1): 54–60.

Lawless, M. and Hart, C., 1983, 'Forces that shape restaurant demand', *Cornell HRA Quarterly*, 24(3): 6–17.

Lee, D.R., 1987, 'Factors of restaurant success: why some succeed where others fail', *Cornell HRA Quarterly*, November, 28(3) 32–37.

Palmer, J., 1983, 'Automatic food service: the meal of the future', *Cornell HRA Quarterly*, May, 24(1): 62–70.

Panyko, F., 1990, 'Challenging directions in food marketing', *Cornell HRA Quarterly*, May 31(1): 54–60.

Robichaud, R. and Khan, M.A., 1988, 'Responding to market changes: the fast food experience', *Cornell HRA Quarterly*, 29(3): 46–49.

Schaffer, J.D., 1984, 'Strategy, organisation structure and success in the lodging industry', *International Journal of Hospitality Management*, 3(4): 159–165.

Shortt, G.B., 1987, 'Organisations (9): Environment (1)', seminar paper, Department of Management Studies, Manchester Polytechnic.

Walsh, D. 1991, 'UK trends', *Caterer and Hotelkeeper*, 18–24 July, 14.

14 Food trends in Europe

G. Valterio

Because their stomachs often cried out for food, peasants in the Middle Ages dreamed only of one thing: to eat until they had a full belly. This state of affairs has now given way to conditions of abundance and prosperity in our corner of the globe, and its removal symbolizes the change that has occurred in the space of three decades. While greasy, copious meals were universally prized in our grandparents' day, two generations later we are 'fussy' about what we eat and swear by 'light' foods.

Today, we do not buy cabbage to make hotpot, but for its vitamin C. Oysters no longer sing to us of the sea, but of the virtues of trace elements. We have bid farewell to midday casseroles, to sugar that gives us tooth decay and unwanted extra pounds, and to butter that blocks the arteries. We distrust our refrigerator, suspecting it of harbouring staphylococcus and salmonella. And we have turned our back on tinned food which, if not properly sterilized, is likely to give us botulism, which continues to claim its share of victims each year.

This being the case, what is there left to put on our plates? Eggs? Beware of cholesterol! Ham? Saturated with phosphates. Oranges? Treated with diphenyl. Fish contains mercury, there are pesticides in fruit, and nitrates in vegetables. The list of cancer-producing foods grows longer every day, until one wonders what is *not* carcinogenic. As for processed foods, they can all be harmful, through a lack of either vitamins, minerals or fibre. In short, in the century of relativity, we are terrorized by our plates and no longer know what to eat, or how to eat.

Spared the fear of 'going without', eating itself has become problematic and, as French sociologist Claude Fischler (1993) points out, 'seems to preoccupy us, and even worry us, more than ever'. This obsessive fear, revealed in polls, is manifested in the following attitudes: for a start, we eat too much; yet we can limit the damage by resisting temptation; so 'watch what you eat', implying the virtues of going on a diet or at least keeping to a balanced diet.

Faced with the task of deciphering this modern-day anguish, sociologists have pinpointed two reasons. The first is our difficulty in coping not with a shortage, but with a plethora. Now that we have independence in choosing what to eat, we have to compare, decide between multiple, mouth-watering enticements, fight our impulses and resist our urges in order to reject the superfluous. The second reason has to do with the excesses of modern life. Despite the tempting appearance of our food, we are increasingly mistrustful of what it contains. The content reawakens or perpetuates age-old anxieties. Anxieties that are often linked to what the eater imagines to be true.

At the end of the Second World War, diet played a central role in social life: people impressed their neighbours by showing them how much they ate. With the spread of the refrigerator in the 1950s, people promptly discovered that they could store food. Tinned food, too; suddenly appeared. This marked the beginning of individualism and democratization: what was on the plate was no longer a reflection of social class.

The movement gathered momentum towards 1960. Women abandoned the kitchen and entered the job market. People began to question traditional customs, ideologies and beliefs. At the same time, great store was set by the return to nature; colourings were hunted down and people rushed to buy 'natural' products. The trend was not towards what was 'good' to eat, but what was 'healthy' to eat. At the beginning of the 1970s, individuals, with their cars, their well-heated apartments and domestic appliances, aspired to leisure activities and holidays, and consumed frantically.

This was a prosperous time for catering outlets and supermarkets, which sprang up like mushrooms and completely changed patterns of consumption and the way of life. Daily shopping tended to disappear in favour of the weekly shopping trip. People planned their shopping and, above all, their meals for the week. People ate more quickly, and more simply, at the works canteen or on a corner of the table. Family meals went out of fashion. The raw food era came just at the right time, and the art of cooking was considered a waste of time. Exeunt, therefore, the ragout, the stew, shepherd's pie, and all the traditional dishes cooked with loving care.

As the 1980s dawned things went into reverse, and people rediscovered that a food product was not purely and simply a question of nutrition: each had its own aroma, feel and taste. New sensations were sought after. With frozen food it even became possible to seal these flavours in ice, a revolution that challenged the seasons and geography: exotic foods could be eaten in the middle of winter even in the remotest village. Henceforth, anyone could travel simply by eating.

However, these vacuum-packed, cellophane-wrapped, dehydrated, frozen and refrigerated foods are increasingly regarded with suspicion. The present-day eater asks himself a number of perplexing questions: although these foods are easy to prepare, are they processed, do they contain colourings, additives, flavourings, or flavour enhancers? It is as though the very act of eating presents the individual with a delicate, difficult, and at times insoluble problem: an individual, moreover, who is submerged under a deluge of dietary advice, often contradictory, dispensed by doctors, nutritionists, manufacturers and consumer watchdogs, and duly relayed by advertising and the media, forbidding certain foods, only to restore them to favour later in the name of cardiovascular prevention, or in the light of revealing statistics or revolutionary scientific discoveries that overturn or modify the ones that came before. As a result, there are signs in the developed countries that eaters, in varying degrees, are reeling under this nutritional cacophony.

Indeed, if we consider the development of modern dietetics, it has to be admitted that it has floundered back and forth between certainties and contradictions. From the religion of steak and salad of the 1970s we have progressed to the salutary fish. For a long time the tiniest mouthful of bread (full of carbohydrates) weighed us down with remorse, while today baguettes and pastry are almost *de rigueur* (full of fibre!). One by one, carbohydrates have been cursed, fatty acids banished, fruit suspect and fibre revered. A food-related terrorism that Gérard Debry (1985), professor of human nutrition at the University of Nancy, denounced even in 1985:

> Many wrong ideas persist. No food is bad in itself. It was said, for example, that sugar caused arteriosclerosis, diabetes and obesity. All this, as with other products, is very poorly expressed . . . We must not find ourselves beset by a dietary dictatorship. We must preserve the idea that food is something to be enjoyed. This notion has been sacrificed on the altar of dietetics. The eater has come to believe that the pleasure of eating is often misleading, if not actually harmful, and that good health requires restrictions, and mastery over urges and desires. In short, one has to suffer, or at least give something up, in order to be healthy.

The religious practices of fasting and going without meat have been forgotten, and when we sit down to eat, all that remains is a vague feeling of guilt that weighs on our stomachs and permeates our vocabulary.

Much remains to be done before we can enjoy our diet as omnivores without these feelings of anguish and obsession. To do this, we need once more to listen to our senses, and remind ourselves that the verb 'to know' in French (*savoir*) is derived etymologically from the word 'flavour' (*saveur*). Perhaps then we can establish a link between what we eat and what we are.

References

Debry, G., 1985, *Le monde aujourd'hui*, April.
Fischler, C., 1993, *L'Homnivore*, Odile Jacob, Paris.

15 Food management: developing a national policy

J. Thomson

Introduction

Feeding is the most intimate thing we do in our lives; three times every day, in public. We eat 1.5 kg of food every day, over ½ tonne every year and over 35 tonnes if we survive our three score years and ten. We spend up to 4 years of our lives just eating. People in the developed nations of the world take the availability of food for granted and are perhaps slightly puzzled when faced with the ravaging effect of hunger and starvation that so regularly plagues the less developed nations. Of all human activities, none is more important than food production and consumption. Food is a source of world energy to be developed, managed and controlled and wielding as much power as more conventional energy sources such as coal, gas or oil. However, an efficient feeding policy requires organisation and structure and is not free from concomitant disadvantages which in other ways can damage the social structure. Illnesses such as kwashiorkor, pelagra and rickets, associated with food shortages of the less developed nations, are paralleled by coronary heart disease and cancer, diseases of feast in the developed nations.

What is needed to protect a feeding population, whether we are thinking nationally or globally, is a planning system, a food and nutritional management structure. Such a system must take into consideration all factors affecting food production and consumption. It must be a flexible management structure, able not only to work effectively when not under stress, but also to change rapidly to meet any crisis situation. The lack of this latter ability is the major cause of much of the suffering caused by malnutrition in this modern world.

The purpose of this chapter is to describe the structure and main elements of such a flexible food and nutritional management policy and the requirement for its formulation and implementation on a national scale to improve the food and nutritional situation for any given population.

The rapid growth of world population aggravates the food problems. As can be seen from Figure 15.1, despite major famines, epidemics and wars, the population of the world will have risen from 1.7 billion in 1900 to 6.5 billion by the year 2000. Obviously, the demand for food will continue to grow; however, current undernutrition, changes in age structure, longevity, rising incomes, desire for greater dietary variety and the fact that where possible food consumption is always greater than strict physiological needs, continue to make the demand for food grow proportionately more rapidly than even the growth of population.

We need a food and nutritional management policy which will be able to function nationally or internationally, which will provide sufficient food to feed all of the people, all of the time and which will not only be feasible and applicable in times of plenty and peace, but also be modifiable quickly to meet the needs of the people in times of want and of war.

A food and nutritional management policy can be defined as an amalgam of measures – educational, technical, economic and legislative – which will enable sufficient food to be produced to meet projected food demand and forecasted food supply (US Department of Agriculture 1967). Such a policy requires to be instantly flexible and should not in its

(Billions of inhabitants)

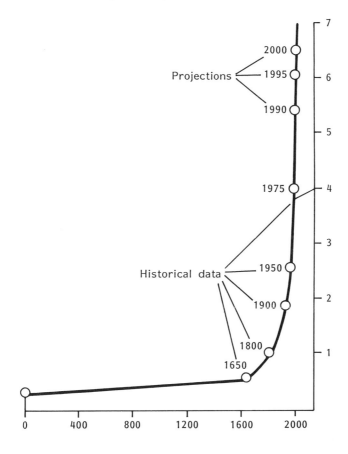

Figure 15.1 *World population growth (billions of inhabitants)*

Source: Sarre 1991, based on data supplied by The Club of Rome

application or flexibility produce side effects which may in other ways damage the health of the feeding population. The measures required have both economic and social impact. They require to alleviate differences which arise between what the consumer physiologically requires, what is available and what is desired.

Production of food in a developed nation

The flow diagram shown in Figure 15.2 is typical of the complex of factors which make up a modern feeding system. The critical factor is the complexity of the path between the farm and the plate; in general the shorter the path the more efficient the feeding system. The whole system exists in times of peace and plenty, but in times of war and want the structure can be rapidly changed to meet the needs of crisis management. In general there are three important factors associated with this modern food production system: first, it is very energy intensive; second it increases the degree of confusion, that is, it is entropy-increasing, thus contributing to an increase in employment; and third, if not managed carefully, it can seriously pollute both the consumer and his environment.

First the problem of energy. The amount of energy used by the farmer and the application of sunlight and photosynthesis, etc., ensure that at the farm gate there is a significant energy surplus. However, the stages involved in processing the food, packaging and distribution to the retail industries, and collection and preparation by the modern consumer, rapidly move the situation into an energy deficit; it has been calculated that the production of the food on our plate requires 7 J of energy for every joule we get out of eating it. An example of a modern processed food product is given in Table 15.1.

We can clearly see that to produce a simple processed can of corn requires the application of about 16 000 kJ of energy. The energy that is received from eating the whole can of corn will not be greater than 1700 kJ, that is nine times as much energy is put into the production as is gained by the consumer. Most modern processed foods fall into this bracket and food production and distribution is a real energy sink. It follows therefore that if any society wishes to follow the structure chosen by the developed world to meet its consumer desires, as shown in Figure 15.2, that society must have an infinite, or as near to infinite as is acceptable, source of energy available and secure. If this is not so, then a time of crisis will find that society unable to feed its population, and it is most unwise of developing countries to consider such an energy-sink food system without being aware or being made aware of the costs involved with such a system. However, if the country has the energy then it can be used to produce the variety of food products which will more than meet the desires of its consumers. Food production should be seen as a consumer-acceptable technique for moving fossil fuel energy sources such as coal and oil and gas into the consumable energy source of food. We are all mobile, self-repairing storage heaters. Such a confusion of complicated

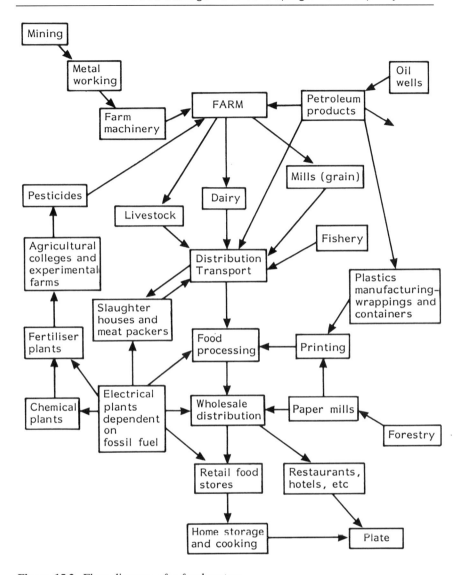

Figure 15.2 Flow diagram of a food system

Source: Scientific American, 1989

processes associated with production, processing, distribution and consumption, although using up energy, does also produce employment. The food industry and those industries involved in packaging, distribution, wholesaling and retailing do employ a very significant number of people. In the UK over 2.6 million people are employed in producing food and, of course, this is a positive factor which is attractive to a developing nation which sees not only what looks like an effective feeding system

Table 15.1 *The energy input required for the production of a can of sweetcorn*

Process	Energy used (kJ)
1. Agriculture (fertilisers, harvesting, pesticides, etc.)	1890
2. Processing (separating, cleaning, canning)	2751
3. Packaging (metal can)	4641
4. Transportation (440-mile trip)	970
5. Marketing	1428
6. Shopping (2½-mile round-trip)	2747
7. Home preparation (including dishwashing)	1806
Total	16 233

but also employment for its significant numbers of unemployed and underemployed people.

However it has never been possible to transfer crude energy to food energy without producing pollution, and Table 15.2 lists the typical pollutants associated with the management of a modern feeding system (Thomson 1983).

Let us return to our definition of a food and nutritional management policy. Our principal aim was to produce sufficient food to meet projected food demand and forecasted food supply. We have noted in passing that the methods used by developed societies are wasteful of energy and pollute the environments of the consumer, while at the same time providing a useful employment source, not an unimportant factor in this day and age. So how can it be managed with particular emphasis on the need

Table 15.2 *Contaminants in food management*

Antibiotics	Lubricants
Antimicrobial	Methane
Cadmium	Micotoxins
Carbon monoxide	Micro-organisms
Carbon dioxide	Nitric oxide
Chlorofluorocarbons (CFC)	Packaging additives
Cyanogens	Pesticides
Detergents	Polychlorinated biphenyls (PCB)
Dirt	Polycyclic aromatic hydrocarbons
Disinfectants	(PAH)
Fumigants	Protein inhibitors
Fungal toxins	Radioactive fall-out
Goutrogens	Rodenticides
Haemagglutinins	Solvent residues
Herbicides	Sulphur dioxide
Hormones	Trace metals
Lead tetraethyl	Veterinary pesticides

for management flexibility in times of crisis? It is clear that a failure to manage in times of crisis, whether that be natural environmental disaster, economic failure or even war, has been the main problem which has led to the serious and unacceptable horrors associated with malnutrition, hunger and starvation.

In the UK, the government, over the past four decades, has managed a 'cheap food policy' ensuring adequate supplies at a price which is acceptable to the population and related to the prevailing world situation. At the heart of such a policy is the possibility of instant and strict government control. This control is of such a nature that in times of plenty the government is not seen to be active in the control of the market, but in times of crisis it can instantly become active and take control. Because of the nature of consumption and its effect on morale and therefore political popularity, it is essential that this control should have the capacity and nature to be at all times proactive and not reactive. Figure 15.3 shows in simplified diagrammatic form some of the elements which make up the management of the UK food system.

In times of peace and plenty, government leaves well alone – little control over production, processing, packaging and distribution, no interference with the marketplace and power to the buyer. However, in times of want and war, government can instantly assume control in expanding and protecting production, reducing energy-wasteful processing and packaging, ensuring efficient distribution, controlling marketing and ensuring supply after controlling demand by use of the means of communication, such as radio and television, to educate the demand function of the consumers. In times of crisis the flow diagram of Figure 15.2 becomes significantly flattened and the farm and plate come closer together. This revised food processing and packaging system and the control of production and distribution produce more efficient food with higher energy ratios and less pollution while at the same time significantly reducing some elements of employment. However, in times of war other employment can be found for most of the people displaced.

An efficient food and nutritional management policy which is to be a proactive complex of educational, economic, technical and legislative measures and which is to respond rapidly to projected food demand, forecasted food supply and nutritional requirements is a policy of many points, some of which are listed in Figure 15.4. The measures are not only of economic but also of social impact. They are directed at palliating demand distortions, which government considers to be detrimental to the public interests, between what the consumer desires, what is available, and what is required physiologically. It is really not surprising that in this complex interactive system, it is essential that government should have control and that the politician has the last word on the choice of priorities. A lack of this essential control is the cause of much of the unacceptable deprivation seen in the world today.

It is possible to develop an interrelated plan that can be applied to the food management of any nation, whether developed or developing. This plan initially requires an accurate knowledge of the food requirement to

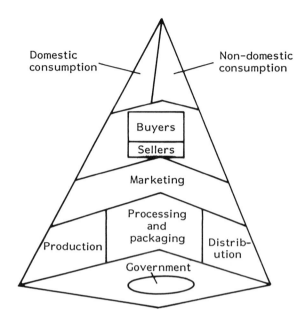

Food management in times of affluence

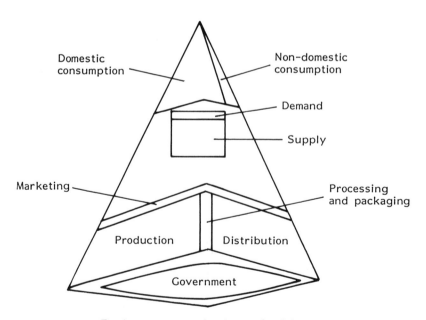

Food management in times of crisis

Figure 15.3 *Modified food management pyramid (including government control)*

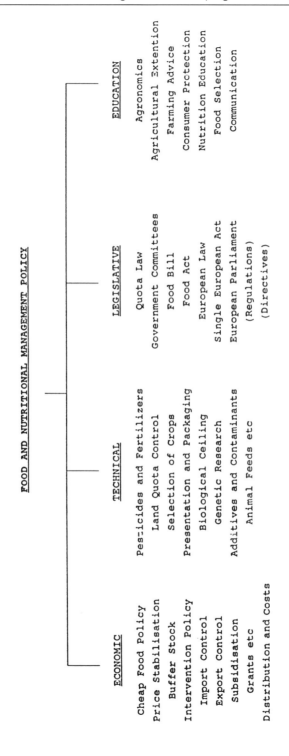

FOOD AND NUTRITIONAL MANAGEMENT POLICY

ECONOMIC

Cheap Food Policy
Price Stabilisation
Buffer Stock
Intervention Policy
Import Control
Export Control
Subsidisation
Grants etc
Distribution and Costs

TECHNICAL

Pesticides and Fertilizers
Land Quota Control
Selection of Crops
Presentation and Packaging
Biological Ceiling
Genetic Research
Additives and Contaminants
Animal Feeds etc

LEGISLATIVE

Quota Law
Government Committees
Food Bill
Food Act
European Law
Single European Act
European Parliament
(Regulations)
(Directives)

EDUCATION

Agronomics
Agricultural Extention
Farming Advice
Consumer Protection
Nutrition Education
Food Selection
Communication

Figure 15.4 *Some of the factors affecting food and nutritional management policy*

feed the nation adequately. This is not simply a matter of demographic statistics but the *population equivalent* of any nation. This is defined as follows:

$$\frac{\text{Population}}{\text{equivalent}} = \frac{\text{Food eaten by the population} + \text{Food eaten by animals}}{\text{Food } requirements \text{ of one person}}$$

Table 15.3 gives examples of population equivalents, and it can be seen that the food demand of any nation is associated not only with the number of people but also with the way in which they feed. For example, a meat-orientated society orientated towards consumption of processed food will require very much larger amounts of food (calculated as cereal equivalent) than a vegetarian society: the USA, with only 28 per cent of the population of India consumes 173 per cent as much food.

The food requirement figures are the initial foundation on which a food production plan can be based. What is then required are indigenous production figures, supply factors affecting importation and transportation, and consumption data. All these factors can then become part of a complex set of interactive variables which need to be controlled by a food and nutritional management policy as shown in Figure 15.5.

Table 15.3 Population equivalents

Nation	Population (million)	Population equivalent (million)	Population factor
UK	60	264	4.4
USA	250	2025	8.1
India	900	1170	1.3

Source: updated from Borgstram 1974

Conclusion

The efficient matching of the food supply to food demand is essential in every nation of the world, but this will only be effective if the development of a food and nutritional management policy is proactive and if the economic, technical, legislative and educational policies are wider in application than simply national needs and always have an element of international awareness built in. If this does not happen, any well-managed nation may not only be seen as efficient but also perhaps as greedy and, whether accurately or not, as a net contributor to the misery of a poorly managed alternative food-management system. It is of prime importance that the well-managed feeding policies developed by the countries in the northern hemisphere should not depend on the misuse by them of world resources.

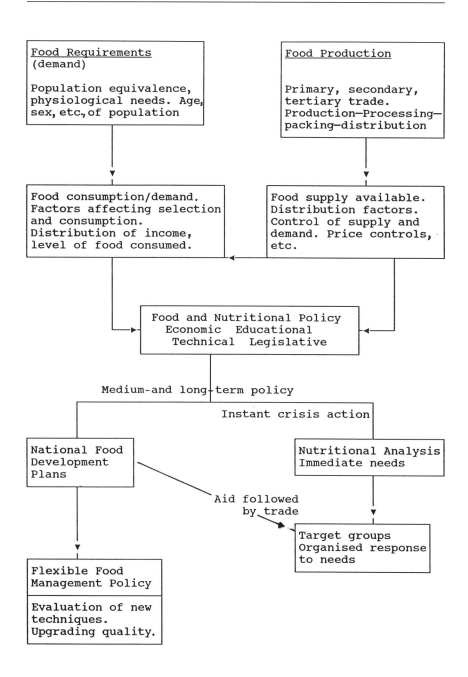

Figure 15.5 *Food and nutritional management policy (basic grid)*
Source: Brandt 1983

Before structuring and implementing a food and nutritional management policy, the planner must possess a coherent frame of control at a national level. There must be an understanding of the demand function, the ability to control supply, the policies to control prices, control over imports, exports, subsidies, etc. In the end, a food and nutritional management policy will be controlled by the political will of whoever is in power. It is no more than an element in an overall economic and social policy but because of the intimate nature of the final product may wield significantly more political power than has hitherto been assumed.

References

Borgstram, G., 1974, *World Food Resources,* International Textbook Company, Washington, DC: 100.

Brandt, W. (ed.), 1983, *Common crisis: North–South co-operation for world recovery* (2nd Brandt Report), Pan, London.

Keyfitz, N., 1989, 'The growing human population', *Scientific American*, 261(3): 70–71.

Leach, G., 1976, *Energy and food production*, IPC Science and Technology.

Sarre, P., 1991, *Environment, population and development*, Hodder & Stoughton, London.

Thomson, J., 1983, 'Should modern food carry a Government health warning?' *Quarterly Review of the Soil Association*, 1: 27–9.

United States Department of Agriculture, 1967, *World food problems*, Report to the President's Scientific Committee, Washington, DC.

16 Culinary heritage in the face of tourism

P. Reynolds

> *The true journey implies a complete change of nutrition, a digesting of the visited country – its fauna and flora and its culture (not only the different culinary practices and condiments but the different imple-ments used ...). This is the only kind of travel that has a meaning nowadays, when everything else visible you can see on television with-out rising from your easy chair.*
>
> (Calvino 1981)

> *The best way to a culture's heart is through its stomach.*
>
> (Chang 1977, p. 4)

Within the discussions of sustainable tourism and development the main thrust appears to be directed at the physical impact rather than social implications. This is perhaps understandable, given that tourism is largely an industry based on natural resources. It is also perhaps easier to measure degradation of a physical resource than something which is more ephemeral – such as social and cultural impact, where the variables are greater and evolution swifter. Key papers such as Pigram (1990) and Griffin and Boele (1993) deal almost exclusively with ecological and physical environment. This is despite the generally accepted definition of sustainable development provided by the Bruntland Report (World Commission on Environment and Development (WCED) 1983): develop-ment that meets the needs of the present without compromising the ability of future generations to meet their own needs.

We now have to move beyond the physical stage in our consideration of sustainability, and fully embrace the more abstract notion of the cultural environment. To this end a recent report by the Pacific Asia Travel Association (PATA) (1992) on *endemic tourism* suggests that the study of tourism has moved beyond the study of the physical and cultural environment, and into the realms of the tangible and intangible impacts of tourism on a particular people native to a country or locality. The concept of endemic tourism encompasses sustainability. It includes recognition of the cultural characteristics of communities and their value as tourism assets. Therefore the areas of anthropology and ethnography must continue to be examined in depth if the full picture of the impacts of tourism on hosts and guests is to emerge.

Many writers over the years have covered the generalities and specifics of impacts that tourism has made or makes on culture and society (see, for instance, Ap 1990; Brayley *et al.* 1990; Jafari *et al.* 1990; or Nash and Smith 1991). It is only recently that the sustainability of cultures in the face of tourism has started to gain prominence (Reynolds 1992). Statements from tourism offices and national tourism plans from around the world now emphasise the sustainable tourism message in both physical and cultural terms. 'Culture' here is usually taken to mean the arts, again usually in their physical form: artefacts, carvings, weaving, painting, etc., although occasionally dance, music and song are mentioned (see Graburn 1982; Jules-Rosette 1985; Litrell 1990; Popelka and Litrell 1991; Craig-Smith and French 1994: 28) and recently the linguistic dimension has been added (Prentice and Hudson 1993). None that have been surveyed have mentioned the sustainability of traditional food patterns, eating culture and the general social significance of food in the face of tourism. The study of food in itself ought to enjoy privileged status in cultural analysis. Food combines the concrete and the ephemeral, it meets physiological and social needs, it provides the free gift of hospitality and the strict requirement of biological survival, all bound up in strict rule systems.

Even in academic literature there is little identifiable sociological literature dealing with culinary practices, menus and manners, the beliefs and concepts and the social organisation of the provision of meals. Yet as Goody (1982) observed, academic concern with these questions is by no means frivolous. As part and parcel of the culture and structure of the societies in which they occur, they have a bearing on attempts either to create change or to appreciate its consequences.

Visser (1991) suggests that food has great significance in the following areas:

1. *Socialisation*: traditionally eating times have been periods where families/tribes have come together to share information as well as food and drink.
2. *Hierarchies and social structure*: the way in which we eat, what we eat with what, whom we eat with.
3. *Cultural heritage*: how we eat and what equipment we eat with, be it knife and fork, spoon and fork, fork only, chopsticks, etc.
4. *Tradition and ritual*: when we eat certain foods, i.e. celebrations, Christmas, Passover.
5. *Courtship*.

The study of food ways and the system of attitudes, beliefs, and practices surrounding food may constitute an important technique in unravelling the complexities of the overall culture pattern of a community. As Visser (1986) states:

> As soon as we can count on food supply (and so take food for granted ...) we start to civilise ourselves. Civilisation entails shaping, regulating, constraining and dramatising ourselves; we echo the preferences and the principles of our culture in the way we treat our food.

She goes on to say:

Changing (or unchanging) food choices and presentations are part of every society's tradition and character. Food shapes us and expresses us even more definitively than our furniture or houses or utensils do.

Eating habits must be viewed as a matter of culture, a product of codes of conduct and of the structure of social relationships. If this is accepted, the disassembling of culture patterns that surround food is probably easier to measure than changing patterns on craft or painting.

There are many pressures on traditional food culture patterns. The internationalisation of fast food, increased communication, access to foods of other nations, commercialisation, changing lifestyles and new technologies of food preparation, storage and presentation all have varying degrees of impact. What also needs to be added to the equation is tourism.

It would seem that tourists are increasingly interested in authentic experiences (see, for example, Gunn 1988; Jenkins 1990; Craig-Smith and French 1994) albeit at low risk, and writers have warned of the impact on the cultural and physical environment of the ecotourist, and the traveller who wants more than just a photograph (Wheeller 1991; 1992; Jones 1992; King 1994). The dichotomy exists in that as authenticity becomes more desired, so it becomes more expensive. Yet as an attraction becomes more popular, so it is often perceived to be less authentic, which therefore decreases its merit and finally, 'social customs and culture become commercialised ... greater weight is inevitably placed on saleability rather than authenticity' (Craig-Smith and French 1994, p. 42).

Food is perhaps one of the last areas of authenticity that is affordable on a regular basis by the tourist. Yet because it is perishable and relies on smell and taste as well as looks for its appeal, it cannot be transported, preserved or put in a gallery. Similarly, because food is perishable, the work of art must be re-created when required. The product can vary from producer to producer and generally cannot be tested (or in most cases even seen) before purchase. The consumer therefore relies on a menu description, which for many tourists is in a foreign language, and is accordingly a further impediment to experimentation. A duality therefore exists in the mind of the tourist: on one hand, the desire to try new experiences which are authentic; on the other, the matter of risk. Food, being so important to our daily well-being, is something we are very particular about. All but the bravest and most allocentric travellers tend to shun new flavours and textures for several reasons. Food is the part of the holiday package that is truly internalised, and is non-optional. It is also something we tend to remember long after the views and cultural shows have vanished from our memory. Factors such as the fear of illness while abroad are also very real. More people are ill on holiday from food-related incidents than any other source (Herniman 1982; Alleyne 1993), and therefore many are inhibited when faced with trying new culinary experiences. As mentioned above, culture has a large part to play in our food choice. If this choice is not available in a foreign and distant place, then dissatisfaction sets in. For these reasons and others, tourists tend to eat safely – even though they may wish to try some new experiences, there are overriding factors which lead to a 'safety first' approach.

There are therefore conflicting interests. Locals wish to preserve their own cultural traditions, yet make money out of visitors to their land. The visitor wants authentic cultural experiences, but only after safe food, shelter and security have been guaranteed (King 1994). A recent study (Reynolds 1993) in a popular tourist destination (Bali, Indonesia) showed that menu offerings over the past five years in 28 restaurants have changed significantly, from predominantly Indonesian foods to little other than copies of Western foods. Many young locals surveyed ate Western products, such as pizza and hamburgers, in preference to their traditional foods. On the other hand, visitors were dissatisfied. Many did not like the local copies of Western foods, and expected a greater range of local foods. In general terms, therefore the interests of both groups were not being met. Income for the producer was not being maximised, the visitor was not being satisfied, and culinary culture was not being preserved.

Conclusion

It is becoming increasing evident, despite tourism being the largest source of employment world-wide and providing work directly and indirectly to millions of people from all strata of society, that the local people are not nearly sufficiently in control over what actually happens within the tourism industry in their communities. Locals, therefore, cannot control cultural impact and the subsequent problems that may flow from a breakdown of traditional patterns of life. It is also clear that there are tremendous pressures on all aspects of traditional culture. MacCannel (1984) suggests several options to serve the tourist craving for authenticity, from 'staged authenticity' to 'reconstructed ethnicity' and perhaps 'museumising' cultural activity at a distinct site with actors re-creating roles and rituals.

The culinary arts are one area where locals do have direct control over purchasing, preparation, display and product conformance. Yet in the face of the internationalisation of food choice and many locals erroneously perceiving customer demand as shifting away from ethnic cuisine, the standards of preparation and number of offerings of local foods are deteriorating.

Traditions and cultures, along with the natural resources which made areas attractive for tourists in the first place, are being rapidly eroded. They are being replaced by a homogeneous product where the sand is massaged into perfection, the 'cultural show' is performed every night at 8 o'clock and Tuesday night offers a 'sumptuous Chinese smorgasbord'.

The culture and customs surrounding food are a central part of our lives, and communities around the world must preserve this resource base for future generations. The Bruntland Report (WCED 1987) pointed out that concern for equity between generations must logically be extended to equity within each generation. Yet we see less and less tradition happening in the home and more foods labelled 'traditional flavour' appearing on the supermarket shelves.

If we are really serious about sustainability, then the erosion of culture, custom and traditional skill must be investigated along with erosion of landscape and degradation of seas. Unfortunately, preservation of something so near to us as food does not usually generate the political concern or economic pressure to raise levels of consciousness enough to ensure sustainability is even considered. If the 'environment is the travel industry's base product' (Cook *et al.* 1992) then a holistic view must be taken of this environment, with culinary tradition growing in importance.

References

Alleyne, G., 1993, 'The health and tourism partners concepts, roles and prospects', *TTRA Conference Proceedings*, 279–87.
Ap, J., 1990, 'Residents' perceptions – research on the social impact of tourism', *Annals of Tourism Research*, 17: 610–15.
Brayley, R., Var, T. and Sheldon, P., 1990, 'Perceived influence of tourism on social issues', *Annals of Tourism Research*, 17(2): 285–8.
Calvino, I., 1981, *Under the jaguar sun*, Minerva, London.
Chang, K.C. (ed.), 1977, *Food in Chinese culture*, Yale University Press, New Haven, Connecticut.
Cook S.D., Stewart, E. and Repass, K., 1992, *Tourism and the environment*, Travel Industry Association of America, Washington, DC.
Craig-Smith, S. and French, C., 1994, *Learning to live with tourism*, Pitman, Melbourne.
Goody, J., 1982, *Cooking, cuisine and class*, Cambridge University Press, Cambridge.
Graburn, N., 1982, 'The dynamics of change in tourist arts', *Cultural Survival Quarterly*, 6(4): 7–11.
Graburn, N., 1984, 'The evolution of tourist arts', *Annals of Tourism Research*, 14(1): 393–419.
Griffin, T. and Boele, N., 1993, 'Alternative paths to sustainable tourism', *2nd American Express Annual Review of Travel*, 13–23, American Express, New York.
Gunn, C.A., 1988, *Tourism planning*, Taylor & Francis, London.
Hernimann, R.H., 1982, 'Travellers diarrhea', *World Health*, April: 5–17, London.
Jafari, J., Pizam, A. and Przeclawski, K., 1990, 'A sociocultural study of tourism as a factor of change', *Annals of Tourism Research*, 17(3): 469–72.
Jenkins, C.L., 1990, 'Tourism: is future demand changing?' in M. Quest (ed.), *Horwath book of tourism*, Macmillan, London: 46–55.
Jones, A., 1992, 'Is there a real "alternative" tourism?', *Tourism Management*, 13(1): 102–3.
Jules-Rosette, B., 1985, *The message of tourist arts*, Plenum Press, New York.
King, B., 1994, 'Bringing out the authentic in Australian hospitality products for the international tourist: a service management approach', *Australian Journal of Hospitality Management*, 1(1): 1–8.
Litrell, M.A., 1990, 'The symbolic significance of crafts for tourists', *Annals of Tourism Research*, 17(2): 228–43.
MacCannel, D., 1984, 'Reconstructed ethnicity: tourism and cultural identity in Third World communities', *Annals of Tourism Research*, 11(3): 375–91.

Nash, D. and Smith, V.L., 1991, 'Anthropology and tourism', *Annals of Tourism Research*, 18(1): 12–25.

PATA Think Tank, 1992, *Endemic tourism: a profitable industry in a sustainable environment*, Pacific Asia Travel Association.

Pigram, S.S., 1990, 'Sustainable tourism – policy considerations', *Journal of Tourism Studies*, 11(2): 2–9.

Popelka, C.A. and Litrell, M.A., 1991, 'Influence of tourism on handcraft evolution', *Annals of Tourism Research*, 18(3): 392–413.

Prentice, R. and Hudson, J., 1993, 'Assessing the linguistic dimension in the perception of tourism impacts by residents of a tourist destination', *Tourism Management*, 14(3): 298–306.

Reynolds, P.C., 1992, 'Responsible cultural tourism: impossible or improbable', paper presented to Pacific Organisation Conference on Environment, Bali. (Unpublished.)

Reynolds, P.C., 1993, 'Food and tourism: towards an understanding of sustainable culture', *Journal of Sustainable Tourism*, 1(1): 48–55.

Visser, M., 1986, *Much depends on dinner*, Penguin, Harmondsworth.

Visser, M., 1991, *The rituals of dinner*, Penguin, Harmondsworth.

Wheeller, B., 1991, 'Tourism's troubled times', *Tourism Management*, 12(1): 91–96.

Wheeller, B., 1992, 'Is progressive tourism appropriate?', *Tourism Management*, 13(1): 104–5.

World Commission on Environment and Development, 1987, *Our common future* (Bruntland Report), Oxford University Press, Oxford.

Contemporary themes

17 Dynamic innovation in the tourism industry

A.-M. Hjalager

Introduction

While market and demand studies, evaluations of impacts on local cultures and studies of the characteristics of particular destinations constitute the main volume of research into tourism, economic investigations and their basic theories and methodologies have received comparatively little attention (Sinclair and Stabler 1991). This also accounts for innovation theories, which were developed primarily in order to explain the dynamics initiated by or affecting manufacturing industries. Only recently have theories emerged which deal with new issues within, for instance, household services (introduced by Gershuny and Miles 1982) and business services (for instance, Barras 1986b).

One possible explanation for the non-transfer of known theories and methodologies to the tourism industry may derive from the fact that the industry is not well defined in the same way as, for instance, the automobile industry. Therefore, the obstacles to the provision of test and comparison data are indeed enormous. The tourism industry will never be as well documented by publicly available data and other quantitative evidence as the manufacturing industries, but this should not delay theoretical discussions. It should also not hamper the collection of data from other sources and by other methods.

This chapter is devoted to theoretical and methodological considerations. Its aim is to present selected theoretical approaches to innovation and to discuss whether and how they apply to the dynamics of the tourism industry. The chapter discusses the following sets of approaches to innovation:

* A typology of innovations at micro (enterprise) level. The typology identifies points of operation for innovating tourist enterprises.
* A typology serving the analysis of meso- and macro-economic impacts of innovations. Based on an inter-organisational mode, it forms a conceptual framework for the analysis of the degree of the transformation effects of innovations.
* An analysis of mechanisms involved in the introduction of innovations. This section will focus on the ways in which innovations are introduced into the tourism industry.
* A template for the analysis of the barriers to and facilitators of the diffusion of innovation.

The various approaches are closely interrelated, but all aim to elaborate a more complex level of analysis. The arguments put forward combine to form a perspective and a platform for research, rather than a sharply defined choice of theoretical definitions.

Definitions of innovations, and the tourism industry

The key concept of this chapter is *innovation*. The term 'innovation' is defined – primarily by Schumpeter (1939) but also by a range of successors – in terms of a close connection to another term: *invention*. Inventions are major scientific or technological developments brought about without any specified industrial use in mind. Frequently mentioned examples are the steam engine and, more recently, the micro-processor. Innovations are further developments of the invention, institutionalising the new methods of production or bringing the new products or services to the market. Thus, the adaptation to markets and production systems is a crucial element which differentiates the concepts of 'invention' and 'innovation'.

Accordingly, the success criterion is *technical* for invention, but *commercial* for innovation. The link between the invention and the innovation is the *entrepreneurial* capability of an individual and/or an organisation (Burgelmann and Sayles 1986).

No doubt, 'classical' inventions and their applications influenced the tourism industry as greatly as they did other industries. For instance, improved transportation opened up a possibility for the urban middle classes to become tourists, expending less time, money and effort on reaching recreational places (Lickorish and Kershaw 1975; Urry 1990). Consequently, the coastal resort can be seen as a conglomerate of innovations responding to (at least) one major technological invention, the steam engine and its heavy implementation in connection with railway systems.

A recent invention, the micro-chip, has had similar consequences for the tourism industry. The possibilities for large-scale information storage and handling result in particular coordination benefits in relation to tourist products, for instance packaged tours, which may be organised in an increasingly flexible manner so as to adapt to specific consumer demands. The opportunities afforded by information technology and the media cannot yet be considered to have been fully exploited by the tourist industry.

As tourism belongs in the service sector, the transformation of inventions into innovations cannot be fully compared to the process usually seen in the manufacturing industries. This fact prevents us from using the same analytical methodologies in order to trace the origins of innovations and to evaluate the consequences of inventions.

For instance, a major part of the innovation literature is devoted to the analysis of patenting. The patenting systems provide excellent opportunities for collecting indicators, which are characterised by stability over time and across national borders (Pavitt 1982; 1984). But these types of data are not available in relation to the tourist industry, as in most cases patenting of inventions or innovations will not be possible.

Other strands of traditional research into innovations are concerned with the study of the size of innovating firms and the sectors to which they belong, the scientific qualifications and the output of research departments within industry and/or of publicly financed research organisations (Tornatsky *et al.* 1983). This approach also cannot be brought to bear on the tourism industry without making considerable modifications. The major obstacle to obtaining relevant evidence concerning the scale and scope of innovation in the tourism industry lies in the fact that this kind of information is not registered by the tourism industry as it is in the manufacturing industries. This must be seen in combination with the fact that the inclination to form R&D departments or laboratories is not widespread in the tourism industry.

A third section of the traditional innovation literature is concerned with government policies – taxes, regulations, subsidies, transaction devices, human resources development initiatives, etc. A number of studies of the tourism industry touch on these subjects (Pearce 1992; Holm-Petersen *et al.* 1993) but usually not with any definite intention of evaluating them or setting a framework for the promotion of innovation.

Finally, a great deal of the innovation literature investigates the processes of innovation and its trajectories. Some studies are concentrated particularly on research into the users' role in the innovation process, and other studies attempt to examine the speed and modes of transfer of innovations from scientific laboratories to industries or from advanced industries/countries to less advanced industries/countries. The interaction between universities and non-universities has also been made the subject of intensive studies and recommendations. Recent attempts tend to combine the views that have thus arisen in order better to understand complex national (or regional) innovation systems. A number of articles in Lundvall (1992) and Mowery (1992) are elaborating on this line of research. In relation to the tourism industry, this type of innovation research represents the most interesting and transferable methodologies.

A typology of innovations at the micro level

On the enterprise or micro level, innovations are usually subdivided into two categories: process innovations and product innovations. This subdivision is classical, though vividly discussed (Uhlmann 1979). At first glance, these categories might also prove useful for analysing innovations in the tourism industry. *Process innovations* would refer to the implementation of new types of equipment aiming at the production of exactly the same services or products as before the innovation. Conversely, within the framework of this typology *product innovations* would consist of changed or entirely new services and products.

However, inspired by Goddard (1990) and Miles (1985) who concentrated their research on the social and spatial effects of information technology, it may be concluded that a wider range of categories is needed to understand entirely the innovation taking place in the service industries and the interactions between process and product innovations.

The following categories of innovations may be considered in order to understand the full range of innovations in the tourist industry:

* classical process innovations;
* transactions innovations;
* innovations of the distribution system;
* process innovations in information handling;
* management innovations;
* product innovations.

Classical process innovations

This type of innovation tends to raise the performance of operations already in the portfolio. On average, the tourism industry is very labour-intensive, and the services provided are very often of a personal, face-to-face nature. Nevertheless, production automation is taking place on a wide scale.

The first introduction of improved equipment tends to take place in sectors and operations not visible to the tourist. For instance, productivity in cleaning has been raised by introducing more efficient equipment and facilities, including new chemicals, accessories and designs suitable for rational maintenance. The introduction of robotic hoovers is about to become a reality. Also in other 'backstage' localities, such as restaurant kitchens, gardens, etc., the use of more efficient technology can lead to productivity gains (Lattin 1990).

Many innovations aim at a combination of purposes. For instance, the increased speed of trains raises the performance and thereby the comfort level of the user, and at the same time the labour assets per distance unit may be reduced. The technology applied in connection with check-in procedures in hotels, airports and attractions may reduce waiting time and raise the flexibility of choice, and therefore be more attractive to the customer. At the same time, technology will create more efficient and labour-saving procedures. Completely automatic check-in procedures are being introduced in several sectors, where personal communication is not required or is less important (Johns and Wheelers 1991).

If automation is entirely inconvenient to the customer, enterprises tend to introduce financial incentives in order to demotivate the use of personalised services.

All types of classical process innovation will help the industry and the individual enterprise to gain in productivity. But process innovations may represent a platform leading to the introduction of other types of innovations.

Transactions innovations

In manufacturing industries, the introduction of flexible production systems has taken place within a time-span of more than a decade. The implementation of the concept of flexible – lean – production methods will reduce the need for the storage of components and products in the individual enterprise. Goddard (1990) also points out that this concept leads to a new division of labour in industry, and it motivates transactions innovation in order efficiently to deal with more frequent commercial interactions by means of relatively smaller amounts of products.

In this respect the operation of most tourist enterprises does not resemble manufacturing. An unsold product of a tourist enterprise cannot be stored for sale at future date, and the product has to be ready for sale at the moment when the customer arrives.

Nevertheless, the concept of flexibility is becoming more evident, but only in certain sectors of the tourist industry – those responsible for the packaging of tours or other combined tourist products. For instance, one or two decades ago the largest tour operators integrated vertically by purchasing fleets of aircraft or entire resorts. In the 1990s a general excess capacity of aircraft seats and hotel beds is causing bankruptcies and heavy losses to the traditional tour operators, a circumstance which opens up possibilities for enterprises operating on more flexible terms without owning any tourist capacity themselves (Mayhew 1987).

Within the sector of cultural attractions the same tendencies are emerging. The excess capacity of concert halls and theatres facilitates the establishment of arranging bureaux; bureaux which also may be identified as *transactions innovations*. However, in culture, losses arising from excess capacity are most often placed on the shoulders of the public authorities.

Transactions innovations are only open to certain types of enterprise within the tourist industry. In their creation of new niches of operation these enterprises utilise the excess capacity of the sector and the planning failures of other sectors.

Innovations of the distribution system

The production of tourist commodities has a spatial perspective important to the concept of innovation. Usually production and consumption cannot be separated in time or space. In comparison to manufactured commodities, this hampers the opportunities for innovating the distribution of tourist products and services.

In one sub-sector of the tourism industry, the airlines distributional innovations can nevertheless be observed. Major carriers tend to develop concepts involving centralised hubs, where the interchange of passengers can take place. The choice of locations for such hubs is crucial; mostly they are aimed at combining of the high service level anticipated by the passenger and increasing the probability of the passenger's choosing to continue the flight with the same airline (Hanlon 1991). The concept of distribution is somewhat similar to what is taking place in retailing, although more visible to customers and therefore more complex. If railways are deregulated and privatised there may be seen a similar development of junctions dominated by the operations of one or more railway companies.

However, if only sales activities undertaken in connection with tourist commodities are considered, the distributional innovations are plentiful, and in this respect the implementation of technically matured innovations have still not taken place on the scale envisaged by futurists (Gilbert 1990). The classical way of purchasing a tourist commodity is to contact a local travel agency personally. On grounds of obtaining personal information this mode of purchasing is still preferred by many customers, as travelling is regarded as a 'high advice' commodity. At the same time however, existing opportunities for information retrieval; purchasing and booking by means of telematics are to an increasing extent being exploited by tourists with access to the relevant equipment. A precondition for a breakthrough in the distance distribution of tourist commodities and information will be a much wider distribution of the necessary equipment into private homes.

Process innovations in the handling of information

Tourism is becoming as information-intensive as other sectors of the economy, and innovation in the handling of large amounts of information is quickly developing. The individual tourist enterprise's possibility of obtaining access to the market depends increasingly on its ability to process information in order either to rationalise and save labour, or to customise and thereby enhance services.

Within the enterprises – particularly in the hotel industry – data systems are implemented for administrative purposes, and tactical decisions (marketing, finance) are being implemented. This step is often the first in the information-handling innovation process, and in most cases it aims at rationalisation only (Lattin 1990; Gamble 1991).

By launching into an interchange of information with outside intermediaries the individual enterprise attempts to gain access to still larger markets. The handling of this kind of information is usually a task too massive for the individual enterprise, as the costs of collecting, storing and transmitting information are considerable and thus have to be shared. Therefore linking into established networks is crucial. Efficient linking will tend to reduce the need for other kinds of information system in the individual firm and may give way to rationalisation of the overall marketing activity.

The most substantial part of the process innovations taking place within the field of information handling does not occur in the tourism industry itself. It does, however, occur in the businesses supplying the hardware, software and information services, i.e. predominantly the large computer reservations systems such as Galileo, Sabre and Amadeus.

Management innovations

Managerial 'revolutions' introduced concepts of decentralisation, particularly as a remedy for increasing job satisfaction and productivity. Informatics revolutions facilitated the ideas further, as decision-making data could be distributed efficiently to the lowest possible level without compromising the planning at strategic and tactical levels. In relation to this kind of managerial innovation, the tourism industry seems to be a late developer.

It could be argued that, compared to manufacturing industry, there never was much room for the concepts of managerial decentralising and job enrichment. Management in most tourism enterprises already depends heavily on the personal judgement, initiative and flexibility of the individual staff member.

On the other hand, a great number of tourist enterprises are not attempting to decentralise, but rather to centralise, primarily in order to increase quality and in order to standardise products and services. Fast food chains are very obvious representatives of this development (Love 1986; Pillsbury 1990) involving the (re)introduction of scientific management models long abandoned by other sectors of industry.

Product innovations

All the above-mentioned types of research on innovations usually deal with the production of tangible commodities. In respect of manufactured commodities, product innovation may be easily understood – a food product with a new flavour, a machine incorporating a new facility or higher performance, or, more radically, an entirely new product which tends to make an earlier product obsolete.

The products and services of the tourism industry cannot be subject to exactly the same type of analysis. Only a simple model is offered, which will be expanded and discussed in the following sections of this chapter.

One mode of product innovation is the activity of making space and traditions accessible to tourists – space and traditions which until the moment of innovation were solely in the hands of the locals. The discovery of new destinations lies within the routine activities of most tour operators. Nowadays this expansion in space is, of course, in most cases purely illusory. European tour operators will discover destinations in the Pacific which were invaded by Australian tourists long ago – and vice versa (Ashworth 1988; Pearce 1991).

The aspect of expanding into the traditions of the locals is more crucial. This may be a question of utilising the facilities otherwise only available to the locals (for example, sports facilities), an approach which has become a strategy in numerous local tourist policies. The opening-up of spectacular but more or less private events (cattle shows, weddings, festivals, production units, etc.) to tourists has also to an increasing extent become a part of tourist policies and enterprise strategies.

In this connection the key word of the innovation process is *commoditi-sation*, which, as anthropologists have not failed to point out, will influence and change the authenticity of the event (MacCannell 1973; Crick 1985; Cohen 1988).

Another mode of product innovation in tourism consists of the incli-nation to satisfy new needs. It is often claimed that the industrialisation of the tourism industry provided opportunities for the population to take a rest from the burden of daily work. The mechanisation and professional-isation of the working environment and the exclusion from the labour market of large groups of the population raised the need to utilise travel not only for purposes of rest, but also to obtain life experience and social esteem.

The modernistic need for self-identity gave rise to the concepts of learning or experiencing being introduced into tourism and resulted in numerous product variations of which some in fact represent only very incremental innovations of something seen elsewhere. The object of these incremental innovations will be to adapt the product or service to specific market segments or local conditions.

In order to satisfy new needs, the act of *staging* is an important feature of this type of innovation. In the same way as a stage play, the experience has to be planned and scripted, the roles of the actors have to be precisely defined, and the *spectacle* needs to be consciously instructed. The process of innovation deals with these tasks along with the commoditisation.

A third mode of product innovation in the tourist industry could be called a *search for substitutes*. In its most radical version, this search will aim at identifying ways of satisfying the need for experiences, learning and relaxation without travelling at all.

Television and other media tend to lead to a change of behaviour in such a way that leisure time is to an increasing extent being spent in the home rather than at the sports field or in the concert hall (Holm-Petersen *et al.* 1993). With less effort and less money it has become possible to experience events and sights previously only available by actually going there. Technical devices may either reduce the inclination to go, or alter-natively increase the appetite for experiencing the real thing. A broader diffusion of advanced equipment into private homes may push the ten-dency towards the former.

In his vision for the future, Krippendorf (1986) suggests that tourism ought to involve less travelling. As part of a strategy for his concept of 'humanising' tourism, he suggests that if the quality of daily life could be raised, spending the vacation at home may be as satisfying as travelling. Environmental concerns may lead to the same conclusion.

Concluding remarks on the typology of innovations

This typology suggests that it is possible to distinguish modes of innovation. For analytical purposes a separation along these lines would be useful. In practice, however, many authors of innovation studies have noticed that product innovations and process innovations in most cases are closely interwoven. For instance, the implementation of new technology will motivate managements to alter work routines, or new technology may facilitate the provision of new products or services.

Many incremental innovations – some of which could never be regarded as an innovating activity if considered separately – tend to constitute steps in a sequence of small and major innovations (Figure 17.1). The typology approach is useful in connection with first step classifications in empirical studies. The division into various types of innovation may lead to the identification of guidelines to be applied by enterprises and authorities attempting to understand the substance of innovation. But the typology approach can only marginally reveal the *dynamics* of innovations. However, general theories on innovation suggest a number of modifications to straightforward typology. They will be presented in the following sections of this chapter in order to arrive at a closer understanding of the dynamics of innovation in tourism.

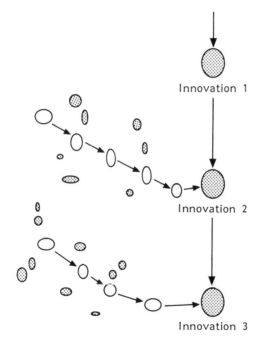

Figure 17.1 *Pattern of incremental innovation*

Radical innovations

The starting point of this section is the hypothesis that some innovations have more far-reaching effects than others. The more important ones tend to dominate the development of not only the individual enterprise, but also the entire economic structure of an industry.

A model developed by Abernathy and Clark (1985), and which Christensen (1990) supplemented by further discussions, seems useful in connection with the conceptualisation of the issue of radical innovations in the tourism industry. The model reflects the notion 'that innovation is not a unified phenomenon: some innovations disrupt, destroy and make obsolete established competence; others refine and improve. Further, the effects of innovations on production systems may be quite different from their linkages to customers and markets' (Abernathy and Clark 1985, p. 4). Thus, the introduction of innovations into a competitive business environment is crucial to any explanation of the concept of the radical degree of innovation described by Abernathy and Clark's model (Figure 17.2).

Architectural innovations

These are based on technology or methodologies that depart from established systems of production, and thus open up new linkages to markets and users. They create new industries and reform the old ones.

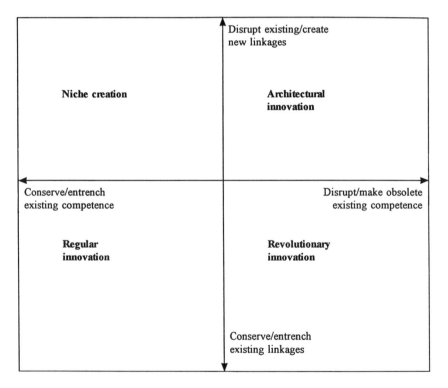

Figure 17.2 *How radical is an innovation?*

Source: Abernathy and Clark, 1985

Innovation of this sort defines the basic configuration of product and process and establishes the technical and marketing agenda that will guide the subsequent development. It lays down the architecture of the industry, the broad framework within which competition will occur and develop. (Abernathy and Clark 1985, p. 7).

Turning to the tourism industry for innovations which disrupt existing linkages and create new ones, and which at the same time disrupt and make obsolete existing competence, we might choose the following cases to illustrate this category of innovation:

• *The fast-food concept*. The organisation of work, the attitudes of the staff towards the customers, the choice of products, the technology, the location of the outlets, are combined factors which form a far-reaching architectural innovation (Love 1986; Pillsbury 1990). When first introduced, the outlets tended to reflect a latent user need to have a meal within a very short time and at a place located conveniently in relation to transport, work, leisure activities, etc.

The fast-food concept greatly influenced eating habits in general. But the innovation also influenced the work processes of the conventional restaurant sector, and the opportunities of suppliers of technology and semi-products.

• *Computer reservation systems (CRS) and related administrative and strategic computer systems*. CRS may be regarded as an architectural innovation as they tend to reorganise the entire marketing approach of the tourist industry. Forming connections to networks of individual enterprises immensely increases exposure to the markets. The computer systems allow the customers more careful selection routines without the need to invest the time and effort that was previously required of them. The customers are able to gain a more complete view of the products and services available.

To the enterprises, connection to CRS not only means better access to the markets, but also implies much heavier competition. It might be argued that with a limited flow of information between customers and enterprises, the individual enterprise will be better protected against its competitors, as customers may not want to spend time and effort gaining knowledge of substitutes. But to an increasing extent the enterprises will come to regard this isolation as having a dangerous effect on their business opportunities. The overall tendency will be the development of more perfect market mechanisms – in a neoclassical sense.

Transport and accommodation services can most often be found as CRS members. But also other services, such as attractions and events, are to an increasing extent finding their way into the systems. This will tend to change the architecture of the business in these sections of the tourism industry.

* *Virtual reality*. Virtual reality is about to justify its existence in, for instance, construction, medical science and teaching (Sherman and Judkins 1992). The possibility of being 'present' in a computer-created reality

could, however, be applied to many situations in tourism. The opportunity of going for a imaginary walk through the tourist resort or the hotel before actually buying the tour will probably be implemented in travel agencies over the next few years.

The more architecturally innovative effects of virtual reality may occur later as the technology improves. The important thing about this technology is that it tends to disrupt the otherwise unbreakable thesis that tourist products should be consumed in the place where they are produced. Virtual reality allows consumption of the tourist experience, in full or in part, at home or in places other than the original.

At the moment we are still not able to assess the full range of consequences in an architecturally innovative sense, but the hypothesis is that the effects of virtual reality will be substantial (Perlmutter 1992).

Abernathy and Clark (1985) claim that three themes are evident in the architectural pattern of innovation: 'The first is the importance of breaking the grip of the prior industries on the technology structure of the new industry'. In tourism we may see the establishment of an entirely new sector of sub-contractors to the traditional tourism industries, a sector which becomes absolutely crucial as an imposer of change. 'The second concerns the durability of the concepts'. The structural effects and the new divisions of labour due to, for instance, CRS and to new catering concepts seem to be durable, but we still lack evidence for the durability of virtual reality in tourism. 'The third theme is the role of science'. Compared to other sectors the role of science in tourism is limited. The scientific elements of the underlying technology are nevertheless more solid, and the scientific advances seem to be transferred in an incidental way to tourism.

Innovation in the market niche phase

The opening up of new market opportunities through the use of existing technology is crucial to this kind of innovation. The effect of production and technical systems is to conserve and strengthen established products and services. In tourism the consumer inclination to launch into more active holidays is the perfect signal for business to start creating niches. The niches tend to disrupt existing linkages, but in a technological sense they will be based on existing competence.

For instance, the opening up of sports facilities, training institutions, local events, etc., to tourists may be regarded as a market niche, but it will not disrupt the competence needed for running the facilities. The marketing linkages will, however, have to be altered and expanded in comparison to a situation where the facilities are only meant to be used by the local population. In the long run, the niches may decrease the provision of services to the original market, if the tourist market turns out to be more profitable.

Bringing the needs of the customers into closer focus may also lead to niche innovations. Constraints on the financial situation of many consumers will increase the inclination to obtain value for money. The reaction of tourist enterprises may be to close market segments where customers do not have the experience of receiving value for money. Other tourist enterprises will attempt to adapt to the consumer's desire to be able to select exactly the products and services needed and to opt out of inessential ones. In this sense the hotel product is very inflexible, and innovations are difficult. The hotel product is settled, and the customer's only choice is between hotels of different standards, locations and prices.

Concerning flexibility *vis-à-vis* the consumer, the camping sector has developed in a very different way. Niche innovations have taken place intensively over the last decades. The range of options open to the consumer is much wider: the choice of the standard of accommodation is completely free and could be either a small and primitive tent, a large and luxuriously equipped caravan, or a rented hut provided by the camping site. The customer will be able to buy complementary services such as showers, meals and activities. The important thing is that the customer will be able to control the mix of products.

The camping sector is not the only one responsible for this development. Equipment suppliers are interacting by widening the range of choice available to the customer. Camping sites respond, for instance, by providing plugs for electricity, pits for autocampers, etc., and by subsequently marketing the opportunities efficiently. The links and interdependencies between the suppliers of consumer durables and the suppliers of attractive opportunities for using these durables are obvious and constitute a precondition for the most innovative niches in tourism.

Regular innovations

Abernathy and Clark state that regular innovations may be almost invisible, yet they have a dramatic cumulative effect on product costs and performance. Some examples of regular innovations were mentioned above in the discussion of typology.

This kind of innovation will not disrupt any linkages, and it will tend to entrench the existing competence.

> It is important to note that these effects will tend to take place over a significant period of time. They require an organizational environment and managerial skills that support the dogged pursuit of improvement, no matter how minor. The effects of a given regular innovation on competition are thus of less concern than the cumulative effects of a whole series of changes (Abernathy and Clark 1985, p. 12).

The cumulative effects of regular innovations in the tourist industry are crucial. While productivity is steadily increasing in the manufacturing industries, productivity gains in services are much slower. An investigation suggests that, compared to 1980, the overall productivity of the Danish tourist and leisure industry actually fell to a lower level in 1990 (Holm-Petersen *et al.* 1993). The study discloses some of the difficulties encountered in connection with obtaining a competitive production situation, and it focuses on the need to develop managerial skills in order to benefit sufficiently from regular innovations.

Revolutionary innovations

Innovations that disrupt and render established technical and production competence obsolete, and which are yet applied to existing markets and consumers, are labelled *revolutionary*. In this connection we may point to the fragmentation of the hotel and air transport markets into a conventional and a 'no frills' category, of which the latter may be considered a revolutionary innovation of the tourism industry. The no-frills innovation implies a utilisation of technology instead of human resources. The check-in procedures are performed automatically, the meals are not available or are self-service, the equipment is as practical and functional as possible. No-frills service involves types of technology, work routines and attitudes to service which differ from those associated with full service. Some hotel chains and transport companies choose to divide their products into a full service and a no-frills in order to fulfil the expectations of all customers.

All the traditional service attitudes will have to be disrupted by the implementation of the no-frills concept, and competence requirements will be altered. This in fact involves staff with a lower level of skills. Communication skills, flexibility and adaptability will be needed less, as the services are integrated in a standardised concept and efficiently communicated by means of technology.

Concluding remarks

This section provides a taxonomy of innovations in which technology and production procedures are related to market competition. The four quadrants of the model allow the transformation effects to be subjected to consideration and illustrated by cases from the tourism industry.

The consequences that innovations have on linkages (the market and competition aspects) and on competence (the internal efficiency) are brought into focus. It is possible to find relevant examples in the tourism industry, which fit into the four quadrants of the model. One interesting observation is the interrelationship between the tourism industry and its innovations, and the activities of other sectors of the economy (for instance, providers of technology and supplementary services). Another interesting observation, which might need further investigation, is the fact that the role of science seems to be very limited in comparison to what Abernathy and Clark observed in the manufacturing industry.

Mechanisms inducing innovation in the tourist industry

The relative importance of technology-push in relation to demand-pull factors is crucial to the research of the mechanisms of innovation. Schumpeter (1939; 1988) and Schmookler (1966) are most often regarded as the creators of the technology-push and the demand-pull thesis, respectively. In Schumpeter's theories, invention and innovation constitute the exogenous factors stimulating economic growth. Science is the initiator of technological development, but the activity and investment of independent entrepreneurs (in Schumpeter's early works) ensure the manifestation of innovations in the industry. In his later works Schumpeter elaborates on the role of the existing enterprises which include systematic innovative activities in their internal organisation in order to hold or develop monopoly profits.

Vis-à-vis this hypothesis Schmookler (1966) undertook some empirical investigations of patenting and on this basis found evidence of the fact that demand or market needs determine the innovations of enterprises much more clearly than the existence of a pool of technological inventions. The inventive activity seems to take place *after* rather than before industry has been stimulated by demand. The demand-pull thesis has been further developed, particularly by Scandinavian research investigating the stimulus to growth of industrial production deriving from the activities of the welfare state (see, for example, Lundvall 1992; Lotz 1993). In more recent research, the two points of view have been increasingly integrated and modified.

Technology-push innovations in the tourism industry

The work of Barras (1986a; 1986b) is a major contribution to innovation theories concerning services. His concept of a *reverse product cycle* helps us to understand the mechanisms of the implementation of major new inventions in the service industries and the subsequent and independent stages of innovation.

According to Barras (1986a, p. 750), the reverse product cycle implies that

> the first applications of new technology devices tend to be designed to improve the efficiency of delivery of existing services; subsequent applications then shift the emphasis towards improving the quality of existing services; and finally the process of service innovation reaches the point at which the devices can be said to be generating new service activities.

In his research Barras was particularly concerned with the effects of information technology. Based on studies of the financial sector, he finds that in the first phase of the reverse product cycle enterprises will concentrate on cost savings and increased efficiency.

> Almost inevitably, given the labour intensive nature of typically pre-industrial service activities, these early applications are of a labour saving, capital

deepening nature, such that the first phase of technological progress in services tends to have a strong labour saving bias. While these labour saving effects may be masked in industries experiencing a continued growth in demand for their services, the competitive pressures to use new technology to save labour and restructure the organisation of production are typically strongest in established sectors suffering from saturated markets (Barras 1986b, p. 166).

The characteristics of the second phase are unfolded by Barras (1986b, p. 167) in the following way:

this second stage movement towards a qualitative improvement in services can be viewed as an interim 'transition phase', between the improved delivery of existing services and the generation of new types of services. These quality improvements begin to encourage some expansion of markets for the improved products, while the competitive emphasis on quality may typically be accompanied by corporate diversification or integration among service providers. Furthermore, while investment in the capital equipment embodying the technology continues at a high rate, there is a shift towards a more neutral form of technical progress, with the capital deepening effects, and the net impact on labour utilization also being broadly neutral.

Barras (1986a, p. 167) elaborates on the impacts of the third phase of the reverse product cycle:

At this stage, product rather than process innovations become dominant, as the competitive emphasis shifts to product differentiation and product performance in order to open up and capture new markets. New industries and new organisations emerge, in parallel with the further diversification of existing organisations, in order to supply the growing range of new services. The overall impact on output and employment is expansionary, investment in new technology becomes predominantly capital widening in effect, and the bias in technical progress may even tend towards capital saving, reinforcing the employment-generation effects of this stage of the cycle.

At the start of this chapter the influence of the steam engine and the railway systems on the development of tourist resorts was mentioned. According to Schumpeter (1939), major inventions and clusters of innovations stimulate the long waves of the economy. The implementation of steam engines/railway systems may be considered the very first innovation affecting and assisting the development of the tourism industry, bringing it from infancy to a stage of adolescence and through all three stages of the reverse product cycle. The age of the expansion of the railways coincided with the age when the tourism industry started to contribute to and later to be integrated into economies with some weight. The importance of the first innovation flattens out as new modes of transportation develop. Air transportation and the private car take over and expand the same kinds of innovation, although they involve an enlargement of the geographical range.

In the catering sector incremental and major technological innovations have been taking place ever since the first attempts to industrialise food processing were made – by the same token also taking part of the household work out of private homes. New modes of food preservation (freezing, cooling, etc.) tend first to rationalise operations, then to widen the range of catering outlets, and to renew the work processes of the restaurant kitchens. Suppliers in the food industry meet restaurants and fast-food establishments with a still wider choice of opportunities, enabling catering outlets to accommodate their production to the new tastes and lifestyles of their customers. The diffusion of the microwave oven dramatically changed the whole mode of production as well as labour-force requirements and market segmentation (Kirk 1989).

Though it might add substantially to insight in the tourism industry, the complete history of technology in the tourist industry is not outlined here. Instead, we will limit ourselves to mentioning the most recent innovation – information technology. In this case it is questionable whether the cumulative effects associated with the second and third phases of innovation have yet been seen.

A major area of implementation for information technology is the administrative area. Only recently a leap forward has taken place within the field of tourist information and booking services comprising a large number of tourist enterprises. This could be seen as an example of the second step in Barras's cycle.

A number of researchers generally regard the micro-chip as the major recent cause of a technology shift and possibly the stimulating factor of a new economic recovery. It is impossible to tell whether information technology will lead to an economic upswing in the tourism industry, but it is certain that this technology has altered and will alter structures and traditions in tourism considerably and that this development has only just started. Over the next decade, technology will change the operations of travel intermediaries and give way to increased flexibility and choice *vis-à-vis* the tourist. This process may be compared to the concept of *lean production* in manufacturing. The challenge is to combine the products and services of many small suppliers into new systems of tourist products, and facilitate production and marketing by means of technology. The tourist industry has certain similarities of production in common with manufacturing industry, for instance the production of product only if and when there is an explicit demand. But crucial differences between tourism and manufacturing limit the application of the concept of lean production to tourism, mainly because production and consumption are linked to one location. Furthermore, the challenge of using information technology in tourism is even greater than in manufacturing industry, as unsold products and services cannot be stored and sold later, and because the production process cannot be subdivided efficiently in time and space.

Nevertheless, the possibilities of implementing already known and developed technology in the tourism industry are still considerable. A wave of technology-push innovations will probably occur within the next decade.

Demand-pull innovations in the tourism industry

In a very general mode, Freeman *et al.* (1991) consider the role of the service sector a part of cultural change processes. They claim that producers in the 'post Fordist' society will no longer want to sell *products* with *attached services*; rather they will want to sell *services* with *attached products*. This increased importance of immaterial commodities will bring all the service industries into focus, including the tourism industries, and this development will definitely require new routes of innovative activity. The starting point for this type of innovation will have to consist of a careful analysis of customer needs rather than of any needs for rationalising production and increasing output (Rosenberg 1976).

Miles (1985) links the use of household technology to the development of demographic structures, changes in labour markets, etc. This development considerably facilitates the utilisation of equipment as an alternative to personal services. Though technology may be used for the benefit of tourists (saving time and widening choices), the need for optimisation rather than demand-pull is initiating this kind of innovation.

In a number of instances, the demand for facilities which are available in the home urges on the innovation process. The installation of hi-fi equipment and the provision of self-catering facilities in accommodation are a result of changes in demand. The building of summer cottages with private pools and spas is a response to the demand for privacy, the need to isolate the family socially for the vacation period.

Turning to the world of attractions, it is possible to find illustrative examples of demand-pull innovations. Based on extensive analyses, Urry (1990) concludes that the development of prospective tourist attractions more than ever requires deep insight not only into social needs but also into the values and ideologies of modern man. The tourist industry must consider not only immediate needs for entertainment, but also ideological and emotional requirements. For the tourism industry this condition of innovation must be considered a factor of success. To mention a few examples:

Nostalgia. A large number of tourist attractions are based on nostalgia. In some historical town centres, museums and other attractions provide visitors with the opportunity for escaping momentarily into another time and place – and perhaps another social class. For instance, agricultural industrialisation, which has taken place in recent decades, has rendered an enormous labour force superfluous. Contemporary generations are excluded from insight into agricultural activities. Visitor centres, agricultural museums, etc., show them a version of agricultural life – usually not the industrialized one but an earlier 'human' version, with which we can more easily identify.

In many cases (such as mining, fishing and the textile industry) fundamental changes in production modes may lay large plants or whole districts idle, thus giving rise to the growth of heritage centres (Hewison 1987; Harmens *et al.* 1992).

The development of nostalgia attractions based on a process of invent-ing or reinventing traditions is vividly described by Hobsbawm and Ranger (1983) and Lowenthal (1985). They find that authenticity is of less impor-tance as interpretation of historic facts reflect contemporary conditions. The tourist industry is often only very superficially influenced by scientific facts and interpretations. Fakes, staged authenticity and modification of history are widely used by tourist enterprises, and with some success (Ashworth 1990; Getz 1991)

The fascination with experiencing the way of life of natives can be seen as part of nostalgia tourism. McCannell (1973) and Urry (1990) provide a number of examples of how the natives (of all times and cultures) are being innovative in their efforts to exaggerate their traditions and to expose them effectively as part of a tourist business strategy.

Patriotism. The fall of the Berlin Wall and the political changes in eastern Europe give way to increased patriotism. These emotions cause violence around the world, but the same emotional expressions may be included in tourist innovations.

The erection in southern Denmark of a museum illustrating the battles of 1864 with German forces is drawing on patriotic emotions. In a way, this museum is self-contradictory: it is successful in spite of the fact (or perhaps because of the fact) that the 1864 battles resulted in a disastrous defeat and the loss of large provinces to Germany.

Linking nations and patriotic emotions together provides particular opportunities for international tourism. For instance, the events celebrat-ing the anniversary of Columbus's voyage to America, motivated people to cross the Atlantic. Americans were supposed to want to see the origins of their ancestors in Europe, and the Europeans could be helped to explore the routes and deeds of their ancestors.

A more distinct expression of ethnic identity, which can presently be traced in Europe, may provide fuel for many future tourist innovations.

Mysticism and religion. A pilgrimage is a particular type of tourism which has been known for centuries. It continues in a modernised version, often where the actual worship is fully or partly replaced by the need for introspection (Cohen 1992). Even well-established religions and sects try to appeal to young generations in new ways. International exchange – and thus touristic experience – often forms part of the game. The fascination for mysticism also creates other innovations, for instance the 'discovery' of new holy or healing places or persons. To travel in order to meet extra-human experience has become still more common.

Space experience can be considered a particular branch of mysticism, mostly practiced by using multimedia facilities. As the technical possi-bilities are developed, rides in space are becoming still more popular, and equipment is provided in most malls and amusement parks.

Sex. Travelling in order to experience sex – either with co-travellers or with prostitutes – is well known and well documented, though a matter which is only mentioned tacitly (Urry 1990). No doubt a considerable amount of creativity and innovative effort is expended if regulations limit prostitution or to combat diseases such as AIDS. Substituting personal sex services for media and other technical devices may be the way in which things will evolve in the future. This paves the way for a much more open business market. In this connection an interesting trend is the admission of sex into the range of respectable attractions, for instance the Museum of Erotica in Copenhagen. The museum is aware of its origins, however: it is situated in the red-light district of the city and has opening hours until late in the evening.

These examples of the role played by emotions and ideologies with regard to innovations in the tourist industry could be supplemented by many more. The important thing to note in relation to the concept of innovation is that demand-pull plays a very important role in the development of tourist concepts and attractions.

Combining the technology-push and the demand-pull factors

Having identified the technology-push factors underlying the adoption of technical devices within the tourist industry, and having identified the demand-pull pressures, the interaction between the two mechanisms must become apparent.

Autonomous processes of social and economic development are continuously redefining the functions of technology. In turn, these functions create demands for improved and new technologies, and trigger the R&D activity of the sectors supplying the tourism industry. The realisation of the importance of the interaction between the two mechanisms rather than the isolated demand-pull or technology-push factors must lead to a discussion of the concepts of national or regional innovation systems. Inspired by the growing research on the subject, we shall define the innovation systems according to Lundvall (1992, pp. 1–2): 'it is obvious that the national system of innovation is a *social* system ... an embedded process which cannot be understood without taking into consideration its institutional and cultural contexts'.

In other words, a better understanding of innovation mechanisms will have to include the mapping and analysis of the substance of different kinds of links:

• Links within the tourism industry itself between enterprises of the same kind (for example, network affiliations of enterprises, nationally or transnationally). It has, for instance, been shown that chains of hotels are more successful than individually owned hotels (Littlejohn and Beattie 1992; Slattery 1992). However, the studies referred to did not investigate whether conglomeration means that there is a larger potential for innovations.

• Links within the tourism industry between enterprises with complementary services (vertical networks). In principle, the institutional set-up at a destination and its consequences in relation to innovation could constitute an important dimension of the system of innovation. The term 'destination' could apply to a region of any size: small regions, nations or even groups of nations. Links are manifested through institutions. 'Institutions provide agents and collectives with guide-posts for action. In a world characterized by innovative activities, uncertainty will be an important aspect of economic life. Institutions make it possible for economic systems to survive and act in an uncertain world' (Lundvall 1992: p. 10).

• Producer–consumer links. Two kinds of producer–consumer link can be identified. One is the link between the individual tourist enterprise and its particular customers. This link may or may not provide impulses for innovative activity. If enterprises actively request opinions from their customers, or if they carefully study the behaviour of their customers, this may lead to information on relevant innovative efforts. The other kind of link is that between tourist enterprises and their suppliers. Examples from the information technology sector and the catering sector were given above. In relation to the innovation issue, these kinds of link need further investigation, for instance relating to the question of the behaviour and the opportunities of small and medium-sized firms

• Links with public or semi-public institutions in a general business environment. The organisation and strategies of the public sector affect the tourism industry. Innovative effects on the tourism industry take place in two different ways. First, the public sector will regulate the industry's terms of existence, for instance safety precautions, environmental protection requirements, hygiene and tax payment. In many cases this will urge the industry to find new and better ways of operation. Second, the public and semi-public sectors provide facilities for the industry such as infrastructure, education and R&D.

On the other hand, the mere fact of specialization and the inclination of the tourist industry to exert active political pressure will influence the strategies of the public sector. With regard to the analysis of national innovation systems, the public sector may be of particular importance to the tourist industry, as a large number of the attractions and facilities are in fact owned or controlled by the public sector

The structure of links and the influence of the mechanisms of innovation – i.e. the relative importance of technology-push and demand-pull – must be considered crucial to further studies of innovation in tourism. A substantial empirical investigation will have to parallel further theoretical developments, in order genuinely to embrace the similarities and differences between manufacturing and tourism industries.

Diffusion of innovations

Literature on diffusion usually takes considerable interest in the institutional framework – its effect on the economy and its efficiency. The functioning of patenting systems, the role of basic university R&D, the effects and efficiency of public programmes and incentive schemes are all crucial elements that must be considered when doing research on this subject. Furthermore, the diffusion between sectors (industries) of the economy and that between countries are important aspects of research (Rosenberg 1976). It is often implicitly assumed that delays in the diffusion of innovation cause severe economic problems and affect the long-term competitive position of the industry.

Barriers to innovation and the rationale behind the reluctance to innovate and to adopt innovations have only recently been considered, primarily within the conceptual framework of transactions costs (Williamson 1985). For an understanding of diffusion problems, it will be necessary to balance two routes of analysis: the analysis of the factors facilitating the diffusion of innovation; and that of factors creating barriers to the diffusion of innovation.

Factors facilitating the diffusion of innovation

A business environment open to entrepreneurship
This Schumpeterian approach assumes that innovation is predominantly carried out by entrepreneurs. Generally, the implementation of a new business idea is simpler in tourism than, for instance, in the manufacturing industries, as investments will in most cases be lower. The above assumption about the role of entrepreneurship must be studied more carefully and will have to be related to facts about turnover rates, which are considerably higher in tourism than in most other industries (Holm-Petersen *et al.* 1993).

An industrial structure with a predominance of large and internationalised enterprises with substantial financial power
The role played by the large and integrated enterprises may be crucial to innovation, though the evidence supporting this view is lacking. The characteristics of innovation as it takes place in large conglomerates may differ from the type of innovation which takes place in an environments of small enterprise, the result being specific modes of specialisation. Corresponding or competing approaches to innovation chosen by large/internationalised enterprises on the one hand and individual enterprises on the other hand finds their spatial consequences in the development of destinations. Therefore, a spatial analysis is crucial to the definition of factors facilitating (or hampering) innovation.

Institutional links
As mentioned above, institutional links include active agents and guide-posts. In an active framework – for instance, a destination or horizontal network – the agents and guide-posts will filter information down to or up from the enterprise level to/from the policy levels, to/from other industries or from R&D to/from the tourist industry.

The composition of private and public R&D and the amount spent on R&D
These are crucial factors in traditional R&D studies. However, innovation in the tourist industry does not take place in departments dedicated to the purpose. This is the case neither in the tourism industry nor in the public sector. It can often be observed that university institutes do not even contribute to the diffusion of innovation in any substantial way.

R&D studies of the manufacturing industry also find that to a certain degree the recruitment and career patterns of R&D staff determine the diffusion of innovation. One cannot be sure about the diffusion effects of career patterns in tourism.

Free copying opportunities
In contrast to many industrial sectors, which are heavily protected by patents or complicated construction procedures, the products of the tourist industry are exposed very extensively to the risk of being copied due to the very nature of the industry. Codification is often easy, but legal protection would be ineffective (Teece 1992). This applies to product innovations as well as management, distribution or process innovations.

The extensive use of licensing (including franchising)
This is probably the most important single diffusion factor in tourism. This mechanism may be observed in catering, accommodation and even in connection with attractions. The need to tie the production units to widespread locations is the main motivating element in this particular mode of innovation diffusion. This mode of diffusion seems to be very efficient (Economist Intelligence Unit 1990).

An active and demanding – even restrictive – public sector
This may speed up innovation or the diffusion of innovation. Recent Scandinavian literature on innovation stresses the importance of public sector demands and requirements. Particular sectors such as medical devices, energy and environmental equipment have been treated in studies which point out that the high public standards required from the service sector are important in relation to the innovativeness of the supplying industry (Porter 1990; and several articles in Lundvall 1992). With regard to the tourism industry, the same line of research has not been sufficiently investigated. In order to ensure the success of the future restructuring and development of the tourism industry this type of research should be undertaken.

Factors creating barriers to innovation

The existence of fixed investments, well-developed routines, accessible markets, and certain traditions of operation
These will tend to moderate the speed of innovation, particularly in existing enterprises. It would be costly to reorganise completely and only

incremental innovations will be adopted. The industry or the individual enterprises observe and react to the existence of transactions costs. Earlier investments and decisions may be more or less irreversible and imply a trajectory from which it will be costly to depart. In the tourism industry the general excess capacity of investments creates very substantial barriers to innovation. However, some types of innovation may be of particular importance because of this very irreversibility of fixed investment – for instance management or organisational innovations.

A business structure consisting of unaffiliated and isolated units
The lack of organisational links tends to limit the channels of information. We have considered the positive effects of links in relation to diffusion above.

Innovation traps
Many enterprises will have to consider how to avoid innovation traps – development trajectories implying the risk of not being able to return to the starting point. This may particularly hamper the most radical innovations in the tourism industry as it does in other industries – up to the point when the whole architecture of the industry is challenged. At this time the enterprises will have to adapt or to leave the business.

Disinclination to learn continuously
The ability to learn may be affected by the recruitment of staff with low qualifications and a high replacement rate. This is the case in large sections of the tourism industry, and it may hamper the organisational learning process in this sector more than in other sectors. The lack of capability for continuous learning may also be correlated with the size of the firms, the position in the input–output structure, the geographical location, etc.

Lack of sufficient information in the right place at the right time
The costs of retrieving and processing information may be higher than the anticipated benefit. The role played by institutions and R&D in relation to the diffusion of information is crucial. Compared to other industries, the tourism industry has been supplied with professional information brokers much later and much more marginally than the manufacturing industries, agriculture and more prominent parts of the service sector.

Exploiting the opportunities of backwardness
One can challenge the hypothesis of the positive effects of innovative advances. It can be pointed out that late-comers to innovation may gain substantial benefits by avoiding the costs of development and avoiding failures. We can advance the two alternative hypotheses that late-comers will ultimately reach higher levels or that late-comers will entirely surpass the original innovators and launch into completely new opportunities. With regard to the tourism industry, no evidence concerning the opportunities

involved in backwardness in general and the specific consequences is available.

Conclusion: a synthesis of research issues

The theories and the cases selected for this chapter show that it is perfectly possible to utilise basic concepts for the tourism industry and that this represents a major academic challenge. Some modifications will, of course, be necessary before applying them to the tourism industry. For instance, the research approaches, based on empirical evidence collected in the patenting system, could never be fully transferred to the tourism industry. The results would be very misleading. Attempts to measure innovative activity and diffusion should find other channels.

Nevertheless, innovation theories may be used as guidelines for a leap forward in the research on the economic aspects on tourism. Traditional studies most often suffered from a lack of understanding of the *dynamics* of the development; it failed to explain why and how changes take place. Most often an analysis of the interlinking between the tourism industry and other sectors of the economy is lacking. The research of Poon (1988a; 1988b) is a prominent and inspiring exception. She introduces the concept of flexible specialization into the study of the tourism industry, thus bringing into focus the architectural innovations transforming the composition of the tourism industry. From this starting point she is able to explain the composition of business strategies and the connections between managerial, process and product innovations.

The concepts of national innovation systems are crucial to the analysis of dynamic innovation, particularly in welfare state systems as the Scandinavian economies, where interrelationships are numerous and where political issues affecting innovative activity have long traditions. The growing concern for environmental sustainability is an issue which should be studied more carefully within the conceptual framework of innovation theory. Only in this way will it be possible not only to observe the threats posed to the tourism industry, but also to identify the opportunities and innovations provoked by environmental awareness. This development will take place by way of a process of structural changes, and this is an essential matter in economic analysis.

In recent years the theoretical renewal and further development of innovation studies have included a *spatial* dimension (for instance, the GREMI group, Camagni 1991). The concept of *industrial districts* has fuelled the research on why some regions are particularly innovative, and why some are not, given the same macro-economic conditions. The research tends to highlight the importance of links and specialization.

The tourism industry is tied to its destinations, and the individual plants are not foot-loose. as manufacturing production processes may be. Therefore, the geographical dimension of analysis is particularly crucial to future research into the economic dynamics of the tourism industry.

References

Abernathy, W.J. and Clark, K.B., 1985, 'Innovation: mapping the winds of creative destruction, *Research Policy*, 14: 3–22.

Ashworth, G., 1988, 'Marketing the historic city for tourism', in B. Goodall and G. Ashworth (eds), *Marketing in the tourism industry*, Routledge, London: 162–75.

Ashworth, G., 1990, 'The historic cities of Groningen: which is sold to whom?', in G. Ashworth and B. Goddall (eds), *Marketing tourism places*, Routledge, London: 138–55.

Barras, R., 1986a, 'New technology and the new services. Towards an innovation strategy for Europe', *Futures*, December: 749–72.

Barras, R., 1986b, 'Towards a theory of innovation in services', *Research Policy*, 15: 161–73.

Burgelman, R.A. and Sayles, L.R., 1986, *Inside corporate innovation. Strategy, structure and managerial skills*, Free Press, New York and London.

Camagni, R. (ed.), 1991, *Innovation networks: spatial perspectives*, Belhaven, London.

Christensen, J.F., 1990, *Produktinnovation i teoretisk belysning*, Projekt Dynamisk Specialisering, Institut for Erhvervs- og Samfundsforskning, Handelshøjskolen, Copenhagen.

Cohen, E., 1988, 'Authenticity and commodization in tourism', *Annals of Tourism Research*, 15(3): 371–86.

Cohen, E., 1992, 'Pilgrimage centres: concentric and eccentric', *Annals of Tourism Research*, 19(1): 33–50.

Crick, M., 1985, '"Tracing" the anthopological self: quizzical reflections on field work, tourism and the ludic', *Social Analysis*, 17, August: 71–92.

Economist Intelligence Unit, 1990, *Fast food in Europe*, Special Report no. 2027, London.

Freeman, C., Sharp, M. and Walter, W. (eds), 1991, *Technology and the future of Europe*, Pinter, London.

Gamble, P.R., 1991, 'Innovation and innkeeping', *International Journal of Hospitality Management*, 10(1): 3–23.

Getz, D., 1991, *Festivals, special events, and tourism*, Van Nostrand Reinhold, New York.

Gilbert, D.C., 1990, 'European tourism product purchase methods and systems', *Service Industries Journal*, 10(4): 664–79.

Gershuny, J.I. and Miles, I.D., 1982, *Service employment: trends and prospects*, FAST, DG XII, EC, Brussels.

Goddard, J.B., 1990, *Storstäderna i informationssam hället*, ERU-rapport 66, Stockholm.

Harmens, A.B., Prak, P. and Ashworth, G.J., 1992, *The role of tourism in water-front regeneration. The case of London Docklands*, Faculty of Spatial Sciences, University of Groningen.

Hanlon, J.P., 1991, 'Hub operations and airline competition', *Tourism Management*, 10(2): 111–24.

Hewison, R., 1987, *The heritage industry. Britain in a climate of decline*, Macmillan, London.

Hobsbawm, E. and Ranger, T. (eds), 1983, *The invention of tradition*, Cambridge University Press, Cambridge.

Holm-Petersen, E., Hjalager, A.-M., Ploughmann, P. and Framke, W., 1993, *Turisme/fritid – en erhvervsøkonomisk analyse*, Erhvervsfremmestyrelsen, ressourceområdestudierapport 2, Copenhagen.

Johns, N. and Wheeler, K., 1991, 'Productivity and performance measurement and monitoring', in R. Teare and A. Boer (eds), *Strategic hospitality management*, Cassell, New York: 45–71.

Kirk, D., 1989, 'Advances in catering industry', in C. Cooper (ed.), *Progress in tourism, recreation and hospitality management*, Vol. 1, Belhaven, London: 232–41.

Krippendorf, J., 1986, *Die Ferienmenschen. Für ein neues Verständnis von Freizeit und Reisen*, Deutscher Taschenbuch Verlag, Munich.

Lattin, T.W., 1990, 'Hotel technology: key to survival', in M. Quest (ed.), *The Horwath book of tourism*, Macmillan Press, London: 219–24.

Lickorish, L.J. and Kershaw, A.G., 1975, 'Tourism between 1840–1940', in A.J. Burkart and S. Medlik (eds), *The management of tourism. A selection of readings*, Heinemann, London: 11–24.

Littlejohn, D. and Beattie, R., 1992, 'The European hotel industry. Corporate structures and expansion strategies', *Tourism Management*, March: 27–33.

Lotz, P., 1992, *Demand-side effect on product innovation. The case of medical devices*, Handelshøjskolen, Samfundslitteratur, Copenhagen.

Lundvall, B.Å. (ed.), 1992, *National systems of innovation. Towards a theory of innovation and interactive learning*, Pinter, London.

Love, J.F., 1986, *McDonald's. Behind the arches*, Bantam Press, New York.

Lowenthal, D., 1985, *The past is a foreign country*, Cambridge University Press, Cambridge.

MacCannell, D., 1973, 'Staged authenticity: arrangements of social space in tourist settings', *American Journal of Sociology*, 79(3): 589–603

Mayhew, L., 1987, 'The travel agent – rise or fall', in A. Hodgson (ed.), *The travel and tourism industry*, Oxford: 49–73.

Miles, I., 1985, 'Social innovation and information technology', unpublished paper, SPRU, University of Sussex.

Mowery, D.C., 1992, 'The U.S. national innovation system: origins and prospects for change', *Research Policy*, 21: 125–44.

Pavitt, K., 1982, 'R&D, patenting and innovative activities. A statistical exploration', *Research Policy*, 11: 33–51.

Pavitt, K., 1984, 'Sectoral patterns of technical change: towards a taxonomy and a theory', *Research Policy*, 13: 343–73.

Pearce, D., 1991, *Tourist development* (2nd edn), Longman Scientific & Technical, New York.

Pearce, D., 1992, 'Tourism and the European Regional Development Fund: the first fourteen years', *Journal of Travel Research*, 30(3): 44–51.

Perlmutter, M., 1992, 'Virtual reality: its future in travel and tourism. Thinking may not be the best way to travel', *Travel and Tourism Association*, 11: 63–6.

Pillsbury, R., 1990, *From boarding house to bistro*, Unwin Hyman, Cambridge, Massachusetts.

Poon, A., 1988a, 'Innovation and the future of Caribbean tourism', *Tourism Management*, 9(3): 213–20.

Poon, A., 1988b, *Flexible specialization and small size – the case of Caribbean tourism*, Discussion paper no. 57, SPRU, University of Sussex.

Porter, M.E., 1990, *The competitive advantage of nations*, Macmillan, London.

Rosenberg, N., 1976, *Perspectives on technology*, Cambridge University Press, Cambridge.

Sherman, B. and Judkins, P., 1992, *Glimpses of heaven, visions of hell. Virtual reality and its implications*, Hodder and Stoughton, Sevenoaks.

Sinclair, T. and Stabler, M.J. (eds), 1991, *The tourism industry: an international analysis*, CAB International, Wallingford, Oxon.

Schmookler, J., 1966, *Invention and economic growth*, Harvard University Press, Cambridge, Massachusetts.

Schumpeter, J., 1939, *Business cycles, a theoretical, historical and statistical analysis of the capitalist process*, MacGraw-Hill, New York.

Schumpeter, J., 1988, *The theory of economic development. An inquiry into profits, capital, credit, interest, and the business cycle*, Transactions Books, New Brunswick, N.J. First published in 1934.

Slattery, P., 1992, 'Unaffiliated hotels in the UK', *EIU Travel and Tourism Analyst*, 1: 90–102.

Teece, D.J., 1992, 'Strategies for capturing the financial benefits from technological innovation', in N. Rosenberg, R. Landau and D.C. Mowery (eds), *Technology and the wealth of nations*, Stanford University Press, Stanford, California: 175–205.

Tornatzky, L. *et al.*, 1983, *The process of technological innovation: reviewing the literature*. National Science Foundation, Washington, DC.

Uhlmann, L., 1979, 'The typology approach in innovation research', in M.J. Baker (ed.), *Industrial innovation. Technology, policy, diffusion*, Macmillan, London: 17–33.

Urry, J., 1990, *The tourist gaze. Leisure and travel in contemporary societies*, Sage, London.

Williamson, O.E., 1985, *The economic institutions of capitalism*, Free Press, New York.

18 Career theory and tourism: the development of a basic analytical framework

M. Riley and A. Ladkin

Introduction

A career is, at its simplest, a series of jobs arranged in a sequence over time. Yet even casual analysis reveals some of the complexity inherent in this phenomenon. Career sequences contain mobility, direction, pace, goals, incentives, barriers, motives, successes and failures, human capital accumulation and many other attributes. Add to this complexity the fact that careers are part of the fabric of industrial activity involving both individuals and organisations, and it is understandable that there is a practical as well as theoretical literature.

'Career theory' is a broad term which refers to a set of exploratory and investigative approaches used to measure and analyse the phenomenon. Numerous disciplines are involved, notably: personality psychology, with its attempts to link personality traits to career outcomes; economics, with job search processes and mobility patterns; organisational behaviour, with structure determinism; and motivation theory; with incentives and psychological-need determinism.

The practical aspects of careers fall into three categories which are closely integrated with theory: first, *career development*, which refers to the outcomes for individuals and organisations and encompasses important issues such as economics, job transitions, mobility, career withdrawal, career compromise and career stages; second, *career planning*, which is concerned, at the individual level, with the relationship between individual planning and career outcomes and, at the organisational level, with organisational needs and human resource planning techniques; third, *career choice*, which dominates the literature and is concerned with the individual's choice of job and organisation, including decision processes, career anchors, career paths and entrepreneurial tendencies.

What follows is a brief overview of some of the main areas of research on careers. This will lead to an attempt to form an analytical framework for the understanding of careers in tourism and for the development of research projects. The framework will be based on principles derived from career theory.

Career theory

A number of reviews of career theory and research provide general overviews of how the subject has developed. Arthur *et al.* (1989) state that career theory is the body of all generalisable attempts to explain career phenomena. They use the qualifier 'generalisable' to distinguish career theory from the more self-specific explanations of career outcomes derived from personal experience. In terms of other disciplines, career theory suggests the dominance of psychological approaches, with sociology confined to the national picture and with job search theory rooted in economic rationality. Organisational theory which is the context of careers, is however, becoming prominent. Sonnenfield and Kotter (1982) identify four types of career theory. The first type is *sociological*, and is concerned with social class determinants of career outcomes (see, for example, Blau and Duncan 1967). The second is *psychological*, and is concerned with static dispositional differences and their occupational implication (see, for example, the very influential work of Holland 1973). The third focuses on *career stages* (Super 1957; Crites 1981; Dalton and Thompson 1986). The fourth is *sociopsychological*, and focuses on the adult life course and the relationship of the career to other major life activities (Levinson 1978).

Feldman (1989) explores some of the important ways in which career research has changed up to 1989 when Feldman was writing, in terms of content areas studies, theoretical and methodological approaches used, and advances in management practices. Content areas studied include job exit, job stability and resocialisation within and across organisations. Theoretical approaches include the adult development perspective, population ecology, attribution theory, small-group behaviour research and the stress/coping paradigm. The picture which emerges from these writers is that career theory is fragmented, but certainly developing rapidly.

Driver (1988) reviews the fragmentation problem and concludes that a look at organisation – person congruence models, societal trends and career management, and the status of career management practice in organisations, all suggest that a combined approach focusing on the individual and the organisation simultaneously is the way to achieve integration. Some see this as impractical (Schein 1978).

Career development

In their extensive review of advances in the measurement of career development constructs, Chartrand and Camp (1991) identify two common themes across definitions for career development. First, career development is viewed as a sequence of positions or stages through which a person progresses over time. Second, the emphasis is placed on the process rather than the content of career development. The processes are either individual or organisational. They identify the major advances in the measurement of career development constructs between 1971 and 1990, with specific reference to measurement issues. Measurement is seen as important because most substantive research developments were associated with improved measurement techniques. They identify four research areas: stage-based and process oriented models; career decision-making; intervention evaluation; and organisational development and career orientation. By contrast, Russell (1991) emphasises organisational intervention practices such as self-assessment tools, information services, assessment centres and career programmes. According to Russell, the field of organisational career development has grown rapidly. The focus of career development interventions and the change in the level of interest among researchers are considerable. Career programmes in organisations now consist of both individual career planning efforts and organisational career management programmes. A broader perspective than the individual's work area now includes non-work issues. Flexible work arrangements have also become more prevalent as interventions which can facilitate the individual's career growth and help meet the organisation's staffing needs.

As careers are essentially a progression, a key element of career development is the notion of the career stage. Despite its importance there is an issue of definition here. Is it something people just pass through or does it have to contribute to development before it counts? There is, however, agreement on many aspects of career stages. Most researchers have found that stages correlate with age.

Erikson (1963), working from the psychoanalytic perspective, identified four stages of adult life, each with its own task that has to be satisfactorily resolved before the person can move on to the next stage: adolescence; young adulthood; adulthood; and maturity. Super (1957) identified four similar stages: exploration; establishment; maintenance; and decline. However, the most influential attempt to map life stages is by Levinson (1978). He proposed three eras of adulthood (early, middle and late) and within these there are alternating stable and transitional periods.

Some writers isolate the career from external variables and examine it purely as an industrial phenomenon (Dalton *et al.* 1986). In this context, concepts such as compromise, withdrawal and maturity become centres of attention.

A second key element of career development is the concept of *career mobility*. Labour economics subsumes careers within its general principles of mobility which are related to the price of labour, market conditions and search processes. The really useful connection between labour economics and career research is in the identification of salary levels as barriers and incentives to mobility.

The task of identifying different career paths is taken up by several writers. For example, Driver (1982) specified four types of career path: steady-state; linear; spiral; and transitory. Gunz (1988) identified the notion of the 'career climbing frame' in organisations whereby managers can move up, along or down the frame to facilitate their movement within an organisation. In this theoretical model of managerial careers, two organisational characteristics (structure and growth) are linked to the pattern of managerial careers within an organisation. Gunz developed three *career logics*: constructional; command-centred; and evolutionary. The first implies mobility to build human capital; the second to take ever bigger responsibility; and the third to change the existing responsibilities organically within a job. The enormous relevance of organisation structure is strongly emphasised by Ghiselli (1969). He evokes a relationship between structure and the homogeneity, or otherwise, of technical knowledge within the structure.

Rosenbaum (1979) describes two conflicting models of career mobility: the first is a historical (path-independent) model whereby earlier career moves have no influence on later career moves; and the second a historical (tournament) model. The empirical analysis supports the tournament model, finding that mobility in the earliest periods of a career has a dramatic influence on its later development. In other words, those who were promoted early rose to higher levels than those who were not. The first group remained in the 'tournament' but those not promoted in the early rounds were effectively eliminated from the later competition. Rosenbaum suggested signalling theory as an explanation of the tournament pattern of mobility. In this sense, early promotion is critical for later promotion, as, in the absence of more objective criteria, decision-makers will rely on current job status in relation to age or tenure as a signal of ability.

In a study of early intra-organisational mobility, Forbes (1987) tests the degree to which early promotions have lasting effects. Only weak support for the tournament mobility model was recorded. Instead, there was support for an alternative historical model using past position, career movement, and functional background as a signal to those who make decisions concerning promotions.

Within the concept of mobility has grown up a powerful core of research which is concerned with *career transitions*. The notion of holding one job and remaining with one work organisation for life has given way to a pattern of periodic job changes. One area of career research which has received increasing attention in the 1980s, according to Feldman (1989) is individuals' decisions to leave organisations, and how employees cope with job loss.

In their study of managers in the UK, Nicholson and West (1988) showed that the frequency of job moves was increasing, that the changes were often quite dramatic (commonly involving changes in employer, status and function), and that many managers were unable to predict their occurrence. They propose a cyclical transition model of job change passing through the stages of preparation, encounter, adjustment, stabilisation, and thence back to preparation.

Louis (1980) defines a career transition to be the period during which an individual is changing roles or changing orientations to a role already held. This approach extends beyond the notion of actual job change as being the sole type of transition. Louis defined nine types of career transition. Transitioners' experience differs between old and new roles, role orientations, and settings; and between anticipations of and experiences in their new situations. The nine types of career transition are divided between two varieties: inter-role transitions and intra-role transitions. The study then attempts to illustrate how individuals cope with career transitions, with an aim to understand how to facilitate the transition process.

Krausz and Reshef (1992) consider the reasons for leaving, choice determinants and search processes involved in managerial job change. They test Nicholson and West's (1988) distinction between three types of motivational basis for job change: circumstantial; avoidance; and practice- or future-orientated. Rather than adopting Louis' (1980) classification of the types of job transition, Krausz and Reshef are concerned with the *reasons* for leaving. The results indicate that the respondents tend to put their leaving a managerial job down to *content*. Managers tend to attribute their job changes to proactive, rather than avoidance or circumstantial motives.

Career planning

Given that careers are a sequence of jobs with connotations of achievement and advancement, the degree to which they are planned by individuals and organisations is salient to our understanding of career development and career outcomes. There is a connection between the question of locus of control and propensity to plan.

Several authors have pointed to the need for individual career planning (Jennings 1971; Bolles 1972; Hall 1976). Career planning has been defined as a deliberate process of becoming aware of self, opportunities, constraints, choices and consequences; identifying career-related goals, and programming work, education and related development experiences to provide direction and timing to attain a specific career goal.

There are three themes evident in the literature concerning individual career planning. The first relates to the general agreement for the need to plan a career. Edmond (1989) states that the days are past when individuals remain with one organisation or specific occupation throughout their working lives, and individuals need to be able to adapt and plan for such changes.

The second examines the notion that individuals who engage in career planning are more likely to succeed and be satisfied with their chosen occupation. Hall (1976) argues that employee career effectiveness is directly related to organisational effectiveness and that career planning activities can lead to a more committed work force. In the organisational context, Granrose and Portwood (1987) question traditional assumptions linking organisational career assistance programmes with increased employee satisfaction with and commitment to organisations. Their study suggests that the extent of perceived matching between individual and organisational career plans is related to individuals' attitudes concerning their careers. Such matches seem to have an influence on satisfaction and desire to leave or remain with an organisation, whereas participation in formal career management programmes does not appear to have such an effect. If the career plans of the individual and the organisation do not match, dissatisfaction and the search for alternatives outside the current organisation occur.

The third theme considers the variables which influence career planning. High among the organisational variables are the opportunity structure and interventions. At the individual level, self-efficacy and locus of control appear as crucial factors (Korman 1971; Greenhaus and Simon 1976; Gould 1979).

Career choice

By far the most extensive part of the literature is concerned with career choice. Two writers who are very influential are Holland (1985) and Schein (1975). The former belongs to the personality differences tradition and the latter to the basic psychological-needs theme.

Holland's six personality types are the conventional, the enterprising, the social, the realistic, the investigative, and the artistic. Holland (1979) developed the self-directed search as a measure of personality assessment for career choice guidance.

Theories such as Holland's describe the content of actual and ideal decisions, but not the *process*. Arnold *et al.* (1991) review how a person can make an effective career decision. They identify a variety of factors: self-awareness; knowledge of occupations; putting self-knowledge and occupational knowledge together; readiness for effective career decision-making; decision-making styles; and self-esteem and self-efficacy.

An alternative approach to the study of career choices has been developed by Schein (1975) with his development of *career anchors*. According to Schein, a person's career choices are determined by some basic psychological needs. Holland's theory has been applied as a justification for this. Schein (1975) defines a career anchor as 'that set of self percep-tions pertaining to your (1) motives and needs, (2) talents and skills, and (3) personal values that you would not give up if you had to make a choice'. (Simonsen 1986) Five anchors are identified: technical/functional competence anchors; managerial career anchors; security and stability anchors; creativity anchors; and autonomy and independence anchors.

Within the literature surrounding career choice, entrepreneurs have received a certain amount of attention. A common theme in the study of entrepreneurs is the focus upon personality types. In other words, what makes an individual choose an entrepreneurial career.

Scanlan (1980) stresses the importance of self-development and entre-preneurship as a distinct career option, in an attempt to move away from models of career choice and development which are orientated towards existing occupations. The study addresses entrepreneurship from the perspective of Holland's theory by administering Holland's vocational preference inventory.

Scott and Twomey (1988) attempt to ascertain what shapes students' career aspirations in relation to entrepreneurship. The results indicate that *predisposing factors* (background, personality, perceptions), *triggering factors* (seeking work, career advice, unemployment effect) and *having a business idea* act collectively to shape career aspirations. Those who aspire to self-employment are significantly more likely to have parental role models, work and hobby experiences, entrepreneurial self-perceptions, a view of small organisations as places for challenge and gain, and a business idea. They draw two main conclusions: first, that role models and a high degree of personal autonomy are major influential variables in entrepreneurial aspirations; and second, that perceptions of the market may influence the individual's decision for an entrepreneurial career.

Roberts (1989) draws on motivational themes to study the personality and motivations of technological entrepreneurs using McClelland's theory of need for achievement, need for affiliation and need for power. McClelland sees the entrepreneur as the one who translates need for achievement into economic development.

Scherer *et al.* (1989) focus on the first step in the process by which entrepreneurial career preference is developed in response to the criticism of the trait approaches to the study of entrepreneurs. A critical assumption of the trait approach is that the entrepreneur is somehow different in terms of personality, and that this inter-individual difference can be used to predict the selection of an entrepreneurial career. Scherer *et al.* (1989) use social learning theory specifically to investigate the link between a parental role model and the development of preference for an entrepreneurial career. Results indicated that the presence of a parental role model was associated with increased educational and training aspirations, task self-efficacy, and expectations for an entrepreneurial career. Entrepreneurial preparedness and expectancy were then identified as two dimensions for career preference.

A structural-technical framework for the analysis of careers in tourism: some basic principles applied

The purpose here is to draw an outline of the structural variables which form the basis of career research. This outline does not incorporate the psychological variables which form the basis of many research approaches, but comment is made on future directions of psychological research in the area. The stance taken here, however, is that any psychological studies must be preceded by structural analysis in order to describe the true context in which the psychological variables apply. To put it simply, tests of suitability for an industry require direct contact to be made with features of that industry.

The first part of this section focuses on purely structural variables. This is followed by an analysis of the central career dimension which sits within the structural variables: the career path. This section concludes with an exposition of the type of career behaviour that is the focus of research.

Structural variables, specificity and knowledge

Structural determinants

It will surprise no one that the literature on career theory and measurement contains few applications to tourism. Most of the principal areas of research are absent. There is a good deal of exhortation as to the benefits of a career in tourism (Metcalf 1988). The studies that exist, however, are confined to the image problem of the industry (Charles 1992; Ross 1992). In addition, the universal problem of staff retention tends to dominate the labour planning literature. There are 'portraits' of human resources levels and jobs, but these are static entities rather than career planning tools (Peroni and Guerra 1991). Ironically, the issue of careers for women appears in the literature, but does so in the total absence of studies on the context in which such aspirations are played out (Guerrier 1986).

From the review of the literature three writers emerge as being of relevance to the construction of an analytical framework: Ghiselli (1969); Gunz (1988) and Riley (1990; 1991). All three agree on a set of structural determinants of the extent of opportunity and the character of career sequences. It is worth reiterating that what follows are structural variables which in no way deny the importance of psychological variables. Table 18.1 is an outline of the four major variables.

Table 18.1 *Structural determinants*

Industrial growth	Expansion–contraction
Organisation size and structure	
(i)	The overall size of the organisation.
(ii)	The height of the hierarchical pyramid.
(iii)	The intra–organisational distribution of sub-units and the height of their hierarchical pyramids and size differential.
Technological specificity	
(i)	The degree of technological specificity between organisations.
(ii)	The degree of technological specificity between the subject industry (here tourism) and other industries.
Dispersion of knowledge	
(i)	The degree of homogeneity of knowledge within the hierarchy. There are three cases here. First, shared knowledge from top to bottom; second, a knowledge cut-off; and third, where knowledge is highly specialised and not distributed either vertically or horizontally.
(ii)	The complexity of the knowledge required by the production, service or management process.

Putting aside expansion–contraction, the structural arguments are based on the principle that the overall size and height of the hierarchy specify the capacity of the organisation to provide careers; in addition, the intra-organisational distribution of sub-units suggest that career paths might be directed between sub-units and between sub-unit and head office.

The arguments surrounding technological specificity are that, on the one hand, if the industry is technologically specific then there exists a barrier to recruitment from outside the industry which encourages upward mobility within. Training is an intervening variable in both sides of the case. However, on the other hand, whatever the degree of specificity it determines the chances of job seekers finding similar jobs in other organisations.

The importance of the homogeneity of knowledge proposition is three-fold. First, at a practical level, it determines the nature of development training. Second and more important, it governs whether or not there is a path from bottom to top. The more homogeneous, the more likely the opportunity for internal promotion. Riley (1991) points out that where such a path exists it has the effect of pulling downwards the level of pay of senior staff. This is not caused directly by competition between the upwardly mobile and the imported outsiders but simply by the existence of a chord, which is difficult to break, running back to the pay economics of the lowest levels. Third, it dictates how individuals collect knowledge to help them progress. If the knowledge is fragmented then the early stages of a career will be governed by moves to 'get relevant experience' in the manner of Gunz's constructional logic. The existence of a cut-off between technical knowledge and managerial knowledge acts against pathways from bottom to top, but also puts the accent on training rather than experience-collecting strategies as a means to jump through the knowledge cut-off barrier.

The knowledge distribution variables and the structural variables work in tandem. If a pyramid is flattened it is likely to increase the shared knowledge throughout. This should increase internal promotion because more people would have the knowledge to get promotion, although prospects are simultaneously being reduced by the flattening itself.

The case of a structure involving distributed sub-units has particular interest for tourism. Such a structure promotes the kind of career path where individuals move upwards through a hierarchy of sub-units. This type of career corresponds to Gunz's notion of a command-centred logic, looking for ever increasing responsibility.

Sequence analysis

The central problem of sequence analysis is that both measurement and interpretation are dependent upon the *classification scheme* applied by the researcher. It again becomes necessary to ask what a career stage is: is it just a period of work, or is some learning required? Does it change the direction or pace of the career?

Approaches to sequence analysis tend to fall into two camps, which are those that measure what happened and what was learnt in each job and those that concentrate on the differences between jobs – putting the accent on the job transitions rather than the job. For the former, the interpretation is additive; while for the latter, it is developmental.

The design of career path research usually has to consider both job content and transition processes. The choice of emphasis determines the form of classification scheme applied to the sequences. (Work in progress at the University of Surrey by H. Salleh includes a job content classification, and Adele Ladkin's doctoral thesis, also in progress, contains a transitional and context schema.)

Table 18.2 identifies the main attributes of individual sequences, aggregate sequences and summary functions. Summary functions refer to the type of phenomena in which people look back and integrate the past into their present motivations.

Table 18.2 *Dimensions of sequences*

Individual sequences	Aggregate sequences	Summary functions
Duration	Historical models	Career logics
Start	Tournament models	Reflective
Direction	Human capital	Satisfaction
Trajectory	Stage salience	Career
Speed		Commitment
Time flow		Success/failure
Success/failure		Reflective
Satisfaction/dissatisfaction		Anchors
Goals		
Job content		
Job content/differentials		
Transitions		
Transitions/differentials		
Stages		
Stage duration		
Interventions		
Human capital changes		

Behaviour and interventions
It is one thing to measure sequence variables, but most career paths are influenced by interventions. The literature review indicates an increasing interest in sequence analysis but by far the dominant approach is that it focuses on a behavioural object of careers. Table 18.3 indicates the main ideas drawn from research on career behaviour and on interventions.

At this juncture it is worthwhile placing tourism in its true context. The players are not simply education, the individual and the organisation. The labour market is also a key player. This perspective brings the additional complication of having to take into account labour turnover which is always problematic.

Riley (1990) has developed a technique for circumventing this problem

Table 18.3 *Career behaviour and intervention*

Behavioural subjects	Interventions
Career success/failure	Training
Career planning	Development
Career commitment	Organisation planning
Career withdrawal	Individual planning
Mobility	Counselling
Entrepreneurship	Mentoring
Career compromise	Assessment
Socialisation	Career programmes
Career choice	

and for allowing career sequences to be analysed as supra-organisational entities. This offers the opportunity to extend *career logics* to embrace market perceptions. This proposition is currently being tested.

Discussion and research

Perhaps the most glaring omission from the literature review is that of social psychology. Personality psychology is there, as are human resources planning and organisational behaviour, but the absence of social psychology is strange because it is the discipline most likely to be able to integrate the structural variables with the career motives.

If one asks why career research should be undertaken at all, the answer goes beyond the subject of careers itself. There are plenty of worthwhile methods for understanding how careers work in industry, but if career research is seen as a form of human resources planning then its additional value is revealed. Sequence analysis can be seen as analysis of labour supply. It is important for an industry to know its stock of management and skilled workers in qualitative terms. Taking the argument further, the study of careers is the study of the dynamic aspects of human resources and it could be seen as a sampling process to understand the complete dynamics of human resources systems. This case is strongly argued by Psacharopoulos (1991). He argues that manpower forecasts are enhanced by knowing how the present position occurred. Tracing occupation career paths and measuring the quality of the stock of skilled labour are essential investigative approaches.

In terms of research in entrepreneurs, an application to tourism may facilitate a progress in this subject which has not yet delivered much beyond the role of family connections and family role models as influential variables.

In addition, as the tourism industry consists of a number of sub-units, and a general transferability of skills, there exist a large number of managers from the variety of sectors. It follows that some kind of analytical framework with which to study the mobility of managers might add to our understanding of careers in the tourism industry.

References

Arnold, J., Robertson, I.T and Cooper, G.L., 1991, 'Career choice and development', in *Work psychology: understanding human behaviour in the workplace*, London, Pitman: 265–83.

Arthur, M.B., Hall, D.T. and Lawrence, B.S., 1989, *Handbook of career theory*, Cambridge University Press, Cambridge.

Blau, P.M. and Duncan, O.D., 1967, *The American Occupational Structure*, Wiley, New York.

Bolles, R.N., 1972, *What colour is your parachute?*, Ten Speed Press, Berkeley, California.

Charles, K.R., 1992, 'Career influences, expectations and perceptions of Caribbean hospitality and tourism students: a Third World perspective', *Hospitality and Tourism Educator*, 4(3): 9–14.

Chartrand, J.M. and Camp, C.C., 1991, 'Advances in the measurement of career development constructs: a twenty year review', *Journal of Vocational Behaviour*, 39(2): 1–39.

Crites, J.O., 1981, *Career counselling: models, methods and materials*, McGraw-Hill, New York.

Dalton, G.W. and Thompson, P.H., 1986, *Novations: strategies for career management*, Scott Foresman, Glenview, Illinois.

Driver, M.J., 1982, 'Career concepts: a new approach to career research', in R. Katz (ed.), *Career issues in human resource management*, Prentice Hall, Englewood Cliffs, NJ.

Driver, M.J., 1988, 'Careers: a review of personal and organizational research', in C.L. Cooper and I.T. Robertson (eds), *International review of industrial and organizational psychology*, John Wiley and Sons, London: 245–77.

Edmond, A., 1989, 'Building a bridge to a new career', *Black Enterprise*, 19(10): 96–100.

Erikson, E.H., 1963, *Childhood and society*, Penguin, Harmondsworth.

Feldman, D.C., 1989, 'Career in organizations: recent trends and future directions', *Journal of Management*, 15(2): 135–56.

Forbes, J.B., 1987, 'Early intraorganizational mobility: patterns and influence', *Academy of Management Journal*, 30(1): 110–25.

Ghiselli, E.E., 1969, 'The efficacy of advancement on the basis of merit in relation to structural properties of the organization', *Organizational Behaviour and Human Performance*, 4: 402–14.

Gould, S., 1979, 'Characteristics of career planners in upwardly mobile occupation', *Academy of Management Journal*, 22(3): 539–50.

Granrose, C.S. and Portwood, J.D., 1987, 'Matching individual career plans and organizational career management', *Academy of Management Journal*, 30(4): 669–720.

Greenhaus, J.H. and Simon. W.E., 1976, 'Self-esteem, career salience, and the choice of an ideal occupation', *Journal of Vocational Behaviour*, 8: 51–8.

Guerrier, Y., 1986, 'Hotel manager: an unsuitable job for women?', *Service Industries Journal*, 6(3): 227–60.

Gunz, H., 1988, 'Organizational logics of managerial careers', *Organizational Studies*, 9(4): 529–54.

Hall, D.T., 1976, *Careers in organizations*, Goodyear, Pacific Palisades, California.

Holland, J.L., 1973, *Making vocational choices: a theory of careers*, Prentice Hall, Englewood Cliffs, NJ.

Holland, J.L., 1979, *Professional manual for the self-directed search*, Consulting Psychologist Press, California.

Holland, J.L., 1985, *Making vocational choices: theory of careers* (2nd edn), Prentice Hall, Englewood Cliffs, NJ.

Jennings, E.E., 1971, *Routes to the executive suite*, Macmillan, New York.

Korman, A.K., 1971, *Industrial and organizational psychology*, Prentice Hall, Englewood Cliffs, NJ.

Krausz, M. and Reshef, M., 1992, 'Managerial job change: reasons for leaving, choice determinants, and search processes', *Journal of Business Psychology*, 6(3): 349–359.

Levinson, D.J., with Darrow, C.N., Klein, E.B., Levinson, M.H. and McKee, B., 1978, *The seasons of a man's life*, Knopf, New York.

Louis, R., 1980, 'Career transitions: varieties and commonalities', *Academy of Management Review*, 5(3): 329–39.

Metcalf, A., 1988, 'Careers and training in tourism and leisure', *Employment Gazette*, 96(2): 86–9.

Nicholson, N. and West, M.A., 1988, *Managerial job change: men and women in transition*, Cambridge University Press, Cambridge.

Peroni, G. and Guerra, D., 1991, *European Community directory of job profiles: occupations in the hotel and tourism section within the European community: a comparative analysis*, CEDEFOP, Berlin.

Psacharapoulos, G., 1991, 'From manpower planning to labour market analysis', *International Labour Review*, 130(4): 459–74.

Riley, M., 1990, 'Role of age distributions in career path analysis', *Tourism Management*, 11(1): 38–44.

Riley, M., 1991, *Human resource management a guide to personnel practice in the hotel and catering industry*, Butterworth Heinemann, Oxford: Chapter 19.

Roberts, E.B., 1989, 'The personality and motivations of technological entrepreneurs', *Journal of Engineering and Technology Management*, 6(1): 5–23.

Rosenbaum, J.E., 1979, 'Tournament mobility: career patterns in a corporation', *Administrative Science Quarterly*, 24(2): 220–41.

Ross, G.F., 1992, 'Tourism management as a career path: vocational perceptions of Australian courses', *Tourism Management*, 13(2): 262–7.

Russell, J.E.A., 1991, 'Career development interventions in organizations', *Journal of Vocational Behaviour*, 38(3): 237–87.

Scanlan, T.J., 1980, 'Towards an occupational classification for self-employed men: an investigation of entrepreneurship from the perspective of Holland's theory of career development', *Journal of Vocational Behaviour*, 16(1): 163–72.

Schein, E.H., 1975, 'How career anchors hold executives to their career paths', *Personnel*, 52(3): 11–24.

Schein, E.H., 1978, *Career dynamics: matching individual and organizational needs*, Addison-Wesley, London.

Scherer, R.F., Adams, J.S., Carley, S.S. and Wiebe, F.A., 1989, 'Role model performance effect on the development of entrepreneurial career preference', *Entrepreneurship Theory & Practice*, 13(3): 53–71.

Scott, M.G. and Twomey, D.F., 1988, 'The long-term supply of entrepreneurs: students' career aspirations in relation to entrepreneurship', *Journal of Small Business Management*, 26(4): 5–13.

Simonsen, P., 1986, 'Concept of career development', *Training and Development Journal*, 40(2): 70–74.

Sonnenfied, J. and Kotter, J.P., 1982, 'The maturation of career theory', *Human Relations*, 35: 19–46.

Super, D.E., 1957, *The psychology of careers*, Harper and Row, New York.

19 Predicting business failure

S. Lewis

Introduction

While numerous reports and studies monitor the incidence and frequency
of business failure, it is remarkable that so little innovative research in
the field of forecasting business failure has been undertaken in recent
years. The most influential studies relating to the predictability of business
failure were undertaken in the late 1960s and early 1970s, and these
studies remain the basis of research in the 1990s.

It has long been possible to approximate the number of businesses
likely to succeed or fail in a given time period, but to predict exactly
which specific business is likely to succeed or fail has proven much more
difficult. The benefits which accrue from the ability to predict specific
business failure with confidence are without question to the potential
investor or creditor.

On the one hand, it is very difficult to predict with accuracy which
specific business will fail. On the other hand, once a business fails very
few express surprise, but often comment 'Well, it was obvious that the
business was in trouble . . .'. Does such anecdotal wisdom *ex post facto*
bear any relationship to theoretical models which aim to predict specific
business failure?

One cannot discuss business failure without reference to Argenti's
(1977) influential research on this topic. According to Argenti, business
failure is a lengthy process which may take large corporations as long as
a decade to achieve. If this is the case, then the symptoms ought to be
recognisable in advance, and the final failure not a surprise. Who, in 1988,
would have been brave enough to predict the failure of Pan Am just three
years before the final bankruptcy? In the early 1990s, there are a number
of large multinationals struggling in the economic climate of the time, but
are these temporary difficulties or fatal symptoms? Which companies will
fail? Which companies will survive? And succeed?

Foster (1986) identifies four key indicators of the likelihood of financial
distress: cash-flow analysis; corporate strategy analysis; financial statement
analysis; and external variables. Argenti (1977) argues that failure occurs
when there is something wrong with the company, 'preeminently with
their top management or with the way they respond to change. Then
they make a mistake. Finally their finances deteriorate.' It is clear that the
analysis of available financial information is important, but so, too, is the
analysis of all aspects of the business.

If financial difficulties are the final stage in the long road to business
failure, financial failure occurs in the context of management style,

industry structure and economic climate. More importantly, as financial failure is the final stage in a lengthy failure process, the evaluation of financial information may provide the ability to predict specific business failure in the short term.

Research in the field of business failure is fraught with difficulties, many of which have not yet been resolved. The purpose of this chapter is to review the research to date on business failure with specific reference to those studies which assess the predictive ability of financial information and ratios, and to evaluate the relevance of financial prediction models to the hotel and catering industry in the economic climate of the early to mid-1990s.

Business failure and the hotel and catering industry

Currently, all economic indicators, including bankruptcy figures, are keenly monitored for signs of an end to the recession. In the United Kingdom, business failures, as defined by the Department of Trade and Industry, reached 44 459 in 1991, 122 per cent higher than in 1983. In addition, Dun & Bradstreet announced a record number of business failures of 66 767 for 1992.

In the period 1983–91, the hotel and catering industry accounted for an increasing proportion of business failures in Britain. In 1991, there were 2229 business failures in the hotel and catering industry, an increase of 372 per cent on 1983 levels.

Interestingly, during the 'boom' years, the level of business failures in the hotel and catering industry did not fall below 1983 levels. During the years 1987–9, business failures in general, and across most other industry sectors, did decline and fall below 1983 levels (Figure 19.1). It also appears that the rate of acceleration of business failures in the hotel and catering industry is much higher than elsewhere. In addition, the second largest hotel operator in Britain is now the Official Receiver. These factors will have an influence on the prospects for recovery in the hotel and catering industry.

While considerable research has been undertaken in the field of business failure in general, minimal research has been undertaken in the field of business failure within the hotel and catering industry. Given that the hotel and catering industry represents a high proportion of UK bankruptcies, it is worth reviewing the key features of those business failure prediction models which have been developed in order to determine their relevance to the hotel and catering industry.

Methodology

The first problem that researchers encounter in the field of business failure is one of definition. What is business failure? The absence of an agreed definition of business failure makes comparison between alternative

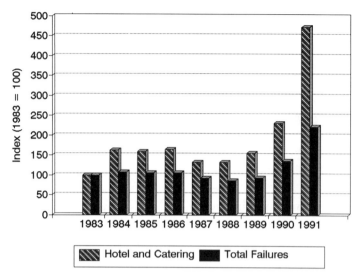

Figure 19.1 *Business failures, 1983–91*

Source: Department of Trade and Industry

studies difficult. The difficulty lies in deciding whether a company has effectively failed or is a failure from a legal point of view. A company may survive for some time while technically insolvent and in financial distress, yet avoid bankruptcy. In the United States, many companies which enter Chapter 11 emerge some years later in a much healthier condition (for example, Continental Airlines has survived two periods under the shadow of Chapter 11).

The primary search for a model which will predict business failure has centred on the evaluation and analysis of financial information relating to failed firms, after failure has occurred. The assumption which underlies most failure prediction models is that the characteristics of firms which have failed historically, do provide a valid basis for predicting specific business failure in the future. Thus, the search is on to identify failed firms together with available financial information, in order to allow comparison with similar firms which have not failed. It is this comparison between failed firms and non-failed firms which has been used to identify the key financial predictors of financial failure.

It is the practical difficulties of compiling a reliable sample of failed firms together with a financial history which has severely limited research in this field. Many of the studies have had to reduce the sample of failed businesses due to the lack of available financial information for many failed businesses. This is not surprising as nearly half of all business failures occur within the first two to five years of operation (Altman 1971), often before a business in difficulty has had time to complete all financial returns. In addition, common symptoms of financial distress include poor financial management and creative accounting (Argenti

1977). This is particularly important for failing businesses who may experience audit problems and delays in finalising the accounts.

In order to identify failed firms, Beaver (1966) used Moody's *Industrial Manual* and information supplied by Dun & Bradstreet and defined business failure as those firms which had been declared bankrupt, insolvent, had defaulted on loan obligations, missed preferred dividend payments or had been liquidated for the benefit of creditors. Beaver (1966) recognised that this was a reluctant sample choice, as it created a bias towards large, publicly owned industrial businesses, ranging in asset size from US $0.6 million to $45 million and with a mean asset size of approximately $6 million dollars.

Alternatively, Altman (1968), Deakin (1972) and Blum (1974) chose to exclude from the definition of business failure those firms which had defaulted on both loan obligations and preferred dividends. This is a much narrower definition which focuses on the legal status of the firm and defines as business failures those which had been declared legally bankrupt and in receivership, or were in the process of reorganisation under the provisions of the National Bankruptcy Act. As a result, Altman's sample of failed businesses ranged in asset size from $0.7 million to $25.9 million with a mean asset size of $6.4 million. Like Beaver before, these studies had a tendency towards the large, publicly owned industrial business.

In the United Kingdom, Taffler and Tisshaw (1977) widened the definition of business failure by considering government intervention as an alternative to business failure. Thus, a failed business is defined as one which had failed legally or would have done so had it not been for government intervention. The resulting sample of failed companies consisted of 46 major quoted manufacturing firms which had failed over an eight-year period.

Selecting failed businesses from published data bases utilising a legal definition of business failure has the important advantage of objectivity and ready availability. However, it excludes a wide range of businesses which came very close to failure, are in financial distress or have failed in a very different way. These studies exclude those businesses in distress and which would have failed in the legal sense had they not been taken over, merged with another business or rescued by government intervention. Also excluded are those businesses which very nearly failed, but did not do so due to timely restructuring and reorganisation which resulted in an effective business turn-around.

The early research (Beaver, Altman, Blum, Deakin) adopted a paired-sample design. Once the sample group of failed companies was determined, a matched sample of non-failed companies was selected. For each failed company, a non-failed company was selected which mirrored, as far as possible, the failed company's size and industry classification. Utilising the dichotomous sample group, the previous studies then adopted differing approaches to identifying the key differences in the financial ratios of failed businesses versus non-failed businesses.

The objective of these studies is to determine whether a model for predicting business failure can be developed from published financial information. The evaluation of financial information in the traditional form of ratio analysis creates a myriad of financial ratios. The next task is to compress this wide range of financial ratios into a much smaller range of key ratios which are significant indicators of the financial health of the firm. Among all studies, there is a consensus that financial health is dependent on a combination of cash flow, profitability, liquidity, solvency and activity, but each study elected to combine and measure these features in alternative ways.

Beaver (1966) adopted a univariate approach, and systematically calculated 30 ratios for each of the 79 companies in both sample groups over a five-year period. The mean of each ratio was calculated for each year for both the failed group and the non-failed group. The resulting means were then compared over the five-year period in a profile analysis. The profile analysis was followed by dichotomous classification test which enabled the conventional financial ratios to be ranked in order of their predictability value. It is worth noting that Beaver did not set out to complete a definitive study on business failure prediction, but to provide a 'bench-mark for future investigations into alternative predictors of failure', and clearly recognised the need for further research using multi-ratio analysis.

Altman (1968), however, recognised that ratios do not perform in isolation; by their very nature they are interactive. He therefore sought to identify the interrelationships of financial ratios by using multiple discriminant analysis (MDA) in order to assign weights to the conventional financial ratios. MDA was selected as a method of analysing the range of characteristics represented by financial ratios simultaneously, recognising the interrelationship of financial ratios. An original selection of 22 conventional financial ratios was reduced to five ratios. The MDA analysis was performed on the resulting five ratios, the group of failed businesses and the group of non-failed businesses in order to create a Z-score for predicting business failure.

Following Altman's study, the use of multivariate techniques replaced Beaver's univariate model. Blum (1974) used MDA to develop his failing company model, and Moyer (1977) used MDA to re-examine the Altman model with a different sample group. In the United Kingdom, Taffler and Tisshaw (1977) utilised linear discriminant analysis in order to develop an alternative model. Ohlson (1980) adopted a different approach, utilising conditional logit analysis.

Research findings

Beaver (1966) set out to provide a starting point for future investigations into business failure, and eventually ranked six key financial indicators according to their predictive ability. The key financial indicators, together with the percentage errors, are shown in Table 19.1. This indicates that over a five-year period preceding failure, some ratios perform better than others in successfully predicting failure. The relationship between cash

Table 19.1 *Percentage of firms misclassified (Beaver)*

Ratio	Year before failure				
	1	2	3	4	5
Cash flow/total debt	13	21	23	24	22
Net income/total assets	13	20	23	29	28
Total debt/total assets	19	25	34	27	28
Working capital/total assets	24	34	33	45	41
Current ratio	20	32	36	38	45
No-credit interval	23	38	43	38	37

Source: Beaver (1966)

flow and debt performs particularly well over time, and is clearly related to the firm's ability to service debt. The need to service debt is closely followed by the need to generate net income from total assets, and the extent to which those total assets have been financed by debt. The predictive ability of the individual ratios ranges from 87 per cent accuracy for cash flow to total debt in the year preceding failure, to 55 per cent for the current ratio five years prior to failure.

This is not surprising, one would expect a successful firm to manage debt prudently, while at the same time fully utilising total assets. What is surprising is the relatively high percentage errors relating to the working capital ratios over time. It would seem from this analysis that working capital related ratios are only reliable in the very short term.

As intended, Beaver's study paved the way for further research in this field. Initially, Altman (1968) took up the challenge and investigated the interrelationships of financial ratios, together with the predictive ability of alternative combinations of financial ratios. Using MDA, Altman created the 'Z-score', based on five key financial ratios together with their relative weightings:

$$Z = 0.012X_1 + 0.014X_2 + 0.033X_3 + 0.006X_4 + 0.999X_5$$

where

X_1 = working capital/total assets
X_2 = retained earnings/total assets
X_3 = earnings before interest and taxes/total assets
X_4 = market value of equity/book value of total debt
X_5 = sales/total assets.

It is therefore possible to calculate the Z-score for a business at any point in time, and it is this score that is used to predict success or failure. A score of less than 1.81 indicates future bankruptcy, a score between 1.81 and 2.68 bankruptcy is more likely than non-bankruptcy, between 2.68 and 2.99 non-failure is more likely than bankruptcy, and a score greater than 2.99 indicates non-bankruptcy. With this benchmark for predicting business failure, Altman achieved a success rate of 95 per cent in the year preceding failure, declining to 36 per cent five years preceding failure (Table 19.2).

Table 19.2 *Percentage of firms misclassified (Altman)*

Ratio	Year before failure				
	1	2	3	4	5
Z Score	05	18	52	71	64

Source: Altman (1968)

When compared to Beaver's analysis, Altman achieves a much higher degree of predictive accuracy in the year preceding failure, although Beaver did achieve a higher degree of predictive accuracy over longer time periods. Altman's Z-score has been used extensively for failure prediction, and has set the standard for research in this field.

Research has also been undertaken to apply failure prediction models in order to meet specific practical needs. Interestingly, Blum (1974) set out to design a model which would predict business failure as defined by the US Supreme Court's Failing Company Doctrine in the case of International Shoe *v* F.T.C. Altman and Loris (1976) successfully developed a modified Z-score specifically for predicting the failure of over-the-counter broker-dealers. Libby (1975), Casey (1980) and Houghton (1984) all investigated the use of financial information by bank lending officers in the decision-making process with mixed results.

In the United Kingdom, Taffler and Tisshaw (1977), developed an alternative Z-score:

$$Z = C_0 + C_1 R_1 + C_2 R_2 + C_3 R_3 + C_4 R_4$$

where

C_0 = a constant
$C_1, \ldots, C_4$ = the ratio weights or coefficients
$R_1, \ldots, R_4$ = the financial ratios appropriately transformed
R_1 = profit before tax/current liabilities
R_2 = current assets/total liabilities
R_3 = current liabilities/total assets
R_4 = no-credit interval.

Unlike Altman, Taffler and Tisshaw did not publish details of the constant, ratio weights or the benchmark Z-score for comparative analysis. In contrast to Altman, they placed considerable emphasis on working capital ratios, and exclude any reference to asset utilisation ratios. However, Taffler and Tisshaw did achieve a 99 per cent success rate in the year prior to failure, declining to just over one-third four years prior to failure. The

Taffler and Tisshaw model has been used commercially to predict business failure.

Much of the subsequent research has focused on testing the validity of the failure prediction models developed by Beaver (1966), Altman (1968) and Taffler and Tisshaw (1977). The results of studies such as those undertaken by Wilcox (1971), Deakin (1972) and Moyer (1977) have been varied.

To summarise, failure prediction models can predict specific business failure with a high degree of accuracy up to two years before failure actually occurs. However, the models place differing degrees of emphasis on working capital and liquidity ratios versus asset utilisation ratios.

Implicit assumptions

The research to date is based on the available published accounts of both failed and non-failed businesses. The use of published financial information automatically implies a wide range of assumptions about accounting policies, standards and practices. Within the same industry, within the same country and legal framework, businesses do legitimately adopt differing accounting practices. As soon as the boundaries for comparison are extended, either geographically or commercially, the range of alternative accounting practices increases dramatically. Accountants with experience of multinational corporations are all too familiar with the difficulties involved in ensuring that apples are compared with apples not oranges. The same difficulties underlie the use of published financial information for failure prediction.

It is assumed that published financial information has been prepared honestly and in good faith, and that such information represents a true and fair view of the business. The potential of window dressing or creative accounting is ignored in most studies, yet the incidence of such practices in failed businesses is known to be high. Taffler and Tisshaw (1977) recognise the potential for window dressing, and argue that their model specifically defeats window dressing and creative accounting. However, it is known that the incidence of creative accounting and window dressing does increase prior to failure (Argenti 1977). The implications of such actions for comparisons between failed and non-failed businesses is unknown and unquantifiable.

The failure prediction models discussed here have been developed by a variety of processes which all involve the comparison of failed businesses with non-failed businesses. This approach to the development of business failure prediction models in itself has disadvantages. First, there is not yet an agreed definition of business failure, and by implication, these studies suggest that success is a non-failed business. Survival may approximate to success in today's economic climate, but it does not necessarily indicate good financial health. As already stated, the legal definition of failure clearly ignores those businesses which have marginally avoided bankruptcy or insolvency for one reason or another. Such businesses would not necessarily be classified as financially healthy.

Second, there is a risk of 'over-fitting' (Foster 1986), resulting from the need to match failed businesses with non-failed businesses. Typically, failed businesses represent a small percentage of businesses as a whole, and they are not necessarily a representative selection. The search for non-failed businesses which correspond with the key characteristics of the failed businesses, compounds this problem and may result in a significant bias.

The samples used in most of these studies have very important characteristics, which result from the need to obtain reliable financial information over a number of years for those businesses in the samples. Therefore, much of the research has been undertaken in the manufacturing sector, with large, publicly quoted companies which have been in existence for a number of years.

It is often said that hindsight has 20/20 vision, and the development of *ex-post* rather than *ex-ante* failure prediction models inevitably results in models which very accurately explain the key factors which distinguish the selected failed businesses from the selected non-failed businesses in the same sample group in the past. However, it is not clear that the key factors identified from historical data will continue to be the factors which distinguish between failed businesses and non-failed businesses in the future.

On a similar theme, the studies inevitably assume *ceteris paribus*, a necessary assumption for model-building. However, failure prediction models do have a particularly practical application, and it is important that changing economic circumstances and financial management practices are incorporated in such models. For example, the management of working capital has become much more aggressive in recent years, to such an extent that a current ratio of 2:1 and an acid test of 1:1 is now a rare event.

In summary, the failure prediction models discussed here are limited by the assumptions implied by their methodologies. It is not clear whether these models can be applied successfully to alternative industry sectors, or to small and medium-sized businesses. It would be useful to develop a common definition of business failure, and to test the existing failure prediction models against alternative industry sectors, business size or time period in order to validate their usefulness.

Relevance to the hotel and catering industry

In addition to the limitations posed by the implied assumptions discussed above, the structure of the hotel and catering industry is very different to the profile of the samples used in the research to date. The hotel and catering industry is top-heavy, consisting of a relatively small number of large businesses, but a large number of small and medium-sized businesses.

Boer (1992) estimates that in the United Kingdom over 75 per cent of businesses in the hotel and catering industry are sole traders or partnerships, and over 90 per cent of businesses have a financial turnover of less than £250 000. This is supported by analysis of the United Kingdom's

Department of Trade and Industry's figures on insolvency which indicate that the majority of business failures in the hotel and catering industry are individual bankruptcies rather than business insolvencies (Figure 19.2).

The fact that the hotel and catering industry is a service industry rather than a manufacturing industry does have important implications for financial ratios. Many businesses in the hotel and catering sector will have negative working capital, which will consist of debtors, cash and trade creditors. There is minimal investment in stock. In comparison, manufacturing companies will normally have positive working capital. For example, the existence of negative working capital will result in a higher Z-score than traditional industries when Altman's model is applied.

The primary component of capital employed for the hotel and catering business is fixed assets, the premises, whereas the manufacturing company will have investment committed in both working capital and stock, as well as land and buildings. The balance sheet value of the property is dependent on re-valuation practice and the accounting policies adopted by the business. The importance of accounting policy and practice regarding property re-valuations has been clearly demonstrated recently by the business failure of Queens Moat Houses plc.

One has to consider whether it is appropriate to apply the models developed in the United States by Beaver (1966) and Altman (1968), primarily based on large-scale manufacturing corporations, to the hotel and catering industry; or whether it would be preferable to apply Taffler and Tisshaw's (1977) United Kingdom model, again based on large manufacturing businesses, to the hotel and catering industry. Intuitively, it is difficult to rationalise the application of these models to the hotel and catering industry.

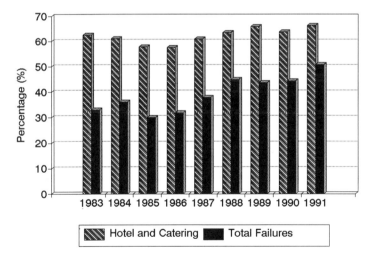

Figure 19.2 *Individual bankruptcies as a percentage of business failures, 1983–91*

Source: Department of Trade and Industry

Both Beaver and Altman place considerable emphasis on asset utilisation ratios. Experience of the hotel and catering industry leaves every general manager with an abiding knowledge of the importance of operating statistics relating to throughput and revenue, such as occupancy rates, average room rate and average spend. Industry reports by consultants such as Horwath & Horwath and Pannell Kerr Forster Associates are valued by many. Neither model in its current form is appropriate, but the compatibility between asset utilisation models and current management practice does provide a basis for further research aimed at identifying whether it is possible to modify these models to reflect the specific characteristics of the hotel and catering industry.

Alternatively, Taffler and Tisshaw place much greater emphasis on the management of working capital. Working capital management in many hotel and catering businesses often receives minimal attention, quite simply because of the relatively low value when compared to the fixed assets of the business. While it is recognised that working capital management is very important to the survival of the hotel and catering business, the primary source of the working capital is through the utilisation of fixed assets. For this reason, the Taffler and Tisshaw model is not suitable for specific failure prediction in the hotel and catering industry.

Given the structure of the hotel and catering industry, the question of whether or not existing failure prediction models can be applied consists of two equally important elements. On the one hand, the transferability of failure prediction models between industry sectors needs to be established, and, on the other hand, the validity of applying such models to small and medium-sized businesses has yet to be demonstrated.

Conclusion and summary

Clearly, it is possible to develop failure prediction models which can predict business failure up to two years before it occurs. This has been successfully proven by Beaver (1966), Altman (1968), Taffler and Tisshaw (1977) and subsequent studies.

As yet, there is no evidence that these failure prediction models in their current form are not suitable for use in the hotel and catering industry. Furthermore, it may be possible to adapt the Beaver and Altman models to meet the needs of the hotel and catering industry. The alternative is to develop an industry-specific failure prediction model.

Failure prediction models have come a long way since Beaver's early research in the 1960s, but they do not yet have a proven track record across a wide range of businesses.

References

Altman, E.I., 1968, 'Financial ratios, discriminant analysis and the prediction of corporate bankruptcy', *Journal of Finance*, September: 589–609.

Altman, E.I., 1971, *Corporate bankruptcy in America*, D.C. Heath, Lexington, Massachusetts.

Altman, E.I. and Loris, B., 1976, 'A financial early warning system for over-the-counter broker-dealers', *Journal of Finance*, September: 1201–17.

Argenti, J., 1977, 'Company failure – long range prediction not enough', *Accountancy*, August: 46–52.

Beaver, W.H., 1966, 'Financial ratios as a predictor of failure', *Empirical Research in Accounting, Selected Studies*, supplement to *Journal of Accounting Research*, Autumn: 77–111.

Blum, M., 1974, 'Failing company discriminant analysis', *Journal of Accounting Research*, Spring: 1–25.

Boer, A., 1992, 'The banking sector and small firm failure in the UK hotel and catering industry', *International Journal of Contemporary Hospitality Management*, 4(2): 13–16.

Casey, C.J., 1980, 'The usefulness of accounting ratios for subjects' predictions of corporate failure: replications and extensions', *Journal of Accounting Research*, Autumn: 603–13.

Deakin, E.B, 1972, 'A discriminant analysis of predictors of business failure', *Journal of Accounting Research*, Spring: 167–79.

Department of Trade and Industry, 1992, 'Insolvency', in *Annual Abstract of Statistics*: 309–10, HMSO, London.

Department of Trade and Industry, 1988, 'Insolvency', in *Annual Abstract of Statistics*: 300–01, HMSO, London.

Foster, G., 1986, 'Distress analysis and financial information', in *Financial statement analysis*, Prentice Hall, Englewood Cliffs, NJ: 559–62.

Houghton, K.A., 1984, 'Accounting data and the prediction of business failure: the setting of priors and the age of data', *Journal of Accounting Research*, Spring: 361–8.

Libby, R., 1975, 'Accounting ratios and the prediction of failure: some behavioural evidence', *Journal of Accounting Research*, Spring: 150–61.

Moyer, C.R., 1977, 'Forecasting financial failure', *Financial Management*, Spring: 11–17.

Ohlson, J.A., 1980, 'Financial ratios and the probabilistic prediction of bankruptcy', *Journal of Accounting Research*, Spring: 109–31.

Taffler, R. and Tisshaw, H., 1977, 'Going, going, gone – four factors which predict', *Accountancy*, March: 50–54.

Wilcox, J.W., 1971, 'A simple theory of financial ratios as predictors of failure', *Journal of Accounting Research*, Autumn: 389–95.

20 Geographic information systems in tourism marketing

S. Sussmann and T. Rashad

Introduction

Previous contributions to this series (Sussmann 1992; 1994) have concentrated on the potential of information technology (IT) to change, decide or influence the tourist's choice of destination and/or transportation. This chapter examines the possible influence of one specific technology, geographic information systems (GIS) on tourism marketing research strategies.

GIS are already well established. The following definition was provided as far back as 1981: 'an automated set of functions that provides professionals with advanced capabilities for the storage, retrieval, manipulation and display of geographically located data' (Ozemoy *et al.* 1981). Demographic statistics in computerised form have been available since the 1970s. It is, however, the combination of demographic information and geographic location – geodemographics – together with the development of high-speed micro-computers and highly sophisticated mapping software, that provide the potential for a new era in consumer information analysis. This chapter concentrates on market research applications and will include some recent research on the GIS awareness of tourism market research organisations. Other interesting applications of GIS, such as recreation research and management (Devine and Kuo 1991) will be briefly reviewed.

What are geographic information systems?

GIS can be seen as just a special case of information systems in general (de Man 1988; Carter 1989), that is, systems that are aimed at the collection and manipulation, including processing and retrieval, of data organised and structured within a certain context which ensures that they are transformed into information for a well-defined group of users. It is not easy to provide a precise and unambiguous definition of GIS, given their rapid rate of development, commercial orientation and diversity (Maguire 1991). The most concise definition found by the authors was provided in a Department of the Environment (DOE 1987, p. 132) report: 'a system for capturing, storing, checking, manipulating, analysing and displaying data which are spatially referenced to the Earth'. There is, however, another approach which transcends the narrow technological definition and takes a wider institutional perspective, exemplified by Carter (1989, p. 3) who defined GISs as follows: 'an institutional entity, reflecting an organisational structure that integrates technology with a database, expertise and continuing financial support over time'. It will be worth returning to this last definition when analysing the results of the survey carried out on usage of GIS by tourism market researchers.

Another alternative postulated by some authors (Maguire 1991) is a classification based on the application of the system, which gives rise to an alternative name. Of these names, those of relevance to various areas of tourism and recreation research are:

- image-based information systems;
- land information systems;
- natural resource management information systems;
- market analysis information systems;
- spatial information systems;
- spatial decision support systems;
- urban information systems.

These diverse application areas are thus connected by common technology and methods, based on a combination of spatially identified location, data-base information and graphical display. The technologies involved in the generation of proper geographic information systems are those of:

○ computer cartography;
○ computer aided design;
○ remote sensing;
○ data-base management.

It is important to emphasise that 'any system that is capable of putting a map on a screen' (Newell and Theriault 1990, p. 42) cannot be rightly called a geographic information system. In such a system, each point in reality is represented according to two data elements: the *spatial element* and its *attribute*, also called the *statistical data element*. The spatial element is generally based on detailed digitised map data – for example, administrative boundaries as the spatial element providing references for demographic data or consumer purchasing power. It is, however, arguable whether current tourism market research applications have reached the stage in which this fundamental distinction has significant practical relevance. Existing alternative systems to retrieve and manipulate geodemographic data will be described in the next section.

GIS in market research

GIS can be applied to many types of problem. Rhind (1990) sets out the following classification of the generic questions GIS are frequently used to investigate

1. Location   What is at ... ?
2. Condition   Where is it ... ?

3. Trend   What has changed ... ?
4. Routeing   What is the best way ... ?
5. Pattern   What is the pattern ... ?
6. Modelling   What if ... ?

If these questions are translated in terms of market research applications, they would correspond to questions of the type:

1. What is the population of a given census tract?
2. Where are all the houses inhabited by a particular pattern of consumer within a two mile radius of a travel agent?
3. What is the change in the percentage of families with two or more children in a certain neighbourhood within the last decade?
4. Which is the nearest international airport?
5. Is there a pattern in choice of holiday period which can be attributed to local types of employment?
6. Which areas of a new destination will be more affected by a new railway link?

There is undoubtedly enormous potential in geodemographics for market research applications. The interesting question is whether the sophistication of a real GIS is necessarily the answer.

In the United Kingdom, for instance, the Royal Mail postcodes provide a very precise location identification, and the Post Office offers PAF (Postcode Address File) as a location tool to interface to data bases. PAF contains both postcodes and Ordnance Survey grid references. A major marketing research company has produced a market segmentation for the British consumer, called Mosaic, based on postcodes (CCN 1993), which distinguishes between 58 different types (or market segments).

In the tourism field, the English Tourist Board (ETB) offers a service called PiN Targeting which provides a complete geodemographic analysis of a retailer's existing customer base, based on customer, visitors or enquiry files (ETB 1992). It is clearly based on the same postcodes principle, combined with census and other demographic data. One of the services offered is a *detailed map* of the customer base, including the possibility of television and local radio boundaries as well as drive times from a specific site or resort. It has the advantage of being a very cheap system, well within the reach of a small travel agency or hotel.

GIS awareness in the tourism market research field

Exeter (1992) asserts that:

> GIS for market research is rapidly maturing, and more business will reach the point where owning GIS becomes cost effective. However, state of the art GIS is not cheap, and most systems are not very useful unless one has a fair amount of training and computer knowledge.

An exploratory study was implemented to test whether Exeter's assertion agreed with the perception of market research companies specialising in the tourism area.

The study investigated the perception of managers of marketing research organisations in the United Kingdom, which have research expertise in travel and tourism, and offer their services to this sector, concerning the potential use of GIS. Only organisations included in the Market Research Society (MRS) guide *Organizations and individuals providing market research services* (MRS 1993) were considered, and only 44 were found to have research expertise in the travel and tourism sector. Because of the small size of the population, it was decided to investigate the whole of the population of those managers (Weiers 1988).

A self-completion questionnaire was sent to each of the senior managers or directors. After a pilot survey, covering five market research organisation managers (11 per cent of the total sample), a final questionnaire was formulated, divided into two sections – the first covering personal and technical information about the manager concerned; and the second exclusively related to managers' awareness and perceptions about GIS. Some secondary data about organisations' usage of GIS were simultaneously collected.

The response rate, after ten weeks, was 57 per cent, that is to say, 25 out the 44 managers responded. Several frequencies were calculated, to build a profile of the respondents and their applications awareness. Figures 20.1–20.3 describe some of the relevant results, giving the percentage of company employees reporting to these managers, the types of computer applications used by the companies and the percentage of annual capital investment in IT. Finally, Figures 20.4 and 20.5 describe the managers' awareness of GIS and the type of data they handle. It is also interesting to point out that 77 per cent of the sample commented that they believed postcodes were very important in facilitating data bases of consumers' addresses. This includes some respondents who expressed little or no knowledge of GIS technology. A significant percentage of those managers who were not yet using GIS believed that GIS applications would represent an important investment in software training, new hardware and software. Cross-tabulations aimed at identifying personal factors of the managers that could be correlated to their attitude towards the introduction of GISs were inconclusive.

Summarising, it appears from this sample that market research organisations specialising in the tourism field see investment in GIS as an expensive project, both in capital outlay and human resources. Most of them, as previously explained, work with some form of geodemographic data and spatial references, but do not perceive the technological advantages of GISs as justifying their perceived high cost.

GIS applications in other areas of tourism or recreation

It is in the area of planning new or improved facilities that the capability to carry out detailed spatial analysis will be justified in cost-benefit terms.

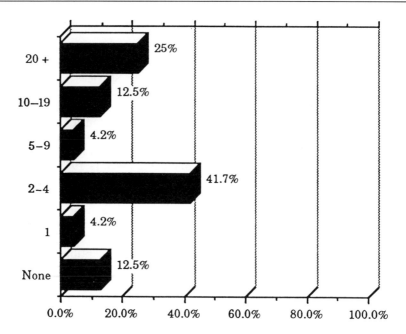

Figure 20.1 *Number of employees directly reporting to the manager*

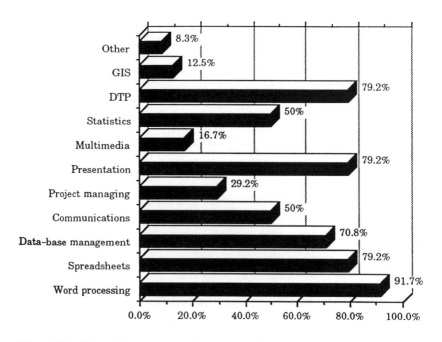

Figure 20.2 *Type of computer applications used*

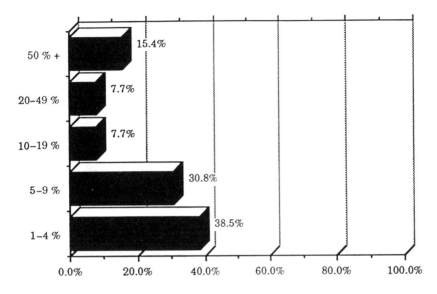

Figure 20.3 *Annual capital investment in IT (per cent)*

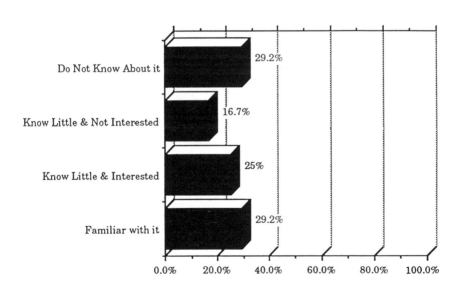

Figure 20.4 *Managers' personal awareness of GIS*

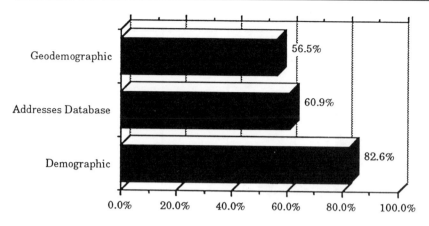

Figure 20.5 *Type of consumer data handled*

As reported by Devine and Kuo (1991), GIS technology holds great promise for expanding the quality of urban recreation planning. They describe a study that was conducted in three stages. First, survey responses were correlated to the location of existing and planned facilities. Second, GIS were used to delimit effective service areas for recreational programmes. Finally, mass transportation routes to support the better utilisation of recreation facilities were evaluated using GIS to determine where existing or proposed routes were potentially available to transport recreation participants. A similar project, not directly related to tourism, was conducted in Shangai to aid urban planning and control unruly property development (Goldstein 1992).

Also, in the electronic marketing of destinations, seen by some tourism researchers as one of the fundamental technological factors of the future (Edgell and Smith 1993), the combination of spatial accuracy and state-of-the-art visualisation could provide a competitive edge, as reported by Hilliard (1993).

Conclusions

Geographic information systems, with their combination of accurate spatial location, data-base information and state-of-the-art visualisation, should provide a powerful tool for tourism marketing. It does appear, however, that their potential has not yet been realised by market research organisations, where they are perceived as too expensive in both financial and human resources terms, as compared to existing location systems based on postcodes.

Their greatest and most immediate impact on the tourism, recreation and hospitality areas appears to reside on transportation and resort planning and update, electronic destination marketing and trip planning.

As has been shown to be the case with most technological advances in the tourism and hospitality field, the potential still runs ahead of the perceived demand.

References

Carter J.R., 1989, 'On defining the geographic information system', in W.J. Ripple (ed.), *Fundamentals of geographic information systems: a compendium*, ASPRS/ACSM, Falls Church, Virginia: 3–7.

CCN Marketing, 1993, *MOSAIC: 1-58 MOSAIC Postcode Types*, CCN, Nottingham.

De Man, E., 1988, 'Establishing a geographic information system relation to its use: a process of strategic choice', *International Journal of Geographical Information Systems*, 2: 245–61.

Department of the Environment (DoE), 1987, *'Handling geographic information'*, Report of the Committee of Inquiry chaired by Lord Chorley, HMSO, London.

Devine, H.A. and Kuo, J., 1991, 'Geographic information systems applications to urban recreation research and management', in C. Sylvester and L. Caldwell (eds), *Abstracts of the Proceedings of the 1991 NRPA Leisure Research Symposium held during the 1991 National Congress for Recreation and Parks*, 17–20 October, Baltimore, Maryland: 83.

Edgell, D.L. and Smith, G., 1993, 'Tourism milestones for the millennium: projections and implications of international tourism for the United States through the year 2000', *Journal of Travel Research*, Summer: 42–7.

English Tourist Board (ETB), 1992, *PiN Targeting and ETB Consumer Database Services*, ETB, London.

Exeter, T.G., 1992, 'The next step is called GIS', *American Demographics*, May: 2–4.

Goldstein, C., 1992, 'Research & innovation: taming Shanghai', *Far Eastern Economic Review*, 155 (47): 74.

Hilliard, J., 1993, as quoted by Di Persio, C. et al in 'Highlights of the 24th Annual TTRA Conference, Whistler, British Columbia, June 12–16, 1993', *Journal of Travel Research*, Summer: 32(1): 55.

Maguire, D.J., 1991, 'The functionality of GIS', in D.J. Maguire, M.F. Goodchild and D.W. Rhind (eds), *Geographical information systems: principles and applications*, Vol. 1, Longman, London: 319–35.

Market Research Society (MRS), 1993, *Organizations and individuals providing market research services*, MRS, London.

Newell, R.G. and Theriault, D.G., 1990, 'Is GIS just a combination of CAD and DBMS?', *Mapping Awareness*, 4 (3): 42–5.

Rhind, D.W., 1990, 'Global databases and GIS', in M.J. Foster and P.J. Shand (eds), *The Association for Geographic Information yearbook 1990*, Taylor & Francis and Miles Arnold, London: 218–23.

Ozemoy, V.M., Smith, D.R. and Sicherman, A., 1981, 'Evaluating computerised geographic information systems using decision analysis', *Interfaces*, 11: 92–8.

Sussmann, S., 1992 'Destination management systems: the challenge of the 1990s', in C. Cooper and A. Lockwood (eds), *Progress in tourism, recreation and hospitality management*, Vol. 4, Belhaven Press, London: 209–15.

Sussmann, S., 1994, 'The impact of new technological developments on destination management systems', in C. Cooper and A. Lockwood (eds), *Progress in tourism, recreation and hospitality management*, Vol. 5, Belhaven Press, London: 289–96.

Weiers, R.M., 1988, *Marketing research* (2nd edn), Prentice Hall, Englewood Cliffs, New Jersey.

21 Comprehensive human resource planning: an essential key to sustainable tourism in island settings

M. V. Conlin and T. Baum

Introduction

The concept of sustainability has its origins in the environmental movement which grew to prominence in the 1960s and which has now become a mainstream issue within most business communities. What began essentially as a fringe protest against the uncontrolled expansion of economic development and its negative impact upon the physical environment has now become a vital issue in national, regional and local planning in many areas, not the least of which is tourism.

Notwithstanding this growth, sustainable tourism policy generation and practice are still in their infancy, and while they have generated a great deal of literature, the full range of their relevance has probably only just begun to be understood by planners (McKercher 1993). Sustainability, if it is to be effective, will need to consider the overall 'environment' in which tourism development takes place, not just the physical environment. This chapter will suggest that human resource development and management are one area of the overall 'environment' which is critical for successful tourism development.

The case for the importance of human resource development for the success of tourism, particularly in those segments of the industry which are labour-intensive, has been made convincingly over the past several years (Baum 1992; Enz and Fulford 1993). These segments would include the accommodation, food and beverage and transportation sectors, among others. This argument, however, has tended to focus upon the impact of human resource management upon levels of productivity and quality of service within various sectors of the industry. This emphasis is important, particularly as the industry becomes more internationally competitive (Baum 1992; Conlin 1991; Goffe 1993).

This chapter, however, approaches the general theme of the importance of human resources for successful tourism from the narrower perspective of human resource development planning in island settings and from the new perspective of sustainability of the industry in this context. The chapter will make the case that the special characteristics of island tourism call for a greater emphasis on the rational use of labour. Given the underlying concept of sustainable tourism, this approach to human resources must be considered as an essential key to sustainability. Ignoring comprehensive planning for human resources in island settings will have profound consequences not only for the local industry but also for the island community, as the experience of Pulau Langkawi in Malaysia demonstrates. Bird (1989, p. 29) states:

> What has emerged in Langkawi is a situation where most local people do not have the necessary experience or skills to take up many of the newly created jobs. Since training is not provided, the people can only fill unskilled positions as cleaners or general workers. Apart from a few ... most islanders lack the contacts, credit, entrepreneurial flair, training and motivation to seize business opportunities. There are also cultural and religious reasons that discourage some locals from certain jobs.

Interestingly, Bird, albeit unwittingly, is alluding to ground covered by Guerrier and Lockwood (1989) in their discussion of the evolution of core and peripheral work roles within the hotel industry. It is clear that, in Bird's view, local islanders are obtaining jobs at the periphery, these being the poorest paid and the most vulnerable to cyclical fluctuations in demand.

Our concept of human resource development, therefore, seeks to counter traditional short-term, operationally orientated approaches to human resource planning and development within tourism which have failed to address the issues of sustainability in the broadest sense. Labour has been seen as a necessary support resource within efforts to develop a tourism industry which has been able to sustain itself in economic and environmental terms. The underpinning issue in this chapter is the need for tourism planning to give recognition to the impact of development on the character and balance within the labour market of local island economies. Lane (1992) touches on this issue by contrasting 'no career structure' and 'employees imported' features of non-sustainable tourism with those, of 'career structure' and 'employment according to local potential' in sustainable tourism development. Development from a human resource perspective should be 'of' island communities and not simply 'in' them as is frequently the case.

The concept of sustainability

The origins of sustainable development, particularly in tourism, are to be found in concerns for the physical environment, as already mentioned. This concern began to broaden during the 1970s to include concerns about the negative impacts of tourism upon the culture of destinations and their indigenous populations. As far back as 1975, concerns about acceptable tourism development in the Caribbean began to include the impact of the industry upon cultural and sociological aspects of the region (Jefferson 1975). As Butler (1993, p. 137) states in his recent analysis of the use of pre- and post-impact assessment of tourism development: 'It is more common now to see references to impact assessment, which implicitly includes both environmental impact assessment ... and social impact assessment'. The broadening emphasis of the sustainability concept to include cultural and social considerations is now widely accepted and has become a fundamental component of the concept.

Several of the more widely accepted definitions of sustainable tourism clearly include this broad focus. The Action Strategy for Sustainable Tourism Development produced at the Globe '90 Conference in Vancouver in 1990 stated that:

> The concept of sustainable development explicitly recognizes interdependencies that exist among environmental and economic issues and policies. Sustainable development is aimed at protecting and enhancing environment, meeting basic human needs, promoting current and intergenerational equity, improving the quality of life of all peoples (*Action Strategy*, 1990, p. 1).

The reference in this important definition to human needs, equity and quality of life is evidence of the broadening of the concept beyond the scope of the physical environment.

Bramwell and Lane (1993, p. 2), in their introduction to the first volume of the *Journal of Sustainable Tourism*, published early in 1993, state that:

> Sustainable tourism is a positive approach intended to reduce the tensions and friction created by the complex interactions between the tourism industry, visitors, the environment and the communities which are host to holidaymakers. It is an approach which involves working for the longer viability and quality of both natural and human resources.

This definition is noteworthy because it stresses the need for long-term perspectives and a concern for the quality of human resources. It clearly underscores the need for the inclusion of human resource development within the ambit of the sustainable tourism philosophy.

In the definitive text on sustainable tourism planning, Inskeep (1991, p. 461) cites the objectives of the concept as applied to the industry in the Action Strategy for Sustainable Tourism Development:

1   To develop greater awareness and understanding of the significant contributions that tourism can make to the environment and the economy;
2. To promote equity in development;
3. To improve the quality of life of the host community;
4. To provide a high quality of experience for the visitor, and
5. To maintain the quality of the environment on which the foregoing objectives depend.

At least three of the objectives clearly involve the importance of comprehensive human resource development in tourism destinations. The notion of equity would seem to preclude tourism development which does not contribute as much to the indigenous population as is feasible. This was not the notion which the Strategy envisioned – it was concerned with equity relative to future generations of travellers – but it is no less relevant and probably more important. The quality of life in the host community is clearly interconnected with the patterns of employment of the host population. It can also be argued, as mentioned in the Introduction, that the human resource component is a vital element in the quality of the tourism product. In addition to these three objectives, it can also be argued that a comprehensive human resource development component in a tourism development plan may contribute to a higher degree of awareness and acceptance of the tourism industry on the part of the local population. This being the case, the first objective also can be seen to be linked with the comprehensive development of human resources in island settings.

The case for the inclusion of indigenous peoples in the tourism planning process has been made very convincingly over the past decade (Murphy 1983). Much of the inclusion strategy, however, has been designed to generate a sympathetic understanding of the importance of tourism within the local community, primarily to ensure tourism's success (Inskeep 1991; Lane 1992; Murphy 1983). As Murphy (1983, p. 118) states: 'An industry claiming to be in the 'hospitality' business can find its product planning and marketing strategies laid to waste through bad service and a hostile reception from local residents'. Murphy appears to be simply confirming the traditional perspective of human involvement in tourism development, namely a 'bottom-line' orientation mainly concerned with marketing and financial considerations.

Indeed, the positive impact on the local community directly in the form of employment, and perhaps more importantly, career development, often seems to be peripheral. The Action Strategy for Sustainable Tourism Development, which provided the definition and objectives discussed above, never mentions employment in its 41 specific action recommendations to governments, National Tourist Organisations (NTOs), international organisations, the tourism industry and the individual tourist. Indeed, the recommendations do not call for any educational or training activity other than those connected with tourism awareness programmes (Action Strategy Committee 1990). Where planning does incorporate considerations of employment, such as the development plan for Trinidad and Tobago, it is almost always confined to a call for the provision of education and training for the tourism industry (Williams 1993).

Much of the discussion concerning community involvement in tourism planning stops short of providing an effective call for mechanisms to ensure that inclusion of local interests means full employment and career development opportunities for indigenous peoples. To date, the emphasis has been on stressing the need for greater education and training opportunities for indigenous populations, particularly in the development of lower-level skills and abilities (Mathiesen and Wall 1990). This has been seen as the most effective means of incorporating locals into the industry and as a possible strategy for encouraging a sense of 'professionalism' in work which is traditionally seen as menial and demeaning (Burns 1994). While no one would argue that the provision of the means for acquiring skills and abilities is not a positive step in involving local populations in the tourism industry, as a strategy it fails to take into consideration cultural and traditional barriers which mitigate against indigenous peoples entering the industry. The Langkawi example already cited by Bird addresses these very issues.

As a further concern, the use of expatriate labour has been identified as one of the factors which mitigates against significant economic impact by tourism on small islands (Fletcher and Snee 1989). If the use of local labour is seen to be discriminatory in the sense that it confines locals to the 'peripheral' jobs, it is unlikely to become a positive force within the economic development of the island as a whole. It will generate employment but it will always be seen as a second-class industry for second-class persons.

This need for more comprehensive planning which fully considers the position of the host population was identified at the First International Assembly of Tourism Policy Experts in November, 1990, at the George Washington University. In its deliberations, the Assembly elaborated 19 broad policy issues which would form the tourism agenda in the 1990s. One of the issues identified – 'Growing dissatisfaction with current governing systems and process may lead to a new framework (paradigm) for tourism' – calls for the integration of tourism planning to reflect more directly the wishes of the host populations. In addition, the need for integrating tourism planning into the overall economic planning for destinations was stressed (Hawkins 1993, p. 198).

What is it about island tourism that sets it apart?

Interest in island tourism is increasing. The success of the two Island Tourism International Forums held in Bermuda in 1992 and 1993 and of the Conference on Sustainable Tourism in Islands and Small States held at the University of Malta in 1993, along with the growth in the number of research centres focusing on island tourism and the growing body of literature on the subject all attest to this. The question can be asked what it is about island tourism that sets it apart from other forms of tourism.

Baum (1992) addresses this question, in part, when he identifies six characteristics of many island tourism destinations, especially in the developing world, which have particular significance in the human resource context. These can be summarised as follows:

- a high economic dependence on a small range of economic sectors, including tourism;
- a focused and limited range of tourism products, generally hedonistic rather than historic/cultural in nature;
- a focus on high-spend, international tourism, with the consequent requirement for five-star or equivalent product standards;

- a restricted pool of skilled labour;
- limited education and training provision for tourism.

To these, we would also add, as pertinent in the present context,

- geographical remoteness;
- a small population base which demands the maximum development of skills, employment and career opportunities;
- political and economic insularity, mitigating against ready mobility of labour;
- cultural intraversion, leading to suspicion and of even hostility to outsiders.

At a practical level, the impact of these characteristics may be manifested in a number of ways. First, economic dependence on tourism and a limited range of alternative economic activities may mean that the effects of the cyclical changes in demand on tourism employment cannot be readily absorbed elsewhere in the local economy. This can clearly be seen in St Lucia, for example, where agriculture is the only significant economic alternative to tourism.

Second, political insularity and physical remoteness may restrict the options open to islanders for example, to seek alternative employment by moving elsewhere within the region in the manner that is open to people in larger land-mass locations. For example, if a hotel closes in St Kitts-Nevis, the ability of the displaced local workers to seek employment elsewhere in the region is hampered by political obstacles relating to immigration policies, financial constraints upon travel and temporary residence, and pressure to maintain the family unit.

Third, the factor of size may mean that educational and training opportunities in tourism are not available locally, while remoteness mitigates against accessing such provision elsewhere. The Maldives provides a good example in this context.

Fourth, the impact of cultural intraversion, or a desire to protect aspects of an island's cultural or historic uniqueness, may act as a barrier to acceptance of the introduction of labour from elsewhere in a way that would not be so common within larger communities which have well developed land-based links at a regional or national level. The Aran Islands, for example, off the west coast of Ireland, have an Irish-speaking community and subscribe to traditional cultural values in many respects. Significant development of the tourism resources of the island would, inevitably, result in the importation of labour, especially on a seasonal basis, without the same cultural and linguistic background. Keane *et al.* (1992) argue the case for sustainability in tourism in the Aran Islands, and cultural aspects are very high on their agenda.

In addition, the emergence of tourism in small islands can have a disruptive effect on their traditional patterns of employment:

> Large scale tourism development in the Caribbean is almost always accompanied by movement of workers out of agriculture into tourism-related

activities to the detriment of the former . . . if the development of tourism is accompanied by the destruction of that sector, through the combined effects of changes in land use and movement of workers away from the farm, the incremental benefits will be minimal and possibly even negative (Jefferson 1975, p. 63)

Phuket, in Thailand, previously self-sufficient in meeting the food needs of the indigenous population, must now import foodstuffs, such as rice, for consumption by local people and visitors alike. Thus, the deployment of personnel, within a finite island labour market, can have an impact which reaches beyond its immediate ambit and impacts on the overall economic balance sheet of the location.

Island tourism is generally seasonal in nature. Thus, permanent full-time employment in the tourism industry is not always available. As a consequence, there is frequently seasonal migration of tourism labour from the island to other locations in search of work. Examples include the migration of workers from the Greek and Spanish islands to the mainland and to other parts of urban Europe and from Ireland to the United Kingdom and Germany. This process, while ostensibly a balanced flow in both directions to reflect the demand for labour in the island's tourism industry, can, in situations where political considerations may allow, result in a net loss to the island, as staff settle permanently elsewhere. This skills haemorrhaging effectively reduces the participation of the indigenous population in the industry with the same ultimate effect as not including them in the first place. A general discussion of this migratory process from peripheral to core tourism areas in the context of Europe is addressed by Baum (1993b).

Island tourism is generally foreign owned, at least in the accommodation area. This has always presented problems, at least two of which were identified in the Caribbean region in 1975:

> foreign ownership represents a source of concentration, reduces the local contribution of any tourism expenditure and reduces the small potential for linkages in these small islands . . . Secondly, and this is most relevant, for Antigua and Barbados where tourism is the dominant economic activity, it encourages the renewal of concepts such as dependency, monoculture and centre/periphery relationship and, as such, inherits a legacy of intellectual criticism and popular hostility (Carrington and Blake 1975, p. 32).

An illustration of this relates to Bali, where it will be interesting to monitor the long-term impact on local businesses in locations such as Kuta and Sanur of the continuing development of Nusa Dua as an international-standard resort. The contrast between traditional local ownership on the island and the more recent influx of international or at least non-Balinese investment, could not be starker and provides an important dimension in our consideration of sustainability in human resource terms. Guerrier (1993), however, discusses strategies which have been brought to bear in Bali designed in part to counter this process through local entrepreneurship training.

These island characteristics form what is essentially a touristic microcosm. This in turn results in a need to view the total touristic experience in holistic terms. Each experience of a 'moment of truth' has far more impact, positive or negative, than may be the case in a larger destination. Therefore, the role of human resources becomes vital to the delivery of a quality touristic experience and to the success of the community as a whole. This link is not always recognised, as Poon (1993, p. 258) argues:

> It seems paradoxical that employees hold the key to competitive success in an industry that has traditionally viewed labour as a cost of production, a replaceable item, an item to dispose of in the low season, an item that can be hired and fired at will. Yet for those companies that have stayed on top of the heap – from Disneyland to the Marriotts to Singapore Airlines – it is the unending drive toward quality and investment in human resources that has made the difference.

The sustainable human resource agenda

The preceding sections have argued that sustainability is important in island settings, that human resources need to be developed in a 'sustainable' manner, and that current tourism development practice does not address fundamentally the issue of sustainable human resource development. What, then, needs to be done in order to ensure the sustainable development of human resources in island settings?

Recognition of the value of human resources

Public sector policy-makers and private sector decision-makers need to recognise that human resources are a necessary element of successful tourism development, particularly that which is sustainable. This may not be easy. Indeed, in a recent study of 66 national tourism administrations, a surprising 14 indicated that they did not see human resource issues to be of concern (Baum 1994). The fact that any NTO would not see human resources to be of concern suggests that there is a need to enhance awareness at this level as to the importance of human resources for success.

This is essential if human resources are to be part of the overall planning for tourism development and not simply an operational consideration after the major policy and planning decisions have already been made. The problem with the inclusion of human resources issues after the planning has been completed is that fundamental changes in public policy and management thinking about human resources become difficult for host countries to instigate.

International funding agencies may provide an incentive in this regard. Generally, aid comes with the requirement for planning which must include some consideration of the human resource factor in the project or programme. To some extent, however, these requirements focus on the need for the provision of education and training without putting into place the necessary framework to motivate full integration. Simply calling for the provision of education and training fails to account for the cultural barriers that may exist in island locations.

Public policy foundations for human resources

Recognition of the value of human resources in itself is not enough. A regulatory framework which seeks to ensure the inclusion of host populations in the tourism industry to the fullest extent feasible is essential to operationalise this recognition at the highest level. The areas of immigration policy and education provide good examples.

Immigration policies generally provide for the training of counterparts. However, this provision can usually be sidelined by any number of clever tactics (Burns 1994) and is generally not strictly enforced. What is needed is a balanced approach to immigration regulation which recognises the legitimate demands of the host population for an appropriate role in the tourism industry based upon ability, balanced against the industry's legitimate right to hire and fire in order to ensure the viability of its product and the sustainability of the economic contribution to the country. In order to obtain this balance, there must be trust and understanding on the part of both the public and private sector representatives.

In the past, governments and administrations in islands have tended to rely on the granting of work permits to promote the use and growth of local employees. At best, this is a confrontational situation which pits locals against expatriates with all its negative consequences. It gives rise to manipulatory practices by management and contributes to the probability of corruptive practices being employed. It is generally the case in island hotel industries that senior management is comprised of expatriates while the junior and supervisory posts are held by locals. The argument which multinational companies usually make to support this practice relates to their own policies for the training of senior managers. They value the far-ranging experience which short-term postings to different properties provide. Assuming that their position in this regard is valid, it would be appropriate for a host island to seek reciprocity whereby talented local employees would have the opportunity to participate in the process by being posted to foreign properties. Burns (1994) discusses the benefits of this process to Sri Lanka where the use of expatriate management is almost non-existent.

What is needed is a recognition that the employment and promotion of indigenous people has a wide range of benefits to both employers and the island communities at large. Greater appreciation of the industry, higher-quality service, more authenticity in the product, and less likelihood of disruption combine with the financial benefits of lower human resource expense and the reduction of salary leakage, particularly at the higher levels of management, to justify changes in the industry's traditional approach to local employment and the use of expatriate labour. This approach would provide a rational basis for local human resource development as opposed to the legislated, coercive system which islands for the most part currently use.

The need for integrated human resource policy structures

A further obstacle to the incorporation of human resource planning into the tourism development process is the fragmentation of responsibility which frequently exists in the public and private sectors for this area. For example, human resource concerns frequently fall within the ambit of several government units, be they ministries (education, labour, tourism, agriculture, home affairs), quangos such as NTOs, and diverse private sector interests (hotel associations, operators, consultants).

In order to counter the consequences of this fragmentation, there is a need for a comprehensive process through which to plan for the development of indigenous human resources in island tourism. Baum (1993a) provides an example of a comprehensive model which addresses many of the concerns mentioned above and which is readily applicable within island contexts. The model calls for the consideration of five areas – the tourism environment; tourism and the labour market; tourism and education; human resource practice in the industry; and tourism and the community – in a comprehensive, integrated and cohesive manner. As Baum (1993a, p. 240) states:

> The value of the approach ... is, primarily, as an aid to policy formulation and the establishment of national, regional and local priorities with respect to human resource concerns in tourism. Where this approach differs from that practised in most tourism environments is in its breadth. The approach is designed to incorporate as many as possible of the diverse influences and considerations which affect the development and management of an effective human resource policy in tourism.

A current example of such an integrated approach to human resource development can be found in the Caribbean. There, the public and private sectors are collaborating to improve the nature of regional participation in the industry. This is being attempted through the use of regional public policy initiatives relating to such issues as immigration policy, the design and installation of coordinating structures and processes such as regional and national tourism education councils, and a prioritisation of education and training within national budgets (Conlin 1993).

Conclusion

This chapter has explored a number of seminal issues relating to the human resource environment within island tourism. It has recommended the use of a comprehensive approach incorporating public policy frameworks to ensure the integration of host populations within the industry. It has provided a model for achieving such integration. What is required is more detailed empirical and case-study research into the various dimensions of human resource policy and implementation which this chapter has addressed.

References

Action Strategy Committee, 1990, *An action strategy for sustainable tourism development*, Tourism Stream, Action Strategy Committee, Globe '90 Conference, Vancouver, British Columbia, Canada, March.

Baum T., 1992, 'Human resources: the unsung price-value issue', in *Proceedings of the First Island Tourism International Forum*, Centre for Tourism Research and Innovation, Bermuda College, Paget, Bermuda.

Baum, T., 1993a, *Human resource issues in international tourism*, Butterworth Heinemann, Oxford.

Baum, T., 1993b, 'Human resource concerns in European tourism: strategic response and the EC', *International Journal of Hospitality Management*, 12(1): 77–88.

Baum, T., 1994, 'National tourism policies: implementing the human resource dimension', *Tourism Management*, 15(4).

Bird, B., 1989, *Langkawi from Mahsuri to Mahathir. Tourism for whom?* INSAN, Kuala Lampur.

Bramwell, W. and Bernard Lane, B., 1993, 'Sustainable tourism: an evolving global approach?', *Journal of Sustainable Tourism*, 1(1): 1–5.

Burns, P.M., 1994, 'Sustaining tourism's workforce: cultural and social-values perspectives with special reference to the role of expatriates', *Journal of Sustainable Tourism*, 1(2).

Butler, R.W., 1993, 'Pre- and post-impact assessment of tourism development', in D.G. Pearce and R.W. Butler (eds), *Tourism research: critiques and challenges*, Routledge, London.

Carrington, E.W., and Blake, B.W., 1975, 'Tourism as a vehicle for Caribbean economic development', in *Caribbean tourism* a publication of the Caribbean Tourism Research Centre (now incorporated into the Caribbean Tourism Organization).

Conlin, M.W., 1991, 'Credible higher education in tourism: a Caribbean example', in *Tourism: building credibility for a credible industry. Proceedings of the 22nd. Annual Conference of the Travel and Tourism Association*, Long Beach, 1991: 227–32.

Conlin, M.V., 1993, 'The Caribbean', in T. Baum (ed.), *Human resource issues in international tourism*, Butterworth Heinemann, Oxford.

Enz, C.A. and Fulford, M.D., 1993, 'The impact of human resource management on organizational success: suggestions for hospitality educators', *Hospitality and Tourism Educator*, 5(2).

Fletcher, J. and Snee, H., 1989, 'Tourism in the South Pacific islands', in C.P. Cooper (ed.), *Progress in tourism, recreation and hospitality management*, Vol. 1, Belhaven, London.

Goffe, P. 1993, 'Managing for excellence in Caribbean hotels', in J.D. Gayle and J.N. Goodrich (eds), *Tourism marketing and management in the Caribbean*, Routledge, London.

Guerrier, Y., 1993, 'Bali', in T. Baum (ed.), *Human resource issues in international tourism*, Butterworth Heinemann, Oxford.

Guerrier, Y. and Lockwood, A., 1989, 'Core and peripheral employees in hotel operations', *Personnel Review*, 18(1): 9–15.

Hawkins, D.E., 1983, 'Global assessment of tourism policy: process model', in D.G. Pearce and R.W. Butler (eds), *Tourism research: critiques and challenges*, Routledge, London.

Inskeep, F., 1991, *Tourism planning*, Van Nostrand Reinhold, New York.

Jefferson, O., 1975, 'Some economic aspects of tourism', in *Caribbean tourism*, a publication of the Caribbean Tourism Research Centre (now incorporated into the Caribbean Tourism Organization).

Keane, M.J., Brophy, P. and Cuddy, M.P., 1992, 'Strategic management of island tourism', *Tourism Management*, 13(4): 406–14.

Lane, B., 1992, *Sustainable tourism: a philosophy*, Rural Tourism Unit, Department of Continuing Education, University of Bristol.

Mathieson, A. and Wall, G., 1990, *Tourism: economic, physical and social impacts*, Longman, Harlow.

McKercher, R., 1993, 'The unrecognized threat to tourism: can tourism survive "sustainability"?', *Tourism Management*, 14(2): 131–6.

Murphy, P., 1983, *Tourism: a community approach*, Methuen, New York.

Poon, A., 1993, *Tourism, technology and competitive strategies*, CABT, Wallingford.

Williams, G., 1993, 'Formulating tourism development strategy in Trinidad and Tobago', in J.D. Gayle and J.N. Goodrich (eds), *Tourism marketing and management in the Caribbean*, Routledge, London.

Tourism statistics

22 Forecasts of international tourism
J. Latham

Introduction

Forecasting any form of business activity, though often necessary, is hazardous, with numerous pitfalls. Even short-term forecasts can be wildly inaccurate due to sudden changes in trend or other unforeseen circumstances. The consequences of, say, the expansion of a business or of tourism development at a resort based on over-optimistic demand forecasts can be severe for individual organisations and states. On the other hand, caution based on a mistrust of projected figures may lead to missed opportunities and a lower market share. There is therefore a need for accurate forecasting, as robust as is reasonably possible. Equally important, though, is the need for a sensible interpretation of forecasts and an understanding of their limitations and potential error. Forecasts can then play a key role in decision-making, say marketing or planning. For greater detail on the need for, and role of, forecasting of international tourism activity, see Wandner and Van Erden (1980), Archer (1987) and Witt and Witt (1992).

Forecasts of effective demand themselves often play a part in influencing that demand. This may result from a change in business behaviour in order to achieve targets based on the forecasts. A hotel, for example, may set its occupancy targets using projections of historical data. By monitoring its bookings, it can increase or reduce its marketing activity or even merely adjust prices, to meet the targets. The forecasts of international tourism made by responsible and respected bodies are taken seriously and affect confidence and investment. In this way, they can be partly self-fulfilling.

The methods used to make forecasts in tourism are wide-ranging, though essentially they are either time series or econometric in nature. Those based on time series make use of past data to produce projections for the future. The econometric forecasting of demand involves establishing a mathematical relationship between demand and a number of other key variables (such as origin population size, personal disposable income, cost of living for tourists, cost of travel); forecasts of these variables are then fed into an equation to derive a forecast of demand. There is evidence (see Witt and Witt 1992) to suggest that, while econometric forecasts provide the greater understanding of the ways in which demand is influenced by other factors, a time-series approach can often produce the more accurate forecasts. Long-term forecasting is less concerned with such statistical techniques; rather a more qualitative approach such as the Delphi technique would normally be taken, based on consensus views. For a detailed explanation and analysis of tourism forecasting, see Archer (1987), Witt and Martin (1989) and Witt and Witt (1992).

The main purpose of this chapter is to provide short- and long-term forecasts of international tourism up to and beyond the year 2000. A global view is taken, broken down into regional analyses; consideration is given to some states, particularly the major origin and destination countries. Three main sources have been used: Economist Intelligence Unit (1992) and World Tourism Organisation (1992; 1993). No detail is given here of the methods used in constructing the forecasts, and the reader is therefore directed to the source material for such information.

Tourism trends to 1992

Since 1950 there has been tremendous growth in international tourism (see Table 22.1). The average annual increase in international arrivals has been about 7 per cent, and tourism is now considered to be one of the top three industries world-wide. Growth has, however, not been even (see Table 22.2). For example, at times of recession in the early 1970s and in the early 1980s, there was a temporary stabilising of demand. These periods were followed by economic recovery, and a corresponding revival in international tourism. The overall performance of tourism has been closely linked with the state of the world economy, and in particular the economies of the major generating countries.

The global experience of almost uninterrrupted growth has not been shared equally by all destinations. Indeed, mainly due to the real and perceived potential of inbound tourism to support a nation's balance of payments, there are a number of countries which have developed tourism on a massive scale, generating increases in tourist arrivals and spend at rates well above the average rates of increase. Notable examples are Turkey, Portugal, Hungary and Greece in Europe; and many countries in the East Asia and Pacific (EAP) region, such as Singapore, Thailand, Malaysia, Korea, Australia and Indonesia. On the other hand, there are countries which have experienced severe downturns in tourism activity. Tourists tend to stay well clear of any destination that they regard as unsafe – this has clearly affected tourism to the Middle East and North Africa in recent years. Some destinations suffer merely because they are no longer fashionable in what were their main generating markets.

The current market shares of regions, in terms of both arrivals and receipts, appear in Table 22.3. These shares have changed somewhat over the years with the growing influence of many countries in the EAP region, mainly at the expense of Europe and the Americas. In the 30 years to 1990, the EAP share of arrivals has increased tenfold, and receipts five-fold. This increasing share is that of an expanding market, and represents remarkable growth in a highly competitive environment. See Latham (1994) for greater detail concerning past and current statistical trends.

Table 22.1 *International tourism trends: arrivals and receipts world-wide, 1950–92*

	Arrivals (millions)	Receipts[1] (US $ million)
1950	25.3	2 100
1960	69.3	6 867
1970	159.7	17 900
1980	277.9	102 372
1981	289.7	104 309
1982	289.4	98 634
1983	293.5	98 395
1984	320.8	109 832
1985	330.5	116 158
1986	340.9	140 019
1987	367.4	171 319
1988	392.8	197 692
1989	427.6	211 366
1990	455.6	255 074
1991	455.1	261 070
1992	476.0[2]	279 000[2]

Notes: [1] Excluding international travel.
[2] 1992 figures are preliminary estimates.

Source: World Tourism Organisation

Forecasts to the year 2000 and beyond

Forecasts in context

Consider the following recent events and some of their direct consequences on international tourism:

* The Chernobyl disaster, terrorist activity, the fall in value of the US dollar, all in 1986: international tourist arrivals to Africa and Middle East down significantly; shift in choice of destinations by many Americans in favour of countries in the Pacific and North America itself.
* The Gulf War, 1990–91: virtual cessation of travel to the Gulf and nearby countries; cancellations increased dramatically; occupancies down and all sectors in the travel industry affected.
* The conflicts in the former Yugoslavia from 1992: almost complete removal of an increasingly popular tourist destination, following a number of years of impressive growth.

International tourism is not only at the mercy of economic performance and the inevitable cycles, but also subject to events such as the above. That similar major conflicts, disasters and upheavals will occur in the future is also inevitable, but their location and timing are often beyond the reach of commentators and are best seen with hindsight. Recent

Table 22.2 *Average rates of growth of international tourism, 1950–90 (per cent per annum)*

	Arrivals	Receipts
1950–60	10.6	12.6
1960–70	8.7	10.1
1970–80	5.7	19.1
1980–90	5.1	9.6
1980–85	3.5	2.6
1985–90	6.6	17.0

Note: The average percentage increase is calculated as the constant annual percentage increase which would result in the overall change over the specified period.

Table 22.3 *International tourism in 1991: regional summary statistics*

	Arrivals (millions)	Share of world total (%)	Receipts * (US $ billion)	Share of world total (%)
Africa	15.8	3.5	4.6	1.8
Americas	97.5	21.4	72.0	27.6
East Asia/Pacific	53.9	11.8	40.3	15.4
Europe	277.9	61.1	138.2	52.9
Middle East	6.7	1.5	4.0	1.5
South Asia	3.2	0.7	2.0	0.8
WORLD	455.1	100.0	261.1	100.0

* Excluding international travel

Source: World Tourism Organisation

history suggests that, barring a world catastrophe on a massive scale, the growth of tourism world-wide is relentless, though in future it will continue at a slower pace than over the past few decades. Economic down-turns and unforeseen events merely act temporarily to dampen growth world-wide or more permanently to influence movements to specific destinations. Most forecasts do take account of likely economic growth. By definition, they do not allow for the unpredictable.

Global forecasts

Table 22.4 provides a simple comparison of two sets of published forecasts of international tourism activity, to the year 2000 and beyond. It can be seen that they are broadly in line with each other. Comparison with Table 22.2 shows that the expected rates of growth are much more modest than those experienced in the previous four decades. Statistically, this follows

Table 22.4 *A comparison of forecasts*

World Tourism Organisation (1993)

661 million international tourist arrivals a year by 2000
937 million international tourist arrivals a year by 2010

Growth rates in arrivals:

1990–1995	3–3.5% per year
1995–2000	4–5% per year
2000–2010	3–4% per year

Economist Intelligence Unit (1992)

A total of 617.2 million trips a year in year 2000
Growth rate in trips:

1990–1995	3.5% per year
1995–2000	5.1% per year
2000–2005	4.0% per year
2005–2010	4.2% per year

the trend of lower rates of increase exhibited in Table 22.2. It can be explained by a number of factors:

> Global growth, both in the past and in the future, is depressed by slow growing market segments, especially short cross-border trips and by the very meagre performance of some big origin countries – most notably Germany in the 1980s and the USA in the 1989–2005 period. A relatively new element of growing importance is that travel from a number of major origin countries, especially in Europe, is expected to be increasingly constrained by ceiling limitations to travel (linked essentially to annual leave entitlements); by 2005 travel from seven of 15 of the largest origin countries, in terms of tourist spending, is likely to be significantly restricted by ceiling effects (Economist Intelligence Unit 1992).

Two possible futures are exhibited in Table 22.5. They are meant to illustrate the different effects of assuming low (pessimistic) and high (optimistic) growth rates in Table 22.4. It is, of course, by no means certain that the true figures will be within the implied ranges.

International tourism receipts are forecast to grow in real terms by an average of between 4 and 5 per cent to the year 2000. This would put receipts (excluding international travel) at around US $500 billion a year, and would almost certainly maintain tourism's position as one of the top three industries world-wide.

Forecasts for regions

Specific elements of growth can be identified. The growth economies of Asia are likely to lead to substantial increases in intra-regional travel, that

Table 22.5 *Forecasts of international tourism arrivals: two futures*

	Arrivals (millions)	
1950	25.3	
1960	69.3	
1970	159.7	
1980	277.9	
1990	455.6	
1991	455.1	
1992	476.0 (E)	
	Forecast A	Forecast B
1994	500	500
1995	520	525
1996	541	551
1997	562	579
1998	585	608
1999	608	638
2000	632	670
2005	733	815
2010	850	990

Notes: (E)   1992 figures are preliminary estimates

Assumptions: 1.   A growth rate of 5% over the period 1992 to 1994.
               2.   Forecast A assumes an annual growth rate of 4% during 1995 to
                    2000; and 3% during 2000 to 2010.
               3.   Forecast B assumes an annual growth rate of 5% during 1995 to 2000;
                    and 4% during 2000 to 2010.

Source: Based on World Tourism Organisation data.

is, international travel within the region. Similarly, the greater freedom of movement of populations in eastern Europe is also likely to result in intra-regional travel, in this case to countries of western Europe. Finally, long-haul travel is set to increase at rates above short- and medium-haul travel, particularly for Japan and the major generators of Europe.

Table 22.6 shows a forecast by the Economist Intelligence Unit of the structure of world travel in the year 2000. It allows comparison with that of 1989. Table 22.7 illustrates trends in market share of arrivals by region. Table 22.8 provides statistics of flows of international tourism between and within different regions in 1990. It is in effect a numerical and practical summary of the complex movement of travellers. Table 22.9 then illustrates the likely growth of each flow. There are a number of key points which relate directly or indirectly to these tables.

* Europe is the leading player in international tourism. Countries in Europe generate over two-thirds of all international trips, and act as destinations for a similar proportion of the global figure. There are many reasons for this – see, for example, Latham (1990) for details.

Table 22.6 *Forecast of the structure of world travel in 2000: total trips* (millions)*

	As destination		As origin	
Europe/Mediterranean	443.8	(279.9)	444.9	(275.6)
North America	70.7	(48.1)	67.3	(60.6)
Central & South America	32.1	(24.1)	35.6	(17.1)
Far East/Pacific	23.8	(25.0)	29.1	(26.7)
South East Asia	18.2	(9.4)	14.9	(6.8)
Caribbean	9.5	(5.6)	3.2	(2.0)
Australia/New Zealand	6.2	(2.4)	4.4	(2.7)
Africa	5.2	(3.3)	6.4	(4.5)
Middle East	4.4	(2.5)	7.5	(3.7)
South Asia/Indian Ocean	3.5	(2.0)	4.2	(4.2)

* Inter- and intra-regional, excluding day trips (1989 figures in parentheses).

Source: Economist Intelligence Unit, 1992

Table 22.7 *Trends in market share of international tourist arrivals, by region (per cent)*

	1970	1990	2010
Europe	68.1	63.4	50.8
Americas	25.3	18.8	22.1
EAP	3.0	11.4	20.3
Africa	1.2	3.4	3.8
Middle East	1.2	2.1	1.9
South Asia	0.6	0.7	1.1

Note: Columns do not necessarily add to 100 per cent, owing to rounding error.

Source: World Tourism Organisation 1993

* Europe's dominance in statistical terms may be eroded to some degree by the year 2000 (Cleverdon 1992); or, on the other hand, be set to increase by a few percentage points (Economist Intelligence Unit 1992). It is, however, commonly accepted that any increase in international tourism to European countries will not be sufficient for it to retain its current high level of market share in the long term. Table 22.7, based on WTO forecasts, shows Europe's share of international tourist arrivals set to fall to about 50 per cent by 2010. Thus, although Europe will continue to be the dominant destination region, it will lose considerable market share, especially to the East Asia and Pacific region.

* The movements of international tourism within regions far outstrips those between regions. Taking the two largest figures in Table 22.8, it is clear that the vast majority of international travel world-wide takes place either within Europe (for example, the British to France or Germans to Spain) or within the Americas (for example travel between Canada and USA). Significant increases in intra-regional travel are expected in travel

Table 22.8 *Flows of international tourism, 1990 (millions)*

	Inbound to:					
	Africa	Americas	EAP	Europe	Middle East	S. Asia
Outbound from:						
Africa	5.9	0.2	*	0.8	1.3	*
Americas	0.6	58.9	4.6	18.8	0.7	0.3
EAP	0.2	5.8	22.3	5.7	0.2	0.4
Europe	5.6	11.0	6.2	240.2	5.8	1.2
Middle East	0.6	0.4	0.1	0.7	4.0	0.2
South Asia	*	0.3	0.9	0.2	0.6	1.0

Notes:
* less than 0.1 million.

1. EAP: East Asia and the Pacific
2. The table shows international tourism flows across regions of the world. Thus, for example, the number of international arrivals from the Americas to countries of Europe in 1990 was 18.8 million.
3. It also shows international flows within regions. For example, the number of international tourist arrivals to countries of Africa from (other) African countries in 1990 was 5.9 million.

Source: Adapted from World Tourism Organisation data

Table 22.9 *Forecasts of growth prospects by WTO region*

	Inbound to:					
	Africa	Americas	EAP	Europe	Middle East	S. Asia
Outbound from:						
Africa	H	M	H	M	M	H
Americas	H	L	M	L	M	M
EAP	H	H	H	M	M	H
Europe	M	H	H	L	M	H
Middle East	H	H	H	L	H	H
South Asia	M	M	H	M	H	H

Key: L   Low; that is below average rates of growth
 M   Medium; that is average rates of growth
 H   High; that is above average rates of growth

Source: Adapted from World Tourism Organisation (1993) data

within Asia by residents of Japan, Korea, Singapore, Malaysia, Hong Kong and Taiwan; and by western Europeans to eastern Europe (Cleverdon 1992). Kearney (1992) and Smeral and Witt (1992) give detailed analyses of the future of European tourism and, in particular, of the likely consequences of recent upheavals and changes.

* Although long-haul travel is forecast to increase from 13.3 per cent of all trips in 1989 to 15.4 per cent in 2000, this is on a relatively low base. Growth prospects are therefore such that intra-regional travel will remain dominant. The long-haul share of tourist nights and money spend is, of course, much higher due to the longer stays involved.

* Outbound growth prospects are particularly high (exceeding 4.5 per cent per annum on average) for the regions of Central and South America, East Asia and the Pacific, and the Middle East. They are low for North America.

* Inbound growth prospects are particularly high (exceeding 4.5 per cent per annum on average) for the regions of the Caribbean, East Asia and the Pacific, and South Asia.

Individual countries

Of course, the situation in individual countries may not be in line with that of a regional overview. It is not the purpose of this chapter to provide a detailed analysis of the likely performance of any particular country. Based on information from a number of sources in the reference section at the end of the chapter, but in particular the Economist Intelligence Unit (1992) and World Tourism Organisation (1992), forecasters and commentators suggest the following trends to the year 2000 and beyond:

* Particularly high growth rates in travel abroad are expected from: Argentina, Australia, Belgium, Chile, China, Hong Kong, Indonesia, Israel, Italy, Japan, Mexico, South Korea, Kuwait, Malaysia, Saudi Arabia, Singapore, South Africa, Spain, Taiwan and Thailand.

* There is a high probability that Japan will overtake the USA and Germany to become the leading country in terms of spend on international tourism. The potential of China to become a major international generator should also be noted – much depends on its economic growth and whether or not its restrictions on travel are significantly relaxed. The growth rates of some European countries may well be slowed by cciling effects during the 1990s.

* Particularly high growth rates in international tourism to the following destinations are expected: Australia, the Caribbean, China, Germany, Greece, India, Indonesia, Malaysia, Portugal, South Korea, Spain, Thailand, the UK and the USA.

By the year 2000, the three leading destinations in terms of receipts are likely to remain the USA, Spain and France, with the USA some way ahead of the other two. These could be followed in rank order by the UK, Italy, Austria, Germany, Switzerland, Canada and Portugal. The ordering by arrivals would naturally show some differences, with France at the top of the list.

Concluding remarks

It is clear that, barring a catastrophe on a world scale, international tourism will continue to grow to the year 2000 and beyond, albeit at average rates lower than those experienced in the 30 years between 1950 and 1980. Forecasts some years ago of half a billion arrivals by the year 2000 now look to be on the low side; the figure is more likely to be close to 650 million. International tourism receipts are projected to be US $500 billion.

This chapter has established that growth will not be uniform. Western Europe and North America will continue to be the leading players, both as receivers and as generators, and in terms of volume and of value. The major growth region will continue to be East Asia and the Pacific, gaining significantly in market share at the expense of Europe.

References

Archer, B.H., 1987, 'Demand forecasting and estimation', in J.R.B. Ritchie and C.R. Goeldner (eds), *Travel, tourism and hospitality research*, Wiley, New York: 77–85.

Cleverdon, R., 1992, 'Global tourism trends: influences and determinants', in J.R.B. Ritchie and D.E. Hawkins (eds), *World travel and tourism review*, Vol. 2, CABI: Oxford: 87–92.

Economist Intelligence Unit, 1992, *International tourism forecasts to 2005*, Special Report no. 2454 (summary), EIU, London.

Kearney, E.P., 1992, 'Redrawing the political map of Europe – the European view', *Tourism Management*, 23(1): 34–7.

Latham, J., 1990, 'Statistical trends in tourism and hotel accommodation', in C.P. Cooper (ed.), *Progress in tourism, recreation and hospitality management*, Vol. 2, Belhaven, London, 117–28.

Latham, J., 1994, 'International tourism statistics, 1991', in C.P. Cooper and A. Lockwood (eds), *Progress in tourism, recreation and hospitality management*, Vol. 5, Belhaven, London: 327–33.

Smeral, E. and Witt, S.F., 1992, 'The impacts of eastern Europe and 1992 on international tourism demand', *Tourism Management*, 23(4): 368–76.

Wandner, S.A. and Van Erden, J.D., 1980, 'Estimating the demand for international tourism using time series analysis', in D.E. Hawkins, E.L. Shafer and J.M. Rovelstad (eds), *Tourism planning and development issues*, George Washington University, Washington, DC: 381–92.

Witt, S.F. and Martin, C.A., 1989, 'Demand forecasting in tourism and recreation', in C.P. Cooper (ed.), *Progress in tourism, recreation and hospitality management*, Vol. 1, Belhaven, London: 4–32.

Witt, S.F. and Witt, C.A., 1992, *Modelling and forecasting demand in tourism*, Academic Press, London.

World Tourism Organisation, 1992, *WTO tourism trends to the year 2000 and beyond*, WTO, Madrid.

World Tourism Organisation, 1993, *Global tourism forecasts to the year 2000 and beyond – executive summary*, WTO, Madrid.

23 The European hotel industry

A. Pizam and T. Knowles

Introduction

International trends in tourism over the past 40 years have shown an average growth in tourist arrivals of just over 7 per cent. The average growth rate in the Asia and Pacific region since the 1980s has been higher than the world average, even though the actual figures started from a lower base.

Europe can be considered the axis of world travel, with an average growth rate of tourist arrivals of 3.7 per cent since the 1980s. It is by far the largest area in terms of tourist arrivals and tourism receipts. Since the 1980s it accounted for 60–65 per cent of world-wide tourist arrivals and 50–55 per cent of receipts. In 1990 the EC countries alone represented 39.2 per cent of world tourist arrivals (167 million) and 37.3 per cent of receipts (US $85.8 billion). From these statistics it is obvious that the industry has exhibited underlying growth despite the jitters created by the economic recession and political and armed conflicts (Latham 1992). The importance in such an analysis of tourism is that such trends are mirrored to some extent within the hotel industry.

World-wide hotel industry

Sources and definition

Any statistical analysis of the hotel industry needs to be viewed with caution as the reliability of data, the variety of sources and the definitions used, vary on a national and international basis. An example of this problem is seen in the UK, where, because there is no statutory requirement for hotel registration, industry size can only be approximated. Such an approximation can be taken from national grading schemes, the Huddersfield University Hotel and Catering Research Centre (Huddersfield University 1992) and official government statistics. The picture is further complicated by the fact that definitions and methods of data collection vary between the UK's national tourist boards.

Industry performance data tend to come from a variety of consultancy reports which are inevitably limited by their sample size, and detailed stockbroker reports, which concentrate on publicly quoted companies. The central problem in these reports is that in some countries the industry is dominated by small independently owned hotels, which are invariably not public limited companies.

Room supply

In 1990 the world-wide hotel room supply stood at 9.2 million rooms (Mars and Company 1992). Over the last 20 years the room supply has grown at an average of 3.5 per cent per year. An examination of product growth by region shows that room supply as a share of the world total decreased in Europe from 49 per cent in 1970 to 39 per cent in 1990. Asia, on the other hand, increased its room supply from 5 per cent of the total to 15 per cent in 1990. North America's share has remained unchanged at 35 per cent.

When analysed by region, the actual room supply figures show a sharp increase in Asia and a modest increase in Europe, North and South America. Room supply grew by an average of 8.5 per cent per year in Asia, from 270 000 rooms in 1970 to 1.38 million in 1990. Europe saw a marginal increase in room supply, from 2.64 million in 1970 to 3.58 million in 1990, an average increase of 1.5 per cent per year. North America increased its room supply from 1.89 million in 1970 to 3.22 million in 1990, an average of 2.7 per cent per year. Finally, South America increased its room supply from 324 000 in 1970 to 552 000 in 1990, an average increase of 2.7 per cent per year. It can be seen that while percentage growth is greatest in Asia, that region's market size is considerably smaller than Europe's.

Hotel market structure

The hotel market structure for upper- and mid-level hotels shows that North America is dominated by chain hotels, both foreign (8 per cent) and domestic (77 per cent). In contrast, Europe is highly fragmented, with independent hotels dominating the market with a 70 per cent share, while domestic chains constitute 19 per cent and foreign chains 11 per cent. In Asia and the Pacific, independent hotels account for 66 per cent, and foreign chains for 20 per cent. Africa and the Middle East have 53 per cent independent, and only a small fragment (11 per cent) of domestic chains. Such statistics show a mirror image between the Americas and Europe. This contrast is even greater when one considers such a country as Italy, with approximately 90 per cent of hotels in independent ownership. With respect to the market structure for lower-level hotels, although regional estimates are not generally available, it is obvious that, with the exception of North America, in all regions this market is highly dominated by independents. In North America, budget chains have been successful for many years, although in terms of occupancy they have been on a steady decline since 1980 (from 78 per cent average occupancy in 1980 to 58 per cent in 1991). In the UK, budget chains (lodges) became established in the latter half of the 1980s and in 1991 their occupancy rates were higher (84 per cent) than in both France (65 per cent) and the USA (58 per cent), the only two other countries that have a sizeable number of budget chains (Mars and Company 1992).

A further expansion of lower-market chains is expected throughout many European countries and other countries with mature markets.

In most places where lower market chains have been established, performance in terms of room occupancy greatly exceeds the average.

Market segments

The two main market segments for most hotels are business and leisure. Generally speaking, the world-wide average distribution between business and leisure guests is currently 60 per cent to 40 per cent (Horwath International 1993). This distribution, however, is not representative of all hotel types. For example in lower-market US chains, the leisure sector dominates the market with more than 68 per cent, while in France and the UK the business sector dominates the market with 70–80 per cent of the market share.

The hotel industry in Europe

Room supply

As can be seen from Table 23.1, in 1990 the top three EC countries in terms of supply of hotel rooms were Italy, Germany and Spain. These three countries had between them 61 per cent of the total EC hotel rooms and 60 per cent of total hotels. A certain degree of caution should be exercised with these figures as both the statistical base and the definition of a hotel vary within Europe.

Key characteristics

Several key characteristics are distinctive of the European hotel industry (Slattery and Johnson 1992). First, it is highly fragmented and dominated by independents. Second, it has a relatively large number of employees (approximately 4 million people). Third, the UK is the most chain-orientated. This orientation is evident at all market levels. Fourth, the penetration by USA-based hotel chains is minimal. Finally, there are differences in the business culture of the hotel industry throughout Europe – one can contrast the 'innkeeping' (or hoteliery) tradition of Switzerland with the 'management and business' orientation of the UK.

Level of concentration

The domination of independent hotels in the mid- and upper market is particularly evident in Austria (95 per cent), Italy (92 per cent), Switzerland (89 per cent), Spain (65 per cent), the Benelux countries (64 per cent), Germany (60 per cent) and France (54 per cent). On the other hand, Scandinavia (66 per cent), eastern Europe (60 per cent) and the UK (56 per cent) are dominated by chains.

Table 23.1 *Supply of hotel rooms in the EC countries, 1990*

Country	Rooms	Hotels	Rooms per hotel
Belgium	66 000	2 200	30
Denmark	35 000	1 165	30
Republic of Ireland	23 000	958	24
France	560 000	22 400	25
Greece	200 000	4 344	46
Italy	975 000	32 500	30
Netherlands	58 000	2 070	28
Portugal	65 000	340	191
Spain	630 000	24 230	26
West Germany	899 000	23 050	39
United Kingdom	550 000	19 640	28
TOTAL (MEAN)	4 061 000	132 897	(31)

Source: Krutick 1991

Market segments and economic factors

As to the origin of hotel guests, European countries in general are dominated by guests outside the host country – 53.4 per cent in 1991 (Horwath International 1992). However, when analysed by individual countries, Germany, the UK, Italy and France are seen to be dominated by domestic guests, while the rest of the countries are dominated by foreign guests. The above is especially true for the lower markets, where domestic guests dominate the market in absolute terms. This suggests that the hotel industry in the above four countries is highly dependent on its domestic economy.

While the performance of the European hotel industry in 1991 was dominated principally by the impact of the Gulf War, the results for 1992 were dominated by the condition of both national and global economies. The European hotel industry is influenced by the economies of the major European countries, along with other major world economies such as Japan and the USA (Salomon Brothers 1993). While the economy in Germany is likely to slip deeper into recession in 1994, as indicated by a projected fall in gross national product, the reverse would seem to be true for the USA, and a slow rise out of recession in Japan appears likely (Salomon Brothers 1993).

Hotel performance

Occupancy
In 1992 the 15 European countries (including both EC and EFTA) reported in the Horwath International data base had an average annual room occupancy rate of 60.6 per cent. This compares with the world-wide

figure of 61.6 per cent, but is lower than the 69.7 per cent occupancy rate reported for Asia and Australasia.

As far as individual countries are concerned in 1991, Germany had the highest occupancy rate (66.2 per cent), followed by Hungary (65.1 per cent), Austria (64.5 per cent), Ireland (64.3 per cent), Portugal (64.0 per cent), Belgium (63.2 per cent), France (62.9 per cent), Netherlands (62.6 per cent), Switzerland (60.9 per cent) and the UK (58.8 per cent). It is the balance of occupancy against average achieved room rate, known as the *yield*, that will reflect in gross operating profit trends within these countries.

Gross operating profit
Compared with other geographical regions, the European hotel industry seems to be doing well in terms of its financial performance. The 1991 average gross operating profit (GOP) as a percentage of sales of European hotels in the Horwath International data base was 27.3 per cent. With the exception of Africa and Middle East, which had a GOP of 38.8 per cent, the European ratio is the highest reported. Asia and Australasia, North America and Latin America had lower ratios (26.3, 24.1 and 19.6 per cent, respectively).

A country by country analysis in Europe shows Hungary having the highest GOP ratio (35.1 per cent) followed by Belgium (31.2 per cent), Portugal (31.0 per cent), France (30.0 per cent), Netherlands (29.5 per cent), the UK (29.4 per cent), Germany (24.4 per cent), Switzerland (23.4 per cent), Austria (19.6 per cent) and Ireland (18.4 per cent).

Major countries analysis: the corporate picture

France

At the end of 1992, quoted hotel companies in France operated 1340 hotels and 115 928 rooms, up 9.6 per cent from 1991. More hotel rooms were added in France during this period (within the major hotel companies) than in all of the continental countries and the UK together. Most of the expansion came from the French companies Accor and Louvre, which jointly added 10 295 rooms, and represented 97.8 per cent of the total net additions to room stock in the country. In contrast to these indigenous companies, foreign chains in net terms added no new rooms to their total in France. The share of room stock owned/operated by publicly quoted companies in the French hotel market is now 22.3 per cent up from 20.4 per cent in 1991 (Slattery and Johnson 1992).

Publicly quoted hotel companies in France are characterised by a high proportion of limited-service and rooms-only hotels. These two segments of the market account for 58.6 per cent of rooms and are dominated by domestic chains such as Accor and Louvre. These chains concentrate on achieving high room volumes in their limited-service hotels and, with few non-room facilities, are able to maintain high margins. Foreign companies, on the other hand, are located at the medium and higher levels of the market.

France is an underdeveloped market for hotel-based leisure clubs (Slattery and Johnson 1993). Only 12.8 per cent of the Kleinwort sample have any formal leisure facility, and of these only 1.8 per cent of the total have facilities with membership potential. Indeed, as far as it can be traced, the practice of attracting fee-paying members is very rare in France. Accor's Novotel brand does have four Thalassa hotels, which specialise in therapeutic beauty and fitness facilities on a charge basis to hotel residents, but they do not operate as clubs. Accordingly the facilities in the hotels that do have leisure clubs are invariably cost centres rather than profit centres.

Germany

At the end of 1992, publicly quoted companies in Germany operated 202 hotels, all but a handful of them in the former West Germany (Slattery and Johnson 1993). Germany is distinct from the other major Western economies such as the USA, UK and France, because its sole quoted domestic hotel company, Kempinski, has only a minor presence in its domestic hotel market. Over half of the hotel rooms in Germany are in major city locations, a high figure for a developed economy. The relatively low exposure to other locations is dominated by Accor, with 67 hotels, and Queens Moat Houses, with 29 hotels. Unlike the UK and France, there is no single dominant city in Germany, which produces a wider geographic spread for foreign companies, international brands and foreign demand. The very high proportion of rooms at the high and medium levels of the market is consistent with the extensive exposure to major city locations and is indicative of an emphasis on the business market. Most of the exposure at the lower levels of the market is from Accor, which has 50 hotels.

The emphasis on full-service hotels is consistent with the paramount importance of the business market to the German hotel industry. It is also consistent with the locational spread and the market-level profile. Derived from these features is the high average size of hotels in Kleinwort Benson's sample which, at 184 rooms, is more than double the average size in the UK and France. The profile of the German hotel industry means that potentially they can attract stronger room occupancies, achieving higher average room rates and higher margins than quoted companies in the UK.

An exceedingly high proportion of publicly quoted hotel companies in Germany have hotels with leisure facilities. Half of all hotels provide facilities, in comparison with 20 per cent in the UK and only 10 per cent in France. The high exposure to international brands and the high proportion of rooms at the middle and higher market levels means that leisure facilities are added to most hotels as a matter of course. Almost all leisure facilities in German hotels are regarded as cost centres rather than profit centres and are used merely as an added attraction for resident customers at no further cost to themselves. Although leisure facilities are used to provide hotels in Germany with a competitive advantage in attracting business and conference demand, it also means that they are underutilised since business travellers are notoriously infrequent users of leisure facilities in hotels.

Spain

The year 1992 was a period of consolidation in Spain for quoted hotel companies following the large increases in hotel supply in time for the Olympic Games and Expo. At the end of 1992 publicly quoted hotel companies operating in Spain accounted for 80 hotels, with 12 503 rooms (Slattery and Johnson 1993). Most expansion in that year came from the domestic group Cofir, adding four more hotels. The overall split between primary and other locations is such that 46 per cent of rooms are in primary cities. Spain has increased the proportion of rooms at the mid-market level from 47 per cent to 54.8 per cent, entirely accounted for by secondary location additions. Spain, like Italy, has no budget hotels in the portfolios of quoted companies. Of the major hotel companies in Spain, 48 per cent of hotels have some form of leisure provision and, as might be expected, nearly two-thirds of these have outdoor facilities. Overall, the market for leisure facilities in Spain in the major companies is embryonic and features mainly resort town hotels. As in other continental countries, leisure facilities are provided for use by resident customers only. They are a cost centre and not promoted in the local markets as leisure clubs.

Italy

Supply
At the end of 1992 the major hotel companies in Italy operated 115 hotels and 19 522 rooms, up 16.2 per cent on 1991. Italy showed the second largest growth of any European country during this period (Slattery and Johnson 1993).

From 1987 onwards the hotel sector as a whole lost numerous businesses, the number of hotels falling from 38 114 at the beginning of 1988 to 36 166 in 1991. However, the number of rooms over the period 1989–91 rose from 922 084 to 938 141, suggesting growth in the average number of rooms per hotel (Mercury 1992).

Demand
The decline in foreign demand in the years 1989 and 1990 (Mercury 1992) represents an important phase in the country, transforming it away from a traditionally tourism receiving country. In the three-year period 1989–91, demand for accommodation by Italians amounted to 66 per cent of total demand. In terms of growth in this demand category, if 1985 is allocated the base index of 100, the 1991 index was 122, which gives an indication of trends in demand over this period.

There are four regions which absorb about half of the internal demand. These are Veneto (13 per cent), Trentino/Alto Adige (11.9 per cent), Emilia Romagna (11.6 per cent) and Tuscany (12.4 per cent). The whole of southern Italy in 1991 accounted for 18.8 per cent.

It has been shown that in the period 1989–91 accommodation demand in Italy by foreigners reduced significantly in terms of both average length of stay and arrivals (Mercury 1992). Demand for accommodation in the coastal zones of Italy fell during the period, while at the same time demand in the main towns and cities grew. Demand within the main towns and cities accounted for 28.6 per cent of total foreign flow in 1988, 30.6 per cent in 1989 and 31.8 per cent in 1990.

In terms of country of origin, the greatest demand for hotel accommodation comes from the European Community (61.7 per cent of the total), with 36.2 per cent from Germany, 7.8 per cent from the UK and 7.6 per cent from France. Demand for accommodation reaches a peak in the summer months and is at its lowest in January.

Geographical distribution
Over half the national accommodation is in the regions of Emilio Romagna, Trentino/Alto Adige, Veneto and Tuscany. Concentration of the major companies has now risen to 6.5 per cent, but the largest number of hotels remain independent resort hotels owned by families. More than 4 per cent of bedrooms in Italy are in the major city locations but the trend is for further expansion in other locations.

Product segmentation
Italy, in terms of publicly quoted hotel companies, continues to be dominated by mid-market hotels, with that proportion increasing in 1992 to 48.2 per cent. Low market-level hotels, according to the Kleinwort data base, continue to be very much in a minority. Italy has no budget lodges (Slattery and Johnson 1993).

Leisure facilities
In Italy, 36.5 per cent of quoted hotels have leisure facilities, the second highest proportion in Europe behind Germany. Of these, 76 per cent are those with primarily outdoor facilities, a statistic indicative of two factors: first, a 33.2 per cent concentration of high market-level hotels; and second, the climate of Italy being conducive to outdoor facilities. Italian hotels provide leisure facilities as an extra amenity for resident customers; they are operated as cost centres and membership is not promoted (Slattery and Johnson 1993).

United Kingdom

Room supply
In 1991 the UK had a supply of approximately 507 000 hotel rooms. Of these, 119 000 (23.5 per cent) were owned/operated by public limited

companies (PLC) (Mintel 1992). Over the last few years the UK PLC hotels have seen a growth in concentration. The ten largest companies in the UK have increased their room supply from 64 081 rooms in 1986 to 89 382 in 1991 (Table 23.2); the latter figure represents approximately 76 per cent of the total PLC hotel rooms and 18 per cent of total UK hotel rooms. The biggest companies are expanding fast at the expense of smaller companies and independents.

Geographical distribution and size
The majority of UK hotels are concentrated in England (75 per cent); Scotland has 16 per cent, Wales 8.5 per cent and Northern Ireland 0.5 per cent (Mintel 1992). The UK hotel industry is dominated by small hotels. In England 86 per cent of all hotels have less than 26 rooms and only 2.2 per cent have more than 100 rooms. The equivalent figures for Scotland are 85 per cent and 2.4 per cent. Wales has 89 per cent of its hotels in the 1–30 rooms category and only 1.2 per cent in the more than 100 rooms category (Mintel 1992).

Classification
One method of analysing the structure of the UK hotel industry is through a consideration of the various classification schemes in existence, despite the fact that such schemes include only a small sample of the UK hotel industry. Within the UK, hotels in the two-star category account for 38 per cent of the total and 3 star for 44 per cent (AA classification). Only 0.6 per cent hotels are in the five-star category. Lodges, which are a form of motel-style accommodation, account for 3.3 per cent (Mintel 1992).

Table 23.2 *The top 10 UK PLC hotels, 1991*

Rank	Company name	Total hotels	Total rooms
1	Forte	328	29 212
2	BIL (Mount Charlotte & Thistle brands)	102	13 830
3	Queens Moat Houses	99	10 427
4	Bass (Holiday Inns & Toby Hotel brands)	37	7 524
5	Rank Organisation (Rank Hotels, Shearing Holidays, Butlins, Rank Motorway Lodges)	72	7 442
6	Ladbroke (Hilton International, Hilton National, Associate Hotels)	35	7 137
7	Swallow	31	3 838
8	Accor	24	3 613
9	Stakis	27	3 255
10	Jarvis	40	3 104
	TOTAL	795	89 382

Source: Krutick 1991

Table 23.3 *UK PLC hotels' financial performance, 1991–2*

	1991	1992	% Change
Year end roomstock	119 443	122 931	+2.9
Occupancy (%)	57.9	57.8	
Room nights sold (million)	25.2	26.0	+3.2
Average achieved room rate (£)	45.59	47.34	+3.8
Rooms turnover (£billion)	1.15	1.23	+6.9
Other turnover (£billion)	1.35	1.39	+2.9
Total hotel turnover (£billion)	2.51	2.62	+4.8
Cost of sales (£billion)	2.04	2.06	+1.0
Operating margin (%)	18.6	21.3	
Gross operating profit (£)	466.3	558.9	+19.9
Trading profit per bedroom (£)	3500	4075	+16.4

Sources: Slattery and Johnson 1992; 1993

Location

Among the non-bed-and-breakfast hotels (more than 11 rooms), Mintel (1992) identifies a number of product categories, of which 37.5 per cent of the total are seaside hotels, 32 per cent older city hotels, 20 per cent country house hotels and 4.5 per cent London hotels.

Demand

The UK hotel industry is highly dependent on the domestic market. In 1991, 60 per cent of guests in UK hotels sampled by Horwath Consulting originated from within the UK, followed by North Americans (15.5 per cent), continental Europeans (13 per cent) and Japanese (4.1 per cent). An absolute majority (61 per cent) of hotel guests in UK hotels are business travellers, and only 19 per cent of them are holiday tourists (Horwath Consulting 1992).

Financial performance

Tables 23.3 and 23.4 list the financial performance of the UK PLC hotels in 1991 and 1992. A cursory examination of these tables shows that after two very poor years (1990 and 1991), UK PLC financial performance improved somewhat in 1992, although the overall performance of individual companies continues to be mixed. Occupancy remained the same but room nights sold increased by a modest 3.2 per cent. This, coupled with an increase in the achieved room rate, caused a 20 per cent increase in gross operating profit (Table 23.3). Impressive as they might be, these figures are misleading as they compare 1992 with 1991, which was one of the worst performing years in the recent UK hotel industry. Because of a major world-wide recession, the years 1991–2 saw a market contraction in the UK hotel industry. This contraction resulted in heavy discounting in both business and leisure sectors to offset reduced discretionary spending. The outcome was low room occupancy and low achieved room rates, which translated into reduced profits and depreciated asset values.

Table 23.4 *Financial performance of the major UK PLC hotel companies, 1991–2.*

	Forte Hotels	Queens Moat	Ladbroke Hotels	Holiday Inns	Swallow
Sales 1992	835		750E	621	77.9
Sales 1991	913		758.1	570	70.4
Operating margin 1992 (%)	9.0		8.7	19.0	16.0
Operating margin 1991 (%)	17.5		21.6	18.1	17.5
Operating profit 1992	75	(0.7)*	140	116	12.4
Operating profit 1991	160	22.4	163.8	103	12.3

Sources: Slattery and Johnson 1992; 1993; *Queens Moat Houses PLC 1993

Note: E = estimated

Profile of six European hotel companies

Forte

Forte Hotels, previously known as Trusthouse Forte Hotels, is a subsidiary of Forte plc. It is the largest UK hotel company. It has 838 hotels and over 29 000 rooms world-wide. In 1991 the company changed its name and restructured its portfolio into three brands and three collections:

- Travelodge: a budget chain operating in the UK and franchised in the USA
- Forte Heritage: small traditional British inns
- Forte Posthouse: three-star hotels
- Forte Crest: four-star business hotels
- Forte Grand: five-star international hotels in city centres and resort locations
- Exclusive Hotels of the World: luxury hotels in major cities, retaining their own names.

To move away from its UK base, Forte plc sold its contract catering division to a management buyout team (1993) and is expanding its hotel operations through joint ventures in Spain, Italy and Ireland, with seemingly its greatest interest being in Italy and its joint venture with Agip (1992). Towards the end of 1993 the company entered into negotiations with the Italian-based hotel company Ciga, in order to establish a joint venture in return for a limited injection of capital (Gordon 1993). The company has also made use of management contracts and recently purchased motorway service station operations from Accor in France (1993).

Queens Moat Houses

Queens Moat Houses plc operates 102 hotels in the UK and 86 in mainland Europe, and is the largest Holiday Inn franchisee on the continent

(Queens Moat Houses plc 1993). Most of its hotels are in the three- and four-star categories. During the 1980s the company expanded rapidly into Europe, where 50 per cent of its profits come from. The company tends to establish national brands in each country rather than one European brand. It owns and operates 25 per cent of Holiday Inns in Europe and so has access to the Holidex reservation system. It has the Queens brand in Holland. In 1991 it purchased the Austrotel brand in Austria. Queens Moat's style is to leave its managers to control the hotels as independently as possible. This policy was widely believed to have created the company's recent financial difficulties which hit the headlines of the trade press in April 1993 (Gledhill 1993). The group reported losses for the year ended 31 December 1992 of £1040.5 million, a substantial part of which was due to the revaluation of the company's properties (Queens Moat Houses plc 1993).

BIL: Mount Charlotte/Thistle

The Mount Charlotte/Thistle Hotels group was purchased by Brierley Investment Ltd (BIL) in October 1990. In 1991, the company had 108 hotels with 14 170 rooms. Most of its hotels are in the three- and four-star categories. The company concentrates on the London market, from where nearly 50 per cent of its turnover is derived. In 1990 the company claimed to have achieved the highest profit per bedroom of any UK hotel group, and in 1992 made a £1.5 million profit after £71 million in interest charges.

Accor

The French-based company Accor has 11 brands world-wide with a total of 229 075 rooms and a market dominance in France. It controls 15 per cent of the market in France and 35 per cent of the group is based in that country. Accor is the largest group of company-owned hotels world-wide, with over 2000 properties on all continents (Accor 1993). With its 11 brands, the company is able to satisfy all demand categories, although the fastest-growing segments are the personal spend leisure markets at the lower market level. While its average growth in room supply over the period 1991–92 was 7.2 per cent, hotels at the lower market level grew by a significantly greater amount. During 1992 the Accor brands grew faster than the brands of the newly acquired company, Wagon-Lits.

Ciga

Ciga, founded in 1906, has since 1985 been controlled by a group of investors headed by the Aga Khan (through a controlling company, Fimpar). All of the company's 36 hotels are at the upper end of the market, and most are situated in European gateway cities. The hotels are located in (in descending order of size) Italy, Spain, Austria, France, Greece and the Netherlands. The demand base for Ciga's hotels is 70 per cent European, 20 per cent North American and 8 per cent Japanese. The company is usually preoccupied with traditional European grand hotels, and relies on the German and Italian markets (Slattery and Johnson 1993).

Jolly

The Italian-based hotel company Jolly, founded in 1949 and floated in 1982, has developed into a chain of 35 domestic mid-market hotels with a limited presence outside Italy. The hotels tend to be situated in areas of high commercial and tourist activity. The nature of the Italian hotel market at this level has meant that the company has enjoyed low levels of competition, although, with Forte's recent joint venture with the Italian company Agip, this situation is likely to change.

References

Accor, 1993, Accor Annual General Meeting, 4 June, France.
Gledhill, B., 1993, 'QMH shock', *Caterer and Hotelkeeper*, 9.
Gordon, R., 1993, 'Strategic alliances for Forte', *Caterer and Hotelkeeper*, 21 October: 23.
Horwath Consulting, 1992, *United Kingdom hotel industry 1992*. Horwath Consulting, London.
Horwath International, 1992, *Worldwide Hotel Industry 1992*, Horwath International, New York.
Horwath International, 1993, *Worldwide Hotel Industry 1993*, Horwath International, New York.
Huddersfield University, 1992, International Hotel Groups Directory 1992, Hotel Portfolio Research, London.
Krutick, J.S., 1991, *The European hotel industry: the race is on*, Salomon Brothers, New York.
Latham J., 1992, 'International tourism statistics', in C.P. Cooper and A. Lockwood (eds), *Progress in tourism recreation and hospitality management*, Vol. 4, Belhaven Press, London: 267–81.
Mars and Company Consultancy Ltd, 1992, Unpublished Internal Report, London.
Mercury, S.R.L., 1992, *Fourth report on Italian tourism*, Italian Ministry of Tourism and Performing Arts, Rome.
Mintel, 1992, *Hotels 1992*, Mintel International Group Ltd, London.
Queens Moat Houses PLC, 1993, *Queens Moat Houses PLC Annual report and accounts 1992, interim report 1993*, 29 October, London.
Salomon Brothers, 1993, 5th Annual European Hotel Industry Investment Conference, The Dorchester, London.
Slattery, P. and Johnson, S., 1992, *Quoted hotel companies: the European markets*, Kleinwort Benson Research, London.
Slattery, P. and Johnson, S., 1993, *Quoted hotel companies: the European markets*, Kleinwort Benson Research, London.

ANNOUNCING A NEW JOURNAL

Progress in Tourism and Hospitality Research

Wiley are pleased to announce the launch of a new journal **Progress in Tourism and Hospitality Research** in the summer of 1995.

In response to many requests from users of **Progress in Tourism, Recreation, and Hospitality Management** we are building on the substantial base of the annual research review to provide an international, refereed research journal of high calibre to reflect the excellence of these rapidly evolving research fields.

If you would like to receive more information on the new journal, fill in your name and address below and return the card.

Lesley Valentine, John Wiley and Sons Ltd, Baffins Lane, Chichester,
West Sussex, PO19 1UD, UK.
Telephone: (0243) 770362 in UK or +44 243 770362 outside UK

Progress in Tourism and Hospitality Research

Yes, I would like to receive more information on this new journal.

Name ....
Position ....
Address...
....
....
Telephone: ....

Return to: Lesley Valentine, John Wiley and Sons Ltd, Baffins Lane, Chichester, West Sussex, PO19 1UD, UK
Telephone: (0243) 770362 UK or + 44 243 770362 outside UK

Lesley Valentine
FREEPOST
John Wiley and Sons Ltd
Baffins Lane
Chichester
West Sussex
PO19 1UD
UK